Scottish Romanticism and Collective Memory in the British Atlantic

Edinburgh Critical Studies in Romanticism
Series Editors: Ian Duncan and Penny Fielding

Available Titles
A Feminine Enlightenment: British Women Writers and the Philosophy of Progress, 1759–1820
JoEllen DeLucia
Reinventing Liberty: Nation, Commerce and the Historical Novel from Walpole to Scott
Fiona Price
The Politics of Romanticism: The Social Contract and Literature
Zoe Beenstock
Radical Romantics: Prophets, Pirates, and the Space Beyond Nation
Talissa J. Ford
Literature and Medicine in the Nineteenth-Century Periodical Press: Blackwood's Edinburgh Magazine, 1817–1858
Megan Coyer
Discovering the Footsteps of Time: Geological Travel Writing in Scotland, 1700–1820
Tom Furniss
The Dissolution of Character in Late Romanticism
Jonas Cope
Commemorating Peterloo: Violence, Resilience, and Claim-making during the Romantic Era
Michael Demson and Regina Hewitt
Dialectics of Improvement: Scottish Romanticism, 1786–1831
Gerard Lee McKeever
Literary Manuscript Culture in Romantic Britain
Michelle Levy
Scottish Romanticism and Collective Memory in the British Atlantic
Kenneth McNeil
Romantic Periodicals in the Twenty-First Century: Eleven Case Studies from Blackwood's Edinburgh Magazine
Nicholas Mason and Tom Mole

Forthcoming Titles
Romantic Environmental Sensibility: Nature, Class and Empire
Ve-Yin Tee
Romantic Pasts: History, Fiction and Feeling in Britain and Ireland, 1790–1850
Porscha Fermanis
William Godwin and the Bibliographic Imagination
J. Louise McCray

Visit our website at: www.edinburghuniversitypress.com/series/ECSR

Scottish Romanticism and Collective Memory in the British Atlantic

Kenneth McNeil

EDINBURGH
University Press

Edinburgh University Press is one of the leading university presses in the UK. We publish academic books and journals in our selected subject areas across the humanities and social sciences, combining cutting-edge scholarship with high editorial and production values to produce academic works of lasting importance. For more information visit our website: edinburghuniversitypress.com

© Kenneth McNeil, 2020, 2022

First published in hardback by Edinburgh University Press 2020

Edinburgh University Press Ltd
The Tun – Holyrood Road
12(2f) Jackson's Entry
Edinburgh EH8 8PJ

Typeset in 11/14 Adobe Sabon by
IDSUK (DataConnection) Ltd

A CIP record for this book is available from the British Library

ISBN 978 1 4744 5546 6 (hardback)
ISBN 978 1 4744 5547 3 (paperback)
ISBN 978 1 4744 5548 0 (webready PDF)
ISBN 978 1 4744 5549 7 (epub)

The right of Kenneth McNeil to be identified as the author of this work has been asserted in accordance with the Copyright, Designs and Patents Act 1988, and the Copyright and Related Rights Regulations 2003 (SI No. 2498).

Contents

Acknowledgements	vi
Introduction: 'So complete a change' (in So Short a Time) – Scottish Romanticism, Modernity and Collective Memory	1
1. Aftermaths: Walter Scott and Imagining Collective Memory in the Transatlantic World	33
2. Memory on the Margins: Anne Grant's Atlantic World	94
3. Indigenous Elsewhere: Lord Selkirk and Native Memory and Resettlement	143
4. Memory, Identity and the Scottish Remembrance of Slavery	201
5. John Galt and Circum-Atlantic Memory	269
References	334
Index	365

Acknowledgements

This book has had a long gestation, and in the process of researching and writing it, I have occurred many debts, more than I can fully account for here. I would like to thank my colleagues at Eastern Connecticut State University, in particular Michèle Bacholle, Reginald Flood, Meredith James and Alison Speicher. They offered their encouragement, time and expertise when it was especially required. Special thanks to Ben Pauley, whose bibliographic savvy helped me track down important leads and whose deft skill with JavaScript saved me no end of frustration.

I also wish to thank my wonderful colleagues in Scottish Romantic and transatlantic studies who have read or listened to parts of the book as it was taking shape. Sam Baker, Andrea Cabajsky (who also helped disentangle my French), Leith Davis, JoEllen DeLucia, Ina Ferris, Evan Gottlieb, Regina Hewitt, James Hunter, Sheila Kidd, the late Susan Manning, Caroline McCracken-Flesher, Michael Morris, Pam Perkins, Murray Pittock, Honor Rieley, Fiona Robertson, Carla Sassi, Jennifer Scott, Juliet Shields, Charles Snodgrass and Matt Wickman offered their enthusiasm for the project and pointed me in the right direction, often, I am sure, without even realising it. Perhaps the greatest of these debts is owed to Ian Duncan, who read an early draft of Chapter 1 and the complete manuscript as series editor at Edinburgh University Press, and who provided invaluable critical input and suggestions. In addition, at no part in the process did his encouragement for the project and great intellectual generosity ever waver. At Edinburgh University Press, I also thank Michelle Houston and Ersev Ersoy for their enthusiasm for the project and careful attention in seeing it through. I also wish to thank my research assistant, Chris Morrison, and my skilled indexer, Lesley Calkins.

I am grateful to library staff who helped me in researching the book, most notably Tricia Boyd in Special Collections at the University of Edinburgh Library; Darlene Wiltsie in Archival and Special Collections at the University of Guelph Library; Amanda Lipson in the Reference Services Library and Archives Canada; Marguerite Ragnow in the James Ford Bell Library at the University of Minnesota; Danielle Funiciello at the New York State Museum in Albany; and Jacquie Aitken at Timespan, Helmsdale, Scotland. Special thanks go to the Interlibrary Loan department at Eastern Connecticut State University and, especially, Kellie O'Donnell-Bobadilla. Without their help, this book would have been a much poorer one. Lastly, I wish to thank my family for their encouragement and patience. Most of all, I thank my wife, Erika McNeil, who, from the very start, read everything and offered advice, encouragement, inspiration and research materials. I am indebted to her for more than she knows, and so this book is for her.

My research was aided by CSU/AAUP Research and Faculty Development Grants and a sabbatical leave award, which gave me the time and focus to work out some key ideas. An earlier version of part of Chapter 2 appeared as 'The Location of Empire: Anne Grant's Memoirs of an American Lady' in *European Romantic Review*, 21(2), April 2010, pp. 205–20. An earlier version of Chapter 5 appeared as 'Time, Emigration, and the Circum-Atlantic World: John Galt's Bogle Corbet' in Regina Hewitt (ed.), *John Galt: Observations and Conjectures on Literature, History, and Society* (Lewisburg, PA: Bucknell University Press, 2012), pp. 299–321. Lastly, a version of part of Chapter 4 appeared as 'Diasporas: Thomas Pringle and Mary Prince' in JoEllen DeLucia and Juliet Shields (eds), *Migration and Modernities: The State of Being Stateless, 1750–1850* (Edinburgh University Press, 2019), pp. 51–76.

The duty of memory is the duty of the descendants

Marc Augé

Introduction: 'So complete a change' (in So Short a Time) – Scottish Romanticism, Modernity and Collective Memory

> We are in fact living in a period characterized by constant, rapid and fundamental change in all the circumstances of life; change that is affecting our modes of thinking and our ideas and beliefs powerfully. Social groups break up, lose their traditions and with them the possibility of surviving amid surroundings no longer favourable to them; they know they are on the wane; sometimes we actually watch them disappear . . . Casting our minds back two or three generations . . . it looks as though the changes that have come about since then are probably bigger and more decisive than those we should see if we went back a further five or six centuries, or even more.[1]

Thus, Maurice Halbwachs characterises the singular aspect of modernity – the crisis of historical continuity – in a work that forms part of his foundational contribution to contemporary memory studies. The accelerated pace of historical change in the modern world has created a rupture in the flow of time, a radical break between the present and the past, threatening the survival of social groups, as it threatens the 'collective memory' – the pool of knowledge and experiences in the memories of two or more persons that can be shared or passed down – that defined them.[2] It is the unprecedentedness of this break which provides the modern age with its distinctive temporal dimension.

By the time of Halbwachs's writing, in the late 1930s, the idea that modernity is distinguished by its break from the past was well established in European and North American thought – as it continued to be the go-to trope to frame a temporality of modernity by writers in succeeding generations. Halbwachs's employment of this trope of historical discontinuity, which, Jeffrey Barash argues, provides a leitmotiv in Halbwachs's writing,[3] is significant for the purposes of the present study for two reasons. First, the modern epoch's unprecedented break with the past is intrinsic, in Halbwachs's formulation, to the study of collective memory, as historical disjuncture not only grants to the work a sense of urgency but also helps make collective memory legible in the first place. Where the vestiges of past conditions retain some hold – in the traditional societies of the country and smaller towns – collective memory, in Halbwachs's account, continues to offer some sense of historical continuity. Only from outside the domain of traditional societies, however, from the perspective of modern civilised society, can the sociologist record and categorise the singular features of collective memory, which at the same time is always in danger of disappearing before our very eyes. Second, the vital link between a consciousness of modernity and a concern with collective memory had already gained common expression, I will argue, in a particular context and time: Scottish writing of the Romantic era. More than a hundred years before Halbwachs, in 1814, Walter Scott, the lion of Scottish Romanticism, situated the writing of his immensely successful first novel within a period of unprecedented historical change: '[t]here is no European nation which, within the course of half a century, or little more, has undergone so complete a change as this kingdom of Scotland'.[4] In *Waverley*, in which Scott would lay claim to fiction's authority to shape historical understanding in the modern world, his own age has seen an unprecedented disjuncture between past and present that, in his formulation, has threatened the integrity not just of a particular social groups within Scotland but of the nation as a whole. Scott's concern is not simply to narrate past events, the fateful episodes of the last failed Jacobite attempt to overthrow the Hanoverian succession, but to give an idea of 'habits, manners, and feelings', the rituals and repeated acts located in in the ephemerality of day-to-day experience rooted in oral tradition and passed down from one generation to another. In this, Scott's historical fiction can be seen as part of a larger shift in British historiography in which Scottish writing played a seminal role, a shift to what Mark Salber Phillips has called 'the historicization of everyday life'.[5] For Scott, who never published his own memoirs, fiction, and the novel especially, proved best suited to theorise and describe the particular moment when collective memory begins to fade, and a new generation adapts to the new ways of the present while assuming responsibility to record and curate the old ways of the past. This responsibility is presented as a solemn obligation, for historicity-as-memory always carries with it the threat of its own annihilation: 'forgetting', which often registers as a moral or ethical failing, a failure to do right by one's ancestors. In *Waverley*, the first 'historical' novel, the past is something that can be remembered (or forgotten), as opposed to learned (or unlearned). Scott, like many Scottish writers of his generation, and like Halbwachs several generations later, framed his study of the past and its relation to the present not as a problem of history but of memory.

Scott's emphasis that Scotland is unique among *European* nations in terms of the pace of change implies an unstated point of comparison to alternative domains for which Scotland's accelerated temporality would provide both an exemplar and analogue. Though the new world of North America was never the primary setting in any of Scott's historical fiction, Scott was certainly aware of the profound social and political transformations in the region, transformations which set the terms for the energies and activities of members of his own family as it did for many others in Scotland. The era of Scottish post-Enlightenment Romanticism, when Edinburgh became a leading site in the British Empire for literary and cultural production second only to London, also saw a wide dissemination of Scottish intellectual and literary ideas, in the context of increasing attention, energies and activities in the British Atlantic.[6] In the context of this 'Atlantic System', Scotland's absorption into the British state was part of a larger narrative of political and economic consolidation and fragmentation. In a bewildering cycle of revolution and counter-revolution within the span of a century or so, existing alliances or affinities became obsolete or shifted as new collectivities and cultural formations displaced older ones. As Scottish intellectual and economic energy continued to be oriented towards Britain's expanding North American empire, Scottish writers were in a unique position to shape modern historical understanding in the British Atlantic. In the Atlantic world of colonial settlement and expansion, emigration and diaspora, indentured servitude and slavery, forced removal and clearance, war between empires, rebellion and military occupation, Scottish writers brought their own imaginings of the relation between past and present. Largely in response to their own national predicament in post-Union imperial Britain, Scots brought to this world a historiography that imagined an unprecedented fissure within the flow of time that had rent the present from the past, a fissure that could be measured in only one or two generations and that was often within reach of, or just beyond, living memory. This sense of an immense gulf between past and present was attended by deep national anxieties but also by a renewed optimism, of something new arising from the old, and of social and cultural reinvention. This book examines this distinct Scottish historiography, in which a temporality of modernity takes shape in the forms, tropes and categories of a mode of historical understanding we now would term collective or cultural memory.[7] I trace this emergent mode in Scottish history writing, both fictional and non-fictional, as it circulated throughout the Atlantic world. In doing so, my study follows other recent studies in making the case for the Atlantic world as a critical site in the making of a culture of modernity while bringing to light the fundamental contribution of Scottish Romantic writing to this culture.[8]

A Scottish Post-Union Post-Enlightenment Romanticism

A present radically dissevered from the past, the defining feature of the historicity of European modernity, made even more insistent the anxiety of an uncertain future. 'A characteristic of a new epochal consciousness emergent in the late eighteenth century', writes Reinhart Koselleck, 'was that one's own time was not only experienced as a beginning or an end, but also as a period of transition'.[9] For Scots living with this new epochal consciousness, the anxious speculation of the future expressed fundamentally as an inquiry into the future viability of the Scottish nation, post-Union, in which the rise and fall of Prince Charles Edward Stuart's Jacobite forces – the revolution that wasn't – was a fixed point of reference. The defeat of Jacobitism in 1745 commonly marked the starting point in Scots' enunciation of the commencement of their own modern age. Current-day historians, writing amid renewed heightened interest in Scotland's future, have given empirical credence to this apprehension of unprecedented social change brought on by rapid industrialisation and urbanisation, summarised by one as a 'dash to modernity': 'Not until forced Soviet state industrialisation in the 1920s and 1930s', writes T. M. Devine, 'could any country in Europe equal the speed and scale of the Scottish transformation . . . from around the 1750s and the 1760s'.[10] For many Scots at the turn of the nineteenth century, some of whom were old enough to have lived through the events, the brutal military campaign of pacification and the series of legislative acts that followed in the aftermath of the Jacobite defeat, which were designed to eradicate the threat of uprising once and for all, seemed to mark the beginning of this unprecedented disruption to the social fabric of the nation. Though the articles of the Act of Union of 1707 had preserved Scottish religious, educational, legal and financial systems, ensuring the continuance of an independent Scottish civil society, post-Jacobite social and economic changes, accompanied by increasing centralisation of state power in London and a wave of often virulent anti-Scotch prejudice in the English public press, provoked anxious fears that Scotland was becoming reduced to second-class status within a unified Great Britain. Anxiety for the nation's future was manifested in a conflicted national culture, which, on the one hand, called for complete Scottish assimilation into the English model (most insistently as it concerned the eradication of linguistic 'Scotticisms') to better effect complete Scottish participation in an Anglocentric Great Britain. On the other hand, Scottish cultural anxieties inspired a particular Scottish brand of cultural nationalism that called for the retention of the markers of distinctive Scottishness (particularly as it concerned the preservation of the Scots vernacular tradition in poetry and folklore), lest Scotland's full integration in the Union bring on a complete loss of national identity.

While many studies at the end of the last century emphasised the constrictive aspects of the 'inferiorisation' of Scottish cultural life post-Union – Scotland's disenfranchisement and march towards provincialism signalled perhaps most dramatically in the pronouncement of the 'death' of Scottish history – follow-on studies have provided a re-examination of Scottish culture of the late eighteenth and early nineteenth centuries to emphasise its more generative features.[11] These accounts show how national anxiety prompted Scots to take the lead in inventing a multinational 'Britishness' on variety of fronts, cultural, economic, legal.[12] Robert Crawford's 'devolved' account of Scottish cultural and literary production charts how Scots did the work of actively 'challenging, interrogating, and even structuring' the British cultural 'centre'.[13] As Susan Manning summarises the case, Britishness offered 'Scottish writers a range of rhetorical resources with which to explore the implications of being "modern" in the post-union period'.[14] Far from being side-lined by a post-Union Anglocentrism, Scottish culture became the wellspring of a modern, imperial idea of Great Britain.

The late eighteenth and early nineteenth centuries saw the rise of a productive enquiry into the unique predicament of modern Scotland, as a stateless nation within a modern, multinational state. The period also saw a dramatic expansion in the forms, discourses and institutions in which this enquiry was brought to a reading public, in Scotland and beyond. In Ian Duncan's compelling account, a distinctive literary field emerged from Edinburgh in the first years of the nineteenth century, introducing innovative publications and genres that would come to dominate the nineteenth-century literary market and that 'shaped an imperial British culture that lasted throughout the century'.[15] Periodicals, including the quarterly review, miscellany and weekly magazine; poetry such as the national ballad anthology and metrical romance; and prose fiction, including the novel on historical and national themes, and the short 'tale', all acquired their definitive forms and associations. The rise of this literary field justifies, for Duncan, the framing of a distinct period, a 'post-Enlightenment', in which the rise of a distinctively Scottish Romanticism took the form – initially at least – as a displacement of Enlightenment cultural formations rather than their replacement. This was in part because a large number of Scottish literary professionals of the period received their educations in the academic institutions of late-Enlightenment Edinburgh – the High School, the University and in the Faculty of Advocates – and in associated intellectual clubs like the Speculative Society.[16] In the tight-knit, not quite amateur and not yet wholly commercial or entrepreneurial literary culture increasingly oriented towards the marketplace but still 'enmeshed in regional patronage networks', Scottish writing was saturated with the discourses of the Scottish 'Science of Man': philosophical history, political economy and conjectural anthropology.[17] At the same time, novelistic and literary concerns informed much historical writing; the conjectural enquiry into the nature and origins of the ancient Scots, which had taken the form of debate as to the authenticity of Ossian in the 1760s – though a committee chaired by Henry Mackenzie had resolved the question by 1805 – had largely devolved into a discussion of Macpherson's imitative skill. The antiquarian rediscovery of 'lost' artefacts had, by the turn of the century, inspired a fascination with ancient and outmoded poetic and song forms, the contemporary imitation of which had become recognised as a merit-worthy genre all its own. The porousness of the border between Scottish literary and historical fields meant that Scott could, in *Waverley*, admiringly reference two essayists, Anne Grant and the Earl of Selkirk – the transatlantic experiences and writings of whom I examine in the present work – as preceding him in drawing attention to the Scottish Highlands and the profound changes in the region since the disintegration of clanship.[18] Indeed, in the opening remarks of his treatise on Highland emigration, Selkirk in 1805 had supplied the trope of unprecedented acceleration of national-historical change that Scott would use to bracket his fictional narrative. At the same time, Scott had traded on public interest in previous literary treatments of this rapid disintegration, such as Alexander Campbell's 1808 poetic elegy on depopulation in the Highlands, *The Grampians Desolate* – also examined in this study. Campbell's copious paratextual commentary on Highland economic policy in turn amounted to a systematic rebuttal of Selkirk's earlier views in the ongoing debate on Highland emigration. Two other transatlantic Scottish writers I examine, Thomas Pringle and John Galt, were both associated with the Edinburgh-based *Blackwood's Edinburgh Magazine* at some point in their careers – Pringle as its first (failed) editor, Galt as frequent contributor. Both would continue their literary careers while establishing alternate but parallel careers in the service of British colonial settlement and administration.

Influenced by the conjectural and comparative methodology of the late Enlightenment Science of Man, Scottish writers took up a cultural preoccupation with progress in the modern age, offering to British Romanticism, and Britishness, a distinctive form of historicism that assumed a stadial model of human social development. If, as Benedict Anderson has argued, the rise of the modern nation-state was attended by a new temporal consciousness, of a 'homogenous empty time' through which people and nations moved calendrically, Scots, in James Chandler's account, offered an added dimension of temporal unevenness, positing a successive range of temporal orders, different 'stages' of social development, that can exist independently and simultaneously within any point in the (universal) movement of time.[19] 'The crucial element in this new Scottish-Enlightenment sense of history', Chandler writes, 'is a dialectical sense of periodization in which particular "societies" or "nations," newly theorized as such . . . are recognized as existing in "states" that belong at once to two different, and to some extent competing, orders of temporality'.[20] The existence of different and competing orders of temporality in a single moment in time – what Koselleck termed the 'contemporaneity of the noncontemporaneous' – registers as the distinctive contribution of Scottish post-Enlightenment historical writing to the temporality of modernity, as the clash of 'backward' and 'advanced' societies becomes its predominant theme.[21] The dialectical sense of periodisation also established the terms for a post-Union understanding of Scottish nationhood, as the competing elements of this dialectic were set, more often than not, along a Highland–Lowland fault-line. Lowland urban Scots expressed themselves as uniquely connected, in various degrees to be sure, to a Highland society that simultaneously fell within the range of Scotland's imagined community but, aided by a heavy military presence and unprecedented government intervention in many aspects of Highland social and economic life, had only just recently climbed from a stage of semi-barbarism. The self-awareness that 'Scottishness' partook of both the primitive and the civilised was an integral feature of Scottish narratives of nationhood in relation to Great Britain, the British Empire and the rest of the world. As their own nation seemed situated in the liminal space between two different and competing orders of orders of temporality, Scots were particularly attuned to the complexity of social development not only among nations but within them as well.[22]

Memory/History

Post-Enlightenment Romantic Scotland defined the times as the immediate aftermath of the last failed resistance to Union, which was at the same time a violent lurch into the modern world, culminating in Scottish participation in the British wars against revolutionary and Napoleonic France. The 1789–1815 struggle, which Linda Colley argues was the historical catalyst for the forging of a British nation,[23] also inspired a widespread psychic after-effect, an anxiety, Richard Terdiman writes, that the 'past had somehow evaded memory, that recollection had ceased to integrate with consciousness. In this memory crisis the very coherence of time and of subjectivity seemed disarticulated.'[24] That Terdiman identifies this post-Revolutionary anxiety as a *memory* crisis, rather than a crisis of history, is telling of the ways in which the Romantic-era discourse of modernity conceived of a break with the past so abrupt and decisive it could easily take place within a single lifetime. Thus, the special vantage point from which one could survey and narrate this crisis was not defined by a particular education, discipline or training, but by a particular age: those who had lived during the earlier time, or who were intimate with the stories of those who had, were in a position to perceive what had changed and what had been lost. Scottish Romantic writers, who were preoccupied both with marking this epoch of change, as well as making sense of its new political, social and cultural landscapes, were uniquely positioned to shape a historical consciousness imagined as memory in Great Britain, and, as I argue, in the emergent nations and colonial settlements of North America.

But what is historical memory, and how does it differ from 'history' proper? What does it mean to describe events of the past in mnemonic rather than historical terms? Our own time has experienced a great upsurge in memory, which has taken on a greater resonance in contemporary culture. It is now commonplace to describe the 'memory' of historical events that lie well beyond a span of several human lifetimes, and the sources of this 'memory' may derive from a wide variety of forms exclusive of oral testimony. But the question of what is memory and what is history has remained insistent for historians and cultural critics, as it has formed the critical foundation for an emergent field of memory studies.[25] Many critics, for example, have argued that delineating and maintaining the distinction between memory and history is essential for maintaining the intellectual integrity of the former, which would otherwise simply be absorbed into the critical field of the older and more established latter. In this vein, Jeffrey Barash argues that 'collective memory essentially concerns the living remembrance of overlapping generations, and this remembrance must be distinguished from all secondary forms of recollection that are bequeathed by the historical past'.[26] Beyond 'a given horizon of contemporaneity', Barash writes, the historical past always lies beyond the pale of collective memory. 'The fluidity and fragmentation sphere of collective memory' distinguishes it 'from that of the methodologically elaborated field of history or codified and institutionally sanctified practices of tradition.' Barash traces the intellectual history of the memory/history debate to return ultimately to the starting point of contemporary memory studies, to Halbwachs, who had insisted on a fundamental difference between collective memory and history. For Halbwachs, history is unitary – though historians may display an 'excessive specialization and fanatic desire for detailed study', they do so under the assumption that there is only one history, and 'in the total record resulting from all these successive summations, no fact will be subordinated to any other fact, since every fact is interesting as any other and merits as much to be brought forth and recorded'.[27] In contrast, collective memory 'by definition . . . does not exceed the boundaries of [the] group' which gives rise to it.[28] Because its chief function is to provide a sense of cohesive group identity, collective memory is about resemblances: 'when it considers its past, the group feels strongly it has remained the same and becomes conscious of its identity throughout time'.[29] In contrast to unitary history, which is interested in differences and does not concern itself with moments when nothing happens, 'when life is content with repetition', memory lives in the domain of the everyday and the commonplace: 'it is a current of continuous thought whose continuity in not at all artificial, for it retains from the past only what still lives or is capable of living in the consciousness of the groups keeping the memory alive'.[30]

More recent critics have wanted to expand the temporal range of Halbwachs's theory of collective memory, moving it beyond the horizon of overlapping generations. Jan Assmann does this by distinguishing between two modes of collective memory – communicative memory, based on everyday oral communications shared by members of a group, and cultural memory, which extends beyond the range of oral history, taking in what Assmann terms the 'objectivized culture' of 'texts, images, rites, buildings, monuments, cities, or even landscapes'.[31] In so far as 'objectivized culture' includes texts, Assmann extends the range of collective memory into what had been considered the exclusive domain of history, the written word. Assmann's work provides a useful framework for understanding the rise of Scottish memory writing, as I outline it in Chapter 1. At the same time, other critics have seen in the recent upsurge of interest in memory a concomitant diminishing of the authority and power of history. Andreas Huyssen, for example, has argued that the current 'hypertrophy' of memory signals a larger shift in temporal consciousness in contemporary culture. 'If the historical past once used to give coherence and legitimacy to family, community, nation, and state,' he writes, 'then those formerly stable links have weakened today to the extent that national traditions and historical pasts are increasingly deprived of their geographic and political groundings, which are reorganized in the processes of cultural globalization'.[32] The problem, nowadays, Charles S. Maier tells us, is that we have too much memory and not enough history. 'Excessive memory', he writes, risks engendering conflict between competing claims of past victimhood, along with a 'complacency and collective self-indulgence' that obscure rather than illuminate past events.[33] Much like the Romantic cult of sentimental melancholy, which it resembles, he writes, 'memory serves less as a mental faculty for recovering the past than as an exercise pleasurable in its own right'.[34] Maier therefore calls for a return to history, with its power not only to relive the past but to explain it, though a narrative of causal sequencing.[35]

For historians like Maier, memory lacks the power of history to make objective sense of the past. Memory is fragmented and ephemeral; established in everyday utterance, it is antithetical to documentation and material artefact. In the dialectic between memory and history, writes Paul Ricœur, history operates as a 'critical authority that is able not only to consolidate and to articulate collective and individual memory but also to correct it or even contradict it'.[36] For Jacques Le Goff, who seeks to rescue history from contemporary 'naïve trends' that would identify memory with history or even elevate memory above history, disciplinary authority is what sets history apart from memory. To those who see memory as a more authentic and therefore truer form of understanding the past, Le Goff responds that, because the workings of memory 'are usually unconscious, it is in reality more dangerously subject to manipulation by time and by societies given to reflection than the discipline of history itself', which 'must seek to be objective and remain based on the belief in historical "truth"'.[37] Memory occupies an integral but subordinate relation to history as its 'raw material'. 'To privilege memory excessively', Le Goff warns, 'is to sink into the unconquerable flow of time.'[38]

In contrast to critics like Maier and Le Goff, who see an excess of memory in contemporary understandings of the past, Pierre Nora argues that real, living memory is no longer to be found. In what amounts to an elegy on authentic remembrance, Nora distinguishes between two kinds of memory, *milieux de mémoire* – 'environments of memory', which are associated with social groups and which most closely resemble the collective memory that Halbwachs described; and *lieux de mémoire* – 'sites of memory', which represent the calcified residue of the real thing, 'shells on the shore when the sea of living memory has receded'.[39] What we now call 'memory', Nora writes, is already history, inscribed in the '[m]useums, archives, cemeteries, festivals, anniversaries, treaties, depositions, monuments, sanctuaries, fraternal orders', which are the 'boundary stones of another age'.[40] Though Nora's work inaugurated an intensive project of cataloguing sites of memory in the modern world, his study in many ways aligns with Halbwachs's insistence on a temporal relation within the memory/history divide: history is what comes after memory is lost. Others, however, have not been prepared to declare the death of real memory and its replacement by history and, while upholding a fundamental distinction between memory and history, have sought rather to blur the dividing line between them. Peter Burke, for example, sees a complex but overlapping process of selection and interpretation in both collective memory and history. He coins the term 'social memory' to stress 'the homology between the ways in which the past is recorded and remembered'.[41] Others have seen the tension between memory and history as a productive one: Patrick H. Hutton, rather than seeing a stark divide between them, argues that contemporary history is an 'art of memory' 'because it mediates the encounter between two moments of memory: repetition and recollection'.[42] Allan Megill, while asserting that 'history and memory' remain 'sharply different', nonetheless argues for the ultimate futility of delineating this difference, concluding that 'the boundaries between history and memory . . . cannot be precisely established' and, in the absence of a single grand historical narrative, 'the tension between history and memory cannot be unresolved'.[43]

Writing Scottish Collective Memory

'Like everything else,' the editors of a recent influential anthology of memory studies remind us, 'memory has a history.'[44] In his study of shifts in the genres of historical writing in eighteenth- and early nineteenth-century Britain, Phillips alerts us to the ways in which the division between memory and history was manifested through competing but overlapping modes of representation, as well as social practices and disciplinary concerns. Phillips examines the generic porousness of eighteenth-century historiography to chart the rise in interest in and acceptance of a history of manners and everyday life. Though this history may have lacked the solidity or coherence of accepted genres of historical writing, it acquired increasing popularity in 'a miscellaneous collection of particular histories in which biographical, antiquarian, or anecdotal interest predominated'.[45]

Phillips situates himself firmly within the disciplinary ranks of historians, and he frames questions of instabilities in the genres of historical writing as questions for a professional historian to answer, yet his study is compelling for the present study on two accounts. For one, it sheds invaluable light on a particular phase in the history of memory, as Phillips shows how features we now associate with collective memory, as opposed to history – its focus on everyday life and repetition; its fragmentation and lack of formal structure; its ephemerality, generationality and rootedness in oral expression – gained a common currency in Britain in the late Enlightenment and early Romantic periods. For another, his study illustrates how Scots led the way in this new historiography. Drawing on a 'discourse of the social', which in large part emanated from the Scottish Enlightenment, in Phillips's account, the work of writers such as James Boswell, William Creech and John Ramsay of Ochtertyre epitomised a new 'history of everyday life', concerned with private manners and private emotions, a history of 'society and sentiment'. In his vast but still largely unpublished memoir, written in the last quarter of the eighteenth century, Ramsay – who was born in 1736 – recounted the profound transformation of everyday rural Scotland, a transformation that was so abrupt, that, '[e]re long', Ramsay writes, 'it must be the province of the antiquary to describe the life and manners of a real Highlander'.[46] Ramsay relied on his own memories, or enquired of those of a previous generation, to catalogue his sense of historical discontinuity, lamenting that much of the texture of the earlier time is now unrecoverable:

> Although some materials may be collected from books and pamphlets, the most precious information would have been from the conversation

of the aged, who were intimately acquainted with those that had a share in the honour and labour of that generous attempt. Had I myself undertaken this work thirty years ago, I might have had much excellent information which is now irrecoverably lost.[47]

Ramsay's lament reveals the paradoxical nature of spoken memory in late eighteenth Scotland. As Penny Fielding writes,

> On the one hand, the oral is something everyone knows, it is shared experience, communal knowledge, the wisdom of the people. On the other hand, the oral cannot really be known at all because of its habit of vanishing without record into the past.[48]

In Ramsay's formulation, orality is the privileged medium for the dissemination of everyday life and manners. At the same, only writing can preserve this 'most precious information' and allow it to be passed down to future generations of Scots.

Writing, however, does not simply supplant orality in Romantic-era Scotland. Oral culture never disappears; instead, as Fielding has demonstrated, it becomes a parallel medium of social discourse that often cross-pollinates with literacy in productive ways.[49] Scotland is like other societies 'in touch with writing'. In these, 'though [w]riting on one level transforms memory, by fixing it,' Fentress and Wickham argue, 'it is also true to say that more memory comes to be structured through a dialectic between oral and written narrative'.[50] Ramsay's work gives utterance to this dialectic, through which memory, poised always at the edge of forgetting, emerges as the sine qua non of the history of everyday life. Ramsay's exercise in memory transcription would be dwarfed by Henry Cockburn's work composed a few decades later, discussed in Chapter 1 of this study, but, as Phillips points out, Ramsay's work provides a crucial example for Scottish Romantic historical writing, most notably Scott's. Ramsay's work, writes Phillips, 'is a prime example of the kind of effort to hold on to local memory and tradition without which *Waverley* and its successors could never have been written'.[51]

The idea of memory as fragmentary and ephemeral, rooted in folklore, legend and tradition as it is passed down from one generation to another, found expression in literature, and it is in literary texts, writes Terdiman, 'where the most striking representations of . . . the nineteenth-century's memory crisis occur'. In particular:

[i]t is the novel that most organizes itself as a projection of the memory function and its disruptions. Novels are exercises in the process of memory. Writers in all periods have turned their imaginations to the past, but nineteenth-century plots particularly presented themselves as the diegesis of history's stress: much more under the sign of a tense exploration of the past's disjunction from the present than the more traditional guise of rehearsing some consecrated mythology symbolic of the community's consciousness of itself.[52]

Under the sign of collective memory and the past's disjunction from the present, literature, especially the novel, becomes the chief vehicle for the exploration of modernity in nineteenth-century France, in Terdiman's account. It was, however, an exploration inaugurated first and most emphatically in Scottish writing of the Romantic era, which imagined memory in ways distinct from other European, and from English, writing.[53]

This book looks at Scottish writers and how they undertook a distinct mode of historical writing separate from 'history', even though this mode of writing had not coalesced into a distinctive genre. While this book suggests we need to pay more attention to an understanding of the past expressed *as memory* in Scottish writing, as it began to explore and make meaning of its proximate past, it does not, however, seek to supplant 'history' with 'collective memory' in its engagement with Scottish representations of the past. Nor does it seek to undertake an exhaustive investigation of what might now be termed 'Scottish collective memory' of the period: either through an examination of oral cultures or traditions or by uncovering the traces of collective memory in monuments, memorials, public commemorations and ceremonies, architecture, or exhibitions and displays – those mostly material artefacts that are the predominant subjects of scrutiny in much contemporary memory studies. Though there is certainly room for these kinds of investigations in the field of Scottish Romanticism, this book instead examines the ways in which Scots imagined the structures of collective memory in their writing, particularly in literature. It focuses on the ways in which Scottish texts, particularly literary texts, developed forms of narrating the past in which they employed tropes of recollection and remembrance to explore the necessity, function and processes of collective memory in the modern world. It therefore looks for the eruptions of 'memory' in a range of works of differing, sometimes overlapping, genres, including the autobiographical retrospective account, personal memoir and retrospective poetry; the novel masquerading as a personal memoir, handed-down oral account, or 'theoretical biography'; the personal memoir/biography; and the treatise on colonial policy. In tracing the operations of historical memory in Scottish writing of the Romantic era, my work follows the work of Catherine Jones, who astutely traces the uses of 'memory', in its various registers, in the Waverley Novels, and Ann Rigney, who charts the progress of Scott's own 'afterlives' as his legacy is woven into the cultural memory of various places around the world.[54] My work draws upon these pioneering studies; however, while also adding to the appreciation of Scott's significance, it seeks to widen the scope, both by looking more closely at Scott's example as it was taken up by writers in various places in North America, and by examining other writers of the Scottish Romantic period, many of whom established reputations in the New World that were equal to, or even greater than, their reputations in Great Britain.

Scotland, Modernity and Transatlantic Historiography

Ian Duncan identifies the perspective on the compressed or accelerated temporality of modernity in the Scottish post-Enlightenment. 'Scots writers articulated their period consciousness', he writes, 'by looking back at the preceding epoch, the half-century from the 1745 rising to the recent French wars covered in first trilogy of "Waverley Novels," in which the drastic if uneven modernization of Scottish life provided the material context for the Enlightenment conception of history as wholesale social change'.[55] My own study mostly concerns itself with the first thirty years or so of the nineteenth century, a period that roughly overlaps with Duncan's chronology of the Scottish post-Enlightenment, in which the middle period 1814–25 – the focus of his study – is the 'post-war' decade. This period commences with the defeat of Napoleon at Waterloo, which marks the ending of Britain's long struggle against revolutionary France, and the beginning of a new expansion of British global power and influence, although the immediate after-effect of the war, however, was to spark a national economic and agricultural crisis, which hit Scotland especially hard. I take up Duncan's account of Scottish Romanticism as a 'Post-Enlightenment' but wish to widen the frame of view to show how the phenomenon spread out beyond Scotland's shores to shape a culture of modernity in the transatlantic world. In the context of this wider frame, I suggest that that we also see a 'post-war' period that marks a related, but different, set of social and geopolitical realignments.

The status of Britain's North American dominions was not settled in 1783, at the end of the American Revolution; instead, the question ground on for several decades, leading to renewed violence between the new American republic and British forces at sea and in the burgeoning settlements of Upper and Lower Canada. Though it was perhaps peripheral to the main theatre of Anglo-French war on the European continent, the Anglo-American War of 1812 – which involved British, American and Canadian colonial forces, and their still-powerful indigenous allies – had a transformative effect on national and regional polities in North America. Sparked by what was perceived in the new republic as British encroachment on American national sovereignty, the War of 1812 has been described by some historians as the second war of American independence. At the same time, repeated American attempts to invade Canada posed an existential threat to Britain's largest remaining North American colony. The year 1815, which saw Napoleon's final defeat at Waterloo, also marked the cessation of hostilities between the United States and Great Britain, while marking the inauguration of a transatlantic 'culture war', fought not on the battlefield but in the Scottish and American review periodicals. The end of the 1812 conflict not only affirmed once and for all American independence and sovereignty but also largely put to rest the threat of American annexation of Canada. As the French continued their long retreat from North America, the British hold on its Canadian colonies was consolidated, if not completely secured, as francophone resistance to British rule in Lower Canada persisted. The status of Britain's West Indian planation colonies, however, remained an ongoing question in the period. The 1807 ban on the slave trade had not brought with it the demise of West Indian slavery, and the 1805 Haitian Revolution had sparked several slave rebellions in the British West Indies and throughout the Caribbean, as the abolitionist movement, relatively inactive in the years following the slave trade ban, began a renewed campaign, calling for total abolition.

All these struggles can be seen in the context of a quarter-century of violent political upheaval, part of what Wim Klooster has described as an epoch of Atlantic revolutions, during which 'seismic waves traveled through the Atlantic world ... linking uprisings on either side of the Atlantic'.[56] This wave had taken shape commencing with the American Revolution in 1775 and spread to France in 1789, Haiti in 1805, and Spanish America in the 1810s and 20s, often descending into a 'dialectic of violence and counter violence'.[57] Klooster's comparative historiography provides a glimpse into the crucible of social and political fragmentation and fracture, as well as consolidation and fusion, in which new collectivities in the Atlantic world were born of revolutionary movements – both failed and successful – against pre-existing orders. An ongoing history of separation, and union, transformed the lives of a diverse population in the Atlantic world, from the Highlands of Scotland and francophone Quebec, to Kingston and Port Royal, Jamaica, and the Cherokee towns of northern Georgia.

The breath-taking dynamism of social and political change in the Atlantic world in the period, which saw great empires defeated and supplanted by others, has become a key component of the recent historiographical imagining of a geographic entity whose conceptual framework is a vast empty body of water. 'The new Atlantic history', writes J. H. Elliott, 'might be defined as the history of the creation, destruction, and re-creation of communities as a result of the movement, across and around the Atlantic basin, of people, commodities, cultural practices, and ideas'.[58] This conceptualising of the 'Atlantic as a particular zone of exchange and interchange' has helped Atlantic historians to reorient eighteenth- and early nineteenth-century historiography away from a nation-state or European-centred focus.[59]

This historiography has brought its influence to bear on recent literary scholarship, providing a space in Scottish studies for work that emphasises the significant contribution that Scots, carried on the wave of British imperialism, made to cultural formations in the Atlantic world. Following the pioneering work of Andrew Hook, Susan Manning and others have emphasised the cross-cultural exchanges between Scotland and anglophone America.[60] This scholarship tends to focus its attention on the eighteenth century and the contributions of Scottish Enlightenment and religious institutions and ideas in pre-revolutionary American culture. More recently, Katie Trumpener, in what might be described as a 'circum-Atlantic' approach to the British Romantic novel, emphasises the importance of Scottish – as well as Irish, Welsh and North American – historical fiction, as it crossed national, colonial and regional borders throughout the English-speaking Atlantic world.[61] The immense scope of Trumpener's study provided a new understanding of the cultural interconnections among various sites in the British Atlantic, which gave rise to new national and historical forms of the novel, and my own work is indebted to hers. My work, which seeks to offer a wider range of view than previous scholarship that has focused largely on the bilateral relationship of exchange between American and Scottish culture, situates examples of Scottish historical writing within a framework of Atlantic historiography that emphasises the economic and cultural systems that continued to tie both the United States and colonies to the British Isles in the Romantic period, fostering common ideologies, institutions and social practices. At the same time, I wish to build upon the work of Duncan and others that understand Scottish Romanticism as a distinctive cultural formation. If, however, Edinburgh is the locus of a post-Enlightenment culture from which circum-Atlantic Scottish writers derived income, training and professional associations, these writers also drew upon materials and examples furnished by the colonial world beyond Scotland's shores. In tracing the conduits of exchange and interchange, circulation and transmission of Scottish literary writing in the Atlantic world I seek to contribute to an ongoing project of uncovering a distinctive thread in its historiography that had been previously subsumed into 'British' history or that had made its appearance in other settler or emergent national historiographies.

Writing on the Transperiphery

Instrumental in the forging of a culturally heterogeneous Great Britain, Scots were also intent on ensuring that empire would become its definitive feature. The preservation of Scottish civil society following the Acts of Union in 1707 meant Scotland was in a much better position than Wales or Ireland to take advantage of the new imperial economy, and by 1815, Devine writes, 'Scots thoroughly and systematically colonized all areas of the British empire from commerce to administration, soldiering to medicine, colonial education to the expansion of emigrant settlements'.[62] Scottish migration to North America substantially increased, especially after the 1760s, transforming the demographic profile in the colonies, and 'on a epistemological level', summarises Michael Gardiner, 'the Scottish contribution was the essence of empire: the practical and spatial attitude to the observation and organisation of the world, the ideal of franchised universalism, the culture of the work ethic, and the necessity of free markets to a nationless state'.[63] At the same time, Devine writes, '[s]o intense was the Scottish engagement with empire that it affected almost every nook and cranny of Scottish life . . . In a word, empire was fundamental to the moulding of the modern Scottish nation'.[64] The outsize role that Scots would play in colonial exploration, settlement, administration and military occupation have led some historians to describe a 'Scottish empire', in which 'the characteristics of the Scottish civil experience can be identified clearly surviving throughout the former British Empire in a range of educational, religious and other institutions'.[65] The history of Scotland's disproportionately large contribution to the British Empire is complicated, however, by an alternate set of realities: between 1830 and 1914, the heyday of the empire, Scotland, Devine writes, 'haemorrhage[ed]' over two million people, 'a rate of outward movement that was around one and a half times that of England and Wales'.[66] If one includes migration to England in the statistics, 'Scotland then emerges as the emigration capital of Europe for much of the period'.[67] Among nations of the British Isles, only Ireland suffered a greater loss of population in the time period, and 'Scotland was almost alone among European nations in having experienced large-scale industrialization and a great outward movement of population'.[68] Modernisation allowed Scotland to become the great supplier of manpower, matériel and intellectual capital for the British Empire in the nineteenth century, but in terms of its anomalous emigration patterns, Scotland resembled an underdeveloped nation more than an industrial-colonial powerhouse.

The contradictions and anomalies of Scotland's relation to empire have led to a recent debate as to Scotland's 'postcoloniality' and whether Scottish literature qualifies as postcolonial literature. The authors of a seminal study on the theory and practice of postcolonial literatures summarise the problematic position of Scottish – and Irish and Welsh – cultures in terms of the coloniser/colonised divide. 'While it is possible', they write, 'to argue that these societies were the first victims of English expansion, their subsequent complicity in the British imperial enterprise makes it difficult for colonized peoples outside Britain to accept their identity as a post-colonial'.[69]

The authors' answer to this conundrum is a 'dominated-dominating' model that 'stresses linguistic and cultural imposition, and enables an interpretation of British literary historiography as a process of hierarchical interchange in internal and external group relationships'.[70] Yet even this model does not adequately account for social and linguistic complexities within Scottish society, or the ways in which Scots of various and multiple backgrounds engage in hierarchical interchanges among groups across fault-lines in Scotland, Britain or the varied spaces of the Atlantic world.[71] Like many scholars of Scottish Romanticism interested in national or colonial categories, I look to a postcolonial methodology to gain a deeper understanding of my subject, but I have tried not to oversimplify the various situations and conditions in which Scots found themselves implicated, or entangled, in the colonial project and which informed their writings. My intent, then, is not to carry the coloniser or colonised debate into the transatlantic arena, but instead to identify what a recent study of Scotland's relation to postcoloniality has described as 'a dual relationship of congruence and conflict centered on the form of the British empire'.[72] In this vein, I would argue, Scottish activities intellectual and otherwise in the British Atlantic, and the conditions that shaped both Scottish and transatlantic cultures in the period, must be understood within the context of global changes in economic development and exchange in an ascendant capitalist 'world economy'. A 'world-system' arrangement of 'core' and 'periphery' accounts for the increasing economic and cultural marginalisation of Scottish society – with its own increasing internal divisions between urban anglophone Lowland areas and a rural Gaelic-speaking Highlands – within an expanding colonial Great Britain, while also emphasising Scotland's integral relation with a London-based core of British economic and political power.[73]

Scotland's increasing peripheral, or semi-peripheral, status within Great Britain set the terms for Scottish political, economic and social power in the Atlantic world, while it also sowed the seeds of Scottish dispossession and displacement. Thus, while colonial or military administrators from the Scottish Highlands were often at the vanguard of colonial settlement projects that resulted in the relentless dispossession of indigenous peoples from their ancestral lands, the bardic poets emanating from the ranks of Gaelic-speaking emigrants gave voice to their own collective dispossession from ancestral lands, on the other side of the Atlantic. For Scottish colonial administrators, settlers and soldiers, the British Empire offered opportunities and outlets that would have otherwise not been available. Often tied together in networks of kinship, professional affiliation or common background, educated Scots disseminated particularly Scottish cultural and social concerns, and Scots in the Atlantic world cast themselves as full-fledged, though perhaps junior, partners in Britain's imperial project. As both beneficiaries and the victims of this emerging world system, Scots manifested a unique historical sensibility, often providing challenges to existing paradigms of both national and imperial culture in the transatlantic world. In a wide-ranging repertoire of writing – critiques of slavery, and defences of it; surveys and statistical accounts of 'unimproved lands' on either shore; retrospectives of transatlantic sojourns and adventures both non-fictional and fictional; proto-ethnographies; and naturalist/ethnographic prose and poetry that catalogued the local fauna, flora and peoples of the New World – Scots helped to shape new paradigms of nation and empire shaped in the British Atlantic world. Steeped in the ideas and discourses of the Scottish Enlightenment Science of Man, combined perhaps with a heightened sensitivity to cultural difference, Scottish writers of the period often display an interest in the nuances of customs, habits and manners among the various groups they encounter, and in the local histories that have given rise to them, while situating taxonomies of 'local' culture within universalised structures of social development and interaction. Scottish writers often sought to mediate the interrelation between local cultural forms and the universal mechanisms that drove all human societies, an interrelation now writ large against the backdrop of global empire. Scottish writing therefore often exhibits a particular attraction to exploring the possibilities and problems of empire, as both a private and public site of improvement and an arena in which old prejudices and assumptions do not always operate: the latter posing both profound challenges and new opportunities. A basic belief in the principle of social and economic progress in these writings often accompanies a keen interest in local cultural forms, deemed outmoded or anachronistic. This interest sometimes took the form of distanced sympathy with the local victims of universal empire, and even something more akin to affinity or identification with their plight. Still, such sentiments rarely amounted to full-fledged resistance to colonial rule but ultimately sought to explore how local traditions and ways of life might somehow be accommodated within the imperial project.

Given Scotland's complicated status as a subsumed entity within an expanding imperial Great Britain, it is possible to characterise the movement, across and around the Atlantic basin, of *Scottish* people, commodities, cultural practices and ideas as more 'transperipheral' than simply 'transatlantic' or even 'transnational'. Like these related terms, 'transperipheral' emphasises the dynamics of exchange and interchange, circulation and transmission that are integral to recent conceptualisations of Atlantic history, while emphasising the crosscurrents occurring between and among peripheral sites in the British Empire, crosscurrents that are not necessarily generated within a London sphere of influence or those that circumvent the core altogether. For example, some of the most strident defenders of Caribbean enslavement were Scots who mounted their polemical attacks on abolitionists in the Edinburgh periodical reviews or the Glasgow press. At the same time, the London-based Scottish Secretary of the Anti-Slavery Society, Thomas Pringle, had come to the abolitionist cause after witnessing the horrors of slavery first-hand – not in the West Indies, but in the Cape Colony of South Africa, where he previously had attempted to settle. A transperipheral conceptualisation of Scottish writing in the Atlantic world provides a way of getting around the limits of national or imperial categories by which much transatlantic study has been organised, while reminding us of the importance of the varying relations of social, economic and political power that attend specific sites of interaction and cultural formation in the British Atlantic. Scottish contributions, and resistance, to colonising projects, both internal and external, did not play out uniformly in the emergent world-system, but in varying forms and with varying intensity. Seen in this regard, the problematic of Scotland's relative status vis-a-vis colonialism becomes a constitutive feature of Scottish writing in the Atlantic world.

Migrant Lives, Scottish Identities

Whether in Scotland, the North American colonies or even in the London core, Scottish writers drew energy from a feeling of living on the margins, which shaped their national and imperial identities. Scottish writers who moved throughout the Atlantic world as soldiers or their dependants, as colonial agents, journalists, activists or emigrants, played a critical role in the formation of Scottish national identity, both for Scottish migrants and for those they left 'back home', but their construction of their 'Scottishness' in relation to others they encountered in the Atlantic world depended on the context in which they wrote, and their own varying experiences of circum-Atlantic travel. Scottish writers expressed multiple and changing allegiances to their 'native' Scotland, to the 'mother country' of Great Britain, and to newly established colonial or national settlements in North America. With the notable exception of Scott, whose work and influence spread across the British Atlantic world but who never left Europe, the writers I take up in this study were themselves part of the Scottish Atlantic network and most spent some time in North America or the Caribbean, often making more than one journey there as they travelled back and forth on a circum-Atlantic circuit. All of the writers I examine strongly self-identify as 'Scottish' in their writings, and many identify Scotland as their 'native land', yet they do so in the context of a general declaration of estrangement, exile or displacement. These writers perhaps epitomise the condition of many migrant Scots, for whom Scotland is a place of deep personal investment but also always 'elsewhere' in relation to their present situation. The complexities of these migrant lives often make for complex national subjectivities, which resist easy labelling.

Situating the complex subjectivities of Scottish writers within the context of the circum-Atlantic allows us to reorient longstanding assumptions in Scottish studies, by placing 'Scottishness' alongside other national or ethnic subjectivities in the Atlantic world. A circum-Atlantic perspective of Scottish subjectivity, for example, provides a new perspective on the post-Union emergence, identified in Scottish literary historiography, of a problematic 'divided' or 'fragmented' Scottish subjectivity – expressed in concepts such as the 'Protean Scot', 'Caledonian antizygny', 'dissociation of sensibility' or Scottish 'paradox'. No less than for others, intercultural exchange was critical to Scottish writers' national self-definition, and the problem and conceptualisations of subjectivity integral to other fields of circum-Atlantic study can shed new light on our understanding of the hybridity, double consciousness and dialogism at work in the making of Scottish identity in the period.

In his study of the Black Atlantic, Paul Gilroy argues that new chronotopes are needed to fit with an analysis that is 'less intimidated by and respectful of the boundaries and integrity of modern nation-states . . .'.[74] For his own part, Gilroy offers as his study's central organising symbol 'ships in motion across the spaces between Europe, America, Africa, and the Caribbean'.[75] Such an image emphasises for Gilroy the fundamental dynamic of the circulation of cultural and political microcosm in the Atlantic world, while also evoking the Middle Passage and Black Diaspora projects that envisioned a 'redemptive return' to a putative African 'homeland'.[76] My own examination draws upon Gilroy's example in many respects, but in place of the chronotope of ships in motion I offer an alternative chronotope – the Border – to conceptualise the Scottish intervention in the transatlantic world. Neither completely within the core or the periphery, Scots occupied the liminal zone between these regimes, mediating between the centre and margin of the British Atlantic world: between union and fragmentation, revolution and evolution, coloniser and colonised, home and away, self and other, empire and nation, and memory and history. Scottish Romantic writing 'on the Border', installs, to paraphrase Duncan, Davis and Sorensen, the 'space-time of a historical modernity that looks backwards in order to move forwards'.[77] My study hopes to shed new light on the ways in which Scottish writers brought this chronotope of historical modernity to the Atlantic world, while shaping collective memory in this world in the process.

My work offers a threefold engagement with Scottish Romantic, transatlantic and memory studies while drawing from the perspectives and insights of other critical frameworks – such as indigenous, Black Atlantic and francophone Canada. In Chapter 1, I introduce a central theme of my study by examining the phenomenal rise to eminence and popularity of Walter Scott's brand of historical fiction in the context of its evocation of collective memory, which was particularly suited to the anxieties of emergent national cultures in the transatlantic world. In *Waverley*, his first novel, Scott employs mnemonic tropes to install a particular mode of modern historical consciousness I label 'aftermath', in which the present time is shaped in terms of its proximate relation (measured out in one or two human lifespans) to a moment of historical crux. The time of the Forty-Five is imagined as the catalyst for abrupt and transformational social and cultural change, which not only determined the nation's present in fundamental ways but altered the very pace of history. I examine the literary development of the 'aftermath' in *Waverley*, and in the Scottish 'memorial' writing of Robert Chambers and Henry Cockburn. I also look at how Scott's example of the 'aftermath' provided tropes, models and theoretical frameworks for North American writers for their own expression of national memory. These include Washington Irving's tale 'Rip Van Winkle'; John Neal's novel *Seventy-Six*, the themes of which are remembering (or forgetting) the American Revolution; and Philippe-Joseph Aubert de Gaspé's francophone novel of the British conquest of Canada, *Les Anciens Canadiens*, in which he calls on his readers to preserve the memory of their forebears.

Chapter 2 explores the memoirs and travel writing of Anne Grant, in which her remembrances imagine the peripheral spaces of the British Atlantic as the unique enclave of a particular mode of human society and of intercultural exchange. One of the most noteworthy transatlantic figures of the Scottish Romantic period, Grant was considered an important recorder on 'regional' or 'local' cultures, in the United States and Britain. Grant wrote widely on her life in the Scottish Highlands, and her published and unpublished letters, poetry and essay writing were deemed important accounts of Highland culture. Grant's *Memoirs of an American Lady* relates her childhood experiences growing up in colonial upstate New York, where her father, a Scottish officer in the British army, was posted. Grant's remembered childhood world is a polyglot world of indigeneity and emergent and receding empires, a world of tangled and shifting allegiances and identities. Examining the *Memoirs* alongside her writing on the Highlands, I look at Grant's retrospective description of the transperipheral circuits of movement and exchange in the British Atlantic world, circuits which make for a complex interplay of national, ethnic and regional identities that are ultimately at odds with her reputation for providing nostalgic renditions of a 'lost world' for discrete readerships on either side of the Atlantic.

My third chapter explores Scottish reconceptualisations of the 'aborigine', as registered most prominently in the writing and resettlement schemes of a pivotal figure in British immigration and settlement history, Thomas Douglas, 5th Earl of Selkirk. Selkirk's proposals to solve the problem of dispossession in the Highlands through planned Highland settlements in the New World brought about a radical transformation in British attitudes to Highland emigration and, in the process, helped reshape a national and imperial imaginative geography, in large part through a reimagining of 'native' folk memory. In contrast to most influential writing on the

Highland 'problem', Selkirk not only saw immigration as inevitable, but actively encouraged it, envisioning ethnically pristine 'National Settlements' that would serve as a bulwark for British interest in the New World, while allowing for the preservation of the collective memory of a people deemed hopelessly anachronistic in their 'native' land. Looking at published and unpublished plans, proposals, prospectuses and essays, I describe how Selkirk lays claim to the value of an 'aboriginal' way of life and argued for the preservation of Highland language and culture, while reconceptualising the idea of 'aboriginal' land rights. Selkirk's ideas on wholesale resettlement of dispossessed Highlanders reset the terms for the Clearance debate in Scotland; at the same time, these ideas, and his ideas on the future of indigenous and First Nations people, also helped to set the parameters of state policy on native displacement and resettlement in the Atlantic world for much of the nineteenth century.

Chapter 4 undertakes a twofold exploration of the contributions of Scottish writing in shaping transatlantic identities through retrospective testimonial accounts of slavery. I first examine the work of two Scottish writers associated with prominent first-hand descriptions of the horrors of transatlantic enslavement: John Gabriel Stedman and Thomas Pringle. Stedman's published and unpublished autobiographical writings and his *Narrative of a Five Years Expedition against the Revolted Negroes of Surinam* recount his experiences as a Scottish mercenary, sent to the Dutch plantation colony to suppress uprisings of the enslaved. Thomas Pringle, as secretary of the London Anti-Slavery Society, arranged, edited and supplemented with his own corroborating material *The History of Mary Prince*. Both Stedman's and Prince's narratives have received much critical attention in recent years, as they exemplify how retrospective accounts of slavery were crucial to the emergence of hybrid, intercultural identities in the transatlantic world. I examine the Scottish dimension of this emergence, a dimension which has been consistently overlooked or elided in critical accounts.

In this chapter I also explore how the memory of transatlantic slavery informed a Scottish national past that was itself imagined as collective trauma. Donald Macleod's *Gloomy Memories of the Highlands of Scotland*, which was a key document in an emergent historiography of Clearance in the late nineteenth century, was an acrimonious response to Harriet Beecher Stowe's travel memoir *Sunny Memories of Foreign Lands*. Stowe had lauded the abolitionist sympathies of her patron, the Duchess of Sutherland, while dismissing out-of-hand Macleod's remembrances of Sutherland cruelty and injustice during the Clearances of the 1810s. Informed by a critical assumption that 'cultural trauma' is forged in the very call to remember particular events in the past as 'traumatic', I argue *Gloomy Memories* represents a key cultural-memory text that continues to shape an understanding of historical trauma – for both Clearance and slavery – in Scotland.

My last chapter is devoted to John Galt, who has been claimed as both a 'Scottish' and a 'Canadian' writer. An important contributor to *Blackwood's* and a key figure in the early settlement of what is now the province of Ontario, Galt's writing underscores the complex and often conflicted elements of Scottish post-Enlightenment thinking on the relation between the past and present – and the future – in the modern world. On the one hand, much of Galt's writing, both fiction and non-fiction, partakes of an empirical-based 'statistical account' mode of regional and national enquiry, adopting the assumptions and speculative stance of a Scottish political economy. On the other hand, *Annals of the Parish* and his Canadian emigrant novels *Lawrie Todd* and *Bogle Corbet* inscribe a complex, and ultimately profoundly unsettling, cultural memory of the circum-Atlantic world. In the 'annalist' fiction that recounts the proximate past of the parish of Dalmailing, the 'theoretical biographies' of the two emigrants, and in other writing, Galt charts the development of a melancholy worldview inspired by a circum-Atlantic memory of constant upheaval and psychic trauma. The ambivalence at the heart of Scottish Atlantic memory, as reflected in John Galt's circum-Atlantic life experiences and writing, provides a capstone for my study of the Scottish Romantic contribution to collective memory in the British Atlantic.

Notes

1. Halbwachs, *Psychology of Social Class*, p. 22.
2. 'Collective memory' is the term Halbwachs developed in his writing of the first half of the twentieth century. Halbwachs's theories on memory culminated in his work *La Mémoire collective*, published posthumously in 1950. (Halbwachs died in Buchenwald in March 1945.)
3. Barasch, *Collective Memory and the Historical Past*, p. 31.
4. Scott, *Waverley*, p. 363.

5. Phillips, *Society and Sentiment*, p. 320.
6. For a historical account on Scotland's contribution to the British Atlantic empire, see Devine, *Scotland's Empire*; Hamilton, *Scotland, the Caribbean and the Atlantic World*; and Richards, 'Scotland and the Uses of the Atlantic Empire'.
7. There does not seem to be consensus on the terms used in critical accounts to describe collective memory. 'Collective memory', 'social memory', 'cultural memory, 'public memory', 'folk memory' and 'historical memory' are often used interchangeably in the study of memory as a group phenomenon. My own study adopts the term 'collective memory', following the editors of an influential reader on memory studies, but I also follow the distinction Jan Assmann makes between 'communicative' and 'cultural' memory, which provides a useful formula to describe the framework in which many of the writers in my study imagined their work. See Olick, Vinitzky-Seroussi and Levy, 'Introduction'. For Assmann, see 'Collective Memory and Cultural Identity'.
8. Many recent studies of the making of modernity are alternatives to Europe-centred studies that have tended to focus on the French Revolution as a critical historical turning point. For Atlantic-centred studies, see, for example, Gilroy, *The Black Atlantic*; and Baucom, 'Introduction'.
9. Kosseleck, *Futures Past*, p. 251.
10. Devine, *Recovering Scotland's Slavery Past*, p. 233. See also Devine, *The Scottish Nation*, pp. 105–23.
11. For inferiorisation, see Beveridge and Turnbull, *The Eclipse of Scottish Culture*. See also Simpson, *The Protean Scot*. For Scottish history's demise, see Ash, *The Strange Death of Scottish History*. See also Kidd, *Subverting Scotlan's Past*; and Nairn, *The Break-Up of Britain*. For an account of the culture of Scotland as a stateless nation, see McCrone, 'Representing Scotland'.
12. See Colley, *Britons*; Crawford, *Devolving English Literature*; Davis, *Acts of Union*; and Pittock, *The Invention of Scotland* and *Inventing and Resisting Britain*. For literary contributions to this work in the eighteenth century, see Davis, *Acts of Union*; Gottlieb, *Feeling British*; and Shields, *Sentimental Literature and Anglo-Scottish Identity*.
13. Crawford, *Devolving English Literature*, p. 13. See also Manning, 'Ossian, Scott, and Nineteenth-Century Scottish Literary Nationalism'.
14. Manning, 'Post-Union Scotland and Britishness', p. 49. See also Colley, *Britons*.
15. Duncan, *Scott's Shadow*, p. xi. In the first decade of the nineteenth century, writes Duncan, summarising Peter Garside's account ('English Novel in the Romantic Era'), Scotland accounted for 'a mere 0.5 percent of all novels published in the British Isles . . . this figure rose to 4.4 percent in

the following decade and to 12 percent in the 1820s, reaching 15 percent, or 54 out of 359 titles, in the peak years 1822–25 – a rate of growth far steeper than the national average' (Ibid. p. 22). For Scottish Romanticism as a distinct cultural formation, see Davis, Duncan, and Sorensen, *Scotland and the Borders of Romanticism*. See also 'Romancing Scotland'.

16. For studies that chart a Scottish Enlightenment culture outside the capital, see Carter and Pittock, *Aberdeen and the Enlightenment*; and Hook and Sher, *The Glasgow Enlightenment*.
17. Duncan, *Scott's Shadow*, p. 24.
18. In Chapters 2 and 3, respectively.
19. See Anderson, *Imagined Communities*, especially p. 26; and Chandler, *England in 1819*, pp. 127–51.
20. Chandler, *England in 1819*, p. 128.
21. Kosseleck, *Futures Past*, p. 249.
22. See Stroh, *Gaelic Scotland in the Colonial Imagination*; Withers, 'The Historical Creation of the Scottish Highlands'; Womack, *Improvement and Romance*; and McNeil, *Scotland, Britain, Empire*. See also Craig, *Out of History*.
23. See Colley, *Britons*.
24. Terdiman, *Present Past*, p. 4.
25. For a recent effort to consolidate and systemise a set of knowledges for the field of social memory studies, see Olick and Robbins, 'Social Memory Studies'.
26. Barash, *Collective Memory and the Historical Past*, p. 35.
27. Halbwachs, *The Collective Memory*, p. 83.
28. Ibid. p. 80.
29. Ibid. p. 85.
30. Ibid. p. 80.
31. Assmann, 'Collective Memory and Cultural Identity', p. 128.
32. Huyssen, *Present Pasts*, p. 4. Huyssen alludes to Nietzsche's argument that his own time suffered from a 'hypertrophy' of history. 'Today', Huyssen writes, 'we seem to suffer from a hypertrophy of memory, not history' (Ibid. p. 3).
33. Maier, 'A Surfeit of Memory?', p. 137.
34. Ibid. p. 138.
35. For other critiques of the upsurge in memory, and the problems associated with memory as substitute for history, see Michaels, '"You Who Never Was There"'; Klein, 'On the Emergence of Memory in Historical Discourse'; Knapp, 'Collective Memory and the Actual Past'; and LaCapra, *Writing History, Writing Trauma*.
36. Ricœur, 'Memory – Forgetting – History', p. 11.
37. Le Goff, *History and Memory*, p. xi.

38. Ibid. p. xii.
39. Nora, *Realms of Memory*, p. 12.
40. Ibid.
41. Burke, 'History as Social Memory', p. 99.
42. Hutton, *History as an Art of Memory*, p. xx.
43. Megill, *Historical Knowledge, Historical Error*, p. 59.
44. Olick, Vinitzky-Seroussi and Levy, *The Collective Memory Reader*, p. 6.
45. Phillips, *Society and Sentiment*, p. 152.
46. Quoted in Phillips, *Society and Sentiment*, p. 158.
47. Ramsay, *Scotland and Scotsmen*, vol. 1, p. 2.
48. Fielding, *Writing and Orality*, p. 4.
49. See Fielding, *Writing and Orality*.
50. Fentress and Wickham, *Social Memory*, p. 97.
51. Phillips, *Society and Sentiment*, p. 157. Lockhart described Ramsay as one of Scott's models for his antiquary Jonathan Oldbuck of Monkbarns in *The Antiquary* (Phillips, pp. 156–7).
52. Terdiman, *Present Past*, p. 25.
53. Recent studies on memory in British writing of the Romantic era and the nineteenth century tend to focus on the individual or phenomenological dimensions of memory and to be limited to the English context. Dames, for example, argues that, in the Victorian and pre-Victorian novel, memory is perceived as a dilemma or a threat, and so they are concerned more with forgetting than remembering. Yet all the writers in his study are English. See Dames, *Amnesiac Selves*. See, however, Jones, 'Scott's *The Heart of Midlothian* and the Disordered Memory'. See also Campbell, Labbe and Shuttleworth, *Memory and Memorials, 1789–1914*; Ferguson, 'Romantic Memory'; Matus, *Shock, Memory and the Unconscious in Victorian Fiction*; Miller, '"Striking passages"'; and Ann C. Colley, *Nostalgia and Recollection in Victorian Culture*.
54. See Jones, *Literary Memory*; and Rigney, *The Afterlives of Walter Scott*.
55. Duncan, *Scott's Shadow*, p. 23.
56. Klooster, *Revolutions in the Atlantic World*, p. 158. Klooster's focus on the Atlantic is in response to Eric Hobsbawm's *The Age of Revolution*. See also Linebaugh and Rediker, *The Many-Headed Hydra*.
57. Klooster, *Revolutions in the Atlantic World*, p. 163.
58. Elliott, 'Atlantic History', p. 259.
59. Armitage, 'Three Concepts of Atlantic History', p. 18. For discussion and examples of this Atlantic historiography, see also Armitage and Braddick, *The British Atlantic World*; Roach, *Cities of the Dead*; Games, 'Atlantic History', Bailyn, *Atlantic History*; Bailyn and Denault, *Soundings in Atlantic History*; Coclanis, 'Drang nach Osten'; Manning and Cogliano, *The Atlantic Enlightenment*; Canny, 'Atlantic History: What and Why?';

and 'Writing Atlantic History'. For a 'Red' Atlantic, see Rediker and Linebaugh, *The Many-Headed Hydra*. For the Black Atlantic, see Paul Gilroy's book of the same name; and Thornton, *Africa and Africans*. For a pan-American approach that examines Britain's relations with the non-anglophone Americas, see Almeida, *Reimagining the Transatlantic*.
60. See Hook, *Scotland and America* and 'Scotland, the USA, and National Literatures in the Nineteenth Century'; Manning, *Fragments of Union* and *The Puritan-Provincial Vision*; and Sher and Smitten, *Scotland and America in the Age of Enlightenment*.
61. See Trumpener, *Bardic Nationalism*.
62. Devine, *Scotland's Empire*, p. xxvi.
63. Gardiner, 'Introduction', p. 3.
64. Devine, *Scotland's Empire*, p. xxvii.
65. Mackenzie, *Places of Possibility*, p. 11. For recent accounts of a 'Scottish empire', see Fry, *The Scottish Empire*; Devine, *Scotland's Empire*; and Smailes, *Scottish Empire*. For a triumphalist account that links Scottish national greatness with its role in the empire, see Gibb, *The Scottish Empire*.
66. Devine, *Scottish Nation*, p. 263.
67. Ibid. p. 468.
68. Ibid. p. 264.
69. Ashcroft, Griffiths and Tiffin, *The Empire Writes Back*, pp. 31–2.
70. Ibid. p. 32.
71. For discussion of the debate and relevance of postcolonial methods to the study of Scottish literature and culture, see Gardiner, McDonald and O'Gallagher, *Scottish Literature and Postcolonial Literature*; and Stroh, *Gaelic Scotland in the Colonial Imagination*.
72. Gardiner, 'Introduction', p. 3.
73. See Wallerstein, *The Modern World-System III*. For an application of Wallerstein's world-system to Great Britain, see Hechter, *Internal Colonialism*. Hechter's conceptualisation of a 'Celtic Fringe' of Scotland, Ireland and Wales has received much scrutiny. For an analysis of the modern world-system and its effects on literary production, see Trumpener, *Bardic Nationalism*; and Sorensen, 'Internal Colonialism and the British Novel'.
74. Gilroy, *The Black Atlantic*, p. 4.
75. Ibid.
76. Ibid.
77. Duncan, Davis and Sorensen, 'Introduction', p. 13.

Chapter 1

Aftermaths: Walter Scott and Imagining Collective Memory in the Transatlantic World

Scott and the Crisis of Memory

There is no European nation which, within the course of half a century, or little more, has undergone so complete a change as this kingdom of Scotland. The effects of the insurrection of 1745, – the destruction of the patriarchal power of the Highland chiefs, and the abolition of the heritable jurisdictions of the Lowland nobility and barons, the total eradication of the Jacobite party, which, averse to intermingle with the English, or adopt their customs, long continued to pride themselves upon maintaining ancient Scottish manners and customs, – commenced this innovation. The gradual influx of wealth, and extension of commerce, have since united to render the present people of Scotland a class of beings as different from their grandfathers, as the existing English are from those of Queen Elizabeth's time.[1]

Waverley's final 'Postscript, Which Should Have Been a Preface' announces Walter Scott's innovative mode of historical fiction, one that would grant the novel an unprecedented authority to narrate the past and make Scott's output immensely influential throughout Britain, Europe and the world. *Waverley* emphasises its claims to narrate history in its subtitle, which, rather than signalling its generic categorisation, instead describes a specific span of years. "Tis Sixty Years Since' establishes the conditions of the novel's own contemporaneity, one in which a fundamental disjuncture between past and present is mediated by the mechanism of an accelerated social and economic progress. This disjuncture between past and present is the temporality of Scott's first novel and the novels that came after, which would come to be known collectively as the Waverley Novels, and has registered in the critical account as a fundamental aspect of its contribution to a culture of modernity in the Romantic era.[2] But it is worth noting the precise nature of the historical distance that Scott's first novel seeks to mediate, for in the Postscript to the novel, quoted above, Scott is not simply seeking to investigate the relation between past and present but, more precisely, the nature of this relation when the distance that separates them is only a relatively short span of years. 'Half a century, or little more', 'sixty years since' – the past is the past, but the past of the modern epoch, *Waverley* alerts us, is more proximate to the present than in previous times.

The time of the Forty-Five, as Scott describes it in his Postscript, represents a unique crux in the nation's history; the campaign to eradicate Jacobite resistance once and for all inspired a succession of dramatic measures in ensuing years designed to effect the complete social and economic integration of Scotland into the British Union. So convulsive was this transformation, in Scott's formulation, that the very pace of modernisation was suddenly and dramatically speeded up, effecting a complete break from the past which can be measured from a distance of only one or two human lifespans. The novel's own present time therefore lies just at the very horizon of living memory, a moment, Scott makes clear, when the 'present people of Scotland' must come to terms with the cognitive frailties of their grandfathers and great-grandfathers and of their imminent passing. *Waverley* thus situates its author within a period of anxious transition between two modes of remembrance: between first-hand oral recollection and second-hand written compilation of this recollection. If the transition is not complete, if the store of remembrances is not collected and preserved, it will be taken to the grave, and the vital link between the nation's past and its present will be lost for ever. *Waverley* therefore speaks as much about the nature of collective memory as it does about the nature of historical change in general.

Poised at the edge of forgetting, *Waverley* installs a particular mode of historical consciousness configured as a crisis of memory. *Waverley* links a temporality of accelerated change, in which the past has been ruptured from the present, with a single historical event that operates as a 'fixed point' of reference by which to identify and gauge the nature of this rupture. I label this temporality 'aftermath', in which the present of the novel is shaped in terms of its proximate relation (measured out in a few human lifespans at most) to a critical turning point, a moment of abrupt and transformational social and cultural upheaval, which not only determined the nation's present in direct and fundamental ways but altered the very pace of history. The momentousness of the turning point defines the aftermath, as the abruptness of change gives shape to the intensity and the emotional weight of remembrances of a yesteryear now in danger of becoming lost to future generations. Those of the 'present time' are made to feel the alienating effects of an accelerated pace of progress, even as those who were actors of this not-too-long-ago are only just departing from the scene. The collective memory of these earlier times, lingering remnants of what used to be, shares attributes of other traces of the past described in Scott's fiction, but, unlike the traces found in artefacts or in ruined features on a landscape, memory is embodied in individuals. As these individuals encompass a discrete group within the community, an entire generation whose lives were redirected or upended by the events of the past, the reminders of the past that they embody resonate in the present perhaps more deeply and more intimately, and the call to preserve their memories is expressed as a solemn duty to commemorate the nation's dead.

Scott's particular imagining of the aftermath in *Waverley* is a key to its phenomenal rise to eminence and popularity in North America, as the insistent call to remember the recent past particularly suited the demands of emergent national cultures in the transatlantic world. For settler communities in North America of the period, the public historical imagination was in large part dominated by the perception that the present generation was living in a moment of acute crisis, as the generation that had experienced a foundational turning point in the nation's history was fast fading from view, endangering the very integrity of a precarious national culture. In the United States, the allure of Scott's particular envisioning of memory took place against a backdrop of several conflicts that put at risk the cohesion of the new republic. Increased political faction, debates over immigration, and, most interminable of all, the persistent clash over slavery threatened to split the new nation into various warring factions. At the same time, a feeling of American cultural provincialism was exacerbated in the transatlantic 'culture wars' that played out in the pages of Scottish and American literary review periodicals, which followed the cessation of open hostilities between Britain and the United States after the War of 1812. Anxieties of national inadequacy or dissolution inspired an outpouring of historical writing that paid homage to the memory of forefathers (and, on rare occasion, the foremothers) of the Revolutionary generation, who themselves had been driven by patriotic zeal to initiate a radical break from previous generations. This writing claimed to represent and preserve the collective memory of the spirit and acts of heroism that brought about the birth of the nation. 'National memory' became the insistent theme of much American writing at a time when a thriving market for historical prose fiction, both foreign and domestic, was built upon the successive publication of each new Waverley Novel.[3] Of Scott's many American emulators, few writers took up and explored the theme of memory in the aftermath moment more deeply and extensively than the two I will focus on here: Washington Irving and John Neal. Both men's work was indebted in great part to Scott's example. Irving's *Sketchbook of Geoffrey Crayon*, and particularly 'Rip Van Winkle', and John Neal's novel *Seventy-Six* take up *Waverley*'s example and continue the exploration of the theme of national remembrance, in the context of a rapidly dwindling Revolutionary generation.

In anglophone British North America, the Waverley Novels provided a historical framework for British Canadians that meshed universal theories of progress associated with empire with a sentimental attachment to all that made local settings culturally distinct. As Trumpener summarised, Scott's 'ability to reconcile nationalist and imperialist mandates, made him popular at once with the British public, with imperial advocates, and with colonial readers trying to understand their own identity' (*Bardic Nationalism* 247). Though they did so on a much smaller scale than was seen in the United States, English-speaking readers in Canada both consumed and emulated Scott's novels in historical fiction writing that reinforced their ties to the 'Mother Country' even as it provided the material for a nascent anglophone Canadian national identity.[4] Yet for francophone *Canadiens*, who also read Scott and emulated his work, *Waverley*'s example of preserving the proximate past was put to very different cultural uses. Unlike their English-speaking counterparts, francophone Canadian writers saw themselves as inheritors of a momentous defeat that had profoundly transformed their way of life. They identified Great Britain not as the mother country but as the homeland of a conquering foreign culture that now threatened to engulf them. After the final military defeat of French colonial forces in Canada in 1759–60, French Canadians found themselves a minority within a colonial periphery, and in this context, francophone writers shaped a distinctive national culture, in the face of relentless anglicisation, preoccupied with the cultivation and preservation of a collective memory that would serve, in part, as compensation for lost sovereignty.[5] As Scott's fiction crossed both spatial and linguistic boundaries in francophone Canada, it provided a mode of historical understanding that demanded, above all, that the present generation must never forget the traditions of their *Canadien* progenitors. Insistent remembrance informs every aspect of the most preeminent example of historical fiction in nineteenth-century French Canada, Philippe-Joseph Aubert de Gaspé's *Les Anciens Canadiens* (*Canadians of Old*). Heavily indebted to its Scott-authored predecessor, *Les Anciens Canadiens* not only adapts the form and thematic concerns of *Waverley* in the rendition of its own momentous national turning point, it enfolds the cultural memory of the time of the Forty-Five into its own. In the last section of this chapter, I examine Aubert de Gaspé's francophone reimagining of national aftermath, and the implications of its 'surrogation' of Scottish collective memory.

Reading Scott's first great novel as an imagining of collective memory in the aftermath moment provides a rethinking of the role of Scott's historical fiction in shaping national and literary cultures in a post-Union Scotland and throughout North America in the early decades of the nineteenth century. Though there is now a large body of critical work on Scott and the historical novel, much of this work has examined Scott's output within the context of a broadly defined field of history writing and along the trajectory of established national literary historiographies.[6] Trumpener's cross-cultural examination of the rise of the British historical novel in the Romantic era widened the geographical frame of view by bringing to light the connections between historical writing, much of which had been previously overlooked, emanating from Britain's peripheries – Scotland, Ireland and Wales – as well as its North American dominions. Trumpener's work provided an invaluable transatlantic reading of Scott's influence on historical fiction, but she limited the North American scope of her study to British Canada and, for the most part, writers in English. By expanding the frame of inquiry to examine more deeply Scott's fiction in the context of the turn to memorial accounts in Scottish writing – and of the pre-eminence of the historical novel as a 'travelling genre' that spoke to heterogeneous reading publics in North America – this chapter can shed new light on a relatively unexamined aspect of Scott's contribution to historical consciousness in the Atlantic world, as he explored the mechanisms, and precariousness, of collective memory.[7] Scott, the great fictionaliser of history, and historiciser of fiction, was also, as Rigney sums, a 'manufacturer of collective memory par excellence'. The key to his huge success, she writes, was 'his forging of a potent alliance between fiction, memory, and identity that was well-adapted to the modernizing conditions of his age'.[8] As subjects of newly formed nations, and of expanding empires, writers in North America were, much like their Scottish counterparts, confronted with particular anxieties about collective memory a generation after a revolutionary epoch that saw both fracture and fusion.[9]

Generations Past

With the publication of *Ivanhoe* in 1819, Scott announced a significant break from the pattern he had established in all nine of his previous, and enormously successful, novels, which had all laid claim to representing a not-too-distant Scottish past. Scott's first three novels had established this pattern of unfolding a proximate past, measuring it in terms of successive generations. As Scott writes in the Advertisement of his third novel, *The Antiquary*, its publication 'completes a series of fictitious narratives to describe manners of Scotland in three different periods. WAVERLEY embraced the age of our fathers, GUY MANNERING of our own youth, and the ANTIQUARY refers to the last ten years of the eighteenth century'.[10] After *The Antiquary*, Scott would continue to journey deeper into the nation's past, but never extend more than a 150 years or so from his present time. When Scott finally makes a break from this pattern, he does so dramatically, setting *Ivanhoe* in twelfth-century England.

Ivanhoe's epoch lies well beyond the range of collective memory; the putative compiler of the tale, Laurence Templeton, makes this clear in the Dedicatory Epistle, suggesting that the enormous historical distances that stand between him and his subject pose a particular challenge. While England's primitive and adventurous past can only be gleaned from 'musty records and chronicles', the Scottish compiler, in contrast, need only reach back 'sixty or seventy years', to find such a past to supply reader interest. 'Many men alive', he laments, 'well remembered persons who had not only seen the celebrated [Rob] Roy M'Gregor, but had feasted and even fought with him' (6). The distant past of *Ivanhoe* is so long unremembered that, comprised of only 'dry, sapless, mouldering and disjointed bones', it cannot readily be re-embodied, made flesh again (7). From the standpoint of Scott's earlier treatment of the Scottish past, the English past poses a conundrum – England's own formative 'turning point' of cultural upheaval and absorption, and thus its aftermath moment, lies in a pre-modern epoch, far beyond the domain of lived experience. No one now alive can recollect this past, or even recollect its recollection; there is no memory of it to preserve.

The past which cannot be accessed through recollection must be told in a different way, and Scott announces his departure from the subject of the proximate past by subtitling *Ivanhoe* a 'Romance', the literary form most associated with the medieval period in Scott's time.[11] With *Ivanhoe*, Scott seems to be contributing to a larger shift among European historians in the early nineteenth century that, in Patrick H. Hutton's analysis, went from seeking to 'reaffirm tradition' – the repetition of the past into the present – to 'reconstruct[ing] images as they must have once existed, beyond the bounds of their own living memories'.[12] *Ivanhoe* seems poised at the moment of this shift in historical writing; its subtitling announces not only a change in narrative form but in the proximity between past and present.[13]

The introductory first chapter of *Waverley* suggests that Scott had in mind this alignment between genre and proximity to the past from the very beginning of his novelistic career: 'By fixing then the date of my story Sixty Years before this present 1st, November, 1805, I will have my readers understand they will meet in the following pages neither a romance of chivalry, nor a tale of modern manners' (4). Scott declares his independence from previous genres, and from previous pasts, while betraying an anxiety that, when it comes to novel reading, the 'present generation' could be much more critical than the one 'sixty years since'. *Waverley*'s proximity to the past both frames its subject and setting and defines it as something new in novel writing, as it takes the measure of its own contemporaneity, its own relation to the past, in generational terms. The generational measure is even more reinforced by Scott's precise dating of his creation, 'this present 1st, November, 1805', which Peter Garside points out is exactly sixty years since the date that Prince Charles set out from Edinburgh on the campaign into England (369).[14] In doing so, Scott places his narrator, Garside notes, precisely at 'a lifespan, or two generations, away from the potentially still painful events he describes' (370).

The novel's final Postscript echoes its beginning chapter and situates the circumstances of its creation within the aftermath of 'still painful events', by figuring history's progress as a 'deep and smooth river' in which 'we are not aware of the progress we have made' drifting down its stream 'until we fix our eye on the now-distant point from which we set out. Such of the present generation as can recollect the last twenty or twenty-five years of the eighteenth century, will be fully sensible of the truth of this statement . . .' (363). Historical awareness is thus a matter of relative perspective; it requires an anchoring point of reference, which only those who have lived a certain number of years truly can perceive. The anchoring point of *Waverley*'s own historical perspective is the Forty-Five, and Scott, in his mid-forties when he completed the work, imagines his own present generation as standing halfway between the generation that directly experienced the events he narrates: 'those who, in my younger time, were facetiously called "folks of the old leaven"' and the 'rising generation', those perhaps still in childhood and as yet unacquainted and oblivious to their own proximate past. Scott's mediating generation thus occupies a 'middle age', and middle-aged, position between the other two. This middle generation can transmit, second-hand, a past recollected by a previous generation to a younger one that would otherwise have no access to it. The subject of this mediating process is a past not so much re-embodied, through historical narrative, but relived, through individual remembrance. The historical fracture of the British union that Jacobitism posed is made material in the presence of the 'folks of old leaven' who were (and perhaps still are) 'living examples of singular disinterested attachment to the principles of loyalty which they received from their fathers, and of old Scottish faith, hospitality, worth, and honour' (363). 'Disinterested attachment to the principles of loyalty', the raw material that once had driven the ideology of rebellion, is imagined in *Waverley* as a kind of present-day inheritance, preserved and passed down in the form of remembrance from preceding generations. The relative proximity of Scott's own generation to the generation of the Forty-Five allows him to lay claim to be the immediate inheritor of that memory, which also provides the impetus to write in the first place: 'To elder persons [the preceding work] will recall scenes and characters familiar to their youth; and to the rising generation the tale may represent some idea of the manners of their forefathers' (364).

Scott's historical schema, measuring time in terms of the lifespans of those who are roughly the same ages, expresses the temporality of 'generationality', which the social historian Ute Daniel has defined as 'an ensemble of age-specific attributions, by means of which people locate themselves within their respective historical period'.[15] That Scott is attempting to represent a particular shared generational *memory* of the past, rather than the past itself, is reflected in the declared nature of its source material. The scenes and characters of *Waverley* are not derived, as Templeton would lament in *Ivanhoe*, from documents written by unreliable scribes now long dead, but from the remembrances of those who actually experienced the times – Scottish Jacobites of the previous generation, with whom the author was acquainted in his younger days and who recounted their experiences to him first-hand. By the time of his writing, however, the author's younger days are themselves a fading memory; he identifies himself as belonging to a generation all too aware that it has already drifted some distance down the stream of time. Standing at the midpoint of human mortality – old enough to be witnessing 'the almost total extinction' of the 'ancient manners' he had heard recounted in his youth, but with enough vitality to 'preserve some idea of these ancient manners' for generations to come – the author of *Waverley* adopts the position not of the historian or antiquarian but of the memorialist: one who activates the past by collecting and preserving the memories of lived experience of an entire generation, 'not taken from individual portrait but from general habits of the period', the remnants of which were witnessed in the author's 'younger days, and partly gathered from tradition' and which are now 'embodied in imaginary scenes and ascribed to fictitious characters' (364, 363).

In its claim to be a synthetic composite of actual remembrance, *Waverley* lays the foundation for the cultural authority of Scott's work as an authentic representation of the past, 'dependent', Jones writes, 'on its relationship to memory that is possessed across generations'.[16]

Waverley, while seeking to open a space for fiction to record and preserve this memory, pays homage to a litany of predecessors who paid their respect to this inheritance by also recording and preserving it – Scott names Elizabeth Hamilton, Anne Grant and Lord Selkirk, who, in his 1805 analysis of conditions in the Highlands, adumbrates the 'aftermaths' trope that Scott would seize upon for his fiction.[17] Yet for the succeeding generation able to record remembrances of the past, their enunciation of these remembrances is imbued with a persistent sense of melancholy, as they grapple with the awareness that the momentous epoch in which their forefathers had lived is forever lost to themselves. Thus, the tone of gentle irony and burlesque that is cast over much of the story proper completely disappears in the Postscript and is replaced by a more sombre sentimental tone, as the author comes to terms with the insurmountable gap between present and past. This melancholia, and the particular historical awareness that gives rise to it, is an example of what Ina Ferris has described as the 'narrative situation' characteristic of much post-Enlightenment Scottish historical writing, in which the well-worn 'trope of generations took on a new resonance', as it became 'historized, attached to a specific historical temporality rather than to the general temporality of common mortality'.[18] As modern history writers imagine the scene of their writing as situated at the moment of generational change, 'history emerges less as a form of knowledge of the past . . . than as a mode of connection in the present posited on the historian's own alienation'.[19] Ferris's description of the particular imagining of the 'narrative moment' brings into sharp focus the historiographical underpinnings of the mood of sentimentality and melancholia, which I suggest is illustrative of the aftermath mode of historical consciousness, but I also wish to pay particular attention to the ways in which – in the relative proximity of the past that *Waverley* represents – alienation from the past was not just an aspect of writing history but, more precisely, of writing *memory*.

Fictions of Remembrance

The narrative moment of *Waverley* is equipoised between the two contrasting modes of collective memory theorised by Assmann: 'communicative' and 'cultural'. Building on Halbwach's theories of the inherent communal aspect of collective memory as an imaginative reconstruction of the past dependent on the 'social framework' in which it is articulated, Assmann sought to expand collective memory's range and scope.[20] For Halbwachs, memory is located exclusively in oral utterance and bound to the lifespans of members of specific social groups. Though the awareness of past events may remain, social memory begins to fade or change as the social framework in which it was sustained ceases to exist. '[S]ince', he writes, 'social memory erodes at the edges as individual members, especially older ones, become isolated or die, it is constantly transformed along with the group itself'.[21] Assmann, however, sought to develop a theory of memory that persisted beyond a single generation, and he defines as 'communicative' the collective memory that manifests itself in the 'everyday' utterances between individuals within small groups. As the memory is passed down from grandparents to grandchildren, it is distinguished by its 'high degree of formlessness, willfulness, and disorganization'. Communicative memory is also distinguished by its very limited temporal horizon, which 'does not extend more than eighty to (at the very most) one hundred years into the past, which equals three or four generations or the Latin *saeculum*'. Communicative memory 'offers no fixed point which would bind it to the ever-expanding past in the passing of time. Such fixity can only be achieved through a cultural formation and therefore lies outside of informal everyday memory' (127). In contrast, 'cultural memory', in Assmann's formulation, is distinguished by its distance from the everyday and its relative formality (126). Cultural memory has a fixed point; its horizon does not change with the passing of time. What constitutes these fixed points in cultural memory, Assmann argues, are 'fateful events of the past', whose memory is expressed and maintained through 'objectivized' cultural formations ('texts, images, rites, buildings, monuments, cities, or even landscapes') and 'institutional communication (recitation, practice, observance)' (128, 129). Through these, cultural memory persists, where communicative memory does not, and so cultural memory plays an integral role in the 'concretion of' group identity as it 'preserves the store of knowledge from which a group derives an awareness of its unity and peculiarity' (130).

To employ Assmann's two-part schema to the operations of social memory in *Waverley*, we can say the novel takes upon itself, through 'imaginary scenes' and 'fictitious characters', the task of transmuting communicative memory into a longer-lasting, more formal and more socially significant cultural memory, that store of knowledge from which Scots can derive an awareness of their own 'unity and peculiarity'. What *Waverley* does to great effect is to provide a fixed point for Scottish cultural memory, its 'fateful event' of the past. The Jacobite Rebellion endows the remembrances of those who happened to be alive at the time with a special valuation as cultural memory. Without it, these remembrances may stand as testaments to the swift stream of time's river, but they would have no purchase on perpetuating the collective identity of the nation.

Assmann's memory schema provides a useful way to conceptualise the historicising strategy of *Waverley*, which purports to describe events that are just beyond the horizon of what Assmann would define as 'communicative memory'. From the raw materials of communicative memory, *Waverley* would erect a cultural memory, which has the power to reaffirm the nation's historical continuity, to remind the present and rising generations who they are and where they have come from. But in situating itself at the moment of transition, when the passing of communicative memory necessitates the move to cultural memory in the first place, *Waverley* self-consciously draws attention to itself as an act of remembrance. 'Lest we forget', the novel implicitly declares. *Waverley*, then, is a commemorative fiction that narrates modernity's *need* for commemorations. It is an archival materialisation of memory in a moment when memory is felt no longer to be able to sustain itself, either through oral transmission or through lived example. As such, *Waverley* represents a critical early expression of what Terdiman has identified as the 'memory crisis' of nineteenth-century historical writing, the feeling that the past has evaded memory, and that traditional forms of memory have become irrevocably disrupted through the processes of modernisation.[22] But, in evoking the call to remember, *Waverley* makes no demand that its readers revitalise or readopt the customs and manners of their forebears sixty years since. On the contrary, to do so is not only impossible, as Halbwachs would argue, it would render its modern readers susceptible to the 'absurd political prejudice' of the era, which Scott warns against in his Postscript. Scott invests his recounting of a turbulent proximate past with 'an ethos of aesthetic detachment', in Ian Duncan's words, that shifts events of the Forty-Five from the domain of the political to that of national culture.[23] Denuded of its ideological content, Jacobitism instead names a set of principles and manners, recalled, but not relived, with fondness and respect. Scott activates a Scottish cultural memory simply by *recalling* the past – the past remembered in *Waverley* still lies firmly in the past. In modernity's 'acceleration of history', which for Nora signals the death of living memory (*lieux de mémoire*) and its replacement with commemoration (*milieux de mémoire*), Scott's brand of historical fiction begins its ascendancy in Britain, North America and the world by positioning itself as a form of cultural memory, as 'living communication crystallized in the forms of objectivized culture' – and, more crucially, as a vehicle for representing the operations of social memory itself.[24] By providing a stable, usable 'memory' of the past in an epoch which perceived itself to be in danger of losing all connection with the past and thereby itself, Scott's mode of historical consciousness in *Waverley* captured the imagination of an anxious modern world.

The Memorial in Post-Enlightenment Edinburgh

A 'historizing retrospect defining the present through reflection of the past' characterises what Duncan has identified as the middle decade (1815–25) of Edinburgh's post-Enlightenment era. This retrospect 'informs not only the Scottish novels of national history and manners and the attention paid to antiquarian and biographical "remains" in the Edinburgh periodicals but also a distinctive genre of cultural memoir'.[25] The two most notable examples of this distinctive genre are Henry Cockburn's *Memorials of his Time* (published in 1856, two years after his death, but compiled largely between 1821 and 1830) and his follow-up *Journal* (published in 1874) and Robert Chambers's 1825 *Traditions of Edinburgh*. Together these writers offer 'a combined discourse of civic and personal memory', Duncan writes, through a focus on individualised recollections of the common and everyday social practices of a bygone era. Scott's desire to lay claim to perpetuating a collective memory through the preservation of individual remembrance in *Waverley* is testament to the significant overlap in these genres of historical retrospect, as writers expanded the contours of historical writing while seeking to delimit which forms seemed best suited to its production.

In a preface that could be said to recast Scott's own generational stance in *Waverley*'s Postscript, Cockburn positions himself in *Memorials of his Time* as belonging to an elder, rather than middle, generation. Looking back from the vantage point of his sixties, in 1840, he can record without mediation his own personal store of remembrance, before it becomes irretrievable. 'It occurred to me, several years ago,' he writes, 'as a pity, that no private account should be preserved of the distinguished men or important events that had marked the progress of Scotland, or at least of Edinburgh, during my day'.[26] The temporality of 'during my day' announces the distance between the narrative's past and present, positioning the author as himself one of the 'folks of the old leaven'. One whose 'youth tasted the close of the last century', and who has so 'lived so far' into the present age, Cockburn positions himself as an eyewitness to the utter break with the past as well as a living repository of the traditional knowledge of a 'purely Scotch' age now vanished.[27] Cockburn's past is measured out in his writing, as it is in *Waverley*, in generations, not in years. In the progressive movement of time, in which a fixed point of reference is ever receding into the distance, the sixty-something Cockburn can lay claim to being in an even better position than Scott to set down the contrast between Scotland past and present.

Although *Memorials* narrates significant public events in the history of Edinburgh, including the 'electric shock of delight' that jolted the city when *Waverley* first appeared, Cockburn's focus is on the commonplace characteristics of everyday life, a life already in the past but that is recalled with fondness and affection. *Memorials* shares with Scott's first novel an investment in calling up the past through an accumulation of the 'habits, manners, and feelings', the mundane but distinctive social practices that are not only often the chief concern of Scottish natural history but also the locus of collective memory, in Halbwach's account. In the same way that *Waverley* insistently reminds its readers that it is sixty years since tea was drunk in the morning, since the dinner hour was two o'clock in the afternoon, since the potato was completely unknown in Scotland, since a horse cost twenty guineas, and so on; so does *Memorials* evoke the gap between present and past lived experience in a hodgepodge of seemingly random, but – in their sheer accumulation – telling details. Recalling the prevalent style in his youth of moving from one room to another to dine, for example, Cockburn writes:

> The procession from the drawing-room to the dining-room was formerly arranged on a different principle from what it is now. There was no such alarming proceeding as that of each gentleman approaching a lady, and the two hooking together. This would have excited as much horror as the waltz at first did, which never shewed itself without denunciations of continental manners by correct gentlemen and worthy mothers and aunts. All the ladies first went off by themselves, in a regular row, according to the ordinary rules of precedence. Then the gentlemen moved off in a single file; so that when they reached the dining-room, the ladies were all there, lingering about the backs of the chairs, till they could see what their fate was to be. (*Memorials*, pp. 34–5)

Delimited by the duration of his own lifetime, Cockburn's writing reveals the passing of time through grandfatherly remembrances of everyday habits and activities that held no special significance at the time but which, in their passing, dramatically mark the present's break with the past.

Chambers's *Traditions of Edinburgh* also begins with an enunciation of its own narrative situation, adopting *Waverley*'s trope of writing in the aftermath of profound change compressed within a relatively short span of years:

> The ancient part of Edinburgh has, within the last fifty years, experienced a vicissitude scarcely credible to the present generation. What were, so late as the year 1773, the mansions of the higher ranks, are, in 1823, the habitations of people in the humblest degrees of life . . . The contemplation of this change is at once melancholy and gratifying, – melancholy, if we look upon the mansions of Nobility left to the possession of mechanics, and gratifying, if we consider the prosperity of our country, which has produced, or, at least, accompanied the change.[28]

The changing Edinburgh cityscape becomes emblematic of Scotland's status as the locus of an accelerated temporality: modernisation is happening so fast and on such a scale that an entirely anterior mode of life now lies just beyond the horizon of living memory. Changing social demographics and changing social practice are aligned with a changing metropolis in both *Traditions* and Cockburn's writing. Much of Cockburn's account of a now vanished way of life is keyed to descriptions of specific buildings and of the urban landscape of Edinburgh, particularly the building of the New Town. An invocation of the past through miscellaneous anecdote and random historical titbits, all tied to changing architecture, is the focus and organising principle of *Traditions*, which is organised not chronologically but spatially; it unfolds its story of the past primarily through a description of old houses and changing urban landscapes. Each space tells its own tale of the past, but even this spatial organisation is loosely jointed, punctuated with miscellaneous chapters on local institutions and social phenomena. Within its chapters, *Traditions* foregrounds a generational frame of historical reference; its author stands in the same relation to past generations as does *Waverley*'s, recalling and preserving in writing the memories of those 'of advanced age' whose imminent passing marks the 'vicissitudes' of accelerated historical change.[29]

Both Cockburn's and Chambers's accounts are instances of what Phillips has labelled an important shift in historical writing in the early nineteenth century: 'the historicization of everyday life', which provided a new retrospective cast for the vogue in memoir and autobiographical writing in the period. Cockburn casts his *Memorials*, Phillips writes, as 'less a traditional autobiography than as a sketch for a social history of the present'.[30] It is an attempt to 'preserve history not simply as a set of events, but as the experience of a generation'.[31] The intimacy of such accounts is illustrative of what Phillips identifies as the increasing interest in a more 'approximative' stance in historical writing, in which past moments are made close and pressing. This approximative distancing in turn is part of a new affective relation in historical writing between figures of the past and readers, in which 'we go to history in order to experience a sense of evocative presence of other places and other times'.[32]

In Scottish memorialist writing of the period, Phillips's approximative distance is not just a formal or generic concern but a temporal one; the genre's superlative historicisation of everyday life is itself a function of the relative proximity between its author and the past he seeks to represent. For his part, Cockburn makes no claim to represent a past that lies beyond the bounds of the memory of one single human being – that is to say, a time beyond his own remembrances. He makes no attempt to contrast, for example, the social spaces of his youth with those of an earlier generation he 'know[s] nothing about' (*Memorials*, p. 30). In the first (1825) edition of *Traditions*, Chambers adopts the more distanced and mediated stance of a compiler of the middle or younger generation – Chambers was only twenty when the first edition was published – who only collects for posterity the recollections of the old. He would later emphasise this stance when describing the plans he made for gathering material for future editions of his work: 'If, I calculated, a first *part* or *number* could be issued, materials for others might be expected to come in, for scores of old inhabitants, even up perhaps to the very "oldest," would then contribute their reminiscences' (*Traditions, New Edition*, p. v). Forty years later, Chambers chose to publish a new edition of the work and in the later edition repositioned himself as one of an older generation, able to reminisce upon the passing epoch of his youth. This shift in narrative stance allowed him to expand the temporal range of cultural memory in the new edition, even into the period of the Forty-Five that is the subject of *Waverley*. In the original edition Chambers tells the story of a remarkable 'lady of advanced age' who lived in a house on the upper floor of the Bowhead tenement in the Lawnmarket. The lady in question was the inheritor of the patent for 'Dr. Anderson's Pills', a popular remedy invented by a physician of Charles I, which has been sold 'upwards of a century past', – the health benefits of the remedy demonstrated by the patent having been passed down 'through no more than three generations of proprietors' (*Traditions*, vol. 1, pp. 255–6). In the 1868 edition, however, Chambers inserts himself into the account, describing his own first-hand experience of the woman's character:

> In 1829, Mrs Irving lived in a neat, self-contained mansion in Chessels's Court, in the Canongate, along with her son, General Irving, and some members of his family. The old lady, then ninety-one, was good enough to invite me to dinner, when I likewise found two younger sisters of hers, respectively eighty-nine and ninety. She sat firm and collected at the head of the table, and carved a leg of mutton with perfect propriety. She then told me, at her son's request, that, in the year 1745, when Prince Charles's army was in possession of the town, she, a child of four years, walked with her nurse to Holyrood Palace, and seeing a Highland gentleman standing in the doorway, she went up to him to examine his peculiar attire. She even took the liberty of lifting up his kilt a little way; whereupon her nurse, fearing some danger, started forward for her protection. But the gentleman only patted her head, and said something kind to her. I felt it as very curious to sit as guest with a person who had mingled in the Forty-five. (*Traditions, New Edition*, p. 39)

Chamber's distinctly personal recollection of the nonagenarian who 'had mingled in the Forty-five' gives this anecdote an immediacy and vitality it perhaps lacked in the first edition, the momentous past suddenly come to life, embodied through remembrances of lived experience. Mrs Irving's recollection of the encounter also reveals the idiosyncratic prioritising of informal, everyday 'communicative memory', which does not always record events or deeds of great historical importance but instead often fixes on small details of no account. For her, the occupation of Scotland's capital by an invading army is reduced to single moment of sneaking a peek up a Highlander's kilt.

Remembrances build upon remembrances, as the recollections of one who witnessed the events of the Forty-Five form part of the recollections of the author, himself now in advanced age. *Traditions'* memorialisation of the past is achieved here through the accumulation and sentimentalisation of often historically naive and insignificant fragments of individual remembrance. The sentimentality of this passage, however, abruptly gives way to emotions of a more intense nature, when an actual visage from the past seems suddenly to make an entrance on the scene:

> [M]y excitement was brought to a higher pitch when, on ascending to the drawing-room, I found the general's daughter, a pretty young woman recently married, sitting there, dressed in a suit of clothes belonging to one of the nonagenarian aunts – a very fine one of flowered satin, with elegant cap and lappets, and silk shoes three inches deep in the heel – the same having been worn by the venerable owner just seventy years before at a Hunters' Ball at Holyrood Palace. The contrast between the former and the present wearer – the old lady shrunk and taciturn, and her young representative full of life, and resplendent in joyous beauty – had an effect upon me which it would be impossible to describe. To this day, I look upon the Chessels's Court dinner as one of the most extraordinary events in my life. (*Traditions, New Edition*, p. 39)

As he recounts the indescribable effect of this striking apparition – the ghost of Mrs Irving's young life seems to suddenly appear alongside her at the dinner party – Chambers's work seems to swerve for a moment into the domain of the gothic. But the general's daughter is no ghost, and the strange juxtaposition that Chambers describes is instead emblematic of the affective power and persistence of memory. In the figure of a little girl costumed in the style of *Waverley*'s 'sixty years since', the modes and manners of her ancestors/forebears are not so much resurrected from the past as they are repeated in the present, and, for a moment, the past is no longer past. In that moment, history itself seems to dissolve, a feeling so alien to its chronicler that it produces in him a reaction of great emotional intensity.

At the same time, both Cockburn and Chambers emphasise the ephemerality of memory, and the precariousness of its archive. Cockburn was particularly anxious about the fragility of his own memory, which gave him the early impetus to set down his recollections in writing. In a letter to his friend he wrote around 1806, before he began his *Memorials* in earnest, he expressed the anxiety of forgetting:

> You have lived nearly 30 years; all this time your mind has been actively employed, and your heart warmly attached to some things or other. Yet if you will sit cross-legged at the fire half an hour I suspect you will be able to make everything you can recollect of past years rise before you. Undoubtedly many delightful thoughts – many happy days and even months – 100ds of curious long established opinions – strange anticipations – and stranger resolutions – vain forebodings – and millions of other things which you would give the world to feel over again are gone from your remembrance, completely and for ever.[33]

The encyclopaedic but scattered collection of things no longer so well remembered is both memory's great value as an immanent expression of the past as well as its profound limitation. Because his work is a recounting of his memory of events rather than a narrative of these events compiled from source material, the veracity of Cockburn's remembrances may be in doubt, but their 'truthfulness' never is. Similarly, Chambers's nonagenarian subject is clearly speaking from the heart. Her recollections of the time of the Forty-Five are completely unselfconscious, and they make no claim to an unbiased reportage of the past. The intimate, unguarded, authentic and unmediated access to the manners and customs of the times makes such recollection of immense value to the memorialist, who seeks not so much to narrate the past itself but the ways in which it is remembered. *Waverley* enshrines this valuation by emplotting it in its Postscript, in which the author privileges not the antiquarian archive or published historical account, which Garside reveals were the actual sources for much of the novel's historical details, but personal remembrance.[34] In the background of all these memorialist accounts, however, is the persistent note of melancholy that Ferris identifies, a sense of impending loss and alienation that is perhaps most emphatic in Cockburn's letter to his friend. The archive of remembrance of a single life does not persist after life ends, and the loss of this store of historical knowledge, if left unrecorded, is 'completely and for ever'.

'Tis (about) Fifty Years Since: Imagining the Aftermath in America

With publication of the first of the Tales of My Landlord, *The Black Dwarf*, in 1816, Scott formalises into his narrative structure his trope of the passing down the remembrances of previous generations, which he had commenced with *Waverley*. Though his next two novels, *Guy Mannering* (1815) and *The Antiquary* (1816), both treated a past more proximate than that of *Waverley*, the subtitle of the shorter, one-volume, work *The Black Dwarf* announces it as the first in what Scott intended to be a collection of short 'tales'. These tales would comprise four Scottish regional stories, each filling a single volume of the four-volume work.[35] Scott did not follow through with his plan – the second work, *The Tale of Old Mortality*, filled up the remaining three volumes of the series. The scheme is, however, illustrative of Scott's generic taxonomy, which aligns particular narrative forms (the 'tale', the 'romance') with the relative proximity of the past he wishes to represent. In addition, the first series of Tales of My Landlord, like the two that followed it, adopts a frame narrative. The series is ostensibly a transcription of tales recounted by the innkeeper of the Wallace Inn in Gandercleugh, taken down by one Peter Pattieson and then received and edited after his death by the parish-clerk and schoolmaster Jedidiah Cleishbotham, who, 'to answer funeral and death-bed expences', presents them before the public (*The Black Dwarf*, p. 8). In this way Scott's early Tales of My Landlord evoke both the immediacy and fragmentariness of collective remembrance, as each 'tale' represents a putative transliteration of an oral recounting from living memory, or of one handed down as tradition from one or two generations previous. Each title in the series is therefore situated within a particular relation to the varying ranges of cultural memory.[36]

Scott's alignment between the form announced on the title page of his works – all later subsumed under the category of the 'Waverley

Novels' – and the proximity of the past he wishes to recount adds a new dimension to our understanding of both the significance and timing of his influence on historical fiction in America, particularly as it bears upon the work of American writers before 1821, a year Americanist critics have identified as a watershed moment in terms of Scott's influence. George Dekker, for example, in his study of the development of the 'historical romance' in America, argues that Scott provides the imaginative form, the 'Waverley-model', which Dekker traces through what he sees as its first successful adaption in the United States, the two-volume novel *The Spy*, published by James Fenimore Cooper in 1821.[37] By dating the commencement of Scott's influence as 1821, and by concentrating on multivolume examples of work he labels 'historical romance', Dekker perhaps undervalues the significance of the work of the author who had perhaps the greatest professional relationship with Scott of any of his American contemporaries: Washington Irving. In two works published before 1820, neither of which he labelled novels or romances, Irving, who often played the role of Scott's interlocutor rather than disciple, provided his own working-out of Scott's experiments with form and narrating cultural memory. In the fictional historiography that comprises his 1809 *History of New York*, a burlesque recounting of the Dutch settlement of the city, Irving established the tropes of narratalogical memory preservation that Scott would develop, perhaps more completely, in *Waverley* a few years later. In the 1819 miscellany of short pieces he published as the *Sketch-Book of Geoffrey Crayon, Gent.* – particularly in 'Rip Van Winkle', the piece that, along with 'The Legend of Sleepy Hollow', would secure his literary reputation – Irving attempts to work out the implications of America's own aftermath moment. He does so in a story that, while rich in observation on the ways in which the proximate past is remembered and recalled, leaves out description of the Revolution entirely.

Amnesia in the Aftermath

The idea that the literary success of the young Irving owed an immeasurable, and one-sided, debt to the Great Unknown was established in large part by Irving himself. In the preface to the 1848 'Author's Revised Edition' of the *Sketch-Book*, the last edition he revised before his death, Irving made Scott the hero of the work. At a moment of professional crisis while residing in Britain, Irving writes, when he despaired of ever achieving a successful writing career, Scott intervened on his behalf 'with that practical and efficient good will that belonged to his nature', promising to speak with Scott's own publisher, Archibald Constable, and securing a (favourable) review of the *Sketch-Book* by John Gibson Lockhart in *Blackwood's* (4–6).[38] 'Thus under the kind and cordial auspices of Sir Walter Scott', Irving concludes,

> I began my literary career in Europe and am but discharging in a trifling degree my debt of gratitude to the memory of that golden-hearted man in acknowledging my obligation to him. But who of his contemporaries who applied to him for assistance ever did not experience most prompt generous and effectual assistance![39]

The relationship between the two men suggested in Irving's preface seems to play out what many contemporary critics identify as a familiar position of American literary endeavour in relation to that of Great Britain in the early nineteenth century. These critics have seen in Irving's confession that he felt unfitted to the task at hand and his lamenting to Scott of the 'desultory' trajectory of his 'whole course of life', a professional malaise that is symptomatic of the nation's 'postcolonial' literary culture after the War of 1812.[40] Though such a reading of Irving's output draws attention to the significance of his work in shaping national culture, it also casts Scott as a kind of colonial father-figure, representing a dominant, and domineering, British literary culture, whom Irving, as the culturally cringing young protégé, can either imitate or resist. Such a reading, however, belies both the complexity of Scott's status as a 'British' author and the examples of transatlantic cross-connection and cross-influence that existed between the two writers.[41]

Several years before publication of the *Sketch-Book*, Scott had taken an early interest in Irving's career and had admired his previous historical fiction. In April of 1813, a time when Scott was at work on *Waverley*, a copy of Irving's *A History of New York* was placed in his hands, although it would not be published in Britain until 1820.[42] In *A History of New York*, Irving introduced the framing device of Diedrich Knickerbocker, the putative antiquarian source for the two American tales in the *Sketch-Book*, 'Rip Van Winkle' and 'The Legend of Sleepy Hollow'. In *A History of New York*'s introductory 'Account of the Author', Knickerbocker is identified as the author of the manuscript, which is placed before the public by his landlord, one Seth Handaside, who is seeking to recoup expenses for Knickerbocker's 'board and lodging' after his sudden and mysterious disappearance from the city.[43] Irving's frame narrative in *A History of New York*, which perhaps could be subtitled 'Tales of my Tenant', therefore bears striking parallels with the frame narrative that Scott would later adapt in the Tales of My Landlord. At the same time, the *History*'s potent style of tragicomic burlesque punctuated with occasion moments of sentimentality, and its stated ambition to 'trace the rise of sundry manners and institutions' of the city (17), rather than provide a chronology of its great events, must certainly have made an impression on Scott, as he set out to develop his own style of historical fiction, in *Waverley*.[44] The prefatory remarks of Irving's history evoke the collective memory of the 'reverend Dutch Burghers' who serve as 'tottering monuments of good old times' and who will soon be 'gathered to their fathers' (16). Knickerbocker presents his historical account at a particular moment of historical anxiety, when 'the twilight of uncertainty' has already thrown its shadows over 'times long past'. Such a moment calls for the intervention of the historian-preserver, 'to rescue from oblivion the memory of former incidents, and to render a just tribute of renown to the many great and wonderful transactions of our Dutch progenitors . . .' (ibid.).

While employing the narrative situation he had already experimented with in earlier verse works and that Irving had developed in his prose work *A History of New York*, Scott would expand Irving's example and adapt it to the particular demands of his story of Scotland sixty years since. A few years later, Irving, with Scott's help and with the success of the Waverley Novels in the background, would return to his own exploration of collective or cultural memory in the *Sketch-Book*, which would ultimately secure his own great reputation in American letters. In 'Rip Van Winkle' particularly, which locates the narrative situation of *A History of New York* explicitly in the post-revolutionary period, Irving refines his ideas on the nature of memory: on its origins in everyday life, its fragility, and its problematic preservation through textual transcription.

'Rip Van Winkle' announces its thematic concerns with a topographical symbol of rupture: the setting of the story is the Kaatskill Mountains west of the Hudson, a 'dismembered branch' of the Appalachians, the narrator tells us. Like the mountains in which he sleeps, Rip Van Winkle is dismembered, cut off from his community, as he is unable to bring to mind, to 're-member', a generation's worth of the past. If the operations of memory establish a continuity between our past and present selves through ongoing acts of remembrance, Rip Van Winkle's epic sleep manifests an intensely personalised crisis of memory, as he must confront a profound gap between the past he remembers and the present world in which he finds himself. Rip has no memory of the past twenty years, and the immediate effects of this gap are an overwhelming sense of alienation and loss of self: 'I was myself last night' he exclaims, 'but I fell asleep on the mountains – and they've changed my gun – and everything's changed – and I am changed – and I can't tell what's my name, or who I am!' (39). Irving links the disruptive psychological effects of Rip's memory loss with the general tenor of the times. Rip's bewilderment upon waking up is exacerbated by the enormous pace of change in post-Revolutionary America. Rip comes down from the mountains to find himself within his country's own transformative moment, defined by the great turning point of which Rip himself, of course, has no actual memory. For Irving's own narrative moment, Rip's tale poses some pressing questions about the nature of collective memory. What happens when the generation of the 'turning point' epoch has no actual memory of the times? And what then are the implications of memory lapse for the cohesion of the new nation if there is nothing to preserve or transmit as cultural memory? The answer, Irving seems to suggest in 'Rip Van Winkle', is dependent both on the mechanisms by which memory is actually transmitted and the relatively flimsy material that the Revolution actually provides to that memory. When it comes to cultural memory, revolutions, it turns out, do not necessarily seem to amount to much.

Rip's enormous gap in memory, which is also the great syncope in the narrative proper, draws attention to the temporal spaces that border it on either side. Before Rip's fateful journey into the mountains, the small Dutch settlement where Rip resides seems a spot where time, if it has not quite stopped altogether, has certainly slowed down. The news of the day is duly received and drawled out by the village schoolmaster, but only when 'by chance an old newspaper fell into their hands from some passing traveller' – after which, Rip and his friends would 'deliberate upon public events some months after they had taken place' (*Sketch-Book*, 1978, p. 32). In the descriptions of a village that lags behind, of 'sages, philosophers and other idle personages' that converse listlessly over village gossip and repeat endless stories about nothing, and through a protagonist who 'displays insuperable aversion to all kinds of profitable labor', Irving mocks the progressive temporality that underlies an ideology of improvement that was transforming the landscape on both sides of the Atlantic. In the time before Rip's enchanted sleep, we get a different kind of temporality, a pre-'American' time that emphasises slow repetition and accumulation of the past rather than its utter remaking in successive stages.[45] The strange ninepin-playing figures that lure Rip into a twenty-year sleep seem to heighten the satire directed towards an ideology of progress, which was both the engine of 'so great a change' in post-Union Scotland and of a manifest destiny that would bring 'civilization' to the vast wilderness, and to its indigenous inhabitants, in post-Revolutionary America.

When Rip is in the mountains he is 'out of time', but this atemporal existence is of a particular kind, strangely anchored, it seems, in the traditions of the earliest European settlement: the strange folk Rip encounters in the mountains wear the seventeenth-century costume of the first Dutch settlers to the region. Furthermore, these beings do not displace Rip from the contours of history altogether: time continues to pass as Rip slumbers, and the fantastic tale of his awakening and return to the village allows Irving to explore the nature of historical change across a relatively short span of years, marking what changes and what remains the same within a single generation. The river and the mountains remain unchanged after twenty years, but this length of time lies beyond the lifespan of Rip's dog, which is nowhere to be found. As Rip ventures into the village, the changes he perceives become much more profound. The political and social landscape of the village, has, in a generation's time, undergone a dramatic transformation, and what seems to have changed most dramatically is the relative distance between the past and the present. In the spot where once stood the village inn, Rip is now confronted with 'the Union Hotel'. The sign outside still displays the 'ruby face of King George', but the King's red coat has been exchanged for a blue one and the figure is now identified as 'GENERAL WASHINGTON' (*Sketch-Book*, 1978, p. 37). The broken windows and rickety construction of the new hotel, which have replaced the 'quiet little Dutch inn of yore', testify to the new building's own insubstantiality and impermanency. The strange elements of the village landscape before Rip's eyes throw into relief the distinct temporalities of village life pre- and post-Revolution. The great tree that once sheltered the inn is also gone and in its place 'reared a tall naked pole with something on top that looked like a red night cap, and from it was fluttering a flag on which was a singular assemblage of stars and stripes – all this was strange and incomprehensible' (ibid.). The picturesque scene of ancient tree and village inn that had emphasised the slow pace of time's passing in the community has been transformed into a scene that represents the disorienting effects of revolutionary change, of fast-shifting ideologies and political loyalties. The substitution of George Washington for George III reminds the reader that the American answer to the question of *Waverley*'s Shakespearean title-page epigraph – 'Under Which King?' – turns out to have been 'No king at all'.

Revolution has transformed the 'very character' of the community and there is now a 'busy, bustling, disputatious tone' about it, instead of the 'accustomed phlegm and drowsy tranquility'. In other words, the community has become more 'Yankee' and less 'Dutch', and the once familiar faces of 'sage' Nicholaus Vedder and Van Bummel have long disappeared, replaced by that of:

> a lean bilious looking fellow with his pockets full of hand bills ... haranguing vehemently about rights of citizens – elections – members of congress – liberty – Bunker's Hill – heroes of seventy six – and other words which were a perfect babylonish jargon to the bewildered Van Winkle. (*Sketch-Book*, 1978, p. 37)

Yet the simple substitutions of the tavern sign – simply replacing the costume and accoutrements of one ruling George for another – suggest that beneath a surface veneer of radical social and political transformation, little of actual substance has changed in the village. Though the success of the Revolution has infused a new political rhetoric into the community, this rhetoric, brought into the village from the outside world and mostly in the form of written documents, remains external to the social workings of the community and has little effect on everyday life. Rather than depicting an unfolding of historical progress in which the Revolution represents a turning point in the movement towards a more perfect political union, 'Rip Van Winkle' instead presents the aftermath of revolution as a moment of a disquieting, but ultimately fleeting, conglomeration of superficial signs and rhetoric. Irving's tale expresses a winking scepticism about the new nation's revolutionary ideals, which are ultimately external to, and intrude upon, the older and longer-lasting remembrances and traditions of local communities. Without its own particular cultural memory, Irving's tale suggests, the 'United States' has no actual purchase on the past, and is revealed to be an abstraction, an ideology, built upon a rather rickety foundation of rhetorical bombast, rather than an organic, cohesive nation.

Irving's deep ambivalence about the flimsy historical underpinnings of the new nation seem symptomatic of the general anxiety that critics have identified in American literary culture of the time: a nation without its own legends and traditions, without its own sense of the past, would ultimately fall to pieces.[46] But if Irving in 'Rip Van Winkle' draws attention to this threat to national cohesion by pointing out the scant material with which it was erected, he also offers the reassurance that, in terms of securing an American cultural memory, the material provided by the Revolutionary epoch is largely irrelevant. For one, even though Rip's long sleep leaves him a virtual shadow of his former self initially, he is quickly reintegrated into the community, a process helped along and sanctioned by 'old Peter Vanderdonk', the village's lore master, who is himself a descendant of the local historian who had written one of the earliest accounts of the province. As 'the most ancient inhabitant of the village and well-versed in all wonderful events and traditions of the neighbourhood', Vanderdonk not only remembers Rip at once, he corroborates Rip's story to everyone's satisfaction by assuring them that it was 'a fact handed down from his ancestor the historian, that the Kaatskill mountains had always been haunted by strange beings' (*Sketch-Book*, 1978, p. 40). The authority to pass down judgement on the credibility and social standing of village members continues to derive not from the handbill or public newspaper but from a member of the elder generation whose own store of remembrance is beyond repute and who has been invested by the village with the task of collecting and passing down the cultural memory of the community. Rip, 're-membered' and reintegrated, ultimately achieves a position of high authority and respect in the village as an oracle of cultural memory himself, particularly among its 'rising generation'. Suffering no long-lasting social effects from his twenty-year absence, Rip is instead 'reverenced as one of the patriarchs of the village and a chronicle of the old times "before the war"' (41).

Stephen Blakemore has described the significance of Irving's use of the term 'rising generation', which had come to serve as a kind of shorthand that linked the increasing power of the United States with the duties and energies of those living in the aftermath of the Revolution.[47] For Blakemore, Rip's abandonment of his former cronies and his popularity with the 'rising generation' signals Irving's rejection of the nation's colonial past and his support for the new post-Revolutionary regime. This patriotism is directed at Irving's readers on both sides of the Atlantic – for American readers, who sought inspiration from their revolutionary past and for British readers, who needed to be reminded of America's growing prosperity and significance on the world stage.[48] Rip, however, achieves his lofty status as village patriarch among the rising generation because of his Revolutionary amnesia, not despite it. Untainted by events that came after 'before the war', Rip has no knowledge of the Revolution, and his recollections are therefore prized because they take on the quality of cultural memory preserved in a kind of suspended animation, unaffected by the experience of what came later. Though Rip's tale became varied in points 'every time he told it', his story also becomes imprinted into the collective memory of the entire community, as 'not a man woman or child in the neighbourhood but knew it by heart' (*Sketch-Book*, 1978, p. 41). Perhaps, then, the greatest irony in a story rife with irony is that the amnesiac becomes an esteemed figure of historical continuity precisely because he slept through the great moment of political fracture that rent the present from the past.

But what exactly is to be preserved for future generations in Irving's post-Revolutionary tale if not the memory of the Revolution? The formation of cultural memory in 'Rip Van Winkle', it seems, is cast as a series of appropriations and substitutions from other cultures, a state of affairs that replicates the appropriation of European folklore that proved a central aspect of Irving's creative method, what Jones aptly describes as a 'predatory folk memory', which gave rise to the best-known tales from the *Sketch Book*.[49] But the persistence of these pre-existing stores of cultural memory suggests something else is at work in 'Rip Van Winkle' besides the appropriation of European folk memory. Cultural memory in 'Rip Van Winkle' works through and around moments of fracture; it persists through slow sedimentation and the stitching together of various fragments of remembrance.

This persistence of memory diminishes the significance of the Revolutionary epoch in a nation that, though established through a violent insurrection, nevertheless derives much of its store of collective remembrance from the empires that preceded it on the continent. Cultural memory in America is the product of the interplay between the various cultural memories of European settlements: successive generations in these settlements continue to pass down their respective traditions, even though these are sometimes interrupted or dislocated. Through the efforts of Diedrich Knickerbocker, and Geoffrey Crayon, the memory of the nation's 'former incidents' will indeed be rescued from oblivion, but the living receptacle of that memory, Rip himself, cannot remember, and therefore will not pass down to the 'rising generation', that fateful epoch which saw the invention of the nation.[50]

Anxieties of Forgetting: Post-Revolutionary Remembrance and John Neal

As Scott's popularity in America reached manic proportions in the early 1820s, authors that sought to emulate his literary example stood in uneasy relation to his success, alternately paying homage to his achievement while seeking to establish a distinct reputation for themselves. James Fenimore Cooper, for example, whose achievement as a novelist would come to be measured by the title that was bestowed upon him as the 'American Scott', ultimately disavowed Scott's influence, distinguishing his own work by its adherence to the egalitarian principles that Cooper found lacking in the Waverley Novels. Catharine Maria Sedgwick boldly subtitled *The Linwoods*, her 1838 novel of the Revolution, '"Sixty Years Since" in America', but then spent much of her Preface peremptorily fending off detractors who might accuse her of the 'insane vanity' of placing her work on the level of the 'great Master'.[51] Although both Cooper's and Sedgwick's sentiments are illustrative of the complex and ultimately ambivalent relations between Scott and his American contemporaries, their particular focus on the Revolutionary period is also indicative of the lasting influence of Scott's imagining of the 'aftermath' moment. Both *The Linwoods* and *The Spy* were part of a litany of historical novels published after 1820 that evoke the call for the present generation to remember their Revolutionary progenitors.[52] Few of these, however, would bring to the subject of generational change the intensity and energy that John Neal provided in his 1823 novel *Seventy-Six*.

Neal's literary career began while he was establishing a law practice in Baltimore but was nurtured in London in the 1820s, when he became part of the transatlantic network of literary exchange of which Scott and Irving were also a part. While in London, Neal became a contributor to *Blackwood's*, recruited as an American infiltrator in the transatlantic culture wars being waged in the periodical literary reviews. As Neal would later relate in his autobiography, he began his writing career consciously seeking to follow in the footsteps of Irving and Cooper, who had both spent many years living and writing in London. Neal's sojourn overseas had been impulsively inspired, he writes, by an offhand comment at a Baltimore dinner party made by an English-born acquaintance, who had taken up Sydney Smith's infamous query in the *Edinburgh Review*: 'Who reads an American book?' In response, Neal writes:

> I told him, 'more in sorrow than in anger,' that I would answer that question from over sea; that I would leave my office, my library, and my law-business, and take passage in the first vessel I could find – we had no regular packets then – and see what might be done, with a fair field, and no favor, by an American writer. Irving had succeeded; and, though I was wholly unlike Irving, why shouldn't I? Cooper was well received; and I had a notion, that, without crossing his path, or poaching upon his manor, I might do something, so American, as to secure the attention of Englishmen.[53]

In London, where two of his novels, *Logan* and *Seventy-Six*, had already been published, Neal, using a pseudonym, went on to write a series of five essays for *Blackwood's* from 1824 to 1825 on 'American Writers' (one of which made some praise of his own work).

Seventy-Six, which Neal later proclaimed to be his best work (even though he also boasted it took him only twenty-seven days to write), was inspired, he wrote in his autobiography, by 'the doings of our Revolutionary fathers', while he was at work contributing material for Paul Allen's *A History of the American Revolution*.[54] *Seventy-Six* is a dramatic two-volume story recounting the adventures and deprivations of its narrator, Jonathan Oadley, who in his younger days had been a soldier in Washington's Continental Army. Depictions of his wartime experiences are interspersed with sentimental scenes of families torn apart and livelihoods destroyed by war and of young love won and lost. In its setting and general themes, *Seventy-Six* could be said to parallel its more successful contemporaries on Revolutionary themes, *The Spy* and *The Linwoods*. But Neal's work differs from the other two by explicitly framing its narrative as the remembrance of one who had directly experienced the pivotal events of the nation's proximate past.

From the vantage point of its 1823 publication, *Seventy-Six* announces, through the unequivocal temporal anchor point of its title, its proximate distance from the turning point it will recount. As a work declaring itself to be the first-person memoir of a veteran of the War of Independence, Neal's novel figures in the widespread sentiment in the 1820s that the nation must remember and commemorate a Revolutionary generation nearing its end. Capturing this sentiment in a eulogy for Charles Carroll, the last living signer of the Declaration of Independence, a Baltimore newspaper editor wrote: 'Thus one after another, the luminaries of the Revolution are leaving the stage of action, and soon the whole of the bright galaxy, which in those dark days, adorned the land, must be numbered with the silent dead . . .'.[55] This generational exit from the stage posed America's own version of the early-century European memory crisis, in which the values and principles that had inspired the call for independence seemed in danger of becoming forever lost to succeeding generations. As a contributor to the *American* wrote upon the death of Carroll: 'The only remaining link which connected this generation with the past, with that illustrious race of statesmen, philanthropists and patriots, the founders of American Independence, and the benefactors of the world, now and for all time hereafter – is broken'.[56]

Without its embodiment in the living figures of the Revolutionary generation, the memory of the nation's past is threatened with complete dissolution in a 'for all time hereafter' that grants no reprieve. Thus, the legacy of a national collective, which had been predicated on a rejection of past traditions in an era of revolution, was now deemed to be threatened with disintegration.[57] Thus the aftermath temporality that dominated American historical consciousness by the mid-1820s was configured acutely as the burden of the 'rising generation' to preserve and carry the memory of past: the patriotic example of the nation's progenitors will 'live only in the grateful recollection of those for whom they have purchased liberty, independence, prosperity and happiness'.[58] The obligation to remember inspired an explosion of commemoration, ceremony and monument building in the decade, all of which helped to form an official memory of the Revolutionary turning point, which – in dramatic contrast to the politics of the past in Scotland during the same period – reflected a widespread desire to commemorate the epochal events of the nation's recent past and thereby re-energise an American patriotism.[59] By memorialising the Revolutionary past, Americans sought to honour the dead, ennoble themselves and secure a polity that was deemed under threat, not by the forces of an invading army but the dissolutive effects of a national forgetting.[60]

Seventy-Six forms a part of this commemorative wave, as Neal's work was one of many accounts, both fictional and non-fictional, ostensibly drawn from the remembrances of actual veterans of the Revolution.[61] In the Preface to *Seventy-Six*, Neal explicitly labels his novel a work of fiction. In attempting to replicate the workings and limitations of the memory of an infirm old man recollecting and recounting events that took place almost fifty years before, however, Neal's fictional account provides a powerful alternative to the 'official memory' that was being erected across the country in the form of monuments, ceremonies, memorabilia and written accounts dedicated to those who answered the Revolution's noble call. Through a digressive, rambling and fragmented recounting of the times, Neal's work offers a form of cultural memory that is more akin to an open wound. Formed by the destructive violence of the past, it remains not fully healed, a permanent trace on the body, and mind, of one who has survived and now bears witness to it.

Fraught Remembrance: Neal's Revolutionary Generation

In its framing Postscript, *Waverley*'s memorialising narrator, like the narrator of 'Rip Van Winkle', is revealed to be invested personally in the past events he describes and is therefore susceptible to occasional outbreaks of melancholia. At the same time, however, he is also able to maintain a critical distance from the past he seeks to narrate, poking gentle fun at the outworn manners and prejudices of his progenitors. Neal's work, while adopting the theme of these two works, preserving cultural memory at a moment of generational transition, differs dramatically from both as it attempts to recreate the actual voice of the preceding generation. Jonathan Oadley, *Seventy-Six*'s first-person narrator, is a septuagenarian veteran of Washington's campaigns in New Jersey and Pennsylvania, whose recollections ostensibly form the material of the work. As a living example of the Revolution's progenitor generation, Oadley is prompted to tell his story by his own awareness that time is soon running out for those like him. Taking the form of an unedited manuscript disseminated first among his children and then to be copied in a 'fair hand' by his son, Oadley's story begins with a direct address to his audience:

> Yes, my children, I will no longer delay it. We are passing, one by one, from the place of contention, one after another, to the grave; and, in a little time, *you* may say – Our Fathers! – the men of the Revolution – where are they? . . . Yes, I will go about it, in earnest: I will leave the record behind me, and when there is nothing else to remind you of your father, and your children's children, of their ancestor – nothing else, to call his apparition before you, that you may see his aged and worn forehead – his white hair in the wind . . . you will have but to open the book, that I shall leave to you – and lay your right hand, devoutly, upon the page.[62]

National memory, figuratively imagined as the remembrance of one's 'forefathers', is made literal in *Seventy-Six*, as Oadley prepares to pass down the story of his own life to his children.

Lacking the ostensible interposition of a middle-generation editor or compiler, memory is represented in Neal's work as raw and unmediated, the 'authenticity' of its enunciation indicated by the narrative's general disorderliness. Against a backdrop of widespread inconsistencies in the novel's orthography and typography, the motives of individual character actions are not always made clear, the depiction of battle is blurred and confusing, and Oadley's narration of the historical events of the Revolution is frequently interrupted by lengthy digressions and asides to his audience. By novel's end, Oadley will apologise for his inability to trace an accurate chronological account of the war, and, giving up entirely, abruptly end his narrative about halfway through his wartime experience. Such problems in plotting and narrative structure have long formed the basis of critical dissatisfaction with *Seventy-Six* and with Neal's work in general and have perhaps contributed to the eclipse of his literary standing.[63] In a recent study, however, Jeffrey Insko has re-examined the narrative 'faults' of *Seventy-Six*, seeing the work as exemplary of Neal's 'antinarrative aesthetic': his attempt to render the actual experiences of life through an 'eye-witness' mode of description that is fundamentally at odds with the dictates of conventional narrative plotting. For Neal, Insko argues:

> the function of a narrator (or author) is thus not to explain, but simply to present incidents with such vividness of interest that the reader becomes 'an eye-witness' . . . [N]arrative is not immanent in our experience, but merely a structure that is imposed upon it retrospectively.[64]

Insko's reading provides a rethinking of the 'eye-witness' narrative structure that allows us to understand Neal's investment in imagining the mechanisms of remembrance and of cultural memory. It might be more precise to say that, in *Seventy-Six*, Neal's antinarrative aesthetic seeks to replicate not so much the way people *experience* events, but the ways in which they *recollect* those experiences. Oadley's eyewitness understanding of the personal and social destructive effects of war are the chief subject of his narrative, but they also determine the manner in which he, as a survivor, recollects them. *Seventy-Six* plays out the vagaries of an old man's memory in ways that *Waverley* does not: Scott will speak for the turning-point generation himself, smoothing out the inconsistencies and biases, and provide an authoritative, if fictive, account of the times. Neal's work, however, grants to the fragmented and sometimes scattered recollections of a wounded elderly veteran the unassailable authority of eyewitness testimony.

As an actual veteran of the Revolution, Oadley claims access to the truth of the past that historians of a younger generation can never have. 'We have had many a history . . . of the revolution,' he declares:

> but none written by men acquainted by participation therein, with our sorrow, and trial, and suffering: not one, where the mighty outline of truth is distinctly visible – no, not one. . . . We wrestled, children as we were, for eight years, with armed giants: and wrenched – *wrenched*! with our own hands, the spoil from the spoiler – overcame them all, at last, after eight years of mortal trial, and uninterrupted battle, even in their stronghold. I was one of them that helped to do this. There is a vividness in my recollection that cannot deceive me. (1:14)

The vividness of his recollection, Oadley writes, grants his narrative both its power and its claim, unrivalled, in his mind, by all other historical accounts, to have unmediated access to the truth. Oadley therefore commands his children that they must not embellish or alter the record he provides. As a result:

> My style may offend you. I do not doubt that it will. I hope that it will. It will be remembered the better . . . You have all had a better education than your father. You have, most of you, a pleasant and graceful ways of expressing yourselves on paper . . . but there is not one among you – not one, that has learnt to *talk on paper*. (1:17)

Beyond the jibes of a disappointed father, Oadley asserts that the very simplicity of his style, its artlessness and directness, will secure its status as sacred testament to the truth, worthy of preservation as cultural memory:

> [L]et [my story] go down with your blood, the patent of your nobility, to the elder son, forever and ever; when you are able, multiply the copies among all that are descended from me, as the last legacy, of one, that it would be an honour to *them*, whatever they become, to be the posterity of. (1:17)

The emotional intensity of recollection, which is the hallmark of its unmediated access to the truth, at times also threatens to overcome its narrator. If Oadley boastfully proclaims that at his bidding the venerable dead of the Revolution will 'harness and array themselves – and stand before you', the act of conjuring them often overwhelms him, forcing him to stop the flow of his narrative. Remembrances of his now dead wife, who had nursed him back to health after he lost a leg in battle, force Oadley to interrupt the narrative and directly address his audience again:

> My children, you can never know her value. From the time you can recollect her, she was feeble and dim. You should have seen her, about the bed of her husband; sick and dying. You should have heard her affectionate voice, soothing him to his short slumber; seen her modest hand, wiping the sweat from his lips! . . . Oh Clara! I am widowed, and way-worn – sorrowing and dark; yet thy image is warmth and brightness – comfort and consolation to me. Yet – ! when shall we meet again? ah *when*! . . . My children, I cannot proceed any further tonight. I feel as if your mother were near me. Good night. (2:153)

In this passage, Neal attempts to recapture both the difficulty in bringing to life the vividness of one's experiences for others, and the processes of memory, which seem to be, for Neal, associative: remembrance of a single moment in their shared experience inspires a general remembrance of their devotion to each other, which in turns jolts Oadley back to his melancholic present and the realisation of his own impending mortality. At the same time, the frequent gaps and digressions in Oadley's narrative are testament themselves to the frailty of his memory, required to call up distressful scenes now fifty years past. Oadley, it seems, is not quite up to the task he set out for himself. He frequently departs from narrating the particular events at hand, sometimes jumping between the Revolutionary past that is the subject of his narrative and more proximate pasts that occurred sometime after, and he is often unable to provide a clear-cut or linear narrative of the events he sets out to unfold. Oadley's memory wanders where it wants to go, and, as he himself admits, often strays from the interest of the audience. The cumulative failings of his memory and the emotional toll required to recollect events culminate at the point at which he gives up narrating his experiences of the war altogether: 'My heart fails me. I never shall be able to carry you through the whole war, as I intended to do when I began. It is out of the question. My own return to the army; the desolation that fell upon us; the darkness – the – no, I cannot' (2:242). The traumatic experiences of war and revolution and its after-effects will not be tidied up for readers of *Seventy-Six*. Instead, Neal offers a glimpse into the psychological and physical toll of war, expressed not in its precise recounting but in the war-wounded memory of its narrator.

After abruptly breaking off the personal recollection of the campaigns of war, Oadley instead finishes his story where it began, near the site of the old family farm, which had been burned to the ground by British troops, who had also murdered Oadley's mother, some three years earlier. It is there that Oadley tries to convince his brother finally to marry his one true love. But this plea is interrupted by his brother, Archibald, who instead asks Oadley to walk with him to a place nearby. Oadley obeys and is led by Archibald to a place where he confesses to the murder of a local man in a duel, fought immediately before he and Oadley were both called off to war. Turning over a heavy rock, Archibald reveals the rusty pistols and bloody handkerchief that gives proof of the deed. The abrupt shift in setting and focus at the end of the novel offers a confusing statement about the nature of the war that Oadley had, up to that point, been recounting. His brother admits to being long haunted by the spectre of the dead – not just of the man he killed on the eve of the war, but of those he killed in battle, and of another man he killed in a duel at the end of the first volume – but Neal introduces the memory of all these deaths in a concluding scene that muddles the meaning of all the Revolutionary violence that had come before. At its end, *Seventy-Six* offers no patriotic 'noble cause' resolution to justify the killing; offering us instead a sudden revelation of, and dramatic conclusion to, a bizarre revenge plot, in which the memory of the dead returns to play havoc with the living.

After his dramatic confession, Archibald seems to voice the novel's sentiment about his entire generation when he says to Oadley:

> We are getting old, brother . . . very old. I feel like one that has worn out his appointment of three score years and ten, outstayed the sojourn permitted to man. Men talk about years and months and days. I measure time by vicissitude – trial – sorrow, blood. Look at me; but a few summers have gone over me. I am what the world calls a young man; but, to my notion, I am older than the patriarchs. I have out lived all the pleasant emotions of the heart, all remembrance of my childhood; the beauty of heaven – the clear water, the green branching tree, the sporting bird – the – the bright lip of woman, and her love – have turned to ashes in my sight. (2:255)

In a narrative premised on the chasm between past and present, time is suddenly compressed in his brother's final lament: the Revolution has already made them bitter old men. Though Oadley had lived many years since the scene he describes, the frail and bitter quality of his narrative suggests that his brother had been right: the body now fails as the spirit did a long time ago. For Oadley's brother, however, there is no future: Archibald agrees to marry his beloved only when he is assured that she knows she will soon be made a widow, a fate confirmed when, as soon as the benediction of their marriage is pronounced, Archibald falls to the floor dead. Oadley has survived the war; he gets to tell his story to his children amid a present time of relative peace and prosperity, but the scars of the Revolutionary epoch are traced on his recollections as well as his mind and body. The domestic tranquility that frames Oadley's story seems to signal the achievement of Revolutionary aims and the establishment of a new national culture in North America, yet Neal's fictive memorial of the war generation draws attention to the costs of that tranquility and the woeful circumstances that attended the nation's origins. In *Seventy-Six*'s mode of collective remembrance, the Revolution is configured not so much as final triumph in the birth of the nation, but as collective trauma, the scars of which take its toll on memory, providing no definitive answers for the 'rising generation'.

Je Me Souviens: French Canada and the Fifty-Nine

In 1863 Phillipe-Joseph Aubert de Gaspé commenced his first and only novel, a tale of the 1759 Conquest, with a prefatory rationale that adopts *Waverley*'s topos of enunciating the past at the very horizon of lived memory:

> Consigner quelques épisodes du bon vieux temps, quelques souvenirs d'une jeunesse, hélas! bien éloignée, voilà toute mon ambition. Plusieurs anecdotes paraîtront, sans doute, insignifiantes et puériles à bien des lecteurs: qu'ils jettent le blâme sur quelques-uns de nos meilleurs littérateurs, qui m'ont prié de ne rien omettre sur les mœurs des anciens Canadiens. 'Ce qui paraîtra insignifiant et puéril aux yeux des étrangers, me disaient-ils, ne laissera pas d'intéresser les vrais Canadiens, dans la chronique d'un septuagénaire, né vingt-huit ans seulement après la conquête de la Nouvelle-France.[65]

> (To set down a few episodes of bygone days, a few memories of youth, alas! long past: that is the sum of my ambition. Many readers will no doubt consider some of these anecdotes trifling and childish. Let them blame a few of our brightest literary lights, who have asked me to leave out nothing concerning the manners and customs of the old Canadians. 'What will seem trifling and childish to strangers', they said, 'will be sure to interest true Canadians in the chronicles of a seventy-year-old, born just twenty-eight years after the conquest of New France')[66]

As Scott had sought to embody and preserve the outmoded principles of 'old Scottish faith, hospitality, worth, and honour' of the nation's forefathers, so would Aubert de Gaspé – who pays homage to Scott in his own work – enshrine French Canadian cultural memory in *Les Anciens Canadiens*.[67] Aubert de Gaspé presents his novel as a kind of technology, par excellence, for the preservation of the traditions and values of the past, a national treasury of remembrance, rendered through its fictive scenes and characters. While adopting the 'proximate past' perspective of *Waverley*, Aubert de Gaspé also vastly extends its range, reaching back all the way to 1759, fourteen years after Culloden but more than a hundred years from the scene of his writing. Born fifteen years after Scott, however, Aubert de Gaspé has survived long enough for his retrospect to stand in the same relation to its historical subject – the British conquest of New France – as Scott stands in relation to his. Only a generation removed from the 1759 turning point he narrates, Aubert de Gaspé, like Scott in *Waverley*, lays claim to representing the proximate past as one who, though he did not directly experience the events he recounts, spent his youth among those who did. The remembrances are handed down to him by family members and by 'les vieillards' and 'les vieilles femmes' he knew in childhood and who were part of his everyday world (328). Already in his seventies when he established his reputation in the literary society of Quebec, Aubert de Gaspé himself was configured as a 'Canadian of Old', a living repository of a memory of an earlier time. Excerpting a passage from the novel, a contemporary commentator summarised the character of its author:

> The reader will have recognized in this extract a translation from a passage of that charming volume *Les Anciens Canadiens*, recently published by our respected townsman, P. A. DeGaspé, Esq., Seigneur of St. Jean Port Joly: himself not a bad personification of the courteous, well-bred, feudal dignitary of former times.[68]

Like the work of the Scottish and American memorialists who came before him, Aubert de Gaspé's work both identifies a historical transition moment when cultural memory becomes in danger of passing into oblivion and intervenes to preserve, and sometimes correct, that memory in its pages. Yet, for de Gaspé, the call to preserve was felt perhaps more acutely as it reminded him of his own advanced age and failing mental acuity. Much like Neal's fictional Jonathan Oadley, Aubert de Gaspé draws attention to the inevitability of the erosion of memory and of death. Aubert de Gaspé's retrospect is infused with a pervasive melancholy, a longing prompted by the awareness of the author's own alienation from a 'youth long past', which his 'trifling' and 'childish' memories only seem to emphasise. In this, Aubert de Gaspé's narrative partakes of, in Svetlana Boym's terms, both a 'restorative' nostalgia, a nationalist revival that 'proposes to rebuild the lost home and patch up the memory gaps', and a 'reflective' nostalgia that dwells 'in longing and loss', and that 'lingers on ruins, the patina of time and history . . .'.[69]

'Communicative' and 'cultural' memory thus overlap in interesting ways in what has been described as the first and most definitive example of the national tale in francophone Canada.[70] *Les Anciens Canadiens* played a seminal role in a literary/antiquarian preservation project that had gathered steam after the 1840 Act of Union, which, after a series of failed uprisings, abolished the separate legislative bodies of Upper and Lower Canada and created a single entity, the United Province of Canada. For many French Canadians, the Act of Union signalled the consolidation of an anglophone agenda to secure what the Conquest had failed to achieve – the destruction of a francophone way of life. Crown policy would impose final political control over Lower Canada through a project of cultural assimilation, a project given doctrinal force in the conclusions of the widely disseminated *Lord Durham's Report*, which had envisioned political unrest in Canada as the clash between two races – between the regressive and vacuous remnants of Nouvelle France and their progressive and enlightened English masters, whose destiny it was to rule all of Canada. 'There can hardly be conceived a nationality', summarised the report

> more destitute of all that can invigorate and elevate a people, than that which is exhibited by the descendants of the French in Lower Canada, owing to their retaining their peculiar language and manners. They are a people with no history, and no literature.[71]

Only by becoming British themselves, concluded the *Report*, would Canadians of French descent reap the benefits of Britain's empire: 'The colony will not be worth our keeping unless it is Anglified'.[72]

In reaction, the francophone elite of Montreal and Quebec embarked on a cultural counter assault, in which they sought to establish the legitimacy of their national identity through the cultivation and preservation of the elements of a distinctly French-Canadian way of life.[73] This way of life was given its historical bona fides with the 1845–8 publication of François-Xavier Garneau's magisterial three-volume *Histoire du Canada*. Garneau's work provided an epic paean to French-Canadian nationhood, seeking to provide a definitive history whose overarching theme was *survivance*. Orphaned by their nation of origin and left to themselves to fend off the relentless attempts of subjugation by an alien invader, in Garneau's account, the *Canadiens* nevertheless persist:

> Abandonné, oublié complètement par son ancienne mère-patrie, pour laquelle son nom est peut-être un remords; connu à peine du reste des autres nations dont il n'a pu exciter ni l'influence ni les sympathies, il a lutté seul contre toutes les tentatives faites contre son existence, et il s'est maintenu à la surprise de ses oppresseurs découragés et vaincus.
>
> (Deserted and completely forgotten by their former mother country, for whom their name perhaps now inspires remorse; scarcely known to other nations, whose influence or sympathies they could never excite, [French Canadians] can only resist all attempts to vanquish them as a people; and they have persisted, much to the surprise of their discouraged and defeated oppressors.)[74]

Secured through the perpetuation of what he defined as the 'trois grands symboles de sa nationalité', Garneau's work inscribes the formation and consolidation of French-Canadian nationhood: as long as the people held on to 'la langue, les lois et la religion', their nation would live on, even while ultimately acceding to the existence of British political institutions and authority.[75] French Canadians, if they could not reverse the Conquest, must resist all attempts at cultural absorption.

The literary field served a vital role in sustaining this growing cultural nationalism, as it provided an ideal mode for the expression of the 'grands symboles' of French-Canadian nationality. The decades following the Act of Union saw an outpouring of work devoted to preserving the nation's heritage, much of which took the form of the literary miscellany. James Huston's collection of French-Canadian poetry and tales, *Le Répertoire national*, for example, appeared in 1848 and was followed by the monthly *Les Soirées canadiennes* in 1861 and James Macpherson LeMoine's *Maple Leaves* – styled by its compiler a *Budget of Legendary, Historical, Critical, and Sporting Intelligence* – in 1863.[76] In the wide range of subjects covered by these publications – traditions, legends, poetry, short tales, bits of folklore and songs, genealogies of surnames and of place names, biographical sketches of notable personages, descriptions of unique social institutions, and, in the case of *Maples Leaves*, ornithological and ichthyological observations – these miscellanies of the mid-century sought to demonstrate a national culture through the sheer accumulation of material. One subject, however, was pointedly left out in these publications. As *Les Soirées canadiennes* proclaimed, within its pages 'les discussions politiques . . . ne devront jamais trouver accès' ('political discussion . . . will never gain entry').[77] Although twentieth-century commentators would criticise the resulting 'watering down' of the national heritage that resulted from this de-politicisation of literary discourse, francophone cultural nationalism in post-Union Canada would mimic in many respects the cultural nationalism of post-Union Scotland, by advancing a nationalist agenda removed from the domain of politics altogether, which would instead concern itself with the recovery and inscription of the nation's cultural memory, particularly through literature.[78]

The prospectus of *Les Soirées canadiennes* encapsulated the aims of this cultural memory project:

> Ce recueil sera surtout consacré à soustraire nos belles légendes canadiennes à un oubli dont elles sont plus que jamais menacées, à perpétuer ainsi les souvenirs conservés dans la mémoire de nos vieux narrateurs, et à vulgariser la connaissance de certains épisodes peu connus de l'histoire de notre pays. (i)
>
> (This collection will be chiefly devoted to protecting our beautiful Canadian legends from an oblivion with which they are threatened more than ever, thus perpetuating the memories preserved in the recollections of our aged storytellers and popularising the knowledge of certain little-known episodes in the history of our country.)

La nationalité would be secured through a critical and aesthetic investment in maintaining a distinct national identity through ongoing acts of collective remembrance, a state of affairs that would shape the course of Canadian francophone literary production well into the twentieth century. As Marilyn Randall writes:

> Literary production until the end of the Second World War was largely at the service of creating and preserving a monolithic national identity, in which the lost Golden Age of New France was to be compensated for by the preservation of the traditions of religion, agriculture, and the French language. That this catholicizing destiny was to be played out in a small corner of the continent only added to the urgency with which the literary-political-clerical elite insisted upon the nation-building function of literature.[79]

The Conquest year of 1759 formed the historical crux of this French-Canadian cultural nationalism, as the pivotal moment when the nation's 'Golden Age' came to a bitter end. Preservation of the nation's cultural legacy became the watchword of literary production in French Canada, legitimising literature, and particularly the novel form, which the Catholic Church had actively discouraged before the 1850s.[80] Even before its publication, Aubert de Gaspé's novel was lauded as a literary expression of the nation's cultural heritage; it also brought the identification of the Conquest as the nation's pivotal moment to the forefront of an emerging national consciousness.[81] In its fond compendium of what could perhaps be summarised as the outmoded principles of 'faith, hospitality, worth, and honour' of the Canadians of Old, *Les Anciens Canadiens* insistently reminds its readers what was lost at the fateful moment of their defeat and what they always must remember.

Culloden on the Plains of Abraham

Only through collective acts of remembrance, Aubert de Gaspé reminds his readers, would the nation's past be protected and preserved, not only against the ravages of time but an anglocentric policy of willed cultural amnesia. But the story that unfolds within the pages of *Les Anciens Canadiens* may prompt the question of just which national turning point its readers are supposed to remember – for the novel incorporates not only the narrative tropes and thematic concerns of *Waverley* but its historical moment as well. Aubert de Gaspé's tale of the D'Habervilles, an old seigneurial family of Quebec, and their travails during the time of the Conquest is related through the actions of the young Scot whom they adopt as one of the family: Archibald Cameron of Lochiel – affectionately known to them as Arché – exiled son of a Jacobite Highland chieftain killed on the field of Culloden. Soon after the defeat of Prince Charles's army, Arché's uncle, having escaped the hangman's noose in Scotland, had fled to France. From there, the novel tells us, he had sent Arché to a Jesuit College in Quebec, where he begins his friendship with Jules D'Haberville and is soon embraced by the rest of the family. After establishing the tragic background of his Scottish protagonist, however, Aubert de Gaspé abruptly turns away from his narrative to address the reader directly on the matter of Culloden's national-historical significance. The battle for which Arché's father gave his life, Aubert de Gaspé writes, represented the dramatic culmination of a centuries-long struggle of the Scottish people against their more formidable English foes. After the defeat at Culloden:

> Un long gémissement de rage et de désespoir par courut les montagnes et les vallées de l'ancienne Calédonie! Ses enfants durent renoncer pour toujours à reconquérir une liberté pour laquelle ils avaient combattu pendant plusieurs siècles avec tant d'acharnement et de vaillance. Ce fut le dernier râle de l'agonie d'une nation héroïque qui succombe. (*Les Anciens Canadiens*, p. 36)
>
> One long moan of rage and despair rang through the mountains and glens, as the children of ancient Caledonia were forced to give up all hope of reconquering the liberty fought for with such fierce heroism over the centuries. It was the death rattle of a brave nation. (*Canadians of Old*, p. 182)

Scotland's complete political disenfranchisement is achieved and encapsulated in one single moment of national tragedy, yet the defeat at Culloden, he continues, was not without its compensations: Scotland's writers, statesmen and warriors have met with acclaim as a nation integrated within one of the most powerful empires the world has seen.

Situating the individual circumstances that brought Arché to New France within a larger narrative of the grand historical progress of nations invites us to read Aubert de Gaspé's summary of Scotland's fateful turning point as analogous to the pivotal events that will follow in his narrative: just as national defeat at Culloden proved beneficial to Scotland, whose citizens had reaped the bounty of empire after their nation's absorption into the British Union, so will the Conquest prove ultimately beneficial to French Canadians, who will similarly be able to play out their ambitions on the selfsame grand imperial stage. In this reading, *Les Anciens Canadiens* seems to echo the political quietism often applied to *Waverley* and that, in earlier French-Canadian political discourse, had configured the Conquest as providential, 'a blessing from heaven', as a writer for *Le Canadien* had put it in 1809.[82] In this earlier formulation, the Conquest bestowed upon a vanquished people of New France the rights and liberties of the British constitution, saving them both from the despotic rule of French colonial governors and the worst excesses of the French Revolution.⁸³ What follows in Aubert de Gaspé's narrative, however, complicates this reading of the defeat of Culloden as historical analogue. Instead the echo of Scotland's 'death rattle', the cultural and psychological after-effects of the battle, reverberate throughout the New World described in *Les Anciens Canadiens*, setting into motion a sequence of events that leads to the despair and ruin of the D'Haberville family and to the bitter failure of Arché's ambition to re-establish his own family fortune in Canada.

Embodied in the character of Arché, whose Scottish past clings to him as he carries the tragic circumstances of his exile to North America, Culloden ties his fate inextricably with the fate of the D'Habervilles. In the climactic last third of the novel, Arché returns to Quebec after an absence of two years, but under very different circumstances from those that had brought him to the colony. Finding his way back to his native country, we are told, Arché had succeeded in recovering what was left of his family fortune after confiscation, and he returns to Canada during the Conquest, as a lieutenant in the British Army, leading a regiment of his clan's own Highlanders. Arché, the novel declares, had 'fait sa paix avec le gouvernement britannique', but his reintegration into its imperial regime does not signal a settlement or reconciliation. Instead, Arché's return initiates the novel's plot of betrayal and divided loyalty, as he revisits the familiar landscape of his carefree college days, but in the service of a conquering army bent on the destruction of his adoptive family's estates and way of life. Carrying his own familial death memento – the sword his father carried when he died, purchased from English spoils taken from Culloden's battlefield – Arché is ordered by his commanding officer to burn the estate and millworks of his adoptive family; afterwards, he witnesses his Canadian foster-brother wounded and lying near death on the Plains of Abraham.⁸⁴ The national trauma of Culloden returns to trouble the following generation on the other side of the Atlantic, but the cruelty and violence of the earlier struggle will not be recompensed by a Scottish/British victory in Quebec. Instead, the bitter memory of death and disenfranchisement and loss of national inheritance is evoked time and again throughout the narrative, albeit, often in altered forms, becoming part of the cultural memory of the 'Canadians of old'. The Jacobite rising and defeat function in the novel less as a historical analogue or exemplar, a figuration of the past signifying in the present, and more a remnant of the past itself, a talismanic scrap of cultural memory that, exiled from its native country, troubles the present elsewhere.

Surrogation of Memory

The traumatic legacy of Culloden and its aftermath are carried across the Atlantic by a Jacobite diaspora, where it becomes part of an alternate cultural memory in the New World. In this way, remembrance of the past is reiterated and preserved, but, as it crosses spatial, linguistic and cultural boundaries, remembrance becomes altered and distorted, serving new contexts and new cultural conditions. Such a transmutation of memory instances a presence of the past that is very different from historical analogue; indeed, it operates very differently from the repetition of the past that has been identified with traumatic memory.[85] Instead, the presence of the Jacobite past exemplifies a surrogation of memory, the term Joseph Roach has used to describe the process by which diasporic cultures of the circum-Atlantic world were reproduced and re-created.[86] 'As actual or perceived vacancies occur in the network of relations that constitutes the social fabric', Roach writes, migrant communities scattered throughout the New World formed their collective memories through substitution and replacement. Cultural memory in one part of the Atlantic world is transported to another, but the 'fit cannot be exact', as the substituted memory is never exactly the same. The 'very uncanniness of the process of surrogation', writes Roach, 'may provoke many unbidden emotions, ranging from mildly incontinent sentimentalism to raging paranoia'. The disruptive social effects of such a reaction may in turn require public enactments of remembering or forgetting, 'either to blur the obvious discontinuities, misalliances, and ruptures or, more desperately, to exaggerate them in order to mystify a previous Golden Age now lapsed'.[87]

The presence of the surrogated memory of Culloden in *Les Anciens Canadiens* has the effect of doubling the intensity of Aubert de Gaspé's account of the pernicious after-effects of the Conquest, reinforcing, rather than diminishing, the momentousness of defeat and, therefore, the anxiety of cultural dispossession. This is illustrated in the middle section of the novel, which forms a relatively bucolic interlude between the introductory material on Arché's Jacobite background and the later scenes of battle and carnage. In these middle chapters the narrative pace is slowed, allowing several excursions into the pre-Conquest milieu of French-Canadian folklore and traditional customs, the raw material that will furnish the novel's treasury of national cultural memory. We learn, for example, that the old Jesuit College of Quebec is now a military barracks, that Canadians of old generally only drank white wine with dessert, that *croquecignoles* are a kind of multi-ringed doughnut made by the cook sticking her fingers through the dough before dropping it into the oil, and that it was the custom of residents in the countryside to end the May Day celebration by shooting up the maypole. Yet the residue of Arché's family past lingers is these chapters as well, as the brutality and dispossession associated with memory of Culloden punctuate the idyll. The faithful retainer of Arche's adoptive family, José – whom Aubert de Gaspé compares to *The Bride of Lammermoor*'s Caleb Balderstone but who, as a reciter of local legend and a repository of oral tradition, figures in Aubert de Gaspé's novel more like *The Antiquary*'s Edie Ochiltree – tells Arché a legend handed down to him by his own father. Walking home late one night and coming to a crossroads near the city, the father had been pressed into the service of the reanimated corpse of a woman executed for the murder of her two husbands, her body having been left to rot in a cage above the roadside. After struggling with the spectre, known as *la Corriveau*, who wants him to ferry her across the St Lawrence to an island to join a witches' sabbath, José's father had fainted dead away, only to awaken at daybreak, with no sign anywhere of the night's encounter.

This 'Tam o' Shanter'-like tale of supernatural encounter exemplifies the kind of pre-Conquest *Canadien* folk legend that Aubert de Gaspé is anxious to transcribe within the pages of his novel, but the historical background supplied in his footnotes on the legend reveal that the spectre's appearance has its basis in the country's more recent, post-Conquest past. Three years after the Conquest, the footnote tells us, with Quebec still under British martial law, Marie-Josephte Corriveau was executed for the murder of her husband and her body was hung in an iron cage at a prominent crossroads in the Pointe-Lévis district, across the St Lawrence. The sight of the dead woman was said to torment passers-by and, when British authorities refused to take her body down, she was secretly buried by some local young men in unconsecrated ground near the cemetery. Telescoped forward in time, from pre-Conquest to the immediate post-Conquest era, the legend of *la Corriveau* evokes the folkloric heritage of the nation's Golden Age while at the same time recording the bloody crackdown of the British occupation army soon after. Even though Aubert de Gaspé is careful to label the legend's appearance in his novel as an 'anachronisme', it nevertheless testifies to the operations of memory within its pages, as the trauma of defeat and its after-effects reverberate through displacement and association rather than strict chronology (*Les Anciens Canadiens*, p. 381).[88]

The discontinuities and misalliances of surrogated memory, and the 'unbidden emotions' they sometimes inspire, are revealed in a later scene in the novel, one which, as Aubert de Gaspé's lengthy footnote tell us, is grounded in the collective memory of his own family. Some years after the destruction of the D'Haberville estates at the hands of the British, a strange visitor suddenly appears at the doorstep of the now impoverished family. This visitor turns out to be a survivor of the historic shipwreck of the *Auguste*, which sank off the coast of Cape Breton Island in November 1761, and he recounts to the family the circumstances of its sailing and the horrible scene of its destruction. The military governor of Quebec, desiring vengeance on the defeated elite families of New France, had arranged for their hasty deportation to France by hiring the unseaworthy and incompetently captained *Auguste* for the purpose. The ship had foundered in a storm and broken apart, amid a remembered scene of abject terror and pandemonium, and all but seven of her passengers had been lost, including friends of the D'Habervilles and the survivor's own brother and two children. Described in the novel as a 'vrai spectre vivant', a living ghost so corpse-like it seemed as if its blood had been drained from its veins by a vampire, this uninvited intruder represents less an actual survivor of the wreck than a figure of the past reanimated (*Les Anciens Canadiens*, p. 279). Appearing before the family suddenly and unbidden, this spectral figure transmits its traumatic memory so that it will never be forgotten. The memory of death, exile and dispossession will be passed on to successive generations, as Aubert de Gaspé himself testifies; though his footnotes reveal that his retelling of the story of the wreck of the *Auguste* – which had taken place more than a hundred years before publication of his novel – had relied on published accounts, the story is nevertheless a personal one for him, as members of his own family had been intimately acquainted with one of the survivors of the wreck, Saint-Luc de La Corne. The scene described in the novel, Aubert de Gaspé writes, directly relates to one between Saint-Luc and the author's grandfather, as recounted fifty years before to the author by his paternal aunt, who was twelve when she overheard it. After hearing Saint-Luc's tale, Aubert de Gaspé recalls, she remembered the family spending the rest of the night weeping and lamenting the loss of their friends and relatives (*Les Anciens Canadiens*, p. 287).[89]

Trauma will attend the scene of remembrance again and again in the novel, as the memory of calamitous events from a different time and place take surrogate form in the present. Opening the chapter on the British burning of Quebec with an epigraph taken from the 'old Scottish song' that Davie Gellatley sings in Waverley, amid the ruins of Tully-Veolan after it is ransacked by British troops, Aubert de Gaspé looks back for a moment from the vantage point of his own time to describe the after-effects of the Conquest. All was not lost in France's terrible defeat, he writes, as the cession of New France to the British may have proved 'un bienfait' to French Canadians who were thus safeguarded from the horrors of the French Revolution some thirty years later (*Les Anciens Canadiens*, p. 218). The condition of Scotland sixty years since may indeed be analogous to the contemporary condition of Canada 114 years since, but the epigraph from Waverley, like the story of *la Corriveau* and the wreck of the *Auguste*, reminds Aubert de Gaspé's readers that they must never forget the heavy price paid by their progenitors and that trauma of the past will continue to intrude upon the prosperity of the living.

Remembering (and Forgetting) in the Aftermath

Surveying the grisly scene of battle's aftermath on the Plains of Abraham, Aubert de Gaspé writes that we must honour the slain on both sides. When the final trumpet sounds, he writes, the French and English buried pell-mell on the Plains of Abraham will rise again, but on Judgement Day, he asks, 'ces soldats auront-ils oublié leurs haines invétérées pendant ce long sommeil ou seront-ils prêts à s'entr'égorger de nouveau . . .?' (*Les Anciens Canadiens*, p. 264) ('Will these soldiers have forgotten their deep-rooted hatred during their long sleep, or will they be ready to slit each other's throats once more?' [*Canadians of Old*, p. 182]). The answer to this question remains unanswered in the novel, reminding us that the Atlantic world reverberates with the memory of death and dispossession; it is a world in which old enmities lie buried under shallow ground, waiting to rise again. In his fictionalised *aide de memoire*, Aubert de Gaspé demands his readers confront the scene of their dispossession and disenfranchisement, describing in some detail the destruction and violence of the Conquest both on the battlefield and among the civilian populace. In this way, *Les Anciens Canadiens* bears witness to the traumatic aftermath of defeat in ways that *Waverley* does not. Scott's narrative demurs from providing its readers with explicit scenes of blood and gore; he alludes to the post-Culloden campaign of brutal suppression throughout Scotland at the hands of the British army but provides no direct description. Edward Waverley is not an eyewitness to the battle and only hears of the defeat while riding back to Tully-Veolan from London. Only as he nears the Highlands do 'the traces of war become visible', and he encounters '[b]roken carriages, dead horses, unroofed cottages, woods felled for palisades, and bridges destroyed or only partially repaired'; the narrative of lives and homes destroyed is left unspoken and reduced to a quick summary that only serves to indicate the movements of unspecified 'hostile armies' (*Waverley*, p. 315). The Bradwardine estate lies in ruins, having suffered the full destructive force of the victorious British army, but its restoration will eventually be achieved, with English money. Scott also alludes to the 'barbaric penalty' paid by defeated Jacobites for their treason – Fergus MacIvor and other Jacobite leaders are hung, drawn and quartered, and their heads displayed on the city gates of Carlisle – but Scott does not narrate the actual scene of execution, and Waverley does not witness it.

Aubert de Gaspé's more aggressive demand that the present must carry the burden of the past is emphasised in his dramatic reworking of Scott's marriage plot. Perhaps predictably enough in a novel that pays explicit homage to its literary progenitor, Arché proposes marriage to the woman he loves, his French-Canadian foster-sister, Blanche D'Haberville. Arché's proposal seems to signal de Gaspe's adoption of Scott's troping of the eventual achievement of cultural and political union through the intermingling and infusion of new blood – enculturated into Scottish and Gaelic ways, the English Edward Waverley weds Rose Bradwardine, daughter of a dispossessed Lowland Scottish Jacobite, thus ensuring future generations of loyal 'British' subjects.[90] Arché's intended betrothed, however, will have none of this. Evoking the still-smoking ashes of the surrounding estates that Arché had helped to destroy, Blanche D'Haberville insists their union would represent the doubling of his betrayal, not its removal. For Blanche, to become Arché's wife would be to become twice conquered. Though her brother, who had already made his sacrifice to *la patrie* on the field of battle, will ultimately marry an English girl, both Blanche and Arché remain unmarried at novel's end. French Canada, embodied in the figure of the maiden who declares 'jamais . . . jamais', will not be reconciled to its conquest, and through her refusal, the shared memory of defeat shared by Scotland and French Canada is abruptly elided in the novel. Rather than the feminine embodiment of reconciliation that Rose Bradwardine becomes at the end of *Waverley*, Blanche D'Haberville is destined to be a transmitter of cultural memory herself – of a recalcitrant nation that accepts its fate but does not forget.[91]

But if *Waverley* emphasises ultimate reconciliation and political settlement though matrimonial union, and refuses to narrate the most horrible aspects of the after-effects of insurrection, the novel does not suggest that we should forget what happened. Instead, the call to remember the social disintegration of the past draws attention to the uncertainties of the present – perhaps reconciliation was not secured; perhaps the Union remains an open sore. In this way, the memorialising impulse of *Waverley* reflects what Alan Megill has described as the common feature of the 'memory wave' of our contemporary culture. Underpinning it, he writes,

> seems to be an insecurity about identity. In a world in which so many opposing certainties come in conflict with each other and in which a multitude of possible identities are put on display, insecurity . . . may be an inevitable byproduct. Such a situation provides ample reason for 'memory' to come to the fore . . . [W]hen identity becomes uncertain, memory rises in value.[92]

The call to remember becomes most acute in times of perceived disruption and crisis. Rising from such moments of uncertainty, cultural memory does not simply transmit national identity; it helps to create it in the first place.

The political and social conditions that would inspire this mnemonic enunciation of national identity are not difficult to locate in the periphery cultures of post-Union, post-Jacobite Edinburgh and of post-Union (of 1840) – but pre-Confederation – Canada. Even in the early American republic, however, the establishment of a public memory dedicated to commemorating the nation's struggle and final achievement of independence from Great Britain was in part inspired by a feeling that internal divisions and fractures that had troubled the colonies long before the Revolution were on the verge of exploding into open conflict. Rufus Choate's famous plea in 1833 – for an American Scott to do for the nation's 'heroic age' leading up to the Revolution what the Wizard of the North had done for the history of his own country – was explicitly framed as no less than a programme to save the Union through literature. A native body of work adopting Scott's model, Choate exclaimed, would be so potent that it 'might do *something* to perpetuate the Union itself', for it would be

> a common property of all the States, – a treasure of common ancestral recollections, – more noble and richer than our thousand million acres of public land; and, unlike that land, it would be indivisible. It would be as the opening of a great fountain for the healing of the nations. It would turn back our thoughts from these recent and overrated diversities of interest, – these controversies about negro-cloth, coarse-woolled sheep, and cotton bagging, – to the day when our fathers walked hand in hand together through the valley of the Shadow of Death in the War of Independence. Reminded of our fathers, we should remember that we are brethren.[93]

In Scotland, America and Canada, the eruption of memory, concomitant with the rise and immense popularity of historical fiction in the early nineteenth century, is a singular feature of a transatlantic crisis of identity in an age of revolution and fragmentation, consolidation and union. In the aftermath moment, what Megill says of our contemporary preoccupation with memory is also true for the aftermath moment, so insistently shaped by Scott's example: '[i]t is easy to imagine that we ought to *remember* the past. But we do not remember the past. It is the present we remember: that is we "remember" what remains living within in our situations *now*'.[94]

We must always remember, *Waverley* announces, but what readers do with remembrance, how they use it to shape their actions and identities, cannot be vouchsafed in Scott's inaugural Waverley Novel, and this uncertainty is transmitted to the vast body of transatlantic writing that Scott's work inspired. Memory of the past, even of the proximate past, ultimately remains an enigmatic cipher whose connection to the present must always be changing and transforming, as we 'remember' only what seems to serve us in making sense of our 'here and now'.

Notes

1. Scott, *Waverley*, p. 363. Subsequent references to this work are given in abbreviated form in the body of the text, or as a page number alone where unambiguous. All references are to the Edinburgh Edition of the Waverley Novels, except when otherwise noted.
2. On Scott and modernity, see Lincoln, *Walter Scott and Modernity*; McCracken-Flesher, *Possible Scotlands*; Duncan, *Scott's Shadow*, especially pp. 96–115; and Chandler, *England in 1819*.
3. For a discussion of Scott's significance to the American literary market, see Todd, 'Establishing Routes for Fiction in the United States'.
4. In its sophistication, geographical range and sheer volume of publications produced, the literary marketplace in the United States dwarfed its counterpart in Canada. Fiona A. Black reports that Scottish publishers, for one, tended to ignore the Canadian market. See 'Bookseller to the World: North America'. For a study of connections between Scottish and Canadian literary traditions, see Waterston, *Rapt in Plaid*.
5. For Scott's influence in the literary and cultural history of French Canada, see Cabajsky, 'The National Tale from Ireland to French Canada'; Hayne, 'The Historical Novel and French Canada'; and Lemire, *Les Grands Thèmes nationalistes*, pp. 241–5.
6. Seminal accounts of Scott and the historical novel, beginning with Lukács, *The Historical Novel* in the 1930s, situate Scott's work in the context of European literary historiographies. The body of scholarship that examines at Scott's work in the context of Scottish or British literature is immense, but for some important recent studies, see Duncan, *Scott's Shadow*; Ina Ferris, *The Achievement of Literary Authority*; Yoon Sun Lee, *Nationalism and Irony*; Lincoln, *Walter Scott and Modernity*; McCracken-Flesher, *Possible Scotlands*; Maxwell, *The Historical Novel in Europe*; Pittock, *The Reception of Sir Walter Scott in Europe*; and Robertson, *Legitimate Histories* and *The Edinburgh Companion to Sir Walter Scott*. For recent studies of Scott's contribution to American literary and cultural historiography, see Robertson, 'Walter Scott and the American Historical Novel'; Dekker, *The American Historical Romance*; Hook, *Scotland and America*, pp. 145–67, *From Goosecreek to Gandercleugh*, pp. 94–115, and 'Scotland, the USA, and National Literatures in the Nineteenth Century'; Manning, 'Did Mark Twain Bring Down the Temple on Scott's Shoulders?'; and Orians, 'The Romance Ferment after

Waverley'. For Scott's profound significance in shaping the book trade in early nineteenth-century America, see Todd, 'Establishing Routes for Fiction'; and Rezek, *London and the Making of Provincial Literature*, especially pp. 40–62.
7. For 'traveling genres', see Cohen's so-titled study. For a study that makes reference to a wide range of texts emanating from four different cultural sites in North America spanning over a hundred years, see Kröller, 'Walter Scott in America, English Canada, and Quebec'.
8. Rigney, *Afterlives*, p. 7. For Scott's contribution to collective memory, see also Rigney, *Imperfect Histories*; Jones, *Literary Memory*; and Barash, *Collective Memory and the Historical Past*, pp. 182–92.
9. See Manning's seminal work on Scottish-American cultural cross-connections, *Fragments of Union*. See also Robertson, 'Historical Fiction and the Fractured Atlantic'.
10. Scott, *The Antiquary*, p. 10.
11. For a discussion of temporal distance and the Waverley Novels, see Barash, *Collective Memory and the Historical Past*.
12. Scott, *Ivanhoe*, p. xxiii. Subsequent references to this work are given in abbreviated form in the body of the text, or as a page number alone where unambiguous. Chandler sees *Ivanhoe*'s Dedicatory Epistle as paradigmatic of the Waverley Novels' 'revivification' of the past (*England in 1819*, pp. 166–70).
13. After *Ivanhoe*, Scott returns to Scottish history for the subject of his next work, but not to the recent past. *The Monastery*, set imprecisely sometime in the mid-sixteenth century, is tellingly also labeled a 'Romance'.
14. By the end of the 1820s Scott himself would establish a tradition on the origins of his historical novel, dating its early genesis to 1805, but this tradition is itself most probably a fiction. Garside has made a convincing case, based on external and manuscript evidence, that drafting of the novel more likely began a few years later, no earlier than 1808. See *Waverley*, especially pp. 367–83; and Garside, 'Popular Fiction and National Tale'.
15. Quoted in Erll, 'Generation in Literary History', p. 386. Erll traces the roots of 'generationality' in popular discourse today to the end of the First World War and the emergence of the 'war' generation. See 'Generation in Literary History'.
16. Jones, *Literary Memory*, p. 23.
17. In the Preface to his *Observations on the Present State of the Highlands*, Selkirk writes: 'It must not be forgotten, that little more than half a century has passed, since that part of the kingdom [the Highlands] was in a state similar to that of England before the Norman conquest. When we look back to the condition of the Highlands before the year 1745, the differences which still exist between that and the

other parts of the kingdom are easily accounted for. There is much more reason to be surprised at the progress that has been made by the inhabitants in these sixty years, than that they should not have accomplished to its full extent the change, which in other parts has been the work of many centuries' (10). For a full discussion of Selkirk's views on historical change and the future viability of the Highland way of life in the British Empire, see Chapter 3.
18. Ferris, 'Melancholy, Memory', p. 78.
19. Ibid. p. 84.
20. Assmann, 'Collective Memory and Cultural Identity'. Subsequent references to this work are given in abbreviated form in the body of the text, or as a page number alone where unambiguous. On Halbwachs and the social frameworks of memory, see *On Collective Memory*, which, though it provides only excerpts of the first four chapters of the original, represents the most complete English translation of Halbwach's *Les Cadres sociaux de la memoire*. See also Halbwach's *The Collective Memory* and *The Psychology of Social Class*.
21. Halbwachs, *The Collective Memory*, p. 82.
22. In Terdiman, *Present Past*.
23. Duncan, *Scott's Shadow*, p. 137.
24. Nora, *Realms of Memory*, p. 128. In *Realms of Memory*, Nora expands on the concept of *lieux de mémoire* to include not just sites, but 'any significant entity, whether material or non-material in nature, which by dint of human will or the work of time has become a symbolic element of the memorial heritage of any community . . .' (1:xvii). For a discussion of the way in which various resonances of 'Walter Scott' became symbolic elements in the memorial heritage of multiple communities, see Rigney, *Afterlives*, especially pp. 1–16.
25. Duncan, *Scott's Shadow*, p. 46.
26. Cockburn, *Memorials of his Time*, p. iii. Subsequent references to this work are given in abbreviated form in the body of the text, or as a page number alone where unambiguous.
27. Cockburn, *Journal*, vol. 2, p. 198.
28. Chambers, *Traditions of Edinburgh*, vol. 1, pp. 1–2. Subsequent references to this work are given in abbreviated form in the body of the text, or as a volume and page number alone where unambiguous.
29. Chambers would extend his memorialising project in his supplement to *Traditions: Minor Antiquities of Edinburgh*, or 'Reekiana', as he termed it on the half title and as the work came to be known. In his Preface, Chambers acknowledges his debt to Scott, who had 'good-humouredly surrendered to me' the title, having already abandoned the idea of penning a similar work himself (vii).

30. Phillips, *Society and Sentiment*, p. 297.
31. Ibid. p. 310.
32. Ibid. p. 28.
33. Cockburn, *Some Letters*, p. 9.
34. For a detailed account of Scott's sources, see *Waverley*, pp. 503–9.
35. See Scott, *The Black Dwarf*, pp. 125–35. Subsequent references to this work are given in abbreviated form in the body of the text, or as a page number alone where unambiguous.
36. For an analysis of the 'tale' in British Romantic fiction of the 1810s and 1820s, see Killick, *British Short Fiction in the Early Nineteenth Century*; and Jarrells, 'Short Fictional Forms and the Rise of the Tale'. Scott, who more than anyone else established the association of the tale as a narrative of the historical past, would return to the 'tales' scheme near the end of his career; but his last series of tales would deviate from the previous three: 'Tales of the Crusaders', published in 1825, comprised *The Betrothed* and *The Talisman*, and both would be set in medieval times.
37. Dekker, *The American Historical Romance*, p. 34. Kröller, 'Walter Scott in America, English Canada, and Quebec', and Kammen, *A Season of Youth*, follow Dekker in seeing 1821 and publication of Cooper's *The Spy* as the moment that marks the beginning of Scott's great influence in America. See Todd, 'Establishing Routes for Fiction', however, which provides a more precise charting of Scott's influence in America, which began with *Waverley*'s publication by Van Winkle and Wiley in January 1815.
38. Irving, *Sketch-Book*, 1978, pp. 4–6. All subsequent references to this work are to the 1978 Twayne edition unless otherwise stated and are given in abbreviated form in the body of the text, or as a page number alone where unambiguous. For problems regarding the Twayne edition of the *Sketch-Book* – a compilation never seen by Irving and never read by a contemporary reader – as definitive, see Manning, 'Note on the Text'. Manning's 1996 edition is based on the 1848 'Author's Revised Edition', the last edition for which Irving himself made revisions. In keeping with my use of the Edinburgh Edition of the Waverley Novels, which adopts the first edition as the most definitive, I have chosen to reference the earliest edition of Irving's work, when this is indicated in the list of emendations in the Twayne edition.
39. Irving, *Sketch-Book*, 1996, p. 7.
40. For studies that see the literary culture of the early republic as postcolonial, see Buell, 'American Literary Emergence as a Postcolonial Phenomenon'; Watts, 'Settler Postcolonialism as a Reading Strategy'; Göbel, 'Washington Irving's "Rip Van Winkle"'; and Yokata, *Unbecoming*

British. For studies that problematise the identification of Irving as a postcolonial writer, see Murray, 'Aesthetic Dispossession'; and Mackenthun, 'America's Troubled Postcoloniality'. For a discussion linking Irving's professional malaise with the identity crisis of the early republic, see Rubin-Dorsky, *Adrift in the Old World*.

41. For an account of the reciprocity of this relationship, see Sutherland, 'Walter Scott and Washington Irving'.
42. Scott received a copy of the work from Irving's close friend Henry Brevoort, who had visited Edinburgh in March and April 1813. Scott would later write to Brevoort praising the work. Comparing it favourably to Swift, Scott wrote, 'accept my best thanks for the uncommon degree of entertainment which I have received from the most excellently jocose history of New York' (*Letters of Sir Walter Scott*, vol. 3, p. 259).
43. Irving, *A History of New York*, p. 5. Subsequent references to this work are given in abbreviated form in the body of the text, or as a page number alone where unambiguous.
44. For an analysis of Irving's use of the burlesque in the *Sketch-Book*, see Giles, *Transatlantic Insurrections*, pp. 142–63.
45. For a discussion of the uses of enchantment and Rip Van Winkle's disruption of linear progressive temporality, see Sizemore, '"Changing by Enchantment"'.
46. See, for example, Rubin-Dorsky, *Adrift in the Old World*; Fliegelman, *Prodigals and Pilgrims*; Horwitz, '"Rip Van Winkle" and Legendary National Memory'; Blakemore, 'Family Resemblances'; and Wyman, 'Washington Irving's *Rip Van Winkle*'.
47. Blakemore, 'Family Resemblances', p. 191.
48. Irving makes this argument more emphatically in 'English Writers on America', the essay that immediately follows 'Rip Van Winkle' and which is explicitly addressed to British readers.
49. Jones, *Literary Memory*, p. 161. For Irving's use of German folklore material, see Pochmann, 'Irving's German Sources in *The Sketch Book*'; Reichart, 'Concerning the Source of Irving's "Rip Van Winkle"'; and Kuczynski, 'Intertextuality in Rip Van Winkle'. For a discussion of Scott's role in reintroducing Irving to German literature and Irving's use of the ballad of Thomas the Rhymer, which he heard from Scott, see Pochmann, 'Irving's German Sources in *The Sketch Book*'.
50. In the 1848 'Author's Revised Edition' of the *Sketch-Book*, Irving extends the depth of this sedimentation of memory into the epoch of pre-European settlement. He does this by adding a 'postscript' to the tale in the form of 'travelling notes from a memorandum book' of his editor-compiler. In it, Knickerbocker reports on 'Indian traditions',

which spoke of a 'kind of Manitou or Spirit, who kept about the wildest recesses of the Catskill mountains, and took a mischievous pleasure in wreaking all kinds of evils and vexations upon the red men' (*Sketch-Book*, 1978, p. 42). For a study of Irving's 1848 Postscript as an example of the 'spectral' Indian in American literature, see Bergland, *The National Uncanny*.
51. Sedgwick, *The Linwoods*, p. 5.
52. Kammen reports that 'more than 100 novels set in the Revolutionary period had appeared by 1850, and still more continued to be published during the next decade' (*A Season of Youth*, p. 154).
53. Neal, *Wandering Recollections*, p. 239.
54. Ibid. p. 224.
55. Quoted in Hay, 'The American Revolution Twice Recalled', pp. 58–9.
56. Quoted in Ibid. p. 61.
57. For the American memory crisis one generation after the Revolution, see Kammen, *A Season of Youth* and *The Mystic Chords of Memory*, especially pp. 41–90.
58. Quoted in Hay, 'The American Revolution Twice Recalled', p. 59.
59. For an overview of Culloden and the Jacobite defeat in British memory, see Pittock, *Culloden (Cùil Lodair)*, especially pp. 137–58.
60. For a study of the 1820s commemorative wave, particularly as it was associated with the return of Lafayette in 1824 to commemorate the forty-third anniversary of the surrender of Cornwallis, see Purcell, *Sealed with Blood*, pp. 171–209.
61. For example, Bloodgood's *The Sexagenary* claims to be an authentic eyewitness account of several Revolutionary campaigns, drawn from the recollections of a sixty-six-year-old New York native. The authenticity of the work, however, became an instant subject of debate. For many years after its publication it was assumed to be a work of fiction. In 1901 John Henry Brandow published an account of the region providing archival proof that the sexagenery must have been an actual person; Becker, *The Story of Old Saratoga and History of Schuylerville*, pp. 180–7.
62. Oadley, *Seventy-Six*, vol. 1, p. 2; ellipses in the original. Subsequent references to this work are given in abbreviated form in the body of the text, or by volume and page number alone where unambiguous.
63. The editors of the 1875 *Cyclopedia of American Literature* wrote that any merit in Neal's novels 'are well-nigh overbalanced by their extravagance and the jerking out-of-breath style in which they are often written' (874). Lillie D. Loshe provided what proved to be a lasting summary of Neal's achievement as a novelist when in 1907 she wrote, 'His fatal defect was a total lack of any idea when to stop. One always

has a vision of him gaily writing away until the ink bottle runs dry, and then scrawling in pencil a few deaths and an insanity or two in order to end the matter' (quoted in Bain, 'Introduction', pp. xix). Later critics, however, would begin to recognise Neal as an important experimenter in narrative forms. For the most recent reassessment of Neal's work, see Watts and Carlson, *John Neal and Nineteenth-Century American Literature and Culture*.

64. Insko, 'Eyewitness to History', p. 64.
65. Aubert de Gaspé, *Les Anciens Canadiens*, p. 27. The 1994 Fides edition is based on the second edition of 1864. Subsequent references to this work are given in abbreviated form in the body of the text.
66. Aubert de Gaspé, *Canadians of Old*, p. 20. Subsequent references to this work are given in abbreviated form in the body of the text.
67. Aubert de Gaspé's nineteenth-century biographer, the historian Henri-Raymond Casgrain, reports that Aubert de Gaspé himself translated almost all of Scott's novels into French and spent many an evening reading them aloud to his family (*Philippe Aubert De Gaspé*, p. 17). Later critics would cast doubt on the story.
68. LeMoine, *Maple Leaves*, p. 64.
69. Boym, *The Future of Nostalgia*, p. 41.
70. For the critical reception of *Les anciens Canadiens*, see Hayne, 'The Historical Novel and French Canada'; Lemire, 'Introduction' and '*Les Anciens Canadiens*'; and Bierly, 'Introduction'. For a bibliography (up to 1980), see Lemire, '*Les Anciens Canadiens*'. See also Deschamps, 'Les "Anciens Canadiens" de 1860'; Paterson, 'Archibald ou Arché? L'alterité dans "Les Anciens Canadiens"'; and Cabajsky, 'The National Tale from Ireland to French Canada'.
71. *Lord Durham's Report*, vol. 2, p. 294.
72. Ibid. vol. 3, p. 289.
73. Lamonde describes the difficulty in launching this counter-assault in the incipient publishing world of francophone Canada in the early nineteenth century. From 1840 to 1850 only five novels were published, and all but one appeared serially at the bottom of the front page of newspapers. With the appearance of James Huston's pointedly nationalistic miscellany *Le Répertoire national*, the publishing world became more open to the novel, and four works appeared between 1850 and 1860, six between 1860 and 1870, and fifteen in the following decade (*The Social History of Ideas in Quebec*, pp. 345–72).
74. Garneau, *Histoire du Canada*, vol. 3, p. 543. Translations from the French are my own (except with regard to *Les Anciens Canadiens*, as noted above), with the invaluable linguistic and scholarly advice of Andrea Cabajsky. Garneau's work was translated into English by

Andrew Bell under the title *History of Canada from the Time of its Discovery till the Union year of 1840–41, translated from 'L'Histoire du Canada' of F.X. Garneau*. Bell, however, admits to having 'reshaped' the work to meet expectations of Anglo-Canadian readers, which required 'retrenchments' of what he saw as Garneau's 'exuberances' (xvii). This resulted in editorial interventions that are intrusive, heavy-handed and politically patronizing.
75. Ibid.
76. Huston's *Le Répertoire national; ou, Recueil de littérature canadienne* comprised two 384-page volumes delivered to subscribers in thirty-two-page installments about every two weeks. The installments began to reach readers on 26 February 1848, appearing with some regularity until the end of the year. *Les Soirées canadiennes* was founded by Casgrain, journalist and lawyer Antoine Gérin-Lajoie, doctor and writer François-Alexandre-Hubert La Rue, and parliamentarian Joseph-Charles Taché. It ran to five volumes from 1861 to 1866. *Les Soirées canadiennes*, along with its rival *Le Foyer canadien* (1863–6) spurred the productivity of francophone writers by making their work more widely accessible. James Macpherson LeMoine, whose mother descended from Scottish United Empire Loyalists, was a bicultural and bilingual writer.
77. *Les Soirées canadiennes*, pp. i–ii.
78. For an astute critique of the politics of mid-century French-Canadian cultural nationalism, see Lemire, 'James Huston'.
79. Randall, 'Resistance, Submission and Oppostionality', p. 22.
80. See Lamonde, *The Social History of Ideas in Quebec*, pp. 368–9.
81. Ducharme in 'Interpreting the Past, Shaping the Present, and Envisioning the Future' provides evidence that the Conquest was not discussed seriously in the colony until the 1840s. Only with publication of *Histoire du Canada* and Garneau's desire to create a 'national public memory' did the Conquest gain common currency in French-Canadian historiography. For a discussion of the Conquest's increasing significance in francophone historical fiction mid-century, see Lemire, *Les Grands Thèmes nationalistes*.
82. Quoted in Lamonde, *The Social History of Ideas in Quebec*, p. 34.
83. Such arguments were more prominent in the early decades of the century, before the Act of Union. See Lamonde, *The Social History of Ideas in Quebec*, pp. 35–40.
84. This incident provides evidence that Arché may have been modelled on Colonel Malcolm Fraser of the 78th Highlanders. Born in Abernethy in 1733, Fraser described in his memoirs the barbarity of his commanding officer at the time, Captain Montgomery. Quoting from Fraser's memoirs in the footnotes to *Les Anciens Canadiens*, Aubert de Gaspé writes that

Montgomery had ordered that all French prisoners be killed 'in a most inhuman and cruel manner'. After the Conquest, Fraser settled in Canada and became a family friend of the Aubert de Gaspé's, who would defend his wartime actions in conversation with Aubert de Gaspé's grandfather (413, 329).
85. See Caruth, *Unclaimed Experience*; and Leys, *Trauma: A Genealogy*.
86. See Roach, *Cities of the Dead*.
87. Ibid. pp. 2–3.
88. For a recent analysis of the *La Corriveau* story, see Ferland and Corriveau, *La Corriveau: de l'histoire à la legend*.
89. Aubert de Gaspé writes of discovering a copy of de La Corne's own published account of the shipwreck, *Journal du voyage de M. Saint-Luc de La Corne*, which helped him to correct 'errors' in the story, as it was told to him in his youth. De La Corne's daughter was the wife of Aubert de Gaspé's uncle.
90. For a discussion of consanguinity as trope of political and cultural union in British anglophone writing, see Corbett, *Allegories of Union in Irish and English Writing*.
91. The noble but impoverished heroine who refuses the hand of her country's vanquisher, thereby demonstrating her devotion to her country, became a common trope in francophone historical novels that followed. For a discussion of this trope (though it elides Arché's Scottishness entirely, labelling him 'English'), see McNamara, 'Fact or Fiction'.
92. Megill, *Historical Knowledge, Historical Error*, p. 43.
93. Choate, *Addresses and Orations*, pp. 36–7.
94. Megill, *Historical Knowledge, Historical Error*, p. 54.

Chapter 2

Memory on the Margins: Anne Grant's Atlantic World

Tales of Other Times

In 1896 the Scottish History Society published a series of letters written in early 1808 by Anne Grant. Grant was duly praised by the editor as 'an authority of some importance on Highland affairs', having published a long poem entitled 'The Highlanders'; a collection of her correspondence while living in the Highlands, *Letters from the Mountains*; and the two-volume *Essays on the Superstitions of the Highlands of Scotland*. In the 1808 letters, written in reply to Grant's friend the antiquarian Henry Steaurt of Allanton, who was preparing a history of the Jacobite cause and who had asked Grant for any material, she furnished a rich trove of anecdote. In her lengthy responses, Grant provided accounts from the Forty-Five – particularly on two of the most famous Jacobite figures of the period – that she herself had remembered being told to her by members of her family and her neighbours in the Highlands, in her younger days: 'I promis'd to send you some anecdotes of Lovat and Lochiel,' she writes. 'This, if my memory does not fail me, is much in my power to do, having liv'd in great intimacy with persons to whom these extraordinary and very opposite characters were very well known'.[1] Many of Grant's sources were not themselves directly involved in the events she would recount to Steaurt, but were of a younger generation and, like Grant herself, were relating the stories they had heard second-hand. 'My authorities for the facts I have given and mean to give you, are very good ones,' Grant writes:

> I knew well two granddaughters of Lochiel's, sisters of the late Clunie, who were our next neighbours at Laggan. I was very intimate, too, with Miss Margaret, daughter to the unfortunate Dr. Cameron, Lochiel's brother. My mother, too, remembers much of the Lochiels, whose memory she adores. ('Letters Concerning Highland Affairs', p. 279)

Her source, however, for perhaps the most dramatic scene in her account – which took place in the house of Lovat's steward Gortulig (or Gorthleck), where Lovat was staying at a critical moment in the rebellion's history – was a direct eyewitness to the events described. 'I have heard' this woman, Grant writes, 'who is still living, describe with great naiveté a scene to which she was witness the day on which Culloden was fought.' This source is Gortulig's own daughter, 'then a girl of ten years old' who, being deemed an encumbrance on the fateful day, was locked away in a closet:

> All of a sudden the tumultuous noise that fill'd the house was succeeded by deep silence. The little prisoner, alarm'd at this sudden stillness, ventur'd out and saw no creature in the house, but Lovat sitting alone in deep thought. Then she ventur'd to the door, and looking down saw about a thousand people in one ghastly crowd in the plain below. Struck with the sudden shifting of the scene and the appearance of this multitude, she thought it was a visionary show of fairies which would immediately disappear. She was soon, however, undeceiv'd by the mournful cries of women who were tearing off their handkerchiefs for bandages to the wounded. In an instant quantities of linen were carried down for the same purpose, and the intended feast was distributed in morsels among the fugitives, who were instantly forc'd to disperse for safety to the caves and mountains of that rugged district. (264–5)

Grant's scene of noisy tumult followed by absolute silence and the solitary figure of Lovat reduced to complete inaction, and the eerie scene of the wounded on the plain that immediately follows, paints perhaps no less a powerful picture of the battle's aftermath than those of Scott's fictional account. Like *Waverley*, and the writing of Cockburn and Chambers, Grant's remembrances of the collective experiences of Jacobite Scotland's twilight generation give life to the aftermath's proximate past, taking the form not of history per se, but of cultural memory. Like the narrator of *Waverley*'s Postscript, Grant is called upon, as part of a 'middle' generation – she was fifty-three – to preserve 'tales of other times' told to her in her younger days. Her account therefore was prized as a historical account because it seems to provide an aspect that conventional document-based histories of the battle could not: the mood of the Jacobite defeat, as captured in the naive account of a ten-year-old girl, 'embodying', in editor J. R. N. Macphail's words, 'what had already become tradition – but tradition of a very rich and special kind' (252).

Throughout her letters to Steaurt, Grant makes clear that she is relying on memory alone for her details, and she makes frequent apologies for the rambling incoherence and disjointedness of her narrative. She also provides frequent signals that the narrative she provides represents an act or remembrance – 'I think', 'I recollect' or 'I can't remember' – acknowledging the inherent unreliability of memory, as she tries to recall and put down on paper the first- and second-hand remembrances of others, told to her in the past. The avowed lack of clarity and faultiness of Grant's memories provide room for Macphail to establish his own historian bona fides in the form of intrusive annotation that is dismissive of many of her details. In footnote commentaries such as 'an obvious mistake', 'wholly inaccurate' and 'this is nonsense', Macphail asserts the authority of more formal and rigorous historical practice over Grant's hazy memory-text. Grant's letters thus reveal both the limits and power of remembrance in shaping the nation's historical consciousness. In publishing Grant's vague recollections of a previous generation's store of memories, such as the scene at Gortulig – told to Grant long ago by a woman who herself was recalling events that had occurred at least thirty years before and when she was only at ten – Grant's editor is careful to dismiss the notion that her letters are 'authoritative statements of historical facts'. At the same time, he recognises its significance in relating something not otherwise accessible in formal chronological narratives of historical events, as Grant's herself recognised in emphasising the naive quality of the daughter's story: the way people of the time actually thought and felt.

As she warms to her topic, Grant can be seen in her letters to Steaurt to be fleshing out subject matter and ideas that would eventually form the basis of her thinking in her *Essays*, published a few years later, in 1811. Yet she also makes passing reference in the letters to a more immediate work-in-progress, which would come to preoccupy her in the latter half of 1808 – *Memoirs of an American Lady*, published in the same year. In this work, Grant draws upon her earliest memories to recapture everyday life in the old Dutch colony in Albany and along the Hudson River in the years before the Revolution, a world which was, by 1808, already receding beyond the horizon of lived memory. Presented in the form of a glowing tribute to the prominent figure who had taken the young Grant into her home more than forty years before – Margaretta (or Margarita) Schuyler, the 'American Lady' of her title – the *Memoirs*, like the Jacobite letters, would be prized as a rich trove of memories that opened a window to a vanished way of life in the nation's not-too-distant past.[2] Also like the letters, Grant's narratives of the past in the *Memoirs* are grounded in the features of localised remembrance – in the lived experiences that Grant herself recalls or that were told to her by family and friends. And as her memories of the Highlands were rediscovered and taken up by later historians and writers in Scotland, so were her memories of old New York rediscovered and taken up by historians and critics in America, who, like their Scottish counterparts, paid due respect to her achievement, while carefully pointing out her many errors of historical fact.

Upon publication of her first work in 1803, *Poems on Various Subjects*, which included 'The Highlanders', Anne Grant had gone from complete obscurity to a fair measure of literary fame. A woman, who, as Pam Perkins neatly summarises, had 'spent most of her adult life in the tiny Highland village of Laggan and had no direct experience of the literary markets of Edinburgh, let alone London', Grant went on to have 'one of the most successful literary careers, both critically and financially, among Scottish women of her generation'.[3] Scott acknowledged her reputation as an authority on Scottish Gaeldom, mentioning her as one of the three Scottish writers 'highly creditable to their country', who were noteworthy predecessors to his own effort to sketch the 'general habits of the period'.[4] By the twentieth century, however, Grant's reputation had long waned and her work had fallen from both popular and critical view. This is regrettable, as Grant's work represents a significant contribution to Scottish Romantic historiography, in both its national and imperial orientations. Writing in a variety of genres both formal and informal, Grant provided richly detailed observations and recollections of a life lived in large part on the margins of the British Atlantic. Her deployment of the comparative methodology of Scottish conjectural historicism to undertake a cross-cultural examination of communities 'in the infancy of society' makes Grant's modest but influential body of work an important contribution to Scottish discourse on modernisation and peripheralisation, and the social and historical contingencies that give shape to these processes.

In recent years, the significance of Grant's writing has received greater critical recognition, but recent studies of her work tend to confine it either to a British/Scottish or American context, replicating the bifurcation of her output into separate national spheres that was established later in the nineteenth century.[5] Bringing together Grant's writing on proximate pasts of the eighteenth-century Highlands and colonial America, however, draws attention to the singular perspective of a writer who lived much of her life on the peripheries of the British Atlantic world, and who drew upon her transatlantic memory of these experiences throughout her writing career. Grant's transatlantic, or more precisely, transperipheral observations – as a young girl accompanying her father, an officer in the 55th Regiment of Foot, to the New York colony during the Seven Years War, and as parish minister's wife in the Highlands in the last decades of the century – offer a more comprehensive picture of disparate localities in the Atlantic world as they become both subject to, and separated from, an imperial British nation-state. In her sympathetic drawing of small rural communities, whether in the Highlands of her married life or the colonial New York of her childhood, Grant conjures a primitive world of rustic simplicity and isolation which fosters deep-felt bonds of affection and loyalty and which represents a stark alternative to the self-interestedness and dissipation that Grant found in more refined society. In posing such a view, Grant's writing represents a recognisable strand of thought in Romantic-era historiography, which traces the universal mechanisms of modernisation through a cross-cultural analysis of disparate locales coming under the forces of imperial expansion and consolidation.[6] At the same time, however, Grant's movements through the British Atlantic world make her alert to the ways in which the processes of historical change work differently and to different ends in different locales.

In the *Memoirs* Grant would provide her richest account of this British Atlantic world, a world comprised of multiple communities on various trajectories of social development brought in contact by the trade in furs, which had cemented relations between colonists and native peoples for several generations; by the West Indian trade, which supplied both goods and slaves; and by a rapid increase in settlement, which brought dramatic and long-lasting social and economic changes. The interactions between these communities take place against the historical backdrop of the long struggle between the British and French for dominance in North America, which reached its culmination in the years that Grant was there, and of the rise of an independent American settler nation, which would soon become a powerful rival to British interests on the continent.[7] The clash of empires, and their expansion and collapse, produces a shifting landscape of national and imperial boundaries, political alliances, and personal loyalties and affinities, as warfare upends the lives of the region's inhabitants. Rather than describing a world in which static and immobile 'primitive' peoples succumb to the forces of modernisation as these relentlessly intrude into their isolated retreats, Grant's *Memoirs* instead paints a more complex picture of the British Atlantic peripheries, in which various groups, as they come into contact with each other, are confronted with disintegration or assimilation but also adapt or accommodate, as they all vie for power in a changing political and social landscape.

The shifting terrain that Grant traces in her writing poses an important question for the cultural memory-text she offers to readers on either side of the Atlantic. Her hazy, incomplete and often fragmented recounting of events she had experienced or that were told to her by her family and by members of the tight-knit community, whether in the Highlands or in New York, fully announces itself as an act of cultural memory, anticipating the memorialist writing of Scott, Cockburn, Chambers and others that would come after. Grant's descriptions of both Highlands and colonial America were valued by readers and historians alike because they seemed to offer a window into the everyday life of the past. Grant, however, offers what amounts to two different sets of cultural memory, as they were taken up by two different sets of readers on opposite shores of the Atlantic. If Grant provides a compelling account of the proximate past of her British Atlantic world, to which community, then, does Grant's store of transperipheral memories belong? Grant's pronouncements of her allegiances suggest a consolidated Scottish/British national identity, as she expresses both a sentimental Scottishness and passionate loyalty to the British Crown. Yet the *Memoirs* reveals a more shifting and contingent understanding of communal belonging, as its author recounts a transitory childhood lived, more or less, on the move.

Modes and Manners: Women Writers and Scottish Post-Enlightenment Historiography

Though in later life Grant became a fixture in fashionable social and literary circles in Edinburgh – her renowned conversational skills established her as a prominent 'Bluestocking' in the city – Grant expressed herself never fully at ease in the cosmopolitan world of the Edinburgh literati, and her work reflects this lifelong ambivalence.[8] On the one hand, she declared that her lack of formal education and early life in remote outposts had made her 'half savage' and irredeemably 'unfit for what the world calls elegant society'.[9] On the other hand she took pride in the rustic, untutored quality of her writing, which had made her a paragon of simple everyday probity and clear sightedness for her many devoted readers, and she traded on her amateur status to build a professional writing career, making public what were originally private expressions intended only, she would claim, for family and friends.[10] The idea that the strengths of her writing lay in its unrefined simplicity of style was confirmed by the prominent men of Edinburgh literary society from whom Grant sought guidance and advice. When Grant, for example, set out to present her considerable knowledge on Highland folk belief in the format of a formal treatise, her long-time supporter and editor George Thomson, the noted collector and publisher of traditional Scottish music, was atypically cool, politely insisting, after reading the proofs of her *Essays*, that Grant was quite out of her depth:

> [I]n Essays of great length, the Public expect a more methodical arrangement, and clearer connection than is suited to your poetical genius and irregular habits of writing. – you occupy the first rank of letter writers: had your American Lady [the *Memoirs*] and the present book been altogether epistolary, be assured that the character of each would have stood far higher; and if the error of the proofs should induce you to reprint the Essays, I venture to submit it to your serious consideration, whether it would not be for the advantage of the Work, and greatly conducive to you reputation, if you were to yet mould the Essays into Letters, . . . addressing them to some of your distinguished English friends . . .[11]

For Thomson, Grant was clearly overstepping the generic boundaries that had made her so successful in the first place, as the weak quality of the *Memoirs* had already indicated. Her undisciplined imaginative powers and great simplicity of style were better suited to the informality of the more recognisably 'feminine' genre of epistolary writing. Yet, as Ina Ferris neatly summarises, Grant in the *Essays* was working already in what was, by the second decade of the century, an accepted and 'well-established matrix of proto-ethnographic eighteenth-century genres of travel-writing, translation, and Scottish historiography'.[12] In the short trajectory of her writing career we can add poetry, diaristic letters, memoir and biography to the matrix that Ferris identifies, but in all of her writing Grant set out to provide experience-based observation and speculation as part of a sustained enquiry into the nature of human social progress, the underpinnings and rationale of which were indebted to late Enlightenment theories of philosophical and conjectural history bequeathed to the Scottish Romantics.

Though Thomson was not the only critic that felt Grant had overreached herself by entering to the masculine arena of the formal essay, Grant's foray into this area reflects what recent scholars have identified as broader opportunities for women history writers of the time.[13] In Scotland in particular, the development of conjectural historiography in the eighteenth century, as Phillips and others have charted, saw a rise in an interest in enquiry into everyday manners and customs of the panoply of human societies, past and present, which allowed for a greater acceptance of historical writing in the more informal genres in which women were more readily published. The conjectural historical method of writers such as Lord Kames, Adam Ferguson, John Millar and Dugald Stewart had formed a wider critique of the restrictive scope of traditional political narrative, 'in favor of a more inclusive conception that would give greater prominence to everyday and inward experience'.[14] At the same time, a shift to an interest in manners and customs – the private realm of everyday social practices that was separate from the public arena of grand political action and momentous historical events – made for greater acceptance of an increasing array of historical writing, particularly by women. Memoirs and biographies would speak to a wider audience as genres that explored domains of experience beyond the private lives of public men.[15] Although conjectural historians such as

Kames, Ferguson, Millar and Stewart drew heavily on the materials of a history of manners, they were not content simply to represent common life 'in all its diversity'. Instead, as Phillips writes, '[i]n their commitment to create a history more systematic and far-seeing, they built a philosophical psychology of the human mind, as well as a comparative study of manners and customs.' Underlying this commitment was the assumption that

> the entire 'history of man' must be unified by fundamental and necessary principles. Whether the origin of these principles was to be sought in workings of human mind, divine purpose, or the methods of natural history, the existence of some unifying principle was a methodological necessity, without which it would be impossible to investigate the scattering of materials that come to hand.[16]

The purpose of the 'grand-narrative' of the conjectural historians, Phillips sums, 'was to represent the vast undocumented history of human experience at every stage of social progress'.[17]

Grant makes explicit her desire to contribute to this 'grand-narrative' of conjectural history in the rich matrix of history writing that is featured in both the *Memoirs* and the *Essays*. Though it is the exemplary outward benevolence of her beloved Aunt Schuyler that provides the 'chief interest' of the *Memoirs*, Grant adds that the reader must excuse her

> for dwelling, at times, on the recollection of a state of society so peculiar, so utterly dissimilar to any other that I have heard, or read of, that it exhibits human nature in a new aspect, and is so far an object of rational curiosity, as well as a kind of phenomenon in the history of colonization.[18]

Three years later in the *Essays*, Grant would declare that all her writings 'derived their chief interest from the fidelity of the delineations they presented, and the images they reflected, of a mode of life more primitive than what is usually met with'.[19] The *Essays* represents perhaps Grant's final, summative retrospection in a lifetime of retrospective writing on the 'character and manners' of isolated primitive societies, their 'customs and even their modes of thinking', a final outlet for 'overflowings of a mind filled with retrospective views of the past, and reflections suggested by deep feeling, and long and close observation among scenes of peculiar interest' (1:iii–iv).[20] Looking back on her life along the margins of Britain's Atlantic empire, devoted to 'long and close observation', Grant establishes her bona fides as source informant for her own contributions to conjectural history, as they provide invaluable insight into the 'arrangements of rude nations' that, Dugald Stewart had argued in 1793, would be otherwise inaccessible.[21] Lacking historical records, Stewart had stated, 'the detached facts which travels and voyages afford us, may frequently serve as landmarks to our speculations; and sometimes our conclusions a priori, may tend to confirm the credibility of facts, which, on a superficial view, appeared to be doubtful or incredible'.[22] In the pushmi-pullyu relationship between 'detached facts' and 'speculations' that Stewart describes – each one furnishing confirmation for the other – travellers' tales become indispensable for the conjectural historian. John Millar had already provided confirmation of their value in *The Origin of the Distinction of Ranks* (1771). '[W]ith regard to the state of mankind in the more uncivilized parts of the world,' Millar had written, 'our information . . . is chiefly derived from the relations of travellers, whose character and situation in life, neither set them above the suspicion of being easily deceived, nor of endeavouring to misrepresent the facts which they have related' (xiii).

In her own writing, however, Grant is dismissive of the quality of just this sort of traveller-based evidence, which she distinguishes from the more authoritative evidence she brings to her own enquiry. In a letter written in 1778, five years after arriving in the Highlands with her mother and father, who was stationed at Fort Augustus, Grant remarks on the curious ignorance of Scotch manners in a country so near as England: 'This comes', she writes 'from confounding the peculiarities, dialect, &c. of the Highlanders with those of the Lowlanders, the two most dissimilar classes of beings existing, in every one particular that marks distinction; the former indeed are a people never to be known unless you live among them, and learn their language' (*Letters*, vol. 2, p. 23). Grant here sets out a key subject of her writing, the social practices and language that define a people, while also establishing a standard of engagement she would later assert sets her own descriptions apart from those of mere travellers – extended residence among the people she wrote about and adoption of their language. Grant was dismissive of accounts of Indian savagery by travellers who spent only a brief time among native peoples. 'Voyagers, who have not their language, and merely see them transiently, to wonder and be wondered at,' Grant writes, 'are equally strangers to the real character of man in a social, though unpolished state' (*Memoirs*, vol. 1, p. 88). In contrast, '[e]arly accustomed to savage life', Grant would boast in a letter written only a month or so after her arrival in the Highlands after her return from North America, 'I have not the horror at it that wiser people have' (*Letters*, vol. 1, p. 53). In both her writing on the Highlands as well as colonial New York, Grant positions herself as something other than a 'traveller' to the 'savage' worlds she describes. The early correspondence appearing in her *Letters* provides what amounts to a 'Highland Tour' depiction of the local landscapes she visited, filtered largely through her teenage enthusiasm for Macpherson's Ossian poetry. But the *Letters* describe a transformation in her relation to the Highland world in which she found herself, as she marries and settles down to raise a large family on a glebe farm in Laggan, where her husband was parish minister. In a residence that lasted nearly two decades, Grant becomes fluent in Gaelic and enculturates herself in the local Highland community, becoming, in her words, 'naturalized'.[23] Grant's Highland letters, as I have argued elsewhere, chart a kind of 'domestic ethnography' of the Highlands for her English-speaking readers, from the liminal vantage point of a writer who would declare herself 'not entirely a stranger nor entirely a native' (*Essays*, vol. 1, p. 10).[24] Grant's stay in North America was, in comparison to her stay in the Highlands, a brief one – arriving in 1758, she left ten years later, at age thirteen, never to return. Yet she would adopt a similar stance of an observer who stands both outside and inside her subject community, which had established her reputation as one who could translate the primitive customs and manners of the peoples she dwelled among. Having lived among her subjects on either side of the Atlantic, and knowing their languages, she parlayed her unusual personal history into a sustained enquiry into the 'real character' of nations in what she termed the 'infancy' of human society.[25]

'Eye and Ear Witness': The Powers of Recall Forty Years Since

In 'their reframing of common life as a domain of pervasive historical change', memoirs, writes Phillips, 'seemed best adapted to overcome the formal restrictions that still surrounded historical narrative'.[26] As the artless descriptions of her day-to-day experiences and thoughts and feelings at the time, Grant's Highland *Letters* were prized because they provided an unmediated, and therefore faithful, glimpse into the Highland world as it had unfolded before her, constituting, like other examples of epistolary writing by women, 'the private archive of everyday life'.[27] Part autobiographical memoir and part biography of her beloved Aunt Schuyler, the *Memoirs*, which Grant herself labelled a 'miscellany of description, observation, and detail', presents a hodge-podge of generic impulses. Yet as she had done in her *Letters*, Grant sought to provide in her *Memoirs* an unmediated account of her experiences and the everyday world of colonial America. For the *Memoirs*, however, Grant would be going back to a period of her life for which she had made no written record – indeed, *Memoirs* would, in part, recount the development of her own literacy. Instead, Grant would rely solely on three self-described aspects of her character that were conspicuous at a very early age: a precocious intellectual curiosity, unusual powers of observation and 'the tenacity of an uncommonly retentive memory'.[28] Despite these claims, however, it was Grant's drawing attention to the *Memoirs* as an act of remembrance that would set the terms for its reception as well as inspiring a chorus of critical commentary that would call into question the very nature of its historicity.

As was the case in Scotland for her writing on the rural Highlands, in the United States Grant's 'charming' and 'faithful' depictions of colonial life – to adopt the most frequent adjectives used to summarise them – would be taken up as source material for a variety of writing, fictional and non-fictional, that served a larger national community. In Scotland, Scott and other prominent Edinburgh men would summarise her contribution to Scottish letters in a petition to George IV to provide Grant, in later life, with a royal stipend:

> We have no hesitation in attesting our belief that Mrs. Grant's writings have produced a strong and salutary effect upon her countrymen, who not only found recorded in them much of national history and antiquities, which would otherwise have been forgotten, but found them combined with the soundest and the best lessons of virtue and morality.[29]

In the United States, the *Memoirs* would have a rich but quite localised afterlife; they would be used as source material for historical fiction, and were reissued and reconstituted throughout the nineteenth century in a variety of writings – from newspaper articles and antiquarian society proceedings to textbooks and educational primers – that were concerned primarily with New York local history.[30]

Beyond, however, its recounting of the comings and goings of interrelated members of prominent old Dutch families – of Schuylers, Cuylers, Cortlands and Van Rensselaers – Grant's account was noted for its particularly rich portrait of the native people who occupied the region. In one particularly resonant portrait of a prominent Indian of the times, which would be reproduced in various formats afterwards, Grant recalls meeting the Mohawk 'King Hendrick', the 'great warrior and faithful ally of the British crown' who was 'then sovereign of the five nations' (*Memoirs*, vol. 1, p. 29). Thirty years before this meeting, she writes, Colonel Phillip Schuyler had convinced the father of this prominent warrior and three other tribal leaders to accompany him to London, where they were granted an audience with Queen Anne, to forge an alliance that would 'counteract the political machinations of the French' in North America and to give them 'an adequate idea of our power and the magnificence of our court' (1:25). The man that Grant recalls meeting was, 'splendidly arrayed in a suit of light blue, made in an antique mode, and trimmed with broad silver lace; which was probably an heirloom, in the family, presented to his father by his good ally, and sister, the female king of England' (1:29). Thus did Grant relate the strange encounter in the colonial hinterlands between a young Scottish girl and an Indian sovereign, a figure whom Eric Hinderaker has described as the 'most famous Indian in the eighteenth-century Anglo-American world'.[31] But the person that Grant met could not have been King Hendrick or his son, because, as more recent historical research has uncovered, 'King Hendrick' was not one man but two unrelated men born into successive generations of separate Mohawk communities.[32] The man who had accompanied 'Phillip' (actually Peter) Schuyler to England was Hendrick Tejonihokarawa, who died around 1735. The other man was Hendrick Peters Theyanoguin, who was killed in the Battle of Lake George in 1755, three years before Grant's arrival in New York. Whom, then, did Grant recall meeting as a child of four or five? Hinderaker surmises it is possible that Grant might have met the grandson of the renowned second Hendrick, whose exploits had been in published accounts of the battle and in a popular portrait engraving entitled *The brave old*

Hendrick, the great sachem or chief of the Mohawk Indians, which appeared soon after his death. Remembering a scene of her childhood after a span of several decades Grant might somehow have conflated this *image* of the second Hendrick and her actual encounter with another man: '[I]n recalling the clothes she saw,' Hinderaker writes, 'it is possible that she was influenced by a memory of "the brave old Hendrick" print, which would have been hanging in Albany homes during the time of her stay'.[33] In putting into print the hazy accumulations of a lifetime of misremembering, Grant thus inscribed into cultural memory the image of a 'King Hendrick' who never was, a portrait that nevertheless shaped transatlantic perceptions of Anglo-Indian relations in the colonial era for more than two centuries.

Hinderaker is perhaps only the most recent example in what is now a long history of scholarly challenges to the *Memoirs*, as a succession of commentators – commencing with the American editors of later editions of the work – have sought to untangle Grant's knots of misremembrance and inaccuracy. This work began in earnest in 1876 when the Albany antiquarian and publisher Joel Munsell sought to rescue the *Memoirs* from oblivion, bringing out the first new edition of the work – complete with extensive commentary, illustrations, maps and a memoir of Grant – since 1846. Munsell directs his historian's gaze on Grant's account of the Dutch families, correcting Grant's frequent errors concerning names, dates and genealogical details. He informs the reader, for example, that the subject heroine of Grant's piece was not named Catalina, as Grant asserts, but Margaretta, Catalina Schuyler's older sister (*Memoirs*, 1876, p. 42).

The more recent examination of Grant's role in perpetuating historical inaccuracy is testimony to shifting historical concerns – from tracing the biographies of European settlers to those of the original occupiers of the land – but also reveals the continuing allure of the *Memoirs* as an artefact of cultural memory, bringing back to life the everyday world of colonial America. Grant herself, despite her confidence in her powers of recall, acknowledged that the passage of time posed profound difficulties when it came time to craft a precise and coherent narrative of events long past. In *Poems on Various Subjects*, Grant had remarked on the deficiencies of memory as raw material for poetic imagination, by way of an apology for the effusiveness of a piece originally meant only for a friend. 'Memory', Grant writes, 'makes no selections; in those retrospections of the most innocent and pleasurable period of life, incidents and characters, serious, pathetic, and ludicrous, rush mingled on the mind. In a composition meant for the public eye, incongruous images should certainly not be mixed together' (254). Several years later, she would offer a similar apology for the *Memoirs*. As she had 'no authorities to refer to, no coeval witnesses of facts to consult', Grant forewarns her reader 'not to look for lucid order in the narration, or intimate connection between its parts' (*Memoirs*, vol. 1, p. 7). Instead, Grant asks, 'in the dim distance of near forty years, unassisted by written memorials, shall I not mistake dates, misplace facts, and omit circumstances that form essential links in the chain of narration?' (1:42). In other commentary, Grant relates the difficulty in producing memoir, which of all the genres, she believes, is the most laborious and slow going:

> Poetry or fiction gives loose reins to the imagination; history is fed by rills of authorities and documents, that flow in from all quarters; epistolary writing is supported by a variety of subjects, the topics which your correspondent suggests, &c.; in travels, if your mind be fertile and cultivated, little more is requisite than to copy with ease and accuracy the picture of nature which that mind reflects, and to record with grace and fidelity the occurrences you meet with. But this retrograde, crablike march over the years that are no more – this tale of other times, where you are neither allowed the liberty of embellishment, nor the collateral lights that in other cases aid research into the past – is a cheerless toil, where all the faculties must needs mount upon the memory. (*Memoir and Correspondence*, 1:157)

As a memoirist who 'must needs mount all the faculties upon the memory', Grant self-reflexively describes the struggle to provide clarity and detail for her 'tale of other times', and frequently intrudes upon her narrative to caution readers that she is unsure as to the specific details or precise dates of the events she describes, or to alert them that she is offering only a partial understanding of events, based on the limited second-hand information that was told to her by Aunt Schuyler or someone else. Many of these interventions seem to operate as a kind of proactive defence, heading off future critique in places where she suspects her details might come under close reader scrutiny. 'Various military characters,' she writes, 'since highly distinguished, whose names I do not recollect, though once familiar to me, obtained introductions to Madame . . .' (2:54). There are also irruptions in the narrative in which Grant seems momentarily to lose herself in a reverie of remembrance, as these represent an escape to pleasanter times; these moments often set her at odds with the putative ethnographic purpose of her descriptions. Recalling bucolic summer evenings in Albany, for example, she writes: 'This picture, so familiar to my imagination, has led me away from my purpose, which was to describe the rural economy, and modes of living in this patriarchal city' (1:47). Alternatively, Grant at times is unable or unwilling to narrate events which are too unpleasant or too painful for her to recollect. She refuses, for example, to provide any detail of the 'dark days' that led to open revolt against British rule in the colonies, both because she feels 'unspeakable pain' in recalling a period of great suffering among her friends and because '[t]hat waste of personal courage and British blood and treasure, which were squandered to no purpose on one side in that ill-conducted war, and the insolence and cruelty which tarnished the triumph of the other, form no pleasing subject of retrospection . . .' (2:278). Narrative intrusions and elisions such as these have become the recognised tropes of memory writing, signalling the intellectual and emotional difficulties of committing to paper the experiences of long ago. In employing such tropes, Grant reminds her reader that the account she provides is a deeply personal, and therefore limited, act of remembrance, or, perhaps more precisely, multiple acts of both remembrance and, sometimes wilful, forgetting that ultimately do not make for a complete and coherent narrative.

At the same time, Grant insists that it is the very unreliability of her retrospection that bears testimony to her claim that it is a true-life picture of the past, 'unassisted by written memorials', just as she had experienced it. When Thomson criticised the *Memoirs* as too praising of its title subject, leaving her actual virtue in some doubt, Grant defended her portrait of Aunt Schuyler as a faithful one, not to the way she actually was perhaps, but to the way the young Grant naively remembered her: 'I speak from the impressions formed in childhood, ever ingenuous and innocent. Time might have diminished these impressions had I continued near the object of them but, as it is, they are just as I received them' (*Memoir and Correspondence*, vol. 1, pp. 182–3). Letters published after her death make it clear, however, that Grant relied on both her large transatlantic network of friends and correspondents – her home in Edinburgh would become a popular destination for a steady stream of American visitors, many of whom had connections with the Schuyler family in New York – and on written accounts to help fill in some of the gaps in her memory, or even supplement it in some instances.[34] Yet readers would accept Grant's own assertion that the very faultiness of her account secured its status as a true-to-life impression of the past, and they would embrace the *Memoirs* as an act of pure retrospection. In an overview of Grant's career in the *North American Review*, Andrews Norton, who corresponded with Grant and visited her in Edinburgh, would provide an explanation of the paradoxical relationship between truthfulness and error manifested in her work, by pointing out a curious detail concerning Grant's retrospective faculties. On three different occasions in her writing Grant gives an account of the moment she came to the attention of Aunt Schuyler, and each version, Norton points out, 'is inconsistent in its details with both of the others', even though Grant stated more than once that the memory of the encounter was 'indelibly fixed in her mind'. Grant's inconsistencies reveal for Norton a fundamental quality of eyewitness testimony:

> [t]hese three passages strikingly illustrate the fact, that a story may be unquestionably true in all its essential characteristics and bearings, though individuals who have been placed in the best possible circumstances for knowing the truth – eye and ear witnesses – may differ from each other irreconcilably in their details of it. We have here three narratives of a single individual relating to an incident adapted to make a deep impression on her memory, and they are irreconcilable.[35]

It would be the task of successive editors and commenters on Grant's work to correct and supplement its many inconsistencies, while at the same time carefully preserving the 'essential characteristics and bearings' of Grant's 'unquestionably true' story of the past. In his sumptuous 1901 edition of the *Memoirs*, for example, the historian and biographer James Grant Wilson, who was also Grant's godson, retains Munsell's 1876 corrections of the work's many inaccuracies, while offering in one case his own gentle explanation for the error, laying the blame on the associative operations of memory. On Grant's confusing of Phillip Schuyler with his uncle Peter, Wilson writes:

She doubtless heard the name Philip repeated often, and that of Col. Peter Schuyler who had died more than thirty years before, comparatively seldom. Philip had become fixed in her memory, and she sometimes uses it erroneously instead of Peter, as in this instance. It is clear from what follows agreeing with historical facts, that Col. Peter Schuyler is meant. (*Memoirs*, 1901, vol. 1, p. 55n.)

In condescending corrections of Grant's faulty memory such as Wilson's, historians and editors would seek to elevate the *Memoirs* into the more authoritative domain of history proper, by filling in the gaps in the narrative between what is historically 'true' and what 'agrees with historical facts'. But in doing so, they highlighted the aspect of the work that made it so invaluable in the first place as an alternative to history. As an 'eye and ear witness', Grant brings experiential knowledge of the past that gives her recounting the quality of unquestionable truth 'in all its essential characteristics and bearings' even as it differs wildly in successive tellings. The very faultiness and narrative incoherence of Grant's original text gave it its powerful quality of immediacy for future readers, as if she wrote it, as a twentieth-century critic put it, 'gazing out a window at the eighteenth-century colonial scenes and citizens she described'.[36]

Nostalgia and the Reign of the Affections

Imbued with 'the living character of by-gone ages', as Francis Jeffrey had claimed for the historical memoir, the *Memoirs* is illustrative of the genre's rising popularity and, like her counterparts Cockburn, Chambers, and Scott, Grant offers her personal, and admittedly faulty, retrospection on a bygone epoch, whose passing can be measured within only a generation or two.[37] But Grant's writing significantly differs from those of her contemporaries in its geographical scope, as she takes in the vast domain of her sojourn along the periphery of the empire. In the *Memoirs*, Grant brings a memorialist historiography to what she identifies as a unique set of local circumstances: a 'kind of phenomenon', she writes, 'in the history of colonization'. Published two years after her *Letters from the Mountains* and three years before the *Essays*, the *Memoirs* represents a new direction for Grant, away from the Highland subject matter that was her greatest source of success.[38] Yet it is also fair to say that Grant's North American experiences both shaped, and were shaped by, her Highland experiences. On the one hand, the *Memoirs* appeared some years after Grant had left the Highlands and after she already had worked out many of her ideas on primitive society. *Letters from the Mountains* had charted the increasing complexity of her thinking: the tourist-like references to sublime landscape and effusive allusions to Ossian of her early letters disappear, as Grant settles down and begins to establish herself as a Gaelic-speaking authority on Highland society and literary traditions, able to speak with some confidence herself on the authenticity of Macpherson's work. Scottish Enlightenment theories of human societal development that Grant had carefully absorbed in her early life through her reading of Ossian continued to inform her own thinking on the isolated rural societies, on both sides of the Atlantic, she had encountered and written about.[39] On the other hand, though Grant began drafting the *Memoirs* sometime in the autumn of 1807 – completing it during a stay on the estate of Sir John Legard outside London – she had been mulling over writing such a work for some years, and traces of her childhood experiences, which she would return to in the *Memoirs*, had already made their appearance in her work on the Highlands.[40] In her 1803 *Poems*, for example, Grant, in a lengthy defence of the authenticity of Ossian, responds by way of a North American analogy to critics who had argued the ancient Scottish Celts were too unsophisticated to write such elevated poetry:

> The clearest way to ascertain the possibility of heroic sentiments being delivered in eloquent language by wandering savages, who subsist by hunting, is to trace the manners of people who still exist in a similar state of society. The banks of the *Mohawk* very lately did, and the borders of the *Huron* and *Oneida* lakes still do, afford an apt illustration: There, heroic friendship, exalted notions of probity and honour; the fondest filial and fraternal affection, and the most enthusiastic patriotism, prevail: There every chief is an orator, and every orator a poet . . .[41]

Grant here adapts familiar comparative methodology of Scottish conjectural history to argue, in effect, that what is the case for one set of 'wandering savages' must be the case for another, regardless of historical or geographical circumstances. At the same time, however, Grant's subtle shift in tense, from 'very lately did' to 'still do' alludes to a divergent history for two sets of native peoples in North America, derived from her personal knowledge: the former a band of

Six Nations Mohawk that she would describe in greater detail in the *Memoirs* and that had been expelled from their ancestral lands after the Revolution.

The overlapping and cross-pollinating influences of both her reading and her transatlantic experiences shaped Grant's ideas on pre-civilised peoples; these culminated in a full-fledged theory in the *Essays* that she had been developing throughout her career and to which she would allude in the *Memoirs*. The 'reign of the affections' encapsulated for Grant both an epoch and a state of mind intrinsic to the primitive societies she had encountered. Isolation and the shared burdens of a harsh existence fostered a total interdependence and deep-felt attachment within their small communities that governed all aspects of their society, from the allocation of labour and division of social ranks and the structures of trade, governance, warfare and entertainments; to the rituals of birth, marriage, and death and the treatment of the young and old. Above all, Grant would emphasise, members of these societies were characterised by their profoundly communal sense of selfhood. 'No highlander ever once thought of himself as an individual', Grant writes in the *Essays*: 'Amongst these people, even the meanest mind was in a manner enlarged by association, by anticipation, and by retrospect. In the most minute, as well as the most serious concerns, he felt himself one of many connected together' (1:51).[42] Of the Mohawk, Grant writes, 'every man was proud of the prowess and achievements of his tribe collectively; of his personal virtues he was not proud, because we excel but by comparison; and he rarely saw instances of the opposite vices in his own nation, and looked on others with unqualified contempt' (*Memoirs*, vol. 1, p. 215). 'This state of life', Grant summarises, 'may be truly called the reign of the affections: the love of kindred and of country ruling paramount, unrivalled by other passions, all others being made subservient to these' (1:215). Though Grant was careful to delineate the social drawbacks of the reign of the affections, which could produce 'the fiercest cruelty and the bitterest revenge', her writing rehearses what were, by 1808, familiar assumptions of Romantic-era primitivism, which set a pre-modern world of deep-felt bonds of affection and intimacy against a cosmopolitan world of overly refined manners and profound self-interestedness. In this way, Grant's writing joins that of many others from both sides of the Atlantic which, while expressing sympathy for the plight of native communities, worked to place these communities on the spatial and temporal margins of a modernising, expanding nation. Grant's fond remembrances of Highland and Mohawk worlds therefore seems a recognisable expression of primitivist nostalgia, as she relives the twilight of a world that has already vanished from sight, a sad but necessary sacrifice on the altar of progress.[43]

But in several ways Grant's account of a life lived on the margins undoes the familiar logic of Romantic-era primitivism. For one, Grant enlarges its scope to include non-natives: it is not just Highland and Mohawk societies that fall into the category of the primitive, but also the Dutch-speaking community in colonial New York, which, she writes, existed in the 'calm infancy of society' (*Memoirs*, vol. 1, p. 36). Against a backdrop of often violent struggle between the British and the French for imperial dominance, the settlements of Albany and along the Upper Hudson Valley, the residue of a once powerful Dutch trading empire, appear in Grant's account as a singular enclave of selflessness, in which the daily privations and dangers of the surrounding wilderness made for a tight-knit community whose members depended on each other for survival.[44] Describing, for example, the custom of the childless Aunt Schuyler to 'adopt' children, including Grant herself, from outside the Schuyler family, Grant links the practice to the particular stage of social development of her entire community. Such a custom, Grant writes,

> was not singular during that reign of natural feeling which preceded the prevalence of artificial modes in this primitive district. The love of offspring is certainly one of the strongest desires that the uncorrupted mind forms to itself in a state of comparative innocence. (*Memoirs*, vol. 1, p. 206)

In the 'primitive district' of the colony, 'Maidens, bachelors, and childless married people, all adopted orphans, and all treated them as if they were their own' (1:117). In Grant's Dutch families, as in her Highland clans and Algonquian tribes, the individual felt herself to be 'one of many connected together', and the settlement was therefore free from internal rivalries and the hunger for individual status and wealth that characterised more polished society.

As Grant ties together three distinct societies – colonial Dutch, Algonquians and Scottish Highlanders – under the sign of the reign of the affections, she provides an alternative to the rigid racial and ethnic dividing that would become a distinct feature of primitivist discourse later in the century. Their status as settlers, however, would set the

Dutch apart from their native counterparts, making them exemplars of what Grant identifies as a peculiar phenomenon in the annals of social progress, arising from the particular circumstances of European colonisation in the region. Long detached from their 'mother country', but not yet assimilated into anglophone culture, the Dutch community along the Upper Hudson had regressed, returned to a more primitive state in relation both to Dutch society of their own time, back home in the Netherlands, and to an increasingly cosmopolitan New York City. Grant summarises the peculiar shift in consciousness characteristic of members of such small and isolated colonial settlements in her account of the founding of William Penn's Quaker colony in Pennsylvania. 'Where nations, in the course of time become civilised,' she writes,

> the process is so gradual from one race to another, that no violent effort is required to break through settled habits, and acquire new tastes and inclinations, fitted to what might be almost styled a new mode of existence. But when colonies are first settled, in a country so entirely primitive as that to which William Penn led his followers, there is a kind of retrograde movement of the mind, requisite to reconcile people to the new duties and new views that open to them, and to make the total privation of wonted objects, modes, and amusements, tolerable. (*Memoirs*, vol. 2, pp. 332–3)

Grant's admiring picture of the 'austere simplicity' of the Quakers leads her train of thought back to her beloved Dutch:

> A kindred simplicity, and a similar ignorance of artificial refinements and high seasoned pleasures, produced the same effect in qualifying the first settlers at Albany to support the privations, and endure the inconveniences of their novitiate in the forests of the new world. (2:333–4)

By comparing the early Quaker colony with the Dutch, Grant makes clear that a colonial 'retrograde movement of the mind' can occur not only at the dawn of empire but at its collapse. New Netherland, like the Iroquois Confederacy and, eventually, New France, will give way to an emergent British imperium in North America, but in Grant's account the residue of former empires linger on, their movement along the axis of social progress taking strange twists and sudden turns, in response to the unique contingencies of their time and place.

Accounts like Grant's helped to ensure the Dutch colony did not disappear from the literature and history of the new American republic. Instead, like their Indian counterparts, the Dutch were inscribed into a new national historiography in the form of a remnant, a ghostly but persistent residue of an earlier society that yet retains some of its distinctive colour, in certain locales, in the present. In works such as Irving's local sketches and tales and his burlesque *History of New York*, James Kirke Paulding's *The Dutchman's Fireside* (1831) and James Fenimore Cooper's *Satanstoe* (1845), the inhabitants of the old Dutch colony became the subject of an armchair nostalgia for a lost pastoral that linked the social relations of the colony with simpler times before the Revolution. The *Memoirs* would provide the inspiration for Paulding's novel, and furnish extensive source material for both his work and Cooper's, yet Grant's work itself represents a stark departure from these nostalgic treatments of the colonial past.[45] Though Grant at times can appear to lose herself in the remembrance of simpler times, her acute observations on the oscillations of empire- and nation-building in eighteenth-century America, and on the widespread turmoil and privations that war brought to the colony, make moments of nostalgic reverie the exception to her larger historical perspective.

In the same vein, Grant, in her descriptions of the ultimate fates of the native peoples she admired, departs from the conventions of much primitivist elegising. She finishes her account of the Mohawk people, for example, in a footnote at the very end of the *Memoirs* that provides a brief but ambivalent description of both communal loss and hope for the future. For those readers who 'will perhaps regret parting with that singular association of people . . . without knowing where the few that remain have taken up their abode', Grant records the Mohawk of the area were given a reprieve from dissolution: 'It is but doing justice to this distinguished race to say, that, though diminished they were not subdued; though voluntary exiles, not degraded.' Instead, 'all that remained of this powerful nation' followed the son of influential British colonial administrator and landowner William Johnson – into 'Upper Canada, where they now find a home around the place of his residence'. 'One old man alone', Grant writes, 'having no living tie remaining, would not forsake the tombs of his ancestors, and remains like "a watchman on the lonely hill"; or rather like a sad memento of an extinguished nation' (2:344). Fittingly at the very end, Grant recounts the diasporic flight of native people, whose passing is reflected in the tragic figure of the 'one old man alone', who is doomed to linger among the graves of his ancestors. But there is nothing in Grant's account to suggest their passing is inevitable, the tragic but necessary by-product of historical progress. Instead, the dispossession and relocation of the Mohawk from lands that belonged to them is a product of what she terms 'the most trying exigencies' of the post-Revolutionary moment. In Grant's account, Mohawk dispossession and relocation, like that of other groups who were loyal to the British Crown – including her own family – is contingent, a product of a particular set of circumstances unique to the time and the place.[46]

In a parallel passage in the *Essays*, Grant declares her scepticism that Highlanders, once displaced from their ancestral lands, 'should, in any foreign land, preserve the poetry and traditions which keep their ancient spirit alive'. Like 'spirits that haunt old towers or manor houses', Grant writes, 'these local muses are inseparably connected with the spot to which they belong – have perpetual reference to the scenes they celebrate – and become unintelligible elsewhere'. Nevertheless, in a summation that echoes her characterisation of the Mohawk as 'diminished' but not 'subdued' or 'degraded' in their migration to Canada, Grant writes that 'though the volatile spirit' of the Highlanders 'should evaporate, much remains that, when they remove in a body together, may be transmitted beyond the Atlantic, and take root in a new soil' (2:172). Grant laments that 'Music, poetry, and, indeed, imagination do not seem to bear transplanting', but 'the love of their ancient home, and their original principles, continue unalterable' (2:177, 175). From the vantage point of their destination, on the other side of the Atlantic, Grant would confirm the success of state-aided schemes – the Earl of Selkirk's is conspicuously noted – to preserve a Highland way of life threatened by dispossession and dislocation by resettling entire Highland communities in undeveloped lands in British Canada. Such schemes signal for Grant a 'new and brighter day' for Gaeldom in the British Atlantic:

> Here . . . are clusters of emigrants, who have fled, unacquainted with the refinements, and uncontaminated by the old world, to seek for that bread and peace, which the progress of luxury and the change of manners denied them at home. Here they come in kindly confederation,

resolved to cherish in those kindred groups, which have left with social sorrow their native mountains, the customs and traditions, the language and the love of their ancestors, and to find comfort in that religion, which has been ever their support and their shield, for all that they have left behind. (*Memoirs*, vol. 2, pp. 341–2)

In what may be described as, at the very least, a profoundly naive underestimation of the lasting individual and social trauma of forced relocation, Grant offers migration as a means for adaptation and the ultimate survival of marginalised societies, in an imperial modernity. Grant's primitives do not vanish, they simply move elsewhere. What matters for her is that is the reign of the affections instilled in such communities can persist, uprooted from the local circumstances that give birth to it, but still intact.[47]

Life on the (Trans)periphery

Isolation and privation in the wild spaces of the British Empire make them the crucible of the reign of the affections for native and non-native communities alike, in Grant's historical philosophy, but, in the multi-ethnic world that Grant envisions in the *Memoirs*, mutual interdependence takes place not just *within* respective communities but also *between* them. This interdependence in turn produces ties of affiliation and affection that reach beyond the boundaries of individual communities, as they must rely on each other for their livelihood and security. By the time of Grant's stay, Mohawk people for generations had traversed the region, trading furs in exchange for wampum at the settlement in Albany, while Dutch settlers had long travelled to Mohawk villages to trade and to live among them. This had created a unique and, for Grant, admirable set of intercultural agents who negotiated between native and European worlds to the benefit of both. The young men of Albany, Grant writes, had long marked the passage into adulthood by undertaking a long sojourn among the Mohawk to establish contacts and to forge alliances that would form the basis for their future success as 'Indian traders'. These young men would display a marked change in character upon their return – 'demi-savages', Grant deems them – 'strange amphibious animals', who 'unit[ed] the acute senses, strong instincts, and unconquerable patience and fortitude of the savage, with the art, policy, and inventions of the European' (*Memoirs*, 1:76–7). After a season spent among Mohawk 'towns' in the wilderness, Grant writes, 'one scarce knows them till they unbend', but 'by this Indian likeness' the young men are not 'by any means degraded'. Instead, their experiences among the Mohawk often formed the basis for their future prosperity in Dutch colonial society (1:87).

Grant's description of intercultural figures such as the 'amphibious' Indian traders of Albany is roughly analogous to the intercultural exchange between European and native cultures, in the context of Western imperialism, that is the defining aspect of what Mary Louise Pratt has termed the 'contact zone', by which she describes 'the spatial and temporal copresence of subjects previously separated by geographic and historical disjunctures, and whose trajectories now intersect'.[48] Like Pratt's contact zone, the terrain of Grant's retrospection is distinguished by cross-cultural contact and exchange, but her account presents an even more complex understanding of cross-cultural encounter, as it describes multiple points of contact between several competing and overlapping imperial cultures – rising British, fading French and residual Dutch – all of which must reckon with the still-pervasive political and cultural influence of the Iroquois Confederacy. In this, Grant's description of native/European interaction seems more closely to anticipate the recent formulation in colonial historiography to describe the region in the seventeenth and eighteenth centuries. The historian Richard White uses the term 'Middle Ground' to describe a time and place in which competing cultures came into contact and in which no single culture has the technological or material means to dominate the region through force alone.[49] The formation of the Middle Ground, White writes, involved a process of 'mutual invention' in which 'the older worlds of the Algonquians and of various Europeans overlapped, and their mixture created new systems of meaning and exchange'.[50]

In the often violently contested space of the Middle Ground, where no single society has the upper hand, intercultural figures are the key to social stability. 'So much of the peace and safety of this infant community', Grant writes, 'depended on the friendship and alliance of these generous tribes; and to conciliate and retain their affections so much address was necessary, that common characters were unequal to the task' (*Memoirs*, vol. 1, pp. 17–18). Grant presents several exemplary individuals, with 'minds liberal and upright', who were able to negotiate between competing and overlapping cultures of this world, beginning with Aunt Schuyler herself. Schuyler, Grant writes,

> early adopted the views of her family, in regard to those friendly Indians [the Mohawk], which greatly enlarged her mind, and ever after influenced her conduct. She was, even in childhood, well acquainted with their language, opinions, and customs; and, like every other person, possessed of a liberality or benevolence of mind, whom chance had brought acquainted with them, was exceedingly partial to those high-souled and generous natives. (1:138)

Active engagement inspired by a mutual respect are the hallmarks of intercultural relations in the region and the distinguishing virtue of several public figures for which Grant provides brief biographical sketches, such as the Scottish-born governor of the colony, Cadwallader Colden, Colonel Phillip Schuyler and, most conspicuously, Sir William Johnson. Born into a landowning Irish family, Johnson, as Superintendent of Indian Affairs, would act as intermediary between the British colonial administration and the Iroquois Confederacy during the Seven Years War. Grant describes 'the justly celebrated' Johnson as 'an uncommonly tall, well-made man: with a fine countenance', noted for his sagacity, discipline and magnanimity (2:56, 57). At the height of his power, Johnson was Britain's sole representative in relations with the Iroquois Confederacy, and he was given immense authority and free rein. Not afraid to enrich himself while serving the greater good, Johnson was, Grant writes, a kind of 'tribune of the Five Nations, whose claims he asserted, whose rights he protected, and over whose minds he possessed a greater sway than any other individual had ever attained' (2:56–7). Living 'like a little sovereign' on a large tract of land along the Mohawk River bequeathed to him by the Mohawk people, Johnson constructed his own special zone of intercultural exchange and affection, wholeheartedly embracing a Mohawk way of life and integrating it into his own. Johnson, Grant writes, 'wore in winter almost entirely their dress and ornaments', and, after the death of his first wife, 'connected himself with an Indian maiden, daughter to a Sachem, who ... whether ever formally married to him according to our usage or not, contrived to live with him in great union and affection all his life' (2:59–60). Johnson would come to serve as prototype for a familiar figure in American writing in the nineteenth century, the white European who has partially adopted 'native' ways – become half-savage – while always retaining his essential superiority, bringing civilisation to the wilderness.[51] Yet, in Grant's account, Johnson's transculturation, like that of the young men of the Dutch colony, makes him neither a figure of degradation nor of white superiority. Instead, a respected and powerful figure who partakes of both European and native communities while able to negotiate the demands of both, Johnson is Grant's beau idéal of the public man in the Middle Ground.

Though Grant gives attention to the masculine arena of public life in her history, most of her focus is in keeping with her other writings and devoted to the more informal and intimate space of the home. Here, too, Grant is an acute and admiring observer of moments of cross-cultural contact. She describes the yearly migrations of 'some detached Indian families', who came to reside on and around the Schuyler family estate every summer; they 'generally built a light wigwam under shelter of the orchard fence on the shadiest side' (*Memoirs*, vol. 1, p. 121). It was during these summer stays that Grant sought to immerse herself in native culture, and the occasion provides one of the earliest examples of her own attraction to intercultural exchange with what she identified as a primitive society:

> Conversing with those interesting and deeply reflecting natives, was to thinking minds no mean source of entertainment.... [T]he Indians had a singular facility in acquiring other languages; children I well remember, from experimental knowledge, for I delighted to hover about the wigwam, and converse with those of the Indians, and we very frequently mingled languages. (1:126)

Of these summer visitors to the colony, Grant would sum, 'never were neighbors more harmless, peaceable and obliging; I might truly add, industrious: for in one way or other they were constantly occupied' (1:121–2). The women and children of this temporary Indian community crafted household wares and finely wrought items of clothing such as belts and shoes – noted for their comfort and refinement, Grant writes – to trade and sell to the colonists. This seasonal domestic economy inspired its own kind of small-scale intercultural community based on the daily interactions of women: [t]he summer residence of these ingenious artisans', Grant writes, 'promoted a great intimacy between the females of the vicinity and the Indian women, whose sagacity and comprehension of mind were beyond belief' (1:124).

Grant also provides examples in which intimacies between native peoples and Europeans are forged not in the arena of domestic trade, but of warfare. In stark contrast to the bucolic scenes of the Indian summer sojourn, Grant recounts a traumatic scene in the wake of Pontiac's Rebellion. After signing a peace treaty, Grant writes, Pontiac agreed to a captives exchange, giving 'permission to the mothers of those children who had been taken away from the frontier settlements', in raids going back ten years in some instances, 'to receive them back again, on condition of delivering up the Indian prisoners' (2:195). Grant's description of the scene of this exchange, which she says Aunt Schuyler arranged to take place on a gentle slope near the Albany fort, is one of the most dramatic in the *Memoirs*. Leery, perhaps, that the 'scene of these pathetic recognitions', so 'impossible to describe and affecting to behold', might raise the spectre of a faulty memory or, worse, outright fictional embellishment, Grant is careful to delineate the accuracy of her account, making clear she was direct eyewitness to the event (2:197). Grant also suggests that the details of the event remain as clear and as vivid as when she first witnessed them, as 'the day is engraven in indelible characters upon my memory' (2:195). What follows is Grant's account of an after-effect of the common wartime practice of taking and adopting captives, which produces a singular scene of anguish among women on both sides of the cultural divide. Grant describes the moment when the settler women who had lost children to captivity, some of whom had travelled 'some hundred miles from the back settlements of Pennsylvania and New England', appeared at the fort 'with anxious looks and aching hearts, not knowing whether their children were alive or how exactly to identify them if they should meet them' (2:197). The ensuing scene is a clash of powerful and contrasting emotions:

> The joy of even the happy mothers was overpowering, and found vent in tears; but not like the bitter tears of those who, after long travel, found not what they sought. It was affecting to see the deep and silent sorrow of the Indian women, and of the children, who knew no other mother, and clung fondly to their bosoms, from whence they were not torn without the most piercing shrieks; while their own fond mothers were distressed beyond measure at the shyness and aversion with which these long lost objects of their love received their caresses. (2:197–8)

Though no historical evidence can be found for the exchange that Grant describes taking place in Albany after Pontiac's treaty signing, hers is nevertheless a compelling account of a captives exchange, which were, by the time of Grant's residence, a common component of Anglo-Indian treaty negotiations.[52] Captivity narratives, however, had a much longer role in shaping the cultural fault line between native and colonial worlds, and, as many critical studies have demonstrated, these narratives provided a powerful set of assumptions about native peoples, which lasted well into the nineteenth century.[53] At the same time, studies on the practice of captive-taking from the perspective of native peoples have emphasised its role in maintaining the vitality of native communities, particularly in times of extended conflict. Captives were considered valuable items of exchange and, more crucially, potential replacements for members lost to warfare. In many cases, captives, once 'adopted' into the community, were expected to assume the pre-existing social and kinship position of the person they had replaced.[54] The tragic interplay of affection and aversion Grant recounts in the prisoner exchange suggests that she is alert to the complexities of native/European exchange and acculturation, describing what amounts to a coercive repatriation to the biological families of children who had lived in Indian villages since infancy and who had known no other life. Unlike many narratives of such a 'release', however, there is no comforting resolution in Grant's account, no notion of cultural or emotional 'return' for the captives. Instead, they remain suspended in the narrative at the point of exchange, the centrepiece of Grant's scene 'impossible to describe and affecting to behold'. Absent as well from Grant's account is the opposition common in captivity narratives between captive and captor, which invites the reader to condemn the (Indian) captor and to sympathise with the (European) captive.[55] Instead, the experience of personal and communal loss of the prisoner exchange is a *shared* one between both native and settler women. Just as settler mothers 'tore off the Indian clothing of their children, dressing them in new clothes they had brought with them, hoping that, with the Indian dress, they would throw off their habits and attachments' (2:198), the native women did not want to relinquish their adoptees: '[i]n the first place, because [the Indians] were grown very fond of them; and again, because they thought the children would not be so happy in our manner of life, which appeared to them both constrained and effeminate' (2:196). In the tragic dynamics of intercultural exchange depicted in the prisoner return, even the most intimate bonds of affection between mother and child, which for Grant was the powerful foundation of communal identity, prove to be adaptive and transferable.

Grant's refusal to condemn or to judge the acts on either side of the cultural divide suggest her own sympathetic disposition towards a non-European culture she both admired and respected. However, attitudes about cross-cultural intimacy in the region are not open-ended, and Grant is much more ambivalent when describing colonial attempts to police such intimacy when it threatens to upset the system of privilege and power within the community. This is particularly the case concerning relationships between members of the Dutch colony and the Africans they enslave. Grant begins her observations on these relationships by declaring 'I have never seen a people so happy in servitude as the domestics of the Albanians', by which she means the enslaved, most of whom labour in the households of well-to-do Dutch families, including the Schuylers (1:51). By way of demonstrating the benign treatment of the enslaved within these households, which often engenders lifelong ties between Dutch and African members of the same household, Grant describes a particular custom of these families:

> When a negroe-woman's child attained the age of three years, the first New Year's Day after, it was solemnly presented to a son or daughter, or other young relative of the family, who was of the same sex with the child so presented. The child to whom the young negroe was given immediately presented it with some piece of money and a pair of shoes; and from that day the strongest attachment subsisted between the domestic and the destined owner. (1:52)

Through such practices as the presentation ritual, 'tender' and 'generous' friendships take hold between the enslaved and their master. These often last a lifetime, as each was dependent on the other in the frontier life of the colony, as evidenced, Grant argues, by extraordinary examples of mutual acts of heroic devotion. Grant recalls one African who, 'at the imminent risk of his life', carried 'his disabled master through trackless woods with labour and fidelity scarce credible; and the master has been equally tender on similar occasions of the humble friend who stuck closer than a brother' (1:53). In the reign of the affections that held sway within the primitive community of the colony, ties between individuals so intimately connected from birth seem to provide a sanctuary, in Grant's account, from the rigid and oppressive hierarchies of racial difference that govern white–black relations elsewhere in the American colonies and beyond. The same vaunted liberality and benevolence of mind that Grant believes inspires Aunt Schuyler's engagement with native peoples also inspires her willingness to hold conversation with 'native Africans brought into her father's family', becoming in the process 'more intimately acquainted with the customs, manners, and government of their native country, than she ever could have been, by reading all that was ever written on the subject' (1:138).

In Dutch Albany, Grant sums, 'the dark aspect of slavery was softened into a smile' (1:51). Yet she also acknowledges the underlying racism that perpetuates it. Though the particular economic and social circumstances of the Dutch colonists may have fomented a 'mild and really tender indulgence to their negroes' compared to others, she writes, as enslavers they 'had not the slightest scruple of conscience with regard to the right with which they held them in subjection' (1:57).[56] 'Mild and really tender indulgence' did not extend to equal consideration. Instead, the Dutch 'sought their code of morality in the Bible, and there imagined they found this hapless race condemned to perpetual slavery; and thought nothing remained for them but to lighten the chains of their fellow Christians, after having made them such' (1:58).[57] A desire to 'lighten the chains' of the enslaved may reflect the general liberality of the Dutch settlement, but the colour line remained scrupulously policed, and acts of cross-racial intimacy that threatened an ideology of European racial superiority were deemed strictly taboo. Grant notes a 'moral delicacy' that distinguishes the Albany settlers from other communities in which the African enslaved and their masters are also brought into close intimate contact: their abhorrence for race mixing. Grant can recall, before the arrival of the British army to the region produced many such examples, only one instance of a 'mulatto': the offspring of a liaison between a member of the Schuyler family, an 'idle bachelor' 'weak and defective in capacity', and 'a favourite negroe-woman' (1:59). Their relationship produced a child, known as Chalk, who, though he was educated and allowed to live on the estate (albeit in a cottage far from the main house), remained an outcast and a living reminder of the family's dishonour. In Albany, the mulatto, Grant sums, is deemed 'an ambiguous race, which the law does not acknowledge; and who (if they have any moral sense, must be as much ashamed of their parents as these last are of them) are certainly a dangerous, because degraded part of the community' (1:59). Even as the mulatto's story highlights what Grant describes as a level of devotion and attachment between Dutch families and the Africans they enslaved that is unparalleled and illustrative of the reign of the affections, the story also brings in stark relief the racial hierarchies that regulate intercultural exchange in the colony.[58]

The Location(s) of Memory

A long-time chronicler of the reign of the affections she identified among primitive peoples, Grant took special note of a common aspect of their way of life: the significance they give to the dissemination and conservation of their collective memory, that store of local history, stories, legends, songs and poetry which is the obligation of the older generations of the community to pass down. Grant's authority to convert a collective memory, through her writing, into a more lasting cultural memory, is predicated on her claim to be one who is 'not entirely a stranger nor entirely a native' – a long-time resident of a particular community in a particular locale who is nevertheless able to observe and describe the community objectively, at a distance. But the question remains, which *particular* locality does Grant's transatlantic *Memoirs* seek to memorialise? For admiring American writers who mined her work for their own literary endeavours and who worked to keep the *Memoirs* before the public, the answer was clear: Grant's work represented a wonderfully rich repository of the traditions of colonial New York. The significance that later writers attached to her work as such, amid what they saw as the dramatic transformations of their own time, is reflected in Munsell's editorial agenda in the 1876 edition of the work. In addition to straightening out Grant's mixed-up family genealogies – not an easy task given the Dutch propensity to reuse Christian names in overlapping generations of the same family – Munsell furnishes precise footnotes, maps and photographs that seek to bring into clearer focus some of the localities that Grant references. Grant's own mapping of the area is in keeping with the general aspect of her narrative. Grant herself provides no maps or illustrations, yet she at times can provide a rich description of the locales in which she finds herself. Her description of the interiors of the Schuyler house on their estate along the west bank of the Hudson and of the journey she took with her father down the Mohawk River to the British fort in Oswego, both of which made a lasting impression on her, are notable for their clarity and rich detail. Overall, however, her geography is hazy and fragmented. In supplementing Grant's geography with detailed accounts of the provenance of local estates, and by providing maps and giving precise distances between sites, Munsell seeks to impose a geographical as well as historical clarity upon her narrative. For example, where Grant notes only that, when you arrived at the Schuyler house, the view on the opposite side of the river 'was bounded by steep hills, covered with lofty pines, from which a waterfall descended' (*Memoirs*, vol. 1, p. 143), Munsell supplies two maps of the area, one providing greater detail of the Schuyler estate, and a more precise description of the landscape, by way of historical comparison:

> This waterfall, known as the Wynant's kill, became, half a century ago, the site of the Albany nail works, whose fires light the skies by night, and send up pillars of smoke by day. The island has acquired a considerable altitude since the time of Mrs. Grant's residence there, and is otherwise changed, being in fact two islands, a narrow creek running between them. (*Memoirs*, 1876, pp. 99–100n.)

Munsell, quite literally, maps Grant's narrative, but by also bringing the landscape up to date, so to speak, his editorial commentary provides more than a simple clarification of historical fact. Munsell's reference to man-made and natural changes to the landscape – wrought 'half a century ago' and in his own time – articulates an antiquarian's vision of sedimented accumulation, in which the traces of preceding generations are left on the landscape for local researchers such as himself to note and record. Through reissues such as Munsell's, Grant's memory-text would become repackaged and resold as a guidebook for the historical-minded tourist and an invaluable catalogue of New York *lieux de mémoire*, sites of memory, in the production of local 'heritage'.[59]

The nineteenth-century rise of the *Memoirs* as the unique expression of an American local tradition is, however, perhaps ironic, given that, with the possible exception of the French, no group receives harsher criticism in Grant's account than the Americans, who ultimately would bring about the greatest 'revolutions in manners and opinion' in the colony (2:248). Americans, particularly from New England, have no sense of communal attachment or belonging, though they come to dominate the region in the last chapters of Grant's narrative. Instead, as they flock to 'every unoccupied spot', their 'malignant and envious spirit' and 'their hatred of subordination, and their indifference to the mother country', begin 'to spread like a taint of infection' (2:220). Her utter disdain for these 'very vulgar, insolent, and truly disagreeable people' is inspired in part by the role they played in her own her family misfortunes – unruly tenants from Connecticut precipitated the ultimate loss of her father's landholdings after the Revolution – but Grant's criticism of American settlers also displays her thinking on the link between a historical connection to a particular locale and patriotic feeling, which she finds utterly lacking in Americans. 'We love our country', Grant writes,

> because we honor our ancestors; because it is endeared to us not only by early habit, but by attachments to the spots hallowed by their piety, their heroism, their genius, or their public spirit. We honor it as the scene of noble deeds, the nurse of sages, bards, and heroes. The very aspect and features of this blest asylum of liberty, science, and religion, warm our hearts, and animate our imaginations. (2:310–11)

'Love of country' is, quite literally, grounded, derived from an ancestral attachment to particular landmarks hallowed by acts of piety, heroism, genius and public spirit on the part of one's forebears. This sense of deep belonging and attachment to a particular location or territory seems antithetical to the general anomie produced by the pattern of settlement that Grant witnessed in New York. Who, Grant asks, can apply 'that sacred appellation, "my country"' to a land 'where one cannot travel ten miles, in a stretch, without meeting detachments of different nations, torn from their native soil and first affections, and living aliens in a strange land, where no one seems to form part of an attached connected whole' (2:313). Indeed, revolutionary fervour, as it begins to establish itself in Grant's rural sanctuary, brings with it seeds of discord and chaos. In Grant's account, the coming of the Revolution signals the birth of a new era and new social order in North America – an end to the reign of the affections – but not a new nation. Lacking its own sense of territoriality, its own sense of communal attachment to specific locale, Grant implies, 'America' will not coalesce.

Unable perhaps – even after a span of more than forty years – to recall without some rancour American interlopers who had wrecked her father's own plans to settle in America, Grant casts them as the antithesis of her communal ideal, exemplified by the Mohawk and the Dutch. Yet the territoriality of Grant's own America remains elusive: her own memoryscape remains a loose collection of sites held together by threads of association, of one who left America for good when she was still a young girl and whose entire experience of the region amounted to a succession of temporary sojourns. The nomadic experiences of Grant's early life perhaps helped shape the psychology behind the insider/outsider perspective she adopted in her writing, as one who had to adapt to the strange and new environments in which she found herself, while never quite feeling that she belonged. This perspective, however, seems at odds with her avowal of 'love of country' as a deep and abiding attachment to a particular locality or community. Instead, Grant's retrospection of her early life in the *Memoirs* reveals her own 'amphibiousness' and the mutability of her own attachments, as she travels the Middle Ground of the eighteenth-century clash of empires.

Grant's expressions of isolation and alienation, which are coupled with an innate sense of her own superiority to – and detachment from – those around her, are perhaps to be expected from an only child in a military family, shuttled from one location to another. Long stretches of her narrative pass without description of meeting anyone her own age; much of her time on the Schuyler estate is spent exploring its environs accompanied only by the family's 'negro girl', Marian. It is Grant's father's military career that governs the migrations of her early life, providing the circumstances for her journey as girl of eight down the Mohawk River with her mother, which Grant recalls with pride: '[w]e were, I believe, the first females above the lowest ranks, who had ever penetrated so far into this remote wilderness' (2:106). The military dictates of empire place Grant in the vanguard of British power in America, but her expressions of isolation and detachment highlight the inherent dynamism of imperial expansion, which forestalls a sense of rootedness to a particular place. Grant herself describes the ways in which the nomadic existence of the army, called upon to enforce the empire's interests in an increasingly global theatre of war, instils in its soldiers a permanent wanderlust. Constant movement infects them, she writes, with 'a love of variety in their wandering way of life'. They 'always imagine they are to find some enjoyment in the next quarters that they have not had in this . . .' and so they chafe at having to keep stationary for any extended time (2:202). Oftentimes, the first and most conspicuous representation of Crown authority, the British soldier situates himself not in a space of the past, his homeland, but in a space of the perpetual future of his own imagination, which can never be fully realised.

For her own part, Grant duly recounts the Scottish imprints on her imagination, derived from the earliest influences of an education provided both by her mother and by members of her father's regiment, which, save for its English officers, she wrote, 'might be considered as a Scotch regiment' (2:120). One of the very first books she remembers reading is Blind Harry's *Wallace*, along with 'Welwood's memoirs of the history of England' (2:120); when a friend of her father's from Argyleshire pays them a month-long visit, he brings with him 'the most endearing recollections of Lochawside, and the hills of Morven' (2:275); and her description of North American flora and fauna inspires a digressive reverie on the distinct charms of Nature in each country, 'which endear it to the natives beyond any other', such as 'the *bonny* broom, such as enlivens the narrow vales of Scotland' (1:170). Yet Grant's attachment to a Scottish native soil, as she herself acknowledges, is contingent on the second-hand accounts of those around her – an image of the Scottish landscape can form no part of her actual childhood memory since she had left her birthplace of Glasgow for North America when she was three. Instead, she describes her developing fondness for the Alpine scenes of Scotland as a 'borrowed enthusiasm', which competes with her growing attachment to an alternate set of scenes in her imagination, of her family's future homestead in the colony. When it becomes more apparent that she might make a return visit to Scotland with her father, she describes being 'talked into a wish for revisiting the land of my nativity' (2:280), a place she admits to 'merely lov[ing] upon trust, not having the faintest recollection of it' (2:290). Only after it becomes clear that her discharged father will not be able to settle in the colony does Grant allow her dreams to be filled 'with images of Clydesdale and Tweedale' to assuage her disappointment at having to leave America (2:289).

The national label that for the most part Grant assigns to herself in the *Memoirs* is 'British', which is perhaps most fitting, as it is the imperial dimension of the British union that formed the basis for her father's livelihood. The role played by affective bonds in her work, established through bonds of commercial and social interaction rather than an ancestral attachment to a particular territory, parallels the role played by sympathy in the formation of a British national identity that Juliet Shields and Evan Gottlieb have traced in eighteenth-century Scottish writing.[60] Yet even Grant's sense of being British, like her sense of being Scottish, is contingent upon circumstance and subject to frequent reconsideration. When her father makes plans to leave the army and stay on in the region, for example, Grant begins to fantasise about the future life of rural simplicity in America that awaits her. In the face of these fantasies 'all the violent love', Grant writes, 'which I had persuaded myself to feel for my native Britain, entirely vanished' (2:211–12). This sudden shift in her affections constitutes a return of sorts to a time in Grant's life a few years before, when acculturation into the local Dutch community in which she resided had made her ashamed of her father and of the uniform he wore.[61] Having up to that point spent most of her time in the Dutch-speaking household of the Schuylers, where she acquired a fluency in the language, Grant had seen little of her father before the journey to Oswego, and the initial sight of his 'scarlet coat', she writes, 'which I had been taught to consider as the symbol of wickedness, disgusted me in some degree' (2:107). When her father actually fails to live up to this image of the wayward soldier, the orientation of her affections abruptly reverses itself:

> I found my father did not swear; and . . . to my unspeakable delight, that he prayed. A soldier pray! was it possible? and should I really see my father in heaven! How transporting! By a sudden revolution of opinion I now thought my father the most charming of all beings; and the overflowings of my good will reached to the whole company, because they wore the same colour, and seemed to respect and obey him. (2:107)

Filial and patriotic devotion are intertwined in Grant's mind, but the easy transfer of her affections reflects the transience of her early life, which is perhaps why the eighteen-year-old Grant can remark to a friend, after only being in the Highlands for a few weeks, 'I now think plaids and faltans (fillets) just as becoming as I once did the furs and wampum of the Mohawks, whom I always remember with kindness' (*Letters*, vol. 1, p. 38).

Substitutions and surrogations of affection, of which the adoption practices of the Mohawk and Dutch communities are a conspicuous example, become a distinctive a feature of Grant's sojourn in North America and play no small role in the development of Grant's own subjectivity. In her isolated enclave on the Hudson, the childless Aunt Schuyler found alternative objects for her surrogate affections, in the children of parents who had been lost or who were unable, like the parents of Grant herself, to provide a stable and secure home for their own. Grant's mother, though she accompanied Grant during much of her stay in America and was an important informant for Grant when she later set down to write the *Memoirs*, receives only small mention and plays only a minor part in Grant's recounting of her own intellectual and imaginative development. Instead, it is the relationship with her adopted 'aunt', which the *Memoirs* of course memorialises, that is the centrepiece of Grant's education in the wilderness. Intensified affection for Aunt Schuyler is intertwined in Grant's imagination with renewed affection for her father in the journey down the Mohawk, in one of the key autobiographical passages in her narrative:

> Sitting from morning to night musing in the boat, contemplating my father, who appeared to me a hero and a saint, and thinking of Aunt Schuyler, who filled up my whole mind with the grandeur with which my fancy had invented her; and then having my imagination continually amused with the variety of noble scenes which the beautiful bank of the Mohawk afforded, I am convinced I thought more in that fortnight, that is to say, acquired more ideas, and took on more lasting impressions, then I ever did, in the same space of time, in my life. (2:108–9)

Grant effects an easy substitution of mother figures in her young imagination, as she reorients her affections to both her father and to Aunt Schuyler. This important moment in the development of her thought also illustrates the complex relationship between sensory impression, affection and the imagination in Grant's construction of her younger self, in her own recounting of 'the growth of a poet's mind'. The image of her beloved Aunt Schuyler is intertwined with the image of her father, and her growing admiration of both is catalysed by the sublime landscape as it impresses deeply upon her young imagination. Though this powerful chain of associations had made a deep and lasting imprint on her memory, many aspects of the associative process of Grant's young mind remain obscure, buried under the accumulation of a lifetime's worth of feelings and experiences. Ultimately, despite her claims to the contrary, the *Memoirs* cannot provide a complete or objective picture of Grant's childhood experiences or emotions exactly as she had perceived them untainted by experiences and emotions that came later in her life. Her picture of colonial America must remain clouded and out of focus, a collection of fragmented and idiosyncratic memories rather than objective observation. Even more, as a world remembered rather than recorded, Grant's colonial America threatens to dissipate with each passing year, as those, like her, who carry it in their memories begin to depart from the scene. Grant herself was confronted with the question of who vouches for a remembered past, when there are few left who had borne witness to it. In 1837, the year before she died at eighty-three, Grant wrote a letter to an American friend who had recently read the *Memoirs*. In it, Grant makes a melancholy observation on her own longevity:

> I am glad to find you so captivated with the character of my Aunt Schuyler. You cannot form to yourself a better model of female excellence. I have, in one sense, outlived her too long; that is, I have outlived those who, at the time the book was written, remembered her, and bore testimony to the fidelity of the picture. (*Memoir and Correspondence*, vol. 3, p. 298)

Perhaps ironically, the transatlantic reminiscences of Anne Grant, who never stayed in any one spot for more than a few years until after she was married, furnished depictions of common life in alternate rural domains that resonated with readers on both sides of the Atlantic. Whether of colonial America or the Scottish Highlands, her observations were prized for their vibrancy, their artlessness and their telling detail, and they would be taken up in complementary Scottish and American historiographies of the local. Yet the very circumstances of Grant's life, particularly her early life, provide no single picture of nation, region or community, but are instead illustrative of the peculiar conditions of her transperipheral world, a world of ceaseless movement through unfamiliar terrains inhabited by strange peoples, a world of isolation and alienation but also one of small communities in which she found safety, affection and some measure of belonging.[62] Grant's depiction of an Atlantic world in flux thus takes its position within the memorialising turn in Scottish Romantic historiography as the 'migrant' retrospection of the daughter of a Scottish soldier in the service of the British Empire, a retrospection that ultimately resists the consolidation of a collective cultural memory.

Notes

1. Grant, 'Letters Concerning Highland Affairs', p. 254. Subsequent references to this work are given in abbreviated form in the body of the text, or by page number alone where unambiguous.
2. Grant pronounced her own family's views on the Jacobites and their cause as mixed. In a letter to her friend George Thomson, Grant characterised her army officer father as the 'bluest' of 'all whigs', who 'taught me to look up to the reigning family as somewhat sublime and celestial'. Though she never knew her mother to express any political views, she 'feelingly lamented the ruin of the families she was connected with, and melted my heart with sad tales of the tragical fate of many of her Stuart relations' (*Essays*, vol. 2, p. 282).
3. Perkins, *Women Writers*, pp. 159, 142. *Poems on Various Subjects* was sold by subscription. Grant managed to gather nearly 2,300 subscribers for her poems, which Pam Perkins has described as 'an extraordinary number under any circumstances' (Ibid. p. 159). Of the works with over 1,000 subscribers in the eighteenth century listed by P. J. Wallis, only three attracted more subscribers than did Grant's. Burn's *Poems Chiefly in the Scottish Dialect*, for example, sold 2,883 copies to 1,536 subscribers.
4. Scott, *Waverley*, p. 364.
5. For example, Devine in *Clanship to Crofter's War* includes Grant in his list of prominent prose writers who 'presented idealised images of heroic Highlanders' in the Romantic era (91). Womack argues Grant belongs to group of writers that included Joanna Baillie, Jane Porter, Mary Brunton and Christian Isobel Johnstone who constructed a 'woman's Highlands'. Perkins argues that in Grant's work 'the Highlands are not so much a static or deliberately aestheticised "other" against which the success (or failures) of a contemporary metropolitan life can be measured as they are a direct source of her own literary and cultural authority' (*Women Writers*, pp. 189–90). Shields, in *Sentimental Literature and Anglo-Scottish Identity*, argues that, in her *Essays*, Grant reconfigures Highland society, making it available for use in a British national imaginary. On the other hand, Perkins in 'Paradises Lost', while acknowledging Grant's transatlantic experiences and Highland

writing, situates *Memoirs* within a distinctly American literary tradition of the pastoral.
6. See Chandler, *England in 1819*, pp. 127–51.
7. For a recent historical account that situates the Seven Years War within a larger context of a global clash of empires, see Anderson, *The Crucible of War*. See also White, *The Middle Ground*; and Axtell, *The Invasion Within*.
8. Grant's conversation was frequently praised by commentators on Edinburgh literary society. In *Peter's Letters to His Kinsfolk*, Lockhart described her character as a departure from the typical 'Blue-Stocking'. Grant is described as plain, modest and unassuming by his narrator, who derived 'sound and rational enjoyment' from his conversation with 'this excellent person' (1:309–10). Lockhart's sentiments were echoed by Cockburn, who described her as 'not too blue', and 'having very considerable intellect, great spirit, and the warmest benevolence . . . Both she and Mrs. Hamilton were remarkable for the success of their literary conversational gatherings' (*Memorials*, pp. 268–9). Scott was more critical, at least in private, describing her in his *Journal* as 'proud as a Highland woman, vain as a poetess, and absurd as a Bluestocking' (21). The American William Tudor remarked on the 'uncommon vivacity' of Grant's conversation, while complaining of its limited scope: 'she has only three subjects, the life and adventures of Mrs. Anne Grant of Laggan, the beautiful lochs, vales, &c. of the Highlands, and the greatness of the British nation. These dishes, the way she serves them up, are very charming the first four or five weeks. But you know, that the emperour Domitian said, that you can't eat lark's tongues forever' ('Letters from Edinburgh', p. 194). For a study of Bluestocking society in the Romantic era, see Rendall, 'Bluestockings and Reviewers'.
9. Grant, *Letters*, vol. 1, p. 81. Subsequent references to this work are given in abbreviated form in the body of the text, or by volume and page number alone where unambiguous. The McCue and Perkins 2017 edition, which is based on the second edition, is definitive. *Letters from the Mountains* forms the first three volumes of this edition. Subsequent references to this work are given in abbreviated form in the body of the text, or by volume and page number alone where unambiguous.
10. For the productive tension between private and public in Grant's writing, see Perkins, 'Anne Grant and the Professionalization of Privacy'. Grant herself stated she was financially compelled into publishing her writing after she was left with eight children to care for after the death of her husband in 1801. Her predicament prompted a sympathetic response and interest in her private life among contemporary readers, though recent studies have cast doubt on her claim she was not

interested in publication until after her husband's death. See Perkins, *Women Writers*; and Hammerschmidt, 'Social Authorship and the Mediation of Memory'.
11. Thomson, Letter to Anne Grant, August 1811, University of Edinburgh Library La.II.357, ff. 202–3.
12. Ferris, 'Translation from the Borders', p. 203.
13. For studies of women and late eighteenth-century and Romantic history writing, see DeLucia, *A Feminine Enlightenment*; and Looser, *British Women Writers and the Writing of History*. See also Phillips, *Society and Sentiment*; Perkins, *Women Writers*, pp. 168–206, and 'Grant: Gender, Genre, and Cultural Analysis'.
14. Phillips, *Society and Sentiment*, p. 173.
15. Ibid. pp. 131–46, 259–94.
16. Ibid. p. 173.
17. Ibid.
18. Grant, *Memoirs*, vol. 1, p. 7. All subsequent references to this work are to the 1808 edition unless otherwise stated and are given in abbreviated form in the body of the text, or by volume and page number alone where unambiguous.
19. Grant, *Essays*, vol. 1, pp. iii–iv. Subsequent references to this work are given in abbreviated form in the body of the text, or by volume and page number alone where unambiguous.
20. As Jeffrey observed in his 1811 review of the *Essays* in the *Edinburgh Review*, 'To illustrate the character and manners of men in remote situations, and in the earlier stages of civilization, may be said to be the object of all her writings . . .' (482).
21. Stewart, *Biographical Memoirs*, p. 34.
22. Ibid.
23. Quoted in a letter to Thomson reprinted in the *Essays* (2:337).
24. McNeil, *Scotland, Britain, Empire*, pp. 150–62.
25. For studies on Scottish Enlightenment theories of the primitive, particularly the Scottish Highlander example, see Hopfl, 'From Savage to Scotsman'.
26. Phillips, *Society and Sentiment*, p. 320.
27. Ibid. p. 205.
28. Grant, *Memoir and Correspondence*, vol. 1, p. 10. Subsequent references to this work are given in abbreviated form in the body of the text, or by volume and page number alone where unambiguous. Grant would begin a memoir of her own life in 1825, but it remained incomplete and unpublished at her death. Her son John Peter Grant would publish it in 1844 as part of *Memoir and Correspondence*. The memoir opens with a statement that explains much of Grant's writing career: 'I

began to live . . . to the purposes of feeling, observation, and recollection, much earlier than children usually do' (1).

29. Quoted in 'Obituary – Mrs. Grant, of Laggan', p. 99. Works by Scottish writers who made use of Grant's Highland material include Stewart's 1822 *Sketches of the Character, Manners, and Present State of the Highlanders of Scotland* and Johnstone's 1815 novel *Clan-Albin*. For a recent historical account that draws on her transatlantic experiences, see Calloway, *White People, Indians, and Highlanders*, pp. 9–10.

30. For examples of historical and antiquarian writing that made use of the *Memoirs*, see, for example, Munsell's multivolume *Annals of Albany* (e.g., vol. 2, pp. 53–60 and vol. 6, pp. 295–301). An article on 'The Aunt Schuyler House' that was originally featured in the *New York Courier and Enquirer* in 1855 describes the *Memoirs* as 'the best sketch of the society of New York, and its local history for the stirring period between the French and the Revolutionary War' (*Annals of Albany*, vol. 6, p. 295). Excerpts from the *Memoirs* also feature in the section on 'Primitive Colonial Life' in Russell, *New-York Class-Book: Comprising Outlines of the Geography and History Of New York . . . Arranged as a Reading Book for Schools* (pp. 509–46). Grant's girlhood in America has furnished material for books written for children and young adults. Her story, the only one whose subject is not male, is featured in 'A Scotch Lassie in America' in a collection of tales by Hope, and, more recently, in Bobbé, *The New World Journey of Anne MacVicar*. For historical fiction that made use of the *Memoirs* as source material, see note 45 below.

31. Hinderaker, *The Two Hendricks*, p. 9.

32. Not until 1996 did genealogical research by Sivertsen in *Turtles, Wolves, and Bears* establish that Hendrick was two different men. See also Snow, 'Searching for Hendrick'. Snow traces the origins of the error to Grant (whom he identifies as Julia). For an overview of the unraveling of the two Hendricks error, see Hinderaker, *The Two Hendricks*, p. 303, n. 2.

33. Hinderaker, *The Two Hendricks*, p. 281.

34. Grant makes one passing reference to relying on information provided by others in the *Memoirs* itself, describing her account of the early history of the colony as 'a sketch, that appears to my recollection (aided by subsequent conversations with my fellow travelers) . . .' (1:117). Grant's letters, however, give reference to meeting visitors from America, some of whom were related to the Schuylers, whom she mined for information. For example, she describes meeting a 'Mrs. Lowe' while working on the *Memoirs*, who was Aunt Schuyler's niece: 'such light, such recollections, such clear and authentic information, such

an affectionate meeting, and affecting retrospections!' (*Memoir and Correspondence*, vol. 1, p. 144). Grant's account of the customs of Algonquian peoples of the region is indebted to Colden's *History of the Five Indian Nations of Canada*, which first appeared in London in 1747 and in subsequent editions throughout the eighteenth and early nineteenth centuries. Colden, who likened Algonquian people to the ancient Romans, provides an example of native oration, a speech made by a figure whom Colden identified as 'one of the chief sachems of the Onandoga's' (65). Grant quoted from this speech in the *Memoirs*. Another possible written source, which she mentions in her letters, is La Rochefoucault Liancourt's *Travels through the United States of North America*, an English translation of which was published in 1800. In a letter dated 21 May 1808, when Grant was working on the *Memoirs*, her friend the historian George Chalmers provided a list of information relating to British military movements during the Seven Years War, in response to her queries (Letter to Anne Grant).

35. [Norton], 'Review *of Memoir and Correspondence of Mrs. Grant of Laggan*', p. 131.
36. O'Donnell, 'Introduction', p. 14.
37. Jeffrey, in his review of the *Memoirs of Lady Fanshawe* in the *Edinburgh Review* (quoted in Phillips, *Society and Sentiment*, p. 295).
38. Grant writes on the success of the *Memoirs* in a letter to her son Duncan in May 1809: 'the whole impression of fifteen hundred copies was sold in three months, and the second edition is now printed, and selling rapidly, I believe' (*Memoir and Correspondence*, 1:212).
39. Later editions of Ossian in the late eighteenth century had included Macpherson's own extensive notes and commentary on the poetry and manners of the ancient Caledonians, as well as Blair's *Critical Dissertation on the Poems of Ossian*, in which Blair argues that the epic verses of the bard exemplify the human imagination in its most unbridled and unsophisticated state. As Stafford has shown in *The Sublime Savage*, Macpherson was also influenced by his courses at the University of Aberdeen where he was introduced to the thinking of Thomas Reid and Thomas Blackwell. Macpherson had himself been influenced by Blair – who would be the prime instigator for Macpherson's search in the Highlands for more Ossianic material – and by other Scottish Enlightenment patrons, such as John Home and Adam Ferguson.
40. In a letter to her friend, Grant describes the attraction of 'leisure and quietness' at the Legard estate, which she hopes will bring a respite from crowded distracting household in Stirling: I 'shall . . . avoid what is always very severe on my nervous frame, the bustle and confusion that so large a family, cooped together in a small house, occasion in

winter, when the younger members cannot go out to play. My room has the nursery above it, and the kitchen below it, and my nerves are torn to pieces with noise and running out and in; the only other habitable room is occupied by my mother' (*Memoir and Correspondence*, 1:118).

41. Grant, *Poems on Various Subjects*, p. 353. Grant's defence appears as a letter prefatory to her translations of some Gaelic poetry, 'to Robert Arbuthnot'. The piece was appended to the third volume of the sixth edition of *Letters from the Mountains* as an 'Essay on the Authenticity of the Poems of Ossian by Mrs. Grant of Laggan', where it is dated October 1802.
42. For a study of Scottish Enlightenment theories of association and its significance for Romantic-era theories of the operations of memory, see Craig, *Associationism and the Literary Imagination*.
43. For Western discourse on vanishing human races, see Brantlinger, *Dark Vanishings*. For a discussion of the Romantic-era shift in the orientation of nostalgia produced by writing on Highland dispossession and displacement, see Shields, 'Highland Emigration and the Transformation of Nostalgia in Romantic Poetry'. See also Daly, '"Return No More"'. For 'vanishing' Indians, see Dippie, *The Vanishing American*; and Bergland, *The National Uncanny*.
44. A citizen of Albany noted the persistence of Dutch culture in the city, even two decades after the Revolution: 'Albany was indeed Dutch, in all its moods and tenses; thoroughly and inveterately Dutch. The buildings were Dutch – Dutch in style, in position, attitude and aspect. The people were Dutch, the horses were Dutch, and even the dogs were Dutch' (Munsell, *Annals of Albany*, vol. 10, p. 193).
45. Paulding, who was a close friend of Irving, acknowledged his direct debt to the *Memoirs*, admitting the idea of the novel was conceived upon reading Grant's work, which he characterised in the novel's advertisement as 'one of the finest sketches of early American manners ever drawn' (*The Dutchman's Fireside*, vol. 1, p. 3). Cooper was less forthcoming about his borrowings from Grant, but his daughter Susan, who edited later editions of his work, was more explicit in recognising the influences of the *Memoirs* in *Satanstoe*, and in other works where Cooper may have drawn upon Grant's depictions of Indian manners. Dondore, in 'The Debt of Two Dyed-in-the-Wool Americans to Mrs. Grant's *Memoirs*', provides a side-by-side comparison of the *Memoirs* and *Satanstoe*, concluding that twenty-one of Cooper's thirty chapters contain examples drawn from Grant's account. For study of the ways in which *Memoirs* presents an alternative to the pastoral in early nineteenth-century American literature, see Perkins, 'Paradises Lost'.

46. After the Revolution, Grant's father lost his claim to lands near Lake Champlain that had been granted to him by the Crown after the Seven Years War, forcing him to abandon his plans to settle in the colony.
47. For a more detailed discussion of Selkirk's Highland settlement schemes, see Chapter 3.
48. Pratt, *Imperial Eyes*, p. 7.
49. See *The Middle Ground*. See also Axtell, *The Invasion Within*. Axtell, like White, resists a teleological reading of eighteenth-century Indian/European contestation in which the ultimate 'winner' is already known.
50. White, *The Middle Ground*, p. x.
51. Johnson appears in Paulding's *The Dutchman's Fireside* and in Cooper's *The Last of the Mohicans*.
52. Though many such return of captives were recorded in the eighteenth century, there seems to be no record of such a return taking place in Albany as part of peace negotiation after Pontiac's Rebellion. Only one such return of captives seems to have been recorded as taking place after the uprising, and the return occurred much farther west, at Fort Pitt, under the authority of Colonel Henry Bouquet after the defeat of Pontiac's allies in the Ohio Valley in late 1764. This return became one of the best known; it was detailed in William Smith's 1766 *Historical Account* of Bouquet's expedition against the Ohio Indians, which was published in both Philadelphia and London, and which featured an illustration of *The Indians Delivering Up the English Captives to Colonel Bouquet* by Benjamin West. It is likely that Grant saw many gatherings of Mohawks in Albany since General John Bradstreet and Philip Schuyler, Aunt Schuyler's great-nephew, often hosted Iroquois delegations at Albany. It is also likely that Aunt Schuyler took an interest in Mohawk politics (Funiciello, personal communication). Grant's recounting of the Albany captives return, however, may be another case of her conflating an illustration of an event with the actual experience of the event. For a detailed account of the Bouquet expedition and Smith's narrative, see Steele, *Setting All the Captives Free*.
53. See, for example, Burnham, *Captivity and Sentiment*, and 'The Journey Between'; Castiglia, *Bound and Determined*; Ebersole, *Captured by Texts*; Marienstras, 'White Children in Captivity Narratives'; and Turner-Strong, *Captive Selves, Captivating Others*.
54. For recent historical accounts of captives taking, see Axtell, *The Invasion Within*, pp. 302–37; Steele, *Setting All the Captives Free*; and Sayre, *Les Sauvages Américains*. The French explorer Joseph-Francois Lafitau described the practice of Indian adoption, or 'requickening': 'If the captive is a man who requickens an Ancient, a man of consequence, he becomes important himself and has authority in the village if he can

sustain by his own personal merit the name which he takes' (quoted in Sayre, *Les Sauvages Américains*, p. 287).
55. More recent studies have rethought the binary structure of eighteenth-century captivity narratives, emphasising their transcultural work in exposing readers to, as Burnham writes, 'alternative cultural paradigms' of native captors (*Captivity and Sentiment*, p. 3). See also Burnham, 'The Journey Between'; and Castiglia, *Bound and Determined*.
56. For a contemporary historical account of enslavement in colonial New York, see McManus, *A History of Negro Slavery in New York*. An 1836 review of the *Memoirs* in *The Southern Literary Messenger* found that Grant's picture of benign treatment of the enslaved 'appl[ies] with singular accuracy to the present state of things in Virginia' (511). The review quotes Grant's account at some length but leaves out entirely her description of Dutch racial attitudes.
57. Underscoring the power of Dutch racism in her account, Grant reports that Indian attitudes were often aligned with those of Europeans. She describes the reaction of those Indians who took up summer residence on the grounds of the Schuyler family. '[T]hough [the Indians] saw the negroes in every respectable family not only treated with humanity, but cherished with parental kindness, they always regarded them with contempt and dislike, as an inferior race, and would have no communication with them' (1:125).
58. Though Grant situates her commentary on enslavement in New York as scrupulously objective, asking her reader that she 'not be detested as an advocate for slavery', Grant's views on slavery in later life suggest she was closer on the political spectrum to apologists for slavery than to abolitionists. Writing to an American friend in 1835, Grant comments on the transatlantic mission of a Glasgow abolition society: 'there is a set of zealous ladies in Glasgow whose prudence and humanity do not seem equal to their piety, who have let loose their anti-slavery agents among you, not warned by the mischief that has resulted both to masters and slaves in the West Indies, from their interference. There seems a passion prevalent just now for gathering fruit before it is ripe. Everything that is permanently good is brought about by a gradual process; and a rash fool may kindle a fire that fifty wise people cannot extinguish. These reformers have certainly set a dangerous stone a-rolling – a freedom bordering on license has been brought into view that is rather alarming' (*Memoir and Correspondence*, vol. 3, p. 275).
59. The *Memoirs*' description of various locales features in local historical accounts. See, for example, the New York State Museum's Online Exhibition on 'The People of Colonial Albany', which features web

pages on Anne Grant, the *Memoirs*, and many of the figures and locations she mentions. The Schuyler House on the Hudson River, where Grant spent many of her summers, burned down in 1962 but is now the site of a cultural park ('Schuyler Flatts').

60. See Gottlieb, *Feeling British*; and Shields, *Sentimental Literature and Anglo-Scottish Identity*. See also Ellison, *Cato's Tears and the Making of Anglo-American Emotion*.

61. For an account of eighteenth-century British–Dutch antagonism, which were exacerbated during the Seven Years War, see Ellis, 'Yankee-Dutch Confrontation in the Albany Area'. Ellis uses the *Memoirs* as source material but erroneously labels Grant the Schuyler family governess. See also Roeber, '"The origin of whatever is not English among us"'.

62. Grant never returned to America, but also expressed no interest in doing so, at least in early adulthood. Looking back some twenty years after she had left, Grant wrote to a friend that her life in North America could not be replicated, because she herself had changed too much. Experience had made her too refined to return to a life that once was (*Letters*, vol. 3, p. 6).

Chapter 3

Indigenous Elsewhere: Lord Selkirk and Native Memory and Resettlement

Landscapes of Memory and Forgetting

In 'Scotchman's Return', the Canadian writer Hugh MacLennan recalls a drive he took high into the Highlands in summer. Taking note of the vast emptiness of the landscape he writes:

> I was in the true north of Scotland among the sheep, the heather, the whin, the mists and the homes of the vanished races. Such emptiness I never saw in Canada before I went to Mackenzie River later in the same summer. But this Highland emptiness, only a few hundred miles above the massed population of England, is a far different thing from the emptiness of our own Northwest Territories. Above the sixtieth parallel in Canada you find that nobody but God has ever been there before you, but in a deserted Highland glen you feel that everyone who ever mattered is dead and gone. Those glens are the most hauntingly lovely sights I have ever seen: they are vaster, more moving, more truly vacated than the southern abbeys ruined by Henry VIII. They are haunted by the lost loves and passions of a thousand years.[1]

'Everyone who mattered is dead and gone' – writing in 1960, MacLennan evokes the legacy of a transatlantic history that links two places, two continents and two cultures. This legacy bears in part the story of the Highland diaspora, of a region emptied out – cleared – of both its native inhabitants and its symbolic and social meaning. The Highlands are an empty landscape of a diasporic memory, haunted by the ghostly presences of people who once belonged there but who were long ago exiled – elsewhere – like MacLennan's own great-grandfather, who had sailed to Nova Scotia from Kintail more than a hundred years before. For MacLennan, the Highlands can be comprehended only through an awareness of what once was. At the same time, his evocation of a primordial Canadian landscape, with its complete absence of human presences – ghostly or otherwise – which so distinguishes it in his mind from the Highland landscape, amounts to a wholesale 'forgetting', an erasure of the First Nations and Inuit peoples who had occupied the land long before his Highland ancestors arrived. MacLennan's transatlantic landscapes then could be said to carry both the present absences of a Scottish diaspora and the absent presences of dispossessed native peoples, as the collective identity of both peoples becomes rooted elsewhere, through their memory of ancestral lands they no longer occupy.

The troubled legacy of Highland dispossession and transatlantic emigration to the New World that MacLennan's description evokes has long been a crucial element in the narrative of Canada's formation as a settler nation. Only recently has this legacy become part of the transatlantic historiography of colonised peoples that often takes the form of tragic irony, as it describes the migration of a set of people dispossessed in one part of the British Atlantic who in turn became complicit in the displacement and dispossession of another set of people in a different part.[2] In this new historiography, the once discrete categories of 'Clearance' and 'Removal' name variations of a phenomenon of transatlantic dispossession taking place in the early nineteenth century in the context of Anglo-colonial expansion and settlement. An immense mobilisation of capital, as John C. Weaver and other historians have described, produced an acceleration of land acquisition and conversion, tying together vast acreages of food-exporting 'neo-Europes' to distant markets throughout the world.[3] This 'great land rush', as Weaver terms it, was underpinned by a systematic consolidation of the idea of private property and the concomitant assumption that land was 'an article to be measured, allocated, traded, and', above all, 'improved' in the name of modernisation. 'Improvement', Weaver writes, 'and its synonyms and antonyms – terms such as betterment, advancement; negligence and waste – were intrinsic to formal and informal practices of taking and allocating land'.[4] This symbolic and material reordering of land under the sign of global capitalism led to the disruption or outright destruction of traditional social and land relations and rationalised the removal of people from lands they claimed and occupied, resulting in the widespread expulsion of peoples and communities. This expulsion in turn prompted a constant uprooting and migration, both across the great ocean but also within regions that comprised the British Atlantic.

Scots were in a unique position to shape not only this symbolic and material reordering of land but to chart its affects within local communities, both as formulators of a transatlantic policy of agricultural improvement and as witnesses to an unprecedented outmigration of the population, especially from the rural Highlands. The influential and innovative intellectual culture of early nineteenth-century post-Enlightenment Edinburgh incubated a vibrant and often contentious combined enquiry on the fate of the Highlands. The collective disruptions that attended the transformation in land relations in the Highlands prompted an intense inquiry into native understanding of land and land rights that also helped to shape attitudes towards tribal peoples and their lands in Canada and the United States. At the core of this enquiry were questions about the very nature of 'nativeness', of belonging and attachment to land. What is the relation between 'the land' and the collective identity of a people who occupy it? What happens to this collective identity when the land becomes a memory, when the people no longer occupy the land they are 'native' to?

This chapter examines the ways in which Scottish ideas on emigration and settlement at the dawn of the great land rush provide a compelling instance of the ways in which a discourse and debate on 'problem' peoples removed or cleared from lands contributed to the emergence of a distinctive geocultural category, the 'aborigine', which identified a particular association between communal identity, memory and land claim deemed outside of – or counter to – the modernising impetus of the Anglo world. My discussion will focus on the writings of one of the most preeminent voices in the Highland debate: Scottish peer and transatlantic landowner Thomas Douglas, 5th Earl of Selkirk, whose 1805 *Observations on the Present State of the Highlands of Scotland* represented a dramatic rethinking on Highland emigration and settlement. Before publication of Selkirk's *Observations*, the prevailing assumption was that Highland emigration ought to be discouraged, as it was detrimental to the well-being of both the region and to Britain as a whole. Selkirk, however, not only saw widespread emigration as the inevitable by-product of the economic transformation of the region, but actively encouraged it, through the establishment of special enclaves in British North America. These 'National Settlements', as he termed them, would allow the preservation of a distinctive way of life that had been passed down from one generation to another for centuries but that was deemed no longer tenable in the Highlands itself, while also serving as a bulwark for British interest in the New World. Through the several settlement schemes that he realised in the early nineteenth century – most ambitiously, in the Red River area of present-day Manitoba – Selkirk paved the way for government-assisted emigration programmes later in the century and established a transatlantic conduit for Highland settlers, for which he is recognised as a founding figure in the history of Canadian settlement.

Selkirk's myriad ideas and plans for solving the problem of displacement and dispossession eventually would come to dominate the emigration debate and, in the process, work to consolidate a transatlantic national and imperial imaginative geography, as they established assumptions about 'aboriginal' land relations that would set the terms for government-inspired polices governing indigenous dispossession, displacement, and resettlement in the nineteenth century. Through the many proposals, prospectuses, position papers and essays he produced on the subject of Highland emigration and settlement, Selkirk on the one hand laid claim to the ongoing value of an aboriginal way of life – and the ancestral memory that sustained it – and sought to preserve that way of life in the modern world. On the other hand, his concern for the continued viability of the aborigine was framed within a broader discourse of national or imperial improvement, which ultimately granted to the state the power and authority to determine the material and territorial conditions for aboriginal preservation. The aborigine's distinctive language traditions, beliefs and, above all, deep attachment to 'the land' would be allowed to live on in the modern world – but elsewhere.

Highland Dispossession and Discontent: Scotland's Problem Aborigine

The discursive formation of the Highland 'aborigine' in anglophone writing emerges from the crucible of resistance to dispossession and displacement in the region, which is particularly illustrated in accounts of those who would be directly implicated in the Highland Clearances. In a May 1816 report James Loch, manager of the vast landholdings of the Countess of Sutherland, described some of the recent practical difficulties and costs associated with ongoing improvements on the estate. In this report, Loch inserted a note by his factor Patrick Sellar, whose name would become a byword for the exploitation and cruelty of the Clearances, in historical accounts and in the historical memory of Gaels on both sides of the Atlantic.[5] Sellar had first come to the estate several years before 1816, charged with executing changes that Loch had drawn up: to remove people from their lands in the interior of the estate and to bring them to the coasts, 'in lotts under the size of three arable acres, sufficient for the maintenance of an industrious family, but pinched enough to cause them to turn their attention to the fishing'.[6] Sellar, a sheep farmer himself who eventually settled on Sutherland lands cleared of their previous tenants, had duly set out in early February 1813 to remove about seventy families from their holdings in the parish of Kildonan. Many of these families, however, refused to leave, protesting that the land they held in common was theirs, by what later observers would identify as a belief in the 'inherited inalienable title to security of tenure in their possessions, while rent and service are duly rendered'.[7] Kildonan tenants resisted efforts to displace them from their lands, petitioning and assembling to confront their evictors and threatening, it was reported, to 'drive the Sheeps out of the country'.[8] As instances of such protest and resistance had led to vandalism and the destruction of livestock and property in the Highlands, the local sheriff depute feared a popular uprising and sent troops into the district, as the people themselves sent petitions to the countess and to the Prince Regent in London asking for just restoration of their lands.[9] At the same time, some families looked to offers of emigration, and these displaced Kildonan people would form the first party of colonists bound for Selkirk's planned Red River Settlement.[10]

Sellar in his note to Loch attempts to make sense of the persistent recalcitrance he encountered on the part of Sutherland tenants, who refused to relinquish their lands to make way for planned sheepwalks. He does this by way of what he saw as a useful cross-cultural comparison, between the condition of the Gaels of Scotland and that of the Indians of North America. With reference to the principles set forth on the subject by 'a Gentleman of great worth and erudition', Adam Smith in *The Wealth of Nations*, Sellar recounts how local dependence on smuggling and the illicit whisky trade had debased their whole way of life, producing a total 'absence of every principle of truth and candour', among the 'several hundred thousand Souls' of the Highlands, who are, he writes:

> the sad remnant of a people who once covered a great part of Europe . . . Their obstinate adherence to the barbarous jargon of the times when Europe *was possessed by Savages*, their *rejection* of any of the several languages now used in Europe, and which being Sprung or at least improved from those of the greatest nations of antiquity, carry with them the collected wisdom of all ages, and have raised their possessors to the most astonishing pitch of *eminence* and *power* – Their seclusion, I say, from this grand fund of knowledge places them, with relation to the enlightened nations of Europe in a position not very different from that betwixt the American Colonists and the Aborigines of that Country. The one are the Aborigines of Britain shut out from the general stream of knowledge and cultivation, flowing in upon the Commonwealth of Europe from the remotest fountain of antiquity. The other are the Aborigines of America equally shut out from this stream . . .[11]

Sellar's use of the term 'Aborigines' to describe both the people who resisted removal on the Sutherland estates and unspecified tribal people coming under colonial control in North America signals, as his self-proscribed debt to Smith implies, an important refinement in the meaning of the term that is testament to dispossession in the context of a global process of world-system expansion and land appropriation taking place under the sign of 'modernisation'. First coined at the end of seventeenth century to distinguish the earliest inhabitants of a land from invading outsiders, 'aborigine' achieved common currency in the conjectural historiography of the Scottish Enlightenment 'Science of Man' as it became synonymous with 'rude nations' encountered around the globe.[12] By the second decade of the nineteenth century, Sellar, employing the comparative methodology of historians like Ferguson, Kames and Dugald Stewart, can rationalise forced eviction of local occupiers of the land by identifying them as aborigines – by which he names a complex but universalised set of social practices and land relations that are untenable in modern commercial society. In the increasingly global reach of a culture of imperial modernity, Scottish Highlanders and other peoples in various locales around the world shared a common fate of domination and land dispossession. The 'aborigine' takes shape in the colonial imagination as a state of incongruity between homeland and residence, of belonging to, and identification with, a 'native' space the aborigine can no longer lay claim to. 'Shut out from the general stream of knowledge and cultivation', Highland aborigines, like their North American counterparts, stand in particular relation not only to space but to time, which placed them outside the stream of progress that was spreading over the remotest corners of the nation and, ultimately, the globe. The anachronistic relation of Scottish and Indian aborigines to the lands they occupied also provides the rationalisation of their discontent, as they struggle against the relentless force of modernisation that would engulf them. As a traditional relation to the land gives way, so must a way of life that is underpinned by that relation. To be an aborigine in the discourse of imperial modernity is to be confronted with the choice of assimilation or extinction, but, regardless of the outcome, the land must be taken.[13]

Land, People and the Wealth of Nations

Selkirk's ideas on Highland emigration combined an abiding sympathy towards the plight of the Gaelic tenantry with the intellectual assumptions of his upbringing and his late Enlightenment Edinburgh education: as a student at the University of Edinburgh, Selkirk had studied under the tutelage of Dugald Stewart and was a member of the Speculative Society, a debating club whose membership had also included Walter Scott, Francis Jeffrey, Henry Cockburn, Henry Brougham, Francis Horner and James Loch.[14] Like those who managed the Sutherland estate, Selkirk had no 'immediate or local connexion with the Highlands' but a keen academic interest in Highland society in his youth had led him, he writes, 'to take a warm interest of his countrymen in that part of the kingdom'.[15] His experience and travels in both the Highlands and in North America made him an acute observer of changes in land use, and his facility in Gaelic allowed him to speak with singular authority on the social and economic upheavals that were transforming the physical and cultural landscape of the Highlands. At the same time, Selkirk's description of this transformation, like those of Loch, Sellar and a host of others on the subject, was informed by Scottish philosophical history and political economy theories in the work of writers such as Lord Kames, James Steuart,

James Anderson, John Knox and particularly Adam Smith. Smith's *The Wealth of Nations*, which emerged as dominant point of reference in the Highland land debate of the late eighteenth and early nineteenth centuries, provided the conceptual framework for Selkirk to identify and map the change in particular notions of land and land use within a universal history of progress and the achievement of national prosperity.

Selkirk, like many others, saw disruption and discontent in the Highlands as an outgrowth of the inevitable processes of modernisation and the consolidation of land as private property, which Smith had identified as a key aspect in the emergence of agriculture, the third stage in his outline of human progress. In turn, the development of a system of laws to safeguard the rights of property owners – as the value of land became derived from its productivity, its ability to provide an agricultural yield that could be bought and sold at market – was for Smith a definitive feature of the final stage, modern commercial society.[16] For Selkirk, this consolidation of land was the root cause of the increasing dissonance in the Highlands between the local people and their titular chiefs. In previous generations, he writes, the value of land was 'to be reckoned not by the rent it produced, but by the men whom it could send into the field' (*Observations*, p. 13). The chief had derived his social status from the number of clansmen he could raise in times of conflict, which established 'an intimate connexion of the chief with his people', as 'their daily intercourse, the daily dependency they had on each other for immediate safety, the dangers they shared, were all naturally calculated to produce a great degree of mutual sympathy and affection' (19). As part of this reciprocal arrangement, Selkirk writes, '[a]ccustomed to transmit their possessions from father to son, as if they had been their property, the people seem to have thought, that as long as they paid the old and accustomed rent, and performed the usual services, their possessions were their own by legal right' (22). Anne Grant, perhaps an even more acute observer on life in the Highlands than Selkirk, summarised the integral role that land tenure performed in defining traditional communities scattered throughout the Highlands. There, she writes:

> [E]very inch of ground was occupied by heads of families, who were perhaps the tenth generation on same spot, and held their lands from a patriarchal chief, to whom and his ancestors they and their forefathers

has performed services the most important. One of these tenants could not be removed to make room for a stranger without giving mortal offence to the whole tribe. Their ideas of morality, as well as of attachment, being outraged by a such proceeding. Thus, though a stranger passing through the country or merely visiting it, was treated with the most liberal hospitality, if he attempted to settle there, he had nothing but prejudice and persecution to expect . . . .[17]

In their accounts of Highland land tenure, both Selkirk and Grant seem to adumbrate the concept of *dùthchas*, a term which has no direct correspondence to any word in English, but which shares etymological roots with *dùthiach* – land or territory. *Dùthchas*, John MacInnes writes, conveys 'ancestral land or family land; it is also family tradition; and equally, it is the heredity qualities of an individual'.[18] To speak of one's *dùthchas*, writes Michael Newton, is to speak of 'one's set of hereditary qualities, one's culture, and one's homeland'.[19] More than a system of land tenure, *dùthchas* is a powerful cultural matrix in which collective identity, ancestral memory, and communal rights to land are interwoven: the land belongs to the community, but the community also belongs to the land. Though the idea of private property, as R. A. Dodgshon has shown, had already transformed the landscape of Gaelic Scotland by the eighteenth century, the notion of *dùthchas*, rooted in the Gaelic oral tradition, remained a powerful ideal among Highland tenantry, and it would form the basis for resistance to eviction and to a new a generation of chiefs 'who came forward', Selkirk writes, 'and feeling more remotely the influence of antient connexions with their dependents, were not inclined to sacrifice for a shadow the substantial advantage of a productive property' (*Observations*, p. 23).[20] These new men, 'reduced to the situation of any other proprietors' (21), indexed the value of their land not to the maximum number of people it could support but to the minimum number required to bring it into maximum commercial productivity.

In Selkirk's account, the introduction of new landed class in the Highlands represents a disavowal of the ancestral memory of reciprocal obligation between the clan chief and his people, as 'men educated under different circumstances' than those of previous generations brought new ideologies and cartographies into the Highlands, the emergence of which Selkirk's account both describes and exemplifies (*Observations*, p. 23). New scientific methods of agricultural experiment and investigation replaced older localised 'mapping' of the land, subjecting it to a universal index that determined its relative potential for bounty, while demarcating with mathematical precision the boundaries of private ownership. In the Scottish-derived 'statistical account', land was quantified through the dense accumulation of empirical observation of climatic and environmental peculiarities – the condition of the soil, the relative topography, seasonal temperature change, rainfall amounts, proximity to markets, and so forth – that allowed for greatest possible productivity and therefore value. At the same time, the cadastral survey or map worked to create, mark, define, retrace or re-establish the boundaries of private and public lands. The survey imposed a new regime of spatial orientation, in which land was reimagined as rigorously demarcated plots whose topographical starting point was often two lines intersecting at right angles, within which respective landowners granted the right to use and manage the land and to derive income by letting others use it or by its sale or transfer to another.[21] The Sutherland Clearances of the 1810s were themselves prefaced by a series of surveys on the estate, which attempted to precisely delimit the value of the lands in terms of their tenancy and potential for productivity. Loch and his agents then used these surveys to map out their eviction and relocation operations.[22]

What the surveyors of Sutherland encountered in the first decade of the nineteenth century was a centuries-old arrangement in which the land 'was laid out not so much to ensure an effective agricultural economy as to stabilize a class structure and to verify mutual obligations'.[23] Highland farmers eked out a precarious existence in small plots of arable land along valleys; land higher up and behind hill crests were held in common, as grazing lands. James Loch, who in 1820 published his own account of the events on the Sutherland estate in an attempt to defend his removal policies against mounting public criticism, recounted the pre-modern 'unimproved' Highland system of runrig:

> The amount of the whole rent was settled by the factors, which, together with the land, was apportioned by an inquest or jury of elders, among the different occupiers. The land was first classed according to its quality; each division was then divided into as many lots as there were occupiers, dispersed over every part of the 'town.' The hill pastures were

held in common; the right of pasturage being regulated by the extent of arable ground which each person held.²⁴

Loch's description of runrig, which places Highland husbandry at the very beginning of the second stage of agriculture in Adam Smith's schematic of human development, signals for Loch the general failure of the Highland land use system, which makes no contribution to national prosperity:

> Such being, until very lately, the condition of the estate of SUTHERLAND, the effect was to scatter thickly, a hardy but not industrious people scattered up the glens and over the sides of various mountains; who taking advantage of every spot which could be cultivated, and which could with any chance of success be applied to raising a precarious crop of inferior oats, of which they baked their cakes, and of bear, from which they distilled their whiskey, added little to the industry, and contributed nothing to the wealth of the empire. (51)

Only through the consolidation of private property – bringing all of the estate's lands and tenants under the inalienable, allodial and exclusive control of the landowner – would the full economic potential of the region be realised, the evidence of which Loch, from the vantage point of 1820, is beginning to see all around him. Modernisation of estate lands thus provides for a powerful correspondence to an increase in the wealth and power of the nation, which in Loch's mind gives all his management activities on the Sutherland estate a patriotic sheen. As he reminds the Sutherland's detractors, the object of eviction and removal was not primarily to increase estate profitability. Rather, it was 'to render this mountainous district contributory, as far as it was possible, to the general wealth and industry of the country, and in the manner most suitable to its situation and peculiar circumstances' (73). Through the discourse of improvement, the Sutherland estate attains a metonymic equivalence to the nation, as Loch indexes the betterment of the estate to the prosperity of the nation at large – as goes the estate, so goes the nation-state. Improvement, taking place simultaneously on estates throughout the Highlands, Scotland and the whole of the British Isles, recognises – but then abolishes – the chronotopic unevenness of the nation. Through the workings of improvement, all lands of the nation will become modernised, integrated into a homogeneous national space, driven by the engine of an expanding market economy.

If a 'denial of coevalness', to paraphrase Johannes Fabian, is a fundamental aspect of Loch's post-Enlightenment view of the Highland aborigine, then the Highlands and the Highlander would be integrated into the space-time of the nation-state through the planned improvement of agricultural lands, encouragement of manufactures, and building of roads, canals, dikes, mills and entire townships. Improvement for Loch guaranteed economic prosperity in the Highlands even if it came at the expense of an outmoded understanding of the relation between the natives and their land. It was a 'policy well calculated to raise the importance, and increase the happiness of the individuals themselves, who were the objects of the change . . . and to promote the general prosperity of nation' (73–4). 'Happiness', like the land itself, is defined by productivity and material wealth, abstracted and unmoored from dictates of tradition and of collective memory. 'The children of those who are removed from the hills will lose all recollection of the habits and customs of their fathers, and it is to be hoped they will never experience that want, to which their parents have been so frequently, and severely exposed' (133). In place of continued remembrance in which the people evoke an ancestral memory of their attachment to the land as part of the assertion of their land rights, Loch offers the metaphor of a collective amnesia, a prosperous contemporaneity in which the relation to the land is indexed only to the outward signs of the material wealth it produces. In this, Loch anticipates a near-future in which Highland people and Highland lands would all be rationalised and economised, integrated into what Koselleck terms the 'Neuzeit' of modernity.[25]

Elegy as Anti-Emigration

The discursive formation of the Highland aborigine emerges from the need to make sense of the intensity of local resistance to the disruptive forces which men like Loch and Sellar helped to unleash, and which Sellar encountered first-hand in the 1810s among tenants on the Sutherland estate. Sellar's 'aboriginising' of their recalcitrance rationalised and legitimated their dispossession and displacement, as the unhappy but inevitable by-product of improvement. The response of Kildonan tenants to their dispossession and displacement was, of course, very different. Faced with the loss of their secure landholdings, Kildonan people, like many others in the Highlands facing the same fate, looked to the possibility of alterative land tenure.[26] The dramatic rise in Highland emigration in the early nineteenth century, however, posed a nagging contradiction within the ideology of Improvement. The outflux of families and, oftentimes, entire communities in the Highlands inspired competing arguments and explanations to account for the peculiar fact that the region's aborigines, characterised by their deep and ancient attachment to the land, were abandoning it in the thousands.[27]

For Loch, who was mainly intent on defending the policy of eviction and clearance that had provoked political outrage and protest and permanently tarnished his reputation and those of his patrons, the greatest problem in the Highlands was not those who left for America but those who remained, resisting all improvement efforts. Loch sees no connection between social protest and emigration, the mention of which comes only as a brief afterthought in his *Account*. Instead, emigration is itself a function of a persistent aboriginal mindset among a recalcitrant few in the Highlands who are simply unwilling to adapt themselves to the new spirit of enterprise: 'They deemed no comfort worth the possessing, which was to be purchased at the price of regular industry; no improvement worthy of adoption, if it was to be obtained at the expense of sacrificing the customs, or leaving the homes of their ancestors' (64). Strong attachment to the land and their traditional way of life actually made it easier for these Highlanders, Loch observes, to abandon Britain's shores entirely:

> So strongly did these feelings operate, that it cost them nearly the same effort to remove from the spot in which they were born and brought up, though the place of their new dwelling was situated on the sea-shore, at the mouth of their native Strath, or even in a neighbouring Glen, as it cost them to make an exertion equal to transporting themselves across the Atlantick. (64)

The Highlanders' deep attachment to the place of their birth paradoxically explains their persistent desire to leave the country entirely. This passage is in keeping with Loch's general disavowal of land claims based on ancestral memory, configured here as an irrational clinging to outmoded ways even when this puts prosperity at risk.

Other writers, however, offered a more sympathetic account of motives for emigration. For these writers, emigration is not the product of an innate Highland inertia but is instead a symptom of widespread melancholic disaffection that was a direct response to displacement of tight-knit communities from lands that were integral to their sense of themselves and their way of life. David Stewart of Garth would echo Anne Grant in arguing that eviction constituted a denial of soul-sustaining nourishment for Highlanders: 'In removing from their homes,' he writes, 'such a people do not merely change the spot of earth on which they and their ancestors lived'.[28] For them, 'even in removing from one part of the Highlands to another, the sacrifice was regarded as severe'. The force of this 'unconquerable attachment to the spot where they first drew breath', Stewart writes, can be demonstrated in any one anecdote, 'selected from hundreds with which every Highlander is familiar' (1:91). He recalls the example of two men of his acquaintance, who had 'occupied the farms on which they were born till far advanced in life, when they were removed' (1:156). Though they got farms 'at no great distance', they were

> afflicted with a deep despondency, gave up their usual habits, and seldom spoke with seeming satisfaction, except when the subject turned on their former life and spot which they had left. They appeared to be much relieved when walking to the tops of the neighbouring hills, and gazing for hours in direction of late homes; but in few months, their strength totally failed, and without any pain or complaint, save mental depression, one died in a year, the other in eighteen months. (1:156)

Migration, in Stewart's account, even of a few miles from location of their birth is tantamount to permanent exile; uprooted, Highlanders are consigned to a hollowed-out life and premature death. Stewart sees the debilitating effects of this exile multiplied a hundred times in the region: 'the evil is extending', he writes, and tenants throughout the Highlands 'are affected by the gloom and despondency ... the natural enthusiasm of the Highland character has, in many instances, been converted into gloomy and morose fanaticism' (1:125).

Aiming in his *Sketches* to provide, like Selkirk before him, an objective scientific enquiry, grounded in the precepts of philosophical history and of political economy, Stewart seems wary of potential accusations of over-sentimentality in his description of removed Highlanders, and he buries the testimony of their suffering in footnotes. But the Highland land debate offered the occasion for other more overtly sentimental accounts, in which the exiled Highlander became an elevated figure of tragic elegy. Perhaps the most sustained example of these is Alexander Campbell's *The Grampians Desolate*, a poem in six books published in 1804 – the year before Selkirk's *Observations* appeared – in which the author sought to diagnose, in poetic form, the current pathology of the Highlands: 'banish'd from their native shore' and 'outcast as poor exiles', the hapless Gael 'roams at large, – their lands to strangers given'.[29] Consigned to a life of ceaseless wandering, Gaels can find no succour for their sufferings, and the melancholia of their dispossession leaves its trace on the landscape. The Grampians are emptied out and now bear the shadow image of the people that once were rooted there: 'See yon deserted glen, of late the bless'd abode of happy men; / 'Tis now a dreary void! – save where yon tree, / By bleak winds blasted . . .' (8–9). The glens are a desert; the Highland landscape can now offer only a memory of once was, as the land passes into the domain of the sheep-farmer: 'How desolate the waste! – / Save where yon shepherd and his dog in haste / Ascend among the mountain's brow . . .' (6).

Campbell's work exemplifies what critics have identified as a Romantic vision of the Highlands in both verse and prose in the era of Clearance.[30] This vision operates wholly on the level of lamentation, as the land and its people enter the popular imagination in the nineteenth-century as subjects of pathos and sympathy. The Highlands is a landscape of ghosts that will be forever haunted by the memory of the natives who were compelled into exile. Forced to abandon their native soil, their overarching relation to the land becomes one of nostalgic remembrance, the Romantic cultivation of which, Shields has argued, takes shape in large part through writing on the Highland emigrant.[31]

In so far as Highland elegy appears to reclaim a pre-existing Highland social order now under duress, it is tempting to read laments such as Campbell's as expressive of what a recent study of the Romantic period has identified as a counter-discourse, a 'melancholy romanticism' that mounts an insistent critique of the 'theoretical realism' of the discourse of political economy, and that is constituted as a specific form of criticism of an ascendant capitalist modernity and the ideology of improvement.[32] But Campbell's literary elegy, no less than the political economy of Selkirk and Loch, upholds an ideology which legitimises the land's appropriation by configuring local notions of land rights as 'aboriginal'. Campbell does this by providing a powerful substitution for the concept of *dùthchas*, upon which local Gaelic resistance to dispossession was based. Campbell's Highland elegy replaces the localised claim to *particular* lands, derived from a notion of hereditary right, with a more generalised affective belonging to *the* land, indexed to the constituent elements of the landscape: the mountains, the glens, or simply the 'native soil'. The evocation of 'native attachment' operates to reduce local land grievances in the Highlands to a collective melancholia that highlights the Gaels' deep and abiding love for an abstracted native 'homeland'.[33] The Highland aborigine, who so passionately 'belongs' to the Highlands, has no actual claim to any particular plot of it.

Thus, though there might be condemnation for the hardened hearts and cruelty of individual landowners and their agents in the Highlands, there is no suggestion from any quarter in the anglophone Highland debate that the customary right to the lands local people had farmed for generations ought to supersede the property rights of the landlords or that the petition claims of local Highlanders for restoration of their land rights were just and reasonable. Instead, both Highland elegy and political economy attempted to shift discussion of Highland discontent from the domain of the political altogether, eliding all notion of inequity or injustice.[34] Even David Stewart, one of the most ardent critics of the actions of the landowners in the Highlands, saw widespread discontent among the populace as a symptom of the Gaels' troubled relation to modern commercial society. Concerned largely with maintaining the supply and quality of military recruits from the region, which he believed were dependent on the preservation of the unique *esprit de corps* found among the Highland regiments, Stewart called not for the recovery of local land rights but for a more gradual transformation of innovation in the Highlands. Evolution not revolution would reduce disaffection and encourage as much as possible acceptance of and participation in the new order on the part of the natives themselves.

In the same vein, though Campbell is pointedly critical of the 'system accurs'd' of conversion to grasslands that had transformed a landscape dotted with small hamlets to a deserted landscape of isolated sheep-walks, his work is not a critique of improvement in the Highlands per se. On the contrary, *The Grampians Desolate* makes a plea for a more active policy of state intervention in the region, to discourage emigration and to entice the local people 'by every possible encouragement to improve and colonize those vast tracts of waste-lands' found in districts throughout the Highlands (202). In his preface, and in the copious notes 'explanatory and historical' which occupy more than half of the work's total pages, Campbell makes clear he intends his work to be taken as much as a dry-eyed dissertation on the proper arrangement of 'rural economy' as a passionate lament for a vanishing Highland world. The poetry, he writes, serves 'to lay open to the imagination' various 'prospects or poetic exhibitions', which will illustrate the suitability of his ideas on 'an improved system of Store-Farms, Manufactures, Fisheries, etc', providing the 'best possible means for the maintenance of private happiness, conjoined with public welfare, national independence, wealth; and true glory' (vi). 'Improved systems' will bring an end to emigration and debilitating melancholia, as they excite a 'spirit of industry and ingenuity' among the native inhabitants, through the benevolent intervention of the state, to which all private interest must ultimately defer: 'For 'tis a maxim sacred, good as great,' Campbell writes, '*all interests are subservient to the State.*' / The State's an Unite Grand, a Perfect Whole, / the General weal must wisely all controul' (14). Elegy in *The Grampians Desolate*, then, does not represent a counter-discourse to political economy; instead, it serves to dramatise and make visible the systems that political economy can only theorise. 'Poetic exhibition', of a Highlands laid waste, becomes the occasion for an enunciation of the proper realignment of the relationship between national subjects and wealth creation in the ongoing refinement of the modern nation-state. At the same time, the poem becomes the vehicle through which Campbell mounts a passionate critique of emigration, as the work describes a landscape that will remain desolate – as long as emigration is allowed to proceed apace.

The ideological alignment between landed class interests and Highland elegy is suggested by Campbell's patronage by the Highland Society of Edinburgh, which championed agricultural improvement in the Highlands while seeing emigration as the gravest threat to the well-being of the nation. Campbell's identification of emigration as symptom of the disarrangement of the Highland rural economy, rather than as a particular response to dispossession, is in keeping with the viewpoint of his patrons in the Highland Society, which was in formed in 1784 and modelled after its senior counterpart in London. Dominated by Highland landowners and by professional men with connections in the Highlands, its membership included not only prominent members of the Edinburgh literati, such as Henry Mackenzie, but some of the most influential and ardent improvement advocates and experimenters. Proclaiming itself committed both to 'the means of the improvement of Highlands' and the 'preservation of language, music and poetry of the Highlands', the aims of the Highland Society gave expression to the collective anxieties of post-Enlightenment Scotland, as the institution offered itself as both a forum for ideas on modernisation in the Highlands and as an agent for the preservation of traditional aesthetic and cultural forms that were thought to be threatened by it.[35] Thus, while the Highland Society would finance Campbell's tour of the Highlands in search of material for the national song collection that would become *Albyn's Anthology*, the society also became the 'established organisation for promoting agriculture in Scotland', through its sponsorship of prizes for agricultural essays.[36]

Selkirk's Anti Anti-Emigration

The Highland Society of Edinburgh was a key institution in shaping state policy on Highland emigration, and at the turn of the nineteenth century it led a campaign in the press and in government to stop Highland emigration. Having issued its own report on the subject in 1802, the Highland Society had been instrumental in pushing through anti-emigration legislation in Parliament, the primary aim of which was not to alleviate conditions in the region but to restrict emigration itself by making it more difficult and costly. The Passenger Vessels Act of 1803, to which Campbell admiringly alludes in *The Grampians Desolate*, was modelled after recent legislation regulating the transportation of enslaved Africans. Ostensibly designed to 'protect' hapless Highlanders from greedy emigrant agents and harrowing conditions at sea, the act set restrictive guidelines on shipboard conditions and had the effect of (temporarily) slowing the flow of emigration, as it more than doubled the cost of transatlantic passage.[37] The Highland Society's efforts to restrict emigration made it Selkirk's arch-nemesis in the *Observations*, as he launched his own controversial and often contentious critique of anti-emigration policies by pointedly condemning members of the society who 'have lent sanction of their names to representations of the most partial nature and have recommended measures', although from 'the purest motives', that are 'inconsistent with every principle of justice' (*Observations*, p. 135). By the time Selkirk published his *Observations* – only a few years before the Sutherlands began to clear their Highland estate – the debate on what to do about the Highlands had already lasted for nearly thirty years. Yet the emigration crisis was considered to have become even more acute, as Britain found itself in a great struggle with France that brought to the foreground the relationship between widespread disaffection and a shrinking population in the Highlands and Britain's relative strength to withstand its enemies.[38] For members of the Society and others, the Highland 'mania' for emigration was an open wound from which the nation's lifeblood poured out, particularly in terms of the manpower needed to maintain the region's labour force and, more urgently, to supply the nation's military ranks with that 'hardy and intrepid race of men' found only in the Highlands.[39] Before publication of the *Observations*, critics of emigration seemed to have the upper hand, and Selkirk's call for *assisted* emigration represented a distinctly minority opinion. The *Observations*, however, would spark a dramatic reversal in public opinion, as Selkirk's arguments shifted the terms of the debate: emigration, previously seen as symptomatic of a pervasive cultural and economic crisis in the Highlands, became, in Selkirk's vision, the instrument of their persistence as a people in the modern world.[40]

Selkirk's advocacy of emigration begins with the insistence that improvement is its root cause. Adam Smith himself, Selkirk writes, foresaw that the processes of modernisation will inevitably drive smallholders everywhere from their lands. Quoting from *The Wealth of Nations*, he writes, 'the diminution of cottagers, and other small occupiers of land, has in every part of Europe been the immediate forerunner of improvement and better cultivation' (*Observations*, p. 36). Improvement and better cultivation, in Selkirk's account, take the form of the consolidation of small landholdings into large holdings and the introduction of the specialised agricultural activity that Campbell so despised: sheep farming, which, 'ever since its introduction', Selkirk himself acknowledges, has produced 'a very unequal struggle between the former possessors of the lands, and the graziers' (30). As smallholdings are consolidated and the value of land increases with the increase in its productivity as grazing land, he writes, the 'old tenantry' becomes unable 'to offer a rent fully equal to that which their competitors would have given' and is driven off the land: 'as fast as current leases expire, the whole or nearly the whole of this body of men will be dispossessed' (33). Dispossession is the inevitable outcome of modernisation, a dynamic Selkirk reiterates throughout the *Observations*, stating 'a number of small occupiers of land must be dispossessed'.[41]

While setting out his argument for the national benefits of planned emigration, Selkirk also dismantles the most common schemes of anti-emigration advocates for keeping dispossessed Highlanders in the Highlands. For one, Selkirk, dismisses as ineffectual most proposals for 'redirecting' the Highland population. He argues, for example, that a plan for cultivation of waste lands – Alexander Campbell's solution to Highland discontent – would amount to little because of the lack of available capital. Likewise, schemes to establish small manufactures in the Highlands would founder because of the extreme distance from markets and the relative isolation of the region, which is supported, Selkirk argues, by the fact that 'no practical manufacturer has ever shown the least inclination to make the attempt' (*Observations*, p. 105). Selkirk most pointed critique, however, is directed at those Highland estate owners who derive a great portion of their income from the kelp industry and who therefore have a 'natural prejudice' against emigration. Estates dependent on kelp manufacture, Selkirk writes, favour a large pool of labourers in the Highlands that also keep wages low (131–4).

Selkirk's continues to take aim at the misguided or self-interested motives of anti-emigration landowners in his careful reading of the socio-economic forces that drive the Highlanders to want to emigrate in the first place. In examining the motives of emigrants, Selkirk, conspicuously for a member of the landed class, offers an account of local agency that directly contradicts prevailing assumptions. For many anti-emigration advocates, the 'mania' to emigrate was spread by unscrupulous emigration agents campaigning in the Highlands and by the disaffection of a particular class in the Highlands – the tacksmen – who, in many anti-emigration accounts, were represented as a superfluous class between landowner and tenant that represented the greatest social obstacle to estate improvement and efficiency.[42] Faced with the loss of their privileged status in the Highland social hierarchy, so the argument went, tacksmen or their agents sought to set the illiterate common people against the rightful owners of the land and duped them into leaving with false images of the prosperity that awaited them in the wilds of North America.[43]

Against this image of a naive people lead astray by disreputable manipulations of an unscrupulous native class, Selkirk offers the image of a populace actively seeking the means to secure its way of life. The belief that preference for emigration in the Highlands has been 'enhanced by the ignorance of the people', Selkirk argues, is a 'delusion' (*Observations*, p. 51). Instead, he writes, '[a]ccustomed to possess land, to derive from it all the comforts [Highlanders] enjoy, they naturally consider it as indispensible, and can form no idea of happiness without such a position' (48).

The primary motive for the 'spirit of discontent and irritation widely diffused' throughout the Highlands, Selkirk argues, is the widespread belief among the tenantry that disregard for their longstanding land rights amounted to a criminal abrogation of the landowners' obligation to safeguard the well-being of the community. On hand in 1813 to witness the protests of the Kildonan tenants whom Sellar had attempted to remove, Selkirk was privately sympathetic: they had 'so much of the Old Highland Spirit as to think the land their own'. The people of Kildonan, he added, were 'only defending their rights and resisting ruinous, unjust, and tyrannical encroachment on their property ... [a]ccording to ideas handed down to them from their ancestors, and long prevalent among high and low throughout the Highlands'.[44] Unlike writers like Loch and David Stewart, who saw assimilation of the Highlander into modern society – gradual or otherwise – as a solution to Highland discontent, Selkirk identifies modernisation itself as the problem, and emigration as the obvious response for tenants who refuse to acquiesce to their dispossession and displacement. If, indeed, forced to remain in the Highlands by draconian anti-emigration legislation, Selkirk writes, the local tenantry 'will not forget that they were once in a higher station, nor will they allow their children to forget they were once on a level with the men who insult them by their superiority' (*Observations*, pp. 118–19). In the new economy of the Highlands, 'intercourse with their superiors' may be 'confined to the daily exchange of labor for its stipulated reward', but at the same time

> they remember not only the very opposite behaviour of their former chiefs; they recollect also the services their ancestors performed for them; they recollect that, but for these, the property could not have

been preserved: they well know of how little avail was a piece of parchment and a lump of wax, under the old system of the Highlands: they reproach their landlord with ingratitude, and remind him that, but for their fathers, he would have no estate. The permanent possession which they had always retained of their paternal farms, they consider only as their just right, from the share they had borne in the general defence, and can see no difference between title of the chief and their own. (120)

The local people, Selkirk insists, will not forget, and his description is a testament to the power of collective memory among the tenantry in the Highlands. Passed down from generation to generation, the memory of their ancestors sustains them in their refusal to accept the dictates of landlords who insisted that they remain in the Highlands, displaced and dispossessed, eking out their living along the coasts as herring fishers or kelp harvesters or as wage-earning labourers in the new order of commercial agriculture. Instead, fully cognisant of the threat posed to their way of life and to their collective identity and guided by the traditional leaders of their communities, many Highlanders chose to emigrate, which, Selkirk recognised, 'requires a great momentary effort; but holds out a speedy prospect of a situation and mode of life similar to that in which they have been educated' (48).

Imperial Modernity and Aboriginal Persistence

Selkirk's acute understanding of the motives for local resistance to dispossession and even sympathy for their plight does not extend, it must be noted, to granting legitimacy to their land claims, and nowhere in his writing does he call for the restoration of the customary or ancestral land rights of small landholders in the Highlands. Ultimately, Selkirk is not an advocate for any particular mode of land tenure in the Highlands, traditional or otherwise. Instead, Selkirk's recognition of the persistence of claims of a hereditary right in the Highlands is one part of a larger imperial vision that seeks to maximise the production and diffusion of wealth and prosperity throughout the British imperial dominions. By actively encouraging transatlantic immigration, Selkirk would find an imperial solution to a regional crisis. If the Highland way of life was incompatible with modernisation in the Highlands, then Highlanders could be redirected to domains elsewhere, where their ancient customs and traditions might better serve the empire. Unable to 'observe without regret' the rapid decline of Highland culture, 'to which the circumstances of the country seemed inevitably to lead', Selkirk writes, 'I thought ... that a portion of the antient spirit might be preserved among the Highlanders of the New World – that the emigrants might be brought together in some part of our own colonies, where they would be of national utility ...' (*Observations*, p. 3).

For anti-emigration advocates, the ultimate destination of the emigrants mattered little. All that signified was the fact of their departure; as 'exiles', Highlanders are to be pitied or disdained, the moment they sail 'beyond the shores'. For these writers, the 'elsewhere' of the Highland emigrant was a blank. Selkirk's call for planned emigration and settlement would, however, reimagine the range and scope of the Highland world, expanding it to encompass the whole of the British Atlantic Empire while making the case for the continued relevance of their 'native' life in the modern world. He does this, first, by accepting the desire on the part of local peoples to leave the Highlands in the face of widespread dispossession, and, second, by converting this desire into the driving force for a new state-sponsored instrument of colonial expansion. Since the people were willing to leave their 'homeland' if it meant a secure stake in lands elsewhere for themselves and their families, Selkirk would devise a plan to yoke this willingness to the British colonial project. Forestalling the plunge into elegy that had characterised much of the anti-emigration rhetoric and imagery – Campbell's desolate landscape and dispirited populace succumbing to what the poet derided as the 'quicksands' of emigration – Selkirk instead deploys the dispassionate yet sunny rhetoric of political economy, expanding the geography of 'national' prosperity through planned settlement in the colonies.

For Selkirk, Highland settlement secured British interests in two 'problem' areas of its imperial domain, on different sides of the Atlantic. As he had argued, emigration was a rational and predictable response on the part of the native Gael to widespread displacement and dispossession. Yet in the present chaos, 'Highlanders were dispersing to a variety of situations, in a foreign land, where they were lost not only to their native country, but to themselves as a separate people' (*Observations*, p. 3). Selkirk would seek to intervene and regulate this dispersion, so that the Highland Gaels, as a separate people, would 'not only be preserved, but actively sustained'.

Highland communities brought to the North America 'should be concentrated in one national settlement, where particular attention should be bestowed to keep them distinct and separate, and where their peculiar and characteristic manners should be carefully encouraged' (162). In these 'national settlements', Selkirk writes,

> It is evident what important services may be derived from such a body of settlers as the Highland emigrants would form . . . not merely from their old established principles of loyalty, and from their military character that they would be a valuable acquisition. It is a point of no small consequence, that their language and manners are so totally different from those of the Americans. This would preserve them from the infection of dangerous principles . . . (161–2)

'National settlement' became the touchstone for Selkirk's ideas on emigration, as it drove most of his public ambitions after 1805. His settlements would be 'national' in the dual sense that they would remain purely 'Highland' in character and they would help secure British interests, as the custom and traditions of the Scottish Gael would act as a kind of antibody to the 'infection' of American principles – a strategic counter against US territorial and cultural expansion in British North America. At the same time, Selkirk's 'settlement' proclaimed both a new project of colonial occupation and reallocation of land, under the sign of modernisation, which would strengthen the empire's rather tenuous hold in North America as well as provide a final answer to the Highland emigration debate – the Highland unrest that Clearance had sparked would be resolved – settled – once and for all. A Highland way of life that for many registered as hopelessly anachronistic in the modern world would contribute to the national prosperity after all, but in new arenas and in new circumstances. For Selkirk, transatlantic emigration became a matter of survival not only for the 'old established principles' of Scottish Gaeldom but for Britain's empire in the New World.

The wealth of nations, in Selkirk's political economy, takes shape not only within the confines of their shores but beyond them, in the realm of empire, and the Highland aborigines, it turns out, are ideally suited to bring prosperity to the colonies even as they are displaced from their titular homeland. In this, Selkirk's emigration schemes represent a stark alternative to the aims and methods of the Highland Society and similar institutions which sought to preserve

Highland tradition, their 'language, music and poetry', in large part through the translation and written transcription of spoken material. Selkirk would also seek to preserve Highland 'tradition', not through the transcription of their ancient poetry but through their lived experiences in National Settlements. The Highland way of life, and the ancestral memory that sustained it – passed down from generation to generation – would go on as it always had, not in the lands of their ancestors but in what Selkirk envisioned as the empty wilderness of North America.

Enclaves of the Aboriginal

In later writings after the appearance of the *Observations*, Selkirk described more fully the settlement schemes he had sketched out in the previous work, in a series of unpublished plans and proposals for Highland settlements in Lower Canada that he submitted to William Pitt and to Lord Windham, Secretary of State for War and the Colonies.[45] These reveal the increasing ambitiousness of Selkirk's plans, and the increasingly grandiose claims he made for his settlements in terms of securing the prosperity of the British Empire in North America, against what he saw as its most serious threat: Britain's former colony to the south. In July 1805, not long after the publication of his *Observations*, Selkirk warns:

> The influx of Amer^n Settlers into U & L. Canada is such that if continued for some years longer the majority of the people in all the remote parts of these provinces will be of that description, and no comments can be necessary to shew how dangerous that will be to the British interests. ('Communications with Government 1805-6-7', 52:13919)

Sounding the alarm at the threat of American incursion, Selkirk proposes a version of his general settlement scheme adapted to the particular geopolitical circumstances:

> [I]f these Provinces were divided into 4 or 5 districts, each inhabited by Colonists of a different nation, keeping up their original peculiarities & all differing in language from their neighbours in the United States, the authority of Government would be placed in the most secure foundation. – This desirable state of things may be brought about with very

little exertion on the part of Gov[t] farther than to lay down a plan of conduct for the Provincial administrations. (52:13919)

Dividing colonial space into discrete territories of national peculiarity in response to the threat of counter colonialism becomes Selkirk's prescription for Highland settlement in North America, the singularity of which would inoculate them from the American infection of 'dangerous principles' he described in the *Observations*.

Selkirk identified a key mechanism by which he believed a colonial government might best cultivate these sites of 'national' antibodies: the strict arrangement and maintenance of their linguistic borders. Second in his six-point scheme is the establishment of a 'division line', within the region, to be taken as a 'boundary':

> Highland Settlers being exclusively encouraged to the Westward of that line & no grants of land being made there to any person who does not speak the Gaelic or the Erse language & on the other hand no person of that description being allowed to receive any grant to the Eastward of that line. (52:13922)

Within this delimited zone of Highlandness, Selkirk writes, the settlers' 'original language must be kept up as the prevailing & established dialect & where they can have no temptation to relinquish their national peculiarities' ('Suggestions Respecting Upper Canada', 52:13930–1).[46] Elsewhere Selkirk had called for the provision of 'a good schoolmaster' as an integral feature of a plan for settlement; however, he cautioned, 'much stress need not be laid on the English language, which in our situation is perhaps a disadvantage: – We should remember that the English language is the American & that in teaching our people English we teach them to become Yankees' ('Plan of Settlement of Baldoon', 55:14652). In what amounts to a dramatic departure from the conventions of colonial discourse, Selkirk here calls for the active discouragement of English in the Highland settlements. James Loch had himself iterated the conventional association between English language education and civilisation, in his *Account* of the Sutherland estate. 'The prevalence of the Celtick tongue', he writes,

> presents a barrier . . . to the improvement and civilization of the district, wherever it may prevail, as it cuts off from the people those means of communication and intercourse enjoyed by the rest of their fellow-subjects.

> The progress of the English language must be rapid and irresistible . . . as the youth . . . who has been taught to read, will never confine himself to the knowledge of a language, in which no book was ever written, and which has never served the purposes of commerce, or of government . . . (44–5)

In Loch's utopian vision of a future Highlands, English language assimilation signals the final integration of the Highlands, and therefore Scotland, into modern British commercial society:

> many years have not to run, when the Celtick tongue, upon the main land of Scotland at least, will cease to be a living language; and that this will happen, without the country losing any of those distinctive nationalities, which nurture and preserve a generous rivalship in the great interests of British policy. (45)

For Selkirk, however, the preservation of the language of the Highlanders is twin skin to the preservation of their identity as a people and to their attachment to their (imperial) homeland:

> If these Highland Emigrants are mixed with other people, they will in a few years lose their peculiar manners & language & blending with the great mass of the American Settlers will by degrees adopt their Sentiments and lose their own attachment of the Mother Country. This mixture may perhaps render them more industrious & better farmers but will destroy that steady dependence, which may otherwise be rested upon them for the security of the colony. ('Suggestions Respecting Upper Canada', 52:13930)

English, the vector of the American disease, would be discouraged in Selkirk's version of a Highlandised colonial North America, as British values are best disseminated there in Gaelic, the continued use of which becomes the very measure of the settlement's viability.

The emphasis Selkirk placed on effecting and maintaining the linguistic integrity of his ethnic enclaves and the lengths he was willing to go to enforce their Highland character is illustrated in his complex and ambitious relocation schemes for settlement consolidation. Highlanders already living in New York State and in Canada eastward of his division line, who would not long be able 'to preserve themselves from the contagion of American manners', would be induced to move to the western districts and to 'combine into one large Settlement, with those who may hereafter be inclined to Emigrate from Scotland' ('Communications with Government 1805-6-7', 52:13921). To encourage the latter to settle in the territory set out for them, Selkirk writes, emigration agents back in Britain must be identified, and legal and financial hindrances to emigration actively circumvented:

> Information should be procured as to the individuals in the Highlands of Scotland most likely to take a lead in future Emigration. They ... may be gained over by private assurances of considerable grants, & to enable them to afford the passage at a lower rate those who go to the United States; permission maybe granted to some individuals to have Transports under the sanction of the name of Government so as to free them from the regulations of the Emigrant [Passenger Vessels] Act. (52:13925)

Immigration of Highlanders already in Canada and the United States to an area where Selkirk would establish his national enclave is combined with the outmigration of US settlers: Americans 'being of a restless and wandering disposition might be induced without much difficulty to sell their lands to Scottish settlers & to remove into some other district' ('Suggestions Respecting Upper Canada', 52:13932–3).

Through various acts of induced migration in and out of colonial spaces in North America, Selkirk would arrange his enclave of Gaeldom, repurposing Highlandness in the service of colonial expansion. Ethnically and linguistically purified and roped off from the rest of the world, Highland emigrants would serve as imperial counters to the pervasive spread of a rootless Yankeeism, which Selkirk, in parallel with Anne Grant's sentiments in the *Memoirs of an American Lady*, describes as a form of settlement lacking in 'all motives of preference for the government or the Country, but merely for the sake of cheap land' (52:13927). For Selkirk, the Highlanders' special relation to the land, which in the categorisation of Highlanders as an aboriginal people had come to be defined as a generalised but profound sense of attachment to the glens and hillsides of their titular homeland, is once again reimagined as both devotion to their 'Mother Country' and to the isolated terrain of their National Settlements in Canada.

Indigenous Elsewhere: Kildonan on the Plains

From the ruins of a world transformed in the name of improvement and the prerogatives of private property arises the transatlantic aborigine, as dispossession on one side of the Atlantic becomes the catalyst for settlement on the other. Selkirk's convergence of colonial theory and praxis is testament to the power and breadth of his particular brand of Scottish empire-making in the Romantic era, as he sought to erect a laboratory of native resettlement that would consolidate vast territories within the dominion of Great Britain. Selkirk's National Settlements grant a strange transperipheral reprieve for Gaeldom; because of his encouragement and authority, entire families and communities in the Highlands would bring themselves to the emigration ships, and their migration across the Atlantic would, in turn, be bound up with the dispossession and migration of many native peoples residing in the New World. By the second decade of the nineteenth century Selkirk had brought several groups of Highlanders to North America as part of attempted settlements, first on Prince Edward Island and later on lands near Lake St Clair in Upper Canada.[47] The first attempt had been a disappointment, the second had failed altogether, but in 1811 Selkirk acquired a controlling interest in the financially troubled Hudson's Bay Company. For a nominal price of ten shillings, the directors of the Hudson's Bay Company deeded to Selkirk a tract of land on the Canadian plains few in Britain even knew existed, but, at some 116,000 square miles (300,000 square kilometres), was four times the size of Scotland, and only some 5,000 square miles (13,000 square kilometres), smaller than the whole of the British Isles.

This unprecedented acquisition, he believed, would give him adequate scope in effecting his settlement theories, with access to vast acreages of land untroubled by pre-existing claims or counter-claims. In early 1813 he inspired several Kildonan families, cleared from their lands on the Sutherland estate, to embark to North America and to lands Selkirk had set aside for Highland emigrants and retired agents of the company at the southern end of his land grant, along the banks of the Red River where it meets the Assiniboine.[48] Selkirk's plan for the Red River Colony was predicated on the possibilities provided by acquisition of Crown or charter lands not yet opened up to settlement – 'empty' lands waiting to be converted into productive private property. But the Kildonan people who fled dispossession and displacement in the Highlands did not become comfortably settled after they arrived at Red River. Instead, the pre-existing occupiers of the 'empty lands' that Selkirk planned to populate with Highlanders worked aggressively to destroy his settlement, which they accomplished only a few years later, after a campaign of pillage, vandalism and open warfare.

The area planned for settlement that the Kildonan people laid eyes on after an eighteenth-month journey – walking a part of the last leg of their journey in the snow single-file, as their piper led the way – was a region of scattered and isolated homesteads and remote outposts of the Hudson's Bay Company.[49] To the west of Red River were outposts of the North West Company, the Hudson's Bay Company's chief rival. The fur trade had established a relation of mutual interdependence between Europeans and Amerindians in the region, and Cree, Ojibwa and Métis people traversed the lands of Selkirk's acquisition as part of their seasonal migration, and in search of furs, which they brought to various outposts of the Hudson's Bay Company and the North West Company.[50] On the flat grasslands near the outpost where Selkirk intended his Highlanders to settle on plots of several acres were small communities of Gaelic-speaking Scots and Orcadians, families of company men of the Hudson's Bay Company. Alongside these were the Métis, the offspring of Ojibwa and Cree women and European fur traders and their descendants, who visited the outpost to trade and acquire supplies and who wintered in small communities near the forks, before setting out in warmer weather on their annual buffalo hunt.

Various livelihoods and interests of these peoples were thus directly affected by Highland settlement in Assiniboia, the name given to Selkirk's acquisition – Selkirk invariably spelled it 'Ossiniboia' – and the coming of the Kildonan people prompted divergent reactions among the previous occupiers of the land. The Salteaux, a local band of Ojibwa people, forged a long-lasting alliance with the settlement, through their spokesman, Peguis, which saved the settlement from attack and threat of starvation several times. For agents of the North West Company and the native and Métis people who relied on trade with the company, however, Selkirk's settlement posed an immediate threat to their livelihood, as it cut through the company's main line of communication and transport. The North West Company and its allies would prove to be the prime obstacle to Selkirk's National Settlement scheme at Red River, and it waged a multi-front war against it. Dominated, like the Hudson's Bay Company, by Highland Scots, the North West Company deployed their tight-knit network of agents in both the colonies and in Britain – based largely on personal ties of kinship and intermarriage – to launch a transatlantic attack on Selkirk's plans. In colonial offices and company boardrooms in London and in newspapers, journals and published pamphlets, the North West Company and its advocates repeated their arguments that settlement was a threat to their lucrative trade. None less than the renowned Scottish explorer Alexander Mackenzie, whom Selkirk admired, opposed the plan, arguing at a meeting of Hudson's Bay shareholders that 'it has been found that Colonisation is at all times unfavourable to the Fur Trade'.[51] Allied with anti-emigration advocates, North West Company agents penned anonymous letters to newspapers in the Highlanders, testifying to the hardships that emigrants would face. They also sent Gaelic-speaking agents into the Highlands to spread rumours of these hardships and of the duplicitous nature of emigration patrons like Selkirk.

In the summer of 1816, right before he sailed for North America to try to regain control of what was left of his dispersed and demoralised Highland colony at Red River, Selkirk mounted a hasty counter-attack to the North West Company's campaign against him, publishing *A Sketch of the Fur Trade in British North America*. In it he sought to ridicule the North West Company and the fur trade itself, as inimical to national prosperity, grounding his argument, as always, in the principles of political economy. Selkirk's *Sketch of the Fur Trade* reveals the influences of his reading of French and American accounts of North American colonisation, in addition to the Scottish influences evident in his *Observations*. Selkirk's own account begins with a backward glance at the origins of the trade during the French colonial period. This period constitutes for Selkirk a kind of Golden Era of European colonialism in the region, when exclusive trading privileges were controlled by provincial governors and handed out to a relative few, who formed a kind of benevolent landed aristocracy in the New World. This system, though it proved a check on the pace of expansion of the trade, worked to secure a more permanent prosperity through the increase of European settlement while at the same time was 'wisely adapted to increase the comforts, and improve the character, of the natives' (*Collected Writings*, vol. 2, p. 49). With the British conquest of New France, however, this system of careful regulation to manage the exchange in furs came to an end, and the trade was 'thrown open to public'. For Selkirk, the abolition of old regime of exclusive privileges inspired an intense competition among rival traders, in which 'every art which malice could devise was exerted without restraint . . .' (2:49). 'Carried on in a very distant country, out of the reach of legal restraint, and where there was a free scope given to any ways or means in attaining advantage', the fur trade produces its own typology of social corruption, the most notable instance of which is the class of free-roaming independent fur trappers, which Selkirk labels the 'Coureurs des Bois':

> [These] French Canadians, who, by accompanying the natives on their hunting and trading excursions, had become so attached to the Indian mode of life, that they had lost all relish for their former habits, and native homes. Of these people . . . they often brought home rich cargoes of furs, but that during the short time requisite to settle their accounts with the merchants, and procure fresh credit, they generally contrived to squander away all their gains. [T]his indifference about amassing property, and the pleasure of living free from all restraint, soon brought on a licentiousness of manners, which could not long escape the vigilant observation of the missionaries, who had much reason to complain of their being a disgrace to the Christian religion. (2:50)

If Selkirk, following Adam Smith, believed that the emergence of land as private property was the hallmark of advanced, and prosperous, commercial society, the fur trade, exemplified in the licentious manners of the coureurs des bois, blocked this emergence. Aligning themselves with their Indian counterparts in the trade, as trappers not traders, the coureurs des bois are tied in Selkirk's account to the early stages of human society, as demonstrated for him by their attachment to 'the Indian mode of life' and their relinquishing of 'their former habits, and native homes'. Nevertheless, as a class that derives all its wealth from the trade in furs, the coureurs des bois are constituted in the commercial world of merchant accounts and credit, in which the riches of the hunt become commodities tied to a lucrative transatlantic market of exchange. The history of the development of the current state of the fur trade in British dominions exemplifies for Selkirk the ways in which, without the guiding hand of state agents, the particular localised conditions in which commercial society arises can distort its progress – the symptoms of which are manifested in the appearance of the transient, half-savage, figure of the Coureur des Bois. Progress and prosperity are not inevitable. They must on occasion be goaded along by the state, acting under the guidance of interested individuals like Selkirk, with the requisite knowledge in political economy.

If the unregulated influx of wealth induces the coureurs des bois to adopt a 'licentiousness of manners', it produces an even more destructive effect among their Indian trading partners: 'Among the Indians it was found that a profuse supply of spirituous liquors was a shorter and more certain mode of obtaining a preference, than any difference in the quality or price of the goods offered for sale' (2:49). Their 'ungovernable propensity . . . to intoxication' being 'well known', Selkirk writes, the Indians were dragged into trader rivalries and feuds and duped into committing acts of ferocity upon imagined enemies. In short, he would write in an earlier piece on the trade, '[I]t is not too much to say that the Fur Trade has contributed to keep up and strengthen the savage habits of the American Indians, as much as the Slave Trade has those of the African Negroes'.[52]

What takes shape in Selkirk's account of the fur trade is a vast space of chaos and disorder, an immense frontier zone between one stage of society and another that is analogous to a Highlands in transition, but to a different degree. While in the Highlands the sudden and dramatic modernisation of systems of land use and land tenure had brought dispossession and discontent, the principles of political economy nevertheless gave Selkirk the confidence to predict that modernisation, secured by rule of law and the enshrinement of private property, inevitably would bring prosperity to the region. In contrast, the fur trade brought to the New World a dramatic and corrupting influx of material wealth while lacking the regulative restraint that the law provided back home. Left unchecked, this unhappy state of affairs in the colonies had produced not prosperity but stagnation:

> [W]hat is this Fur Trade . . .? A trade of which the gross returns never exceeded £300,000, and often not £200,000. A branch of commerce which gives occasion to the exportation of 40, or £50,000 of British manufactures! A trade, in which three ships are employed! This is the mighty object, for which, not only the rights of private property are to be invaded, but a territory of immense extent, possessing the greatest natural advantages, is to be condemned to perpetual sterility! (*Collected Writings*, vol. 2, p. 97)

The world of the fur trade is thus the antithesis of well-ordered and prosperous colonial domain envisioned in Selkirk's 'National

Settlement' scheme, which promised the replication of British social order in the New World through the establishment of discrete linguistic and cultural communities. Instead, the fur trade foments a zone of perpetual liminality, in which the interrelation between two cultures, two stages of social development, has produced an unsettling – because it is never quite 'settled' – degradation of both modes of life.

For Selkirk, the harmful effects of unregulated and uncontrolled intermingling of peoples and cultures brought together through the fur trade are quite literally embodied in the emergence of a new type of mixed people, whom Selkirk later describes in his own attempt to narrate the events surrounding his Red River Settlement as 'half-breeds'. In Selkirk's account, it is these people, living 'at a distance from the restraints of civilized society' and therefore 'ignorant of any law but that of the strongest', who were responsible for the campaign of intimidation and destruction against his Red River Colony on behalf of their North West Company masters (*Collected Writings*, vol. 2, p. 114). 'These half-breeds', Selkirk writes,

> (or Bois Brules as they were now to be called) . . . the sons of [the company's] Canadian and other servants by Indian women . . . have been described as a Nation of independent Indians: but they are in fact with very few exceptions in the regular employment and pay of the North West Company, mostly as canoemen, some as interpreters and guides, and a few of better education as clerks. (2:113)

'[B]red up in the most entire dependence on the Company', Selkirk continues, these half-breed men are all willing to undertake 'acts of violence' on its behalf.

Though utterly dismissive of their status as a separate 'Nation' of Indians, Selkirk's account reveals the significance of resistance to colonial settlement and land appropriation in consolidating a Métis identity, as the mixed peoples of Red River staked their claims to the region based on their ancestral memory of rights passed down to them through their native forebears.[53] Under the newly devised banner of their nation and led by Cuthbert Grant, the son of a Strathspey-born trader and a Cree or Assiniboine woman, the Métis allied themselves with the North West Company and led a campaign of open warfare against Selkirk's colony. With a sentiment that echoed those of the Kildonan families that had petitioned the Countess of Sutherland for just restoration of their land rights only a few years before, Grant promised to drive Selkirk's people from the region 'and never see any of them in the Colonizing way in Red River'.[54] This struggle achieved an iconic status in an emergent Métis collective memory, in the songs and oral history that established the Métis as a people with inalienable rights to the land.[55]

For Selkirk, however, enunciating a racial script that would persist long after, the Métis were outcasts – neither European nor Indian, they belonged nowhere and to no one. Instead, miscegenation between the two groups tropes the licentious condition of the fur trade as a whole, as it has produced a new 'bastard' class of criminal savagery let loose upon the landscape.[56] The conspicuous violence of 'half-breed' agents of the North West Company was illustrated, for Selkirk, in the June 1816 clash north of the settlement at Seven Oaks – or *la Grenouillière* (Frog Plain) – when the territorial governor and twenty others were killed in battle when they rode out to confront a party of Métis led by Grant. After the 'massacre' at Seven Oaks, Selkirk writes, 'the wounded men were lying on the field incapable of resistance, and calling out for mercy, when the half-breeds came up, and butchered them with the most horrid imprecations, stripping them of their bloody clothing, and in several instances, mangling the bodies in wanton cruelty' (*Collected Writings*, vol. 2, p. 123). 'Wanton cruelty' is the hallmark of half-breed people who in turn are the product of a corrupted system of trade that seeks to secure 'by means of violence and intimidation, a monopoly which is not yet secured by law ... a monopoly by which the native Indians are held in worse than Turkish slavery, and an extensive and valuable country is condemned to endless sterility' (2:130).

Indigenous Elsewhere: Indian Country

Selkirk imagines a relation between Europeans and indigenous peoples in his Ossiniboia that is governed by their respective relation to the land. Europeans, through the regime of private property, are the land's proprietors, given title to the land by purchase through treaty and company charter. As the original occupier of the land, the native is due some deference, but the ultimate control of the land – to establish a system of trade, build outposts, or divide it up into lots and distribute it to individuals – belongs to the proprietor, the European. Selkirk extends this native relation to the land that is other-than-proprietorship to the North West Company which, he writes, 'seeks the maintenance of exclusive possession where they have no exclusive right' of title (*Collected Writings*, vol. 2, p. 95). Without right of title, the whole of the fur trade perpetuated by the North West Company in the region is a 'gigantic system of *poaching*' (2:98). The distinction that Selkirk makes, between those who have title to the land and those who do not, establishes a critical understanding of land rights by which neither Indian occupation nor North West Company possession grants any claim of authority. Instead, power over the land is given to whom it is deeded under charter – that is, Selkirk – and it is the need to reassert these rights of landed property, as he explicitly states in the *Sketch of the Fur Trade*, that prompted him to undertake the long journey to Red River, as much as the desire to provide support to his beleaguered Highlanders (2:47).

Selkirk believed the Hudson's Bay Company charter granted him the power to expel the North West Company, or to place its operations under legal sanction, and to come to terms with Indians who remained on the land, even though they had no actual claim to it.[57] Selkirk's ultimate authority over the inhabitants of his land grant would prove expedient for his solution to the pacification and reordering of domains under his control, which, as was the case for the Highlands, demanded a wholesale relocation of its native populace. Circumstances in the colonies, however, called for not so much introduction of new regimes of land relations, but a return to older ones:

> It appears that the British Government acted on mistaken views when the old system of the French was abolished. – It would be advisable that we should retrace our steps, and re-establish that system . . . For this purpose, let the whole extent of Indian territory, be divided into districts of a convenient extent. Let the Hudson's Bay Company be confined within the bounds of the property legally vested in them. Let the rest of the Indian districts be leased for a period of years nearly . . . assigning to the lessees the exclusive trade of their respective districts, together with any other emoluments that can be derived from the paramount rights of landed property during the period of their lease, but under such regulations as may protect the Indian natives from oppression, and preclude them from the use of spirituous liquors which has proved the greatest bane to their improvement. (*Collected Writings*, vol. 2, p. 99)

With rhetorical flourish, Selkirk conjures a paternalistic return to an earlier Edenic arrangement in the colonies in which the ascension of landed property, along with the preservation of the natives, is derived from the active intervention of the state. Within lands set aside for them, Indians would be given 'permanent tenure of their hunting grounds, as nearly as practicable on the footing of private property' (2:99).

In an enthusiastic response to the London publication of a *Proposal for Forming a Society for Promoting the Civilization and Improvement of the North-American Indians Within the British Boundary* in 1806, Selkirk published a short piece that introduced some of the ideas he would develop later in his treatise on the fur trade. In this piece, Selkirk also sketched out his ideas on establishing a discrete Indian domain within British dominions in North America. No plan to civilise and improve the native in British North America would be possible, he wrote, without first isolating native populations from the pernicious influences of the trade in furs, as it both 'holds out a constant encouragement to hunting, which serves to divert the Indians from any more industrious pursuit' while allowing for the easy availability of 'spirituous liquors', which adds to their further debasement (*Observations on a Proposal*, p. 7). To protect Indian populations from the contagion of the fur trade, Selkirk proposed the establishment of what he termed an 'Indian country', divided into separate 'districts', which would replicate what he presumed were the pre-defined boundaries of tribal lands: 'The country within the Indian boundary should be laid out into districts of considerable extent, each coinciding, as nearly as possible, with the territories of a tribe or nation of the Indians' (16). At the same time, Selkirk called for the relocation of tribal peoples if necessary and the imposition of strict limits on the interaction between European and native to secure the integrity and purity of his all-native domain. In doing so, Selkirk was adapting and refining more generalised schemes that had circulated in North America since the 1763 Royal Proclamation, by which the Crown, after the defeat of New France, had sought to impose informal borders between white and Indian territories to regulate trade and settlement while ostensibly safeguarding Indian interests.[58] For his part, Selkirk writes:

> A boundary line must be drawn between the Indians and the Whites. That part of Canada, which has been purchased from the Indians by Government, and laid out for settlements, must be distinguished from

> the lands still occupied by the original natives. The Indians should be discouraged from resorting to the settled districts; and on the other hand, the settlers should be prohibited by law from going into the Indian country, without a license from Government. (15)

Wealth, prosperity and the safeguarding of native peoples will be secured in Ossiniboia by the benevolent hand of the state, acting through its agents, the Hudson's Bay Company and Selkirk himself, as long as the domains of European settlement and the aborigine be rigorously kept apart. In the vast anterior space of 'Indian country', the natives would be free to continue their way of life unmolested. Elsewhere, Selkirk called for the establishment of schools in Indian country as a force of gradual acculturation, 'to excite among them a general desire for improvement', but he emphasised that at these schools Indians should be taught in their native languages and their way of life respected, free to pursue their own path to civilisation (*Collected Writings*, vol. 2, p. 4).[59] 'Indian country' thus names for Selkirk a different order of colonial space entirely than that of the wild, untamed frontier beyond European civilisation. Instead, Indian country is analogous to the Highland National Settlement, a kind of landed set-aside, an indigenous preserve, marked out and operated by its white proprietors and thus strictly integrated into the regime of private property, securing the interests of empire while staving off the aborigine's immediate demise.

Preservation of native ways through the creation and maintenance of native enclaves, all in the service of settlement and expansion – this idea lies at the heart of Selkirk's various colonial schemes, all of which are dependent upon removing and relocating people from ancestral lands. Selkirk's idea to establish a series of districts in an Indian country, as would most of his schemes, came to naught, but the belief that the march of progress could somehow accommodate the Indian way of life through the creation of special enclaves, would become the justification for the greatest single act of dispossession and forced removal of native peoples in North American history. In the United States, the debate on what to do about the aborigine 'problem' roughly paralleled that in Britain, though it was of much greater intensity and scope. By the late 1820s a solution had coalesced from the observations of a group of influential writers who, like Selkirk, were widely respected because of their long experience with the native population.

Thomas McKenney and Lewis Cass were Selkirk's intellectual counterparts: both men expressed their great sympathy towards the plight of native peoples while dismissing their specific land claims.[60] Indebted to Scottish Enlightenment theories of the stadial development of human society, particularly those of William Robertson – whose *History of America* had become the standard reference on Indians in the United States in the nineteenth century – McKenney and Cass agreed that the only way to alleviate the 'present degraded, scattered, and withering condition' of aboriginal Indians was to remove them from their ancestral lands and to consolidate and relocate them in a single territory, far away from the corrupting influences of white civilisation.[61] In the crosscurrents of transatlantic intellectual exchange, Selkirk and his US counterparts arrived at similar conclusions about the native peoples of their respective countries: that the taking of ancestral lands necessitated by dictates of improvement could be made compatible with the continued preservation of native way of life through the paternalistic establishment of indigenous enclaves, 'islands of tribalism', as Charles F. Wilkinson terms them.[62] At the same time, the borders of this new domain would be rigorously secured and maintained by the US government. The conclusions of McKenney and Cass would become the foundation of arguments in Andrew Jackson's administration and its supporters in Congress, which culminated in the passage of the Indian Removal Act of 1830. The act inaugurated a long process of US expulsion of Cherokee, Chickasaw, Choctaw, Creek and Seminole people from ancestral lands in the southern United States, and their relocation to 'Indian Territory', west of the Mississippi. Perhaps thousands died on the long march to lands reserved for them, known to history as the Trail of Tears.

Like its counterpart in Britain, the discursive formation of the aborigine in America was shaped through the circumstances of relentless taking of land and its opening up in the name of improvement and modernisation. In turn, the emergence of an 'aboriginal' relation to the land shaped new topographies in the imperial imagination – Selkirk's 'National Settlement' and 'Indian country', and Jackson's 'Indian Territory' and their late-century offspring, the tribal 'reserve' and 'reservation'. In these, the terms of the continued survival of indigenous people were established in a geography not of their own making. These geographies delimited the preservation of the native way of life under the benevolent protection of the state and in the service of the relentless dispossession of their lands, in the empire of the modern world.

Indigenous Elsewheres and Modern Memory (the River of Now and Then)

In ways therefore that Hugh MacLennan only partially realised, the Atlantic world is etched with the remembrances of dispossession, of a transatlantic collective memory that bespeaks a rootedness in a land and community elsewhere. For Gaels, displacement brought on renewed hardships and remembrance of lands and homes they had left. As Highlanders negotiated their way into North America, reshaping their identities in response to new surroundings and new conditions, they expressed ambivalence about the world they had left behind and the new one in which the settled. Oral tradition and written poetry on both sides of the Atlantic testify to the psychic toll of Clearance and emigration and to continuous acts of remembering and forgetting. In the crucible of dispossession was forged a transatlantic collective memory of Clearance, as the poems and songs composed by Gaelic speakers in the New World were transmitted back to Scotland – and vice versa – via antiquarian society collections, newspapers and periodicals, and on the lips of those who made the journey back.[63] As Margaret MacDonnell writes, almost all emigrant songs, even those which reveal a deep sorrow at leaving home, describe the conditions that made emigration 'inevitable and irresistible to thousands of Highlanders'.[64] Those that recounted the transatlantic experience of the emigrants make frequent reference to increased rents, the introduction of sheep and new landlords and their agents, and the general disregard for local tenantry, which had compelled the people to leave. Many of these songs evince the hope that the people might find a new and prosperous land where they could perpetuate the ways of their ancestors without hindrance, throwing off the yoke of landlord tyranny and become land proprietors themselves. On the other hand, some emigrants describe finding themselves in a cruel New World of a dark and foreboding wilderness, in which the past provides no purchase in the present. One of the best-known examples of this sentiment, *A' Choille Ghruamaich* ('The Gloomy Forest'), written by John MacLean, Am Bàrd MacGhillEathain, originally from Tiree, is a statement of betrayal at the hands of the emigration agents who made false promises of the virtues of the New World and of the psychic and social costs of dispossession:

> Gu bheil mi am ònrachd 'sa' choille ghruamaich,
> Mo smaointinn luaineach, cha tog mi fonn:
> Fhuair mi an t-àit so an aghaidh nàduir,
> Gu'n d' thréig gach talent a bha 'nam cheann.
> Cha dèan mi òran a chur air dòigh ann,
> An uair nì mi tòiseachadh bidh mi trom:
> Chaill mi a' Gàidhlig seach mar a b'àbhaist dhomh
> An uair a bhà mi 'san dùthaich thall[65]

(I'm all alone in this gloomy woodland, my mind is troubled, I sing no song; against all nature I took this place here and native wit from my mind has gone. I have no spirit to polish poems, my will to start them is dulled by care; I lose the Gaelic that was my custom in yon far country over there.)

The miasma of dislocation is combined with a palpable homesickness, 'the ache of memory [which] grows more and more . . . each night and day and in very task I turn to', as MacLean fondly recalls the 'dear land beside the ocean' where 'now no sea laps my dwelling's shore': 'Gach là is oidhche is gach car a nì mi / Gu'm bi mi cuimhneachadh anns gach am / An tìr a dh' fhàg mi tha an taic an t-sàile, / Ged tha mi an dràsd ann am bràighe ghleann'.[66]

The traumatic circumstances of the unhappy departure of the Highland people delimit the parameters of what has been identified as a Scottish diaspora culture in contemporary Canada – for MacLennan the ghosts of the dispossessed in the deserted Highland landscape bear the memory of his own exiled ancestors, but he can see only a memory-less landscape back 'home' in Canada.[67] But, for others, the spirits that MacLennan sees only in the Highlands haunt the contested landscape of the New World itself. Margaret Laurence, in *The Diviners*, describes the persistence of the ghosts of dispossession, not only in the imaginative rendering of the memory of the Highland ancestors of her Manitoba-born protagonist, but also of First Nations and Métis people dispossessed by white settlers.[68] In the 'memorybank movies' of her childhood, Morag Gunn remembers the stories told to her of her progenitors, the Kildonan people brought to the Red River region by the Earl of Selkirk. These stories recounted their struggle: the single-file journey in the snow as their piper, a Gunn, 'led them with his pipes blaring' and the hardships and violent conflict they faced once they arrived; but also the cruelty of the 'bitch duchess', the Countess of Sutherland, who burned them out of their homes in the Highlands.[69] At the same time, Morag's lover, Jules Tonnerre, recalls to her the stories of his Métis ancestors, who fought with Cuthbert Grant and, later, Louis Riel in the struggle to reclaim the lands lost to their people at Red River. *The Diviners* offers a complex exploration of the cultural legacy of dispossession, emigration and migration in both the Old and New Worlds.[70] On the one hand, the novel describes a persistence of memory of, and identification with, a time and place elsewhere, which continues to insinuate itself in the national psyche, and which forms a critical component of the collective memory of a Scottish diaspora in contemporary Canada.[71] Laurence's novel, however, also evokes the persistence of an aboriginal or indigenous memory, bringing awareness of the Métis as a distinct peoples and of their history of dispossession engendered by white colonialism in lands they still inhabit.

Reading Laurence's contemporary rendering of the memory of dispossession in the New World in the context of Selkirk's writings and plans for colonial settlement allows us to see parallels in the status of two distinct peoples from opposite ends of the Atlantic world brought together and subjected to similar conditions as they become conflated through a discursive category of the 'aborigine'. After they come into contact in the New World, however, the histories of these two 'aboriginal' peoples diverge. Selkirk's elaborate plans for the preservation of Scottish Gaels in the New World were based in part on his paternalistic denial of their claims on land tenure in the Highlands. But in British Canada, Highlanders faced no such widespread denial and were free to acquire and work the land as they desired, subject to the same conditions and travails of any other settler. Fully integrated into the regime of private property, as landowners and participants in the great nineteenth-century rush to settle Indian lands, Highland Scots helped shape the landscape of settler nations in the New World.[72] In a similar vein, Selkirk's proposal for an Indian set-aside in British North America was premised on his belief that the natives had no title to the lands they occupied; however, Selkirk himself would eventually acquiesce to pressure that he negotiate a formal treaty with representatives of various tribal peoples in the Red River area to establish and regulate relations between Indians and his settlement.[73] The common recourse to treaties and treaty-making to establish and regulate relations between indigenous people and whites in Canada and in the United States and other settler countries has formed, in turn, the basis for a historical memory that has shaped contemporary indigenous political struggles to reclaim sovereignty over their ancestral lands. The 'discourse of treaties', Chadwick Allen writes, 'since it operated within a paradigm of nation-to-nation status . . . provides one of the few interpretive frames within which contemporary indigenous minority activist and writers can stage formal dialogue with dominant settler interests on (potentially) equitable terms'.[74]

The contemporary discourse on indigenous struggle over sovereignty and the 'discourse of treaties' is testament to a conspicuous shift in the terms used to describe native peoples: the 'aborigine' has become the 'indigene', and a conceptual frame that gained common currency in a colonial discourse that arose from the historical circumstances of widespread dispossession and discontent has been constructively refashioned, put to new uses and to serve new cultural paradigms.[75] What once named a particular kind of problem, a disruption, in the modernising project of nation-states has been seized upon by anticolonial resistance movements around the world to serve as the discursive foundation for an insistent critique of native dispossession and the ongoing struggle for the recovery of ancestral land rights. The distinctiveness of indigenous peoples and their relation to European and settler colonialism has in part inspired the call for a new international category, the 'Fourth World': a term, as Allen summarises, used to distinguish particular historical contexts and the contemporary concerns of indigenous minorities from those of majority populations of so-called Third World nations, as well as from those majority-settler populations that now control most of traditional territories claimed by indigenous minorities. 'The Fourth World condition', Allen writes, 'is marked by a perennial struggle between "native" indigeneity and "settler" or "New World" indigeneity'.[76] To live in the Fourth World is to stand in a relation to colonialism that is akin to but distinct from a Third World identity: simply put, for indigenous peoples colonialism is not yet 'post'. Therefore, while the postcolonial paradigm provides useful ideas and a framework for a critique of a colonial discourse, many native studies critics and activists take issue with its critical emphasis on the ambivalence or hybridity of this discourse and on the constructedness of national, ethnic or racial identities. For these critics and activists, a postcolonial perspective is an insufficient weapon in the ongoing struggle for native self-determination, in which the recovery of tribal perspectives and the re-recognition of the authority of white treaty discourses (rather than their deconstruction) form a significant part.[77]

In the Highlands the struggle to recover communal land rights that were lost in the Clearances would continue long after Selkirk's settlement schemes became history.[78] This resistance to land appropriations, which has now lasted for over two centuries, helped consolidate and stabilise a sense of local, native, shared community in the Highlands which has only recently been linked to the Fourth World indigenous movement. Although the status of Highland crofting community as an indigenous one remains contested, many see parallels between the movement in the Highlands to reclaim ancestral lands once held communally and indigenous movements elsewhere, particularly those of the Sammi people of northern Scandinavia.[79] The Western Isles, write Bryden and Geisler, have become the 'epicentre' for a 'community-centric' reform movement, 'significant for its strong embrace of culture and community', in which lands are purchased and held in trust by the local people.[80] Such reclamations, A. Fiona D. Mackenzie writes, are part of a 'commoning' of lands taking place in the Highlands that is reversing the entrenched practice of enclosure and dispossession that began in the early modern era. This commoning of land hearkens back to previous generations' expressions of *dùthchas*, encapsulated by a crofter living in Lewis:

> There is no sense of ownership; it is a sense of belonging. You are part of the land . . . It is your heritage . . . In Gaelic you never think about the land belonging to you; it is you that belongs to the land. The people belong to the land. That's the only connection that's made in relation to people and land . . . People belong to that land . . . Not just the land, but the whole concept of belonging to that land, everything that goes with life we live here . . . These are inherited rights that nobody can argue with.[81]

The memory of past ways and past practices, whose nature is perhaps not easily communicated outside the Gaelic in which it originates, nevertheless is testament to a notion of collective identity expressed as the interplay of ancestral memory, land and kinship inherent in the concept of *dùthchas*, which had formed the ideological basis for Highland resistance to dispossession in the late eighteenth and early nineteenth centuries. Analogous to the 'blood/land/memory complex' which Allen argues plays a critical role in indigenous activist discourse of the contemporary era, the expression of continuity of language and of community in the face of dispossession also provides a framework for a contemporary land reform movement in the Highlands.[82] In celebrations marking the recovery of communally held lands, which hearken back to ancient land practices in the Highlands, Calum MacMillan, spokesperson for the Stòras Uibhist land trust, evoked the memory of displaced but hopeful Highlanders as they sailed to North America: 'This is where the New World is now!'[83] Highland land reform encompasses the global community of Gaels, as it looks to the past while moving into the future.

But what is at stake in contemporary land reform taking place in the Western Isles for the New World descendants of those dispossessed Kildonan families who departed the Highlands on Selkirk's ships two hundred years ago? How does the present-day communing of appropriated lands and the re-emergence of the Highland aborigine, as a Fourth World indigene, shape or alter our understanding of those in North America whose Highland identity is coterminous with the 'elsewhere' of where they live now? How does diasporic memory overlap with indigenous memory, if at all? The fate of the emigrant and crofter long ago diverged, but their descendants continue to maintain formal and informal associations, lines of communication, and a shared sense of a history and collective memory, which constitute a shared communal identity across the Atlantic. This transatlantic communal identity also shares with tribal peoples in North America a troubled past of dispossession and dislocation, a shared past that is becoming increasingly recognised within both Scottish, emigrant and native communities.[84] The transperipheral history of the Highland 'aborigine' in Scotland in the nineteenth century, and increasingly instances of affiliation and identification between tribal peoples and Gaels, suggests that the past of Highland dispossession and emigration cannot be understood within a diasporic frame or an indigenous one.[85] Instead, the Highlander in the New World lies somewhere, as always, in the space between these categories, the subject of a powerful transatlantic discourse of nativity, by which vast communities were systematically dispossessed, dislocated and resettled.

Notes

1. MacLennan, *Scotchman's Return, and Other Essays*, p. 7.
2. For recent historical accounts of Highlanders in North America and their relations with Indians, see Calloway, *White People, Indians, and Highlanders*; Hunter, *A Dance Called America*; Ferenc Szasz, *Scots in the North American West*, especially pp. 49–77; Margaret Connell Szasz, *Scottish Highlanders and Native Americans*; and Newton, *We're Indians Sure Enough*.
3. Weaver, *The Great Land Rush*, p. 4. See also Belich, *Replenishing the Earth*.
4. Weaver, *The Great Land Rush*, p. 5.
5. For Gaelic commentary on Sellar, see Dòmhnall Bàillidh's 'Aoir air Pàdraig Sellar' (Satire on Patrick Sellar), in which the poet describes Sellar as 'ceàrd dubh' ('black rogue'), adding:

    Nam faighinn-s' air an raon thu
    Is daoine bhith gadf cheangal,
    Bheirinn le mo dhòrnaibh
    Trì òirlich a-mach dhed sgamhan

    (If I could get at you on an open field, / with people tying you down, / I would pull with my fists three inches (of flesh) out of your lungs') (Meek, *Tuath Is Tighearna*, p. 54, trans. p. 190). Meek reports that the poem was preserved in Prince Edward Island, and that no version appears to have survived in Scotland.
6. Quoted in Adam, *Papers on Sutherland Estate Management*, vol. 1, p. 156.
7. 'Napier Commission', p. 8.
8. Quoted in Richards, *Highland Clearances*, p. 132.
9. For recent accounts of Highland reaction to Clearance, see Meek, *Tuath Is Tighearna*; Richards, *The Highland Clearances*; Withers, *Gaelic Scotland*; and Hunter, *The Making of the Crofting Community*.
10. For a recent account of the Sutherland Clearances, see Hunter, *Set Adrift upon the World*. For Selkirk's offer to the Countess of Sutherland to relocate cleared Kildonan tenants in Red River, see Bumsted, *Lord Selkirk: A Life*, pp. 222–30; and Adam, *Papers on Sutherland Estate Management*, vol. 1, pp. 142–3. The Countess politely rebuffed Selkirk's offer, believing it would pose greater difficulties for the tenants and would undermine her plans for their relocation elsewhere on the estate.
11. Quoted in Adam, *Papers on Sutherland Estate Management*, vol. 1, pp. 175–6.
12. According to the *OED* online, the first use of term, in plural form, is in R. Hyrde's ?1529 translation of Juan Luis Vives's *The Instruction*

of *Christen Woman*, referring to the people or race who first inhabited Latium before the ascendancy of the Roman Empire. In later use, it more generally connoted the earliest known inhabitants of a particular country: Bolingbroke distinguishes between 'the ancient Britons' who 'are to us the Aborigines of our Island', and subsequent Roman and Anglo-Saxon invaders, in Letter 12 of his 1735 *Dissertation upon Parties*. In a 1799 entry included in *A Walk through Some of the Western Counties of England* (1800), Richard Warner suggests the antiquarian can discriminate 'between the vallations of Celtic aborigenes and the huge mounds of their Saxon invaders'. The first use of the term to connote 'a member of an ethnic group inhabiting or occupying a country before the arrival of European colonists and those whom they introduced' appears in a 1722 entry of the *Letter-Book* of Massachusetts merchant and jurist Samuel Seawall, who used the term in reference to Indians of New England ('aborigine, n and adj.').

13. Even those who were sympathetic to the plight of local tenants in the Highlands termed them 'aboriginal' in the sense that Sellar employs. David Dunoon, minister of parish of Killearnan, in Sinclair's *Statistical Account of Scotland* laments the plight of the 'poor aborigines' who are compelled to emigrate 'friendless and unprotected', though his answer to their plight, is, like many other commentators, not to question the validity of agricultural improvement but rather the pace in which it is implemented in the Highlands (17:344–45). Ironically, Dunoon's son emigrated to America and settled in Pictou, where he became an important landowner who sought to arrange emigration for other Highlanders around the turn of century (Bumsted, *The People's Clearance*, p. 88). For the discourse of aboriginal extinction, see Brantlinger and Dippie, *The Vanishing American*.

14. A year older than Scott, Selkirk joined the Speculative Society in 1789, the year before Scott did. Selkirk's first opportunity to speak in the society was on the topic of the benefits of the French Revolution, for which Selkirk, his biographer writes, 'weighed in on the affirmative side' (Bumsted, *Lord Selkirk*, p. 36). At the end of the eighteenth century, the society was dominated by Whigs. Brougham, Horner and Jeffrey, who first met while members, would go on to found the *Edinburgh Review*. (Loch joined in 1798 and became the society's president the year after.)

15. Selkirk, *Observations on the Present State of the Highlands of Scotland*, p. 1. The second, 1806, edition of the *Observations* is included in Bumsted's 1984 authoritative edition of Selkirk's collected writings. Before publication of this edition, the most readily available version of the *Observations* was a 1969 reprint of the first edition, published as part

of the *Canadiana before 1867* series. All references are to the first, 1805, edition, except when otherwise noted, and are given in abbreviated form in the body of the text, or by page number alone where unambiguous.
16. Smith, *Lectures on Jurisprudence*, p. 23.
17. Grant, *Essays*, vol. 1, pp. 70–1.
18. MacInnes, 'The Panegyric Code in Gaelic Poetry', p. 279.
19. Newton, *Gaelic Handbook*, p. 209.
20. See Dodgshon, *From Chiefs to Landlords*. For a discussion of *dùthchas* as the underpinning of an ideology of protest and resistance in the Highlands, see Withers, *Gaelic Scotland*, pp. 77–8, 389–91; and Mackenzie, *Places of Possibility*, pp. 34–78.
21. Selkirk relied heavily on statistical accounts and the surveys in the establishment of his Red River Colony. The universal typology used to index lands in the statistical account presumed that land in any locations that was subject to similar conditions of climate, terrain, soil type and so forth would produce similar crops and yields. Hence, in his prospectus for the colony, Selkirk writes that in Red River 'there is more reason to expect that hemp may be raised with success, as the soil and climate of . . . appear to bear a near resemblance to those of the Ukraine, and the other Russian provinces, from whence the chief supplies are now drawn' (*Collected Writings*, vol. 2, p. 17). (All subsequent references to the *Collected Writings* are given in abbreviated form in the body of the text, or by volume and page number alone where unambiguous.) Selkirk employed Peter Fidler, a surveyor for the Hudson's Bay Company, to conduct the first survey of the intended area of Red River Settlement shortly before the first settlers arrived. The date of his work is uncertain, but Fidler, who 'insisted upon running one of his lines through the middle of the garden' of the post of the North West Company, the Hudson's Bay Company's chief competitor, likely completed his work in the summer of 1813 or 1814. Fidler's survey would provide the basis for the pattern of settlement in the area for years to come (Archer, *The Hudson's Bay Company's Land Tenures*, p. 108).
22. For an account of the extensiveness and timing of the surveys, which immediately preceded the evictions, see Fairhurst, 'The Surveys for the Sutherland Clearances'. Local people in the Highlands, like native peoples in North America, were often aware that the early presence of surveyors signalled the eventual disruption of their land tenure, and Loch reported in 1813 that Kildonan tenants, who had disregarded the lot boundaries established by the estate surveyor, were now actively chasing surveyors and valuers off the land. See Richards, *Highland Clearances*, p. 132; Adam, *Papers on Sutherland Estate Management*, vol. 1, p. 207. Similarly, the 1869 Red River Resistance in what had been Selkirk's

North American land grant, began when a party of armed Métis led by Louis Riel destroyed survey chains and stopped Canadian surveyors from establishing a baseline, in the lead-up to Canadian annexation of the region (Weaver, *The Great Land Rush*, p. 230).
23. Gray, *The Highland Economy*, p. 23. For pre-capitalist agrarian society in the Highlands, see Hunter, *The Making of the Crofting Community*, especially pp. 6–14; Richards, *The Highland Clearances* and *A History of the Highland Clearances*; and Dodgshon, *From Chiefs to Landlords*.
24. Loch, *An Account of the Improvements*, p. 50. All subsequent references are given in abbreviated form in the body of the text, or by page number alone where unambiguous.
25. See Kosseleck, *Futures Past*.
26. Bumstead describes the willingness of Gaels with means to emigrate, rather than eking out a living elsewhere on the estate landless and under the landlord's terms, as the 'people's clearance'. Bumsted's work represented an important revision of the historiography of the Clearances, which had seen them in the stark terms of agentless victims succumbing to the cruelty of merciless landlords (*The People's Clearance*). See also McLean, *The People of Glengarry*.
27. In 1802, for example, a party of 445 people, consisting of equal numbers of men, women and children under thirteen, emigrated to Glengarry County in Lower Canada from the west Highlands. The relatively large number of women and children in the party demonstrated 'the wholesale transference of large parts of the Highland communities' at the turn of the century to the new Gaelic settlement in Canada (McLean, *The People of Glengarry*, pp. 139–40).
28. Stewart, *Sketches*, vol. 1, p. 91. All subsequent references are given in abbreviated form in the body of the text, or by volume and page number alone where unambiguous.
29. Campbell, *The Grampians Desolate*, pp. 8–9. All subsequent references are given in abbreviated form in the body of the text, or by page number alone where unambiguous.
30. See Shields, 'Highland Emigration and the Transformation of Nostalgia in Romantic Poetry'; and Daley, '"Return No More!"'.
31. See Shields, 'Highland Emigration and the Transformation of Nostalgia in Romantic Poetry'.
32. For an analysis of the signifying structure of European Romanticism as a critique of modernity, see Löwy and Sayre, *Romanticism against the Tide of Modernity*. See also Baucom, *Specters of the Atlantic*; Makdisi, *Romantic Imperialism*; and Womack, *Improvement and Romance*. The terms 'theoretical realism' and 'melancholy romanticism' are Baucom's.

33. The figure of the (invariably male) Highlander profoundly attached to his mountain homeland became a prime example in an emergent discourse on nostalgia, which in eighteenth-century medical writing was deemed a physical malady. First coined by a Swiss doctor, Johannes Hofer, in his medical dissertation in 1688, 'nostalgia' was diagnosed as a mental derangement, noticed in some soldiers stationed far from their home for whom sensory impulses associated with their homeland – especially sound – afflicted the imagination in ways thought to incapacitate the body. By the late eighteenth century nostalgia was termed a 'national disease' that afflicted those who lived in mountainous climes – Scottish Highlanders and Swiss were the most common examples – most acutely. Few European accounts of nostalgia in the eighteenth century are complete without mention of the Swiss succumbing to the disease upon hearing their native 'Ranz-des-Vaches', or of Scottish Highlanders who fall victim to its effects upon hearing the sound of the bagpipe far from home. For the origins of nostalgia, see Austin, *Nostalgia in Transition*; Boym, *The Future of Nostalgia*, especially pp. 3–18; Goodman, 'Romantic Poetry and the Science of Nostalgia'; Illbruck, *Nostalgia*; Rosen, 'Nostalgia: A "Forgotten" Psychological Disorder'; Starobinski, 'The Idea of Nostalgia'; and Turner, 'A Note on Nostalgia'. For a discussion of the general shift in attitudes toward nostalgia and 'local attachment' in the Romantic era, see McKillop, 'Local Attachment and Cosmopolitanism'.
34. For one of the rare anglophone indictments of landowner behaviour of the time, which called for a return to lower rents and the traditional relations between tenants and titular chieftains, see *The Present Conduct of the Chieftains and Proprietors of Lands in the Highlands of Scotland*.
35. Black, 'The Gaelic Academy', pp. 2–3.
36. Ibid. p. 3.
37. The cost of passage to Nova Scotia, the cheapest North American destination from the west Highlands, 'rose from £4 to £10 after June 1803' (McLean, *The People of Glengarry*, p. 145). Many Highland families able to liquidate their assets, however, could still manage to finance emigration.
38. In 1773, the same year in which the *Hector* departed for Nova Scotia, one of the earliest significant sailings of Highland emigrants to North America, Samuel Johnson reported that, much to his dismay and regret, an 'emigration mania' was overspreading the Highlands. 'Some method', wrote Johnson, 'to stop this epidemick desire of wandering, which spreads its contagion from valley to valley, deserves to be sought with great diligence' (*A Journey to the Western Isles of Scotland*, p. 102). The

Highland mania for emigration was epitomised by the new phenomenon that he and Boswell observed during their stay in Skye, the dance called 'America' in which each of the couples 'successively whirls around in a circle, till all are in motion; and the dance seems intended to show how emigration catches, till a whole neighborhood is set afloat' (327).

39. See Clyde, *From Rebel to Hero*; Womack, *Improvement and Romance*, pp. 27–60; and McNeil, *Scotland, Britain, Empire*, pp. 83–116.

40. By the 1830s Selkirk's pro-emigration stance became predominant throughout the British Empire. As Clearance progressed unabated in the Highlands, it combined with famine to create widespread social distress and impoverishment. Highland landowners began to accept emigration as a necessary check on the distress caused by problems of Malthusian 'overpopulation' and social intransigence. As early as 1819 one of Selkirk's agents in Scotland wrote to Selkirk in Canada on the prescience of Selkirk's views on emigration. With perhaps some exaggeration, the agent wrote: 'Highland proprietors . . . find (as your Lordship predicted) that their estates are consumed by a superabundant, increasing, poor, useless population, who have wasted the means at home that might formerly have enabled them to transport themselves to another quarter of the globe, where they might be of service to themselves & to our manufacturers at home, instead of starving & hanging now as a dead weight upon the industry of others' ('Alex. Macdonald to Selkirk', 18:6009–10, MG19-E1, 18, Microfilm reel C-6, Library and Archives Canada). In 1826 Lord MacDonald assisted the emigration of about 1,300 from his North Uist estate (Devine, *Clanship to Crofter's War*, p. 185). The Passenger Vessels Act was repealed in 1827, and by the 1830s landowners in the Highlands actively sought government support of emigration assistance schemes.

41. In the second edition, Selkirk would add emphasis to this point, writing, 'For these reasons, it is an unavoidable consequence that a great portion of the small occupiers of land must be dispossessed' (*Collected Writings*, vol. 1, p. 115).

42. Tacksmen, or *fir-tasca*, occupied a middle position in traditional Highland society and, often bilingual and literate, had in many instances emerged as the spokesmen and leaders of their communities in resisting landowner action in the era of Clearance.

43. In addition to tacksmen and opportunist emigration agents, Alexander Irvine, minster at Rannoch, locates the source of Highland discontent in the 'perturbation of their mind'. The cause of 'this mental derangement', Irvine writes, may be difficult to trace, but its effects 'are visible, and deserve the serious regard of every true politician' as it has led to a widespread distrust of landowners, flagrant disregard for private property, and

a desire to emigrate throughout the region (*An Inquiry into the Causes and Effects of Emigration*, p. 54).
44. Quoted in Bumsted, *Lord Selkirk*, p. 230.
45. These, like many of Selkirk's unpublished writings on North American settlement, are housed in the Library and Archives of Canada, as part of the Selkirk Papers collection. This collection, which runs to fifty-four volumes, consists primarily of transcripts of Selkirk's correspondence, made in 1906. The originals, held on St Mary's Isle in Scotland, were destroyed by fire in 1940. For convenience, references to these writings are included in the main body of the text and in abbreviated form.
46. Selkirk also would propose 'national' settlements comprised of Irish, Welsh, Dutch, German and Swiss emigrants in his writing at various times, but, by a wide margin, the majority of his writings on national settlement involved Scottish Highlanders.
47. Selkirk brought over 800 passengers mainly from Skye to an area near present-day Belfast, Prince Edward Island, in the summer of 1803. In the summer of the following year, he brought some one hundred people, mostly from the Hebrides to a settlement he named 'Baldoon', in reference to his family's Scottish estates. The swampy land proved not conducive to the planned sheep farms, but very conducive to malaria. The settlement was destroyed by an invading American militia in July 1812 (see Bumsted, *Lord Selkirk*).
48. The initial arrangements for Kildonan communities to leave for Red River were confused and incomplete. Selkirk had originally envisioned establishing a colonial regiment comprised of Kildonan men, whose emigration would be funded by the government. Their families would initially remain on their Kildonan lands until they could be sent over after a year or so. When government support of a Kildonan regiment fell through, Selkirk found himself in the position of appearing to have broken his agreement. However, thirteen families, well over ninety people, did agree to set sail for Red River. For a historical account of Selkirk's negotiations, see Hunter, *Set Adrift upon the World*; and Bumsted, *The People's Clearance*, pp. 188–213.
49. After an ocean journey that saw widespread sickness, Kildonan settlers arrived in August 1813 at Fort Churchill on Hudson's Bay, where they were forced to winter. After an arduous 150-mile (240-kilometre) overland trek to York Factory, the settlers set out for Red River Settlement by boat in May 1814 and made landfall on 22 June 1814.
50. For a history of the fur trade in the region, see Binnema, Ens and Macleod, *From Rupert's Land to Canada*; and Ens, *Homeland to Hinterland*. For an analysis of the fur trade and the formation of an intercultural 'middle

ground' between natives and Europeans, see White, *The Middle Ground*, pp. 94–141.
51. Quoted in Bumsted, *Lord Selkirk*, p. 201.
52. Selkirk, *Observations on a Proposal*, p. 8. All subsequent references are given in abbreviated form in the body of the text, or by page number alone where unambiguous.
53. For a history of Métis land claims, see Flanagan, *Metis Lands in Manitoba*.
54. Quoted in MacLeod and Morton, *Cuthbert Grant of Grantown*, p. 36.
55. Selkirk's plan to 'settle' once and for all the problem of Highland dispossession marked the birth of the struggle for Métis recognition, as it signalled commencement of a long history of state-sponsored native dispossession. For a discussion of the ways in which resistance to Selkirk's colony shaped a distinctive Métis identity in the second decade of the nineteenth century, see Peterson, 'Many Roads to Red River'. See also Peers, *Gathering Places*; and Barkwell, Dorion and Hourie, *Metis Legacy II*. See MacLeod's discussion of 'La Bataille des Sept Chenes', or 'La Chanson de la Grenouillère', penned by Pierre Falcon, Grant's son-in-law, to commemorate the Métis victory over the settlement party at the June 1816 Battle of Seven Oaks (*Songs of Old Manitoba*, pp. 1–9).
56. On 17 August 1816 Selkirk wrote to Upper Canada's Attorney-General, D'Arcy Boulton, that he was sending to him a group of captive militants, 'A Cargo of Criminals of a larger Calibre than usually came before the Courts at York ... mainly bastard Half-Breeds' (quoted in Bumsted's introduction to *Collected Writings*, vol. 2, p. lviii).
57. Selkirk's assertion of rights against the North West Company took place in courts of law in Canada, and in the court of public opinion through various publications, in which Selkirk asserted his magistrate authority under Hudson's Bay Company charter. Legal jurisdiction in the region, however, was ill-defined and contradictory, and Selkirk ultimately had to defend his arrest and imprisonment of North West Company agents against accusations that he had exceeded his authority in doing so.
58. The Royal Proclamation of 1763 marked the first official British attempt to establish a boundary between Indians and whites. Intended in part to resolve conflicts between colonists and Indians in the aftermath of the Seven Years War, the proclamation established the Appalachians as the boundary between Indian lands and British settlement. Colonial administrators were forbidden to permit surveys or to grant lands west of the Appalachian watershed, which was to be reserved for Indian nations. Settlers who had already settled in the region demarcated as Indian would be forced to relocate. The Crown, however, retained its

soverignty over the newly established Indian territory, 'reserving' unexplored lands for the use of the tribes. The Proclamation of 1763 and establishment of an 'Indian Country' represented a significant consolidation of colonial space in North America. In the early years of the republic, the United States adopted similar Indian relations policies; the Intercourse Act of 1796 was the first designation of Indian Country in a statute law. It forbade whites to cross over the Indian boundary line to hunt or to drive their cattle there to graze, on penalty of a $100 fine or up to six months' imprisonment. (See Prucha, *American Indian Policy in the Formative Years*, pp. 20–50, 145; Hoxie, 'Why Treaties?', pp. 96–7.) Perhaps one of the earliest suggestions for the establishment of a boundary between whites and Indians comes from Samuel Sewall of the Massachusetts Bay Colony. In 1722 he wrote: 'I have been of the Opinion these Twenty years, that unalterable Bounds, such as rivers and Rocks and Mountains, should be fixed between the Aborigines and us; to free them from all suspicion of our having a design to root them out' (*The Letter-Book of Samuel Sewall*, p. 142).

59. These ideas are taken from a fifteen-page pamphlet on Indian education, published in 1807, which Selkirk's editor discovered in the Ontario Archives. Though Selkirk's authorship cannot be absolutely established, the ideas in the pamphlet, his editor argues, are in keeping with Selkirk's, and the style and publication circumstances of the pamphlet lend weight to the argument that the work is Selkirk's.

60. McKenney, head of the Office of Indian Affairs within Andrew Jackson's War Department, and Cass, governor of the Michigan territory, were regarded as the nation's chief authorities on Indian matters. Cass wrote extensively on Indians in several articles for the *North American Review*. Prompted by the Jacksonians, McKenney founded the New York Board for the Emigration, Preservation, and Improvement of the Aborigines of America in 1829. McKenney had been an early believer in Indian assimilation into white society, but a tour of the frontier in 1827 convinced him that the only way to preserve the North America aborigine was by removal. After passage of the Indian Removal Act, however, when it became clear that Cherokee people would not be encouraged to leave but actively coerced, McKenney condemned Jackson's Indian policy and was curtly dismissed from office.

61. For the importance of William Robertson and Scottish Enlightenment thinking in late eighteenth and early nineteenth-century America, see Manning, *Fragments of Union*; and Hook, *Scotland and America*. For the influence and popularity of Robertson's work on shaping white attitudes towards Indians in the United States, see Berkhofer, *The White Man's Indian*; Konkle, *Writing Indian Nations*, pp. 9–13;

Pearce, *Savagism and Civilization*, pp. 76–104; and Lenman, '"From Savage to Scot" via the French and the Spaniards'. Lenman's account offers intriguing evidence for the ways in which Robertson ignored or undermined contributions of informants that did not fit in with his assumption that North American Indians should be consigned to the very earliest stage of human social development.

62. Wilkinson, *American Indians, Time, and the Law*, p. 14. Wilkinson points out that ideas on establishing tribal enclaves to preserve native culture are as old as the republic. George Washington wrote to his Secretary of War, John Knox, in 1796 that nothing short of 'a Chinese Wall or line of troops will restrain Land jobbers, and the encroachments of settlers upon the Indian Territory' (quoted in Ibid. p. 146). Indeed, much of the work of the first United States Congress was devoted to laws on Indian affairs and treaty making, 'the central thrust of which', writes Wilkinson, was 'to create a measured separatism. That is, the reservation system was intended to establish homelands for the tribes . . . largely free from interference by non-Indians or future state governments' (14).

63. One of the most significant published examples of this transatlantic collective memory is *Gloomy Memories of the Highlands of Scotland*, Donald Macleod's eyewitness account of the Sutherland clearances of the 1810s and 1820s, which gained worldwide recognition in the late nineteenth century. For more on *Gloomy Memories*, see Chapter 4. For the emigrant literary tradition in Gaelic, see Newton, *Seanchaidh Na Coille*; MacDonell, *The Emigrant Experience*; Creighton and MacLeod, *Gaelic Songs in Nova Scotia*; Dunbar, 'The Poetry of the Emigrant Generation'; and Kidd, 'Caraid nan Gaidheal and "Friend of Emigration"'. For a summary of Gaelic-language use in Canada, see Nilsen, 'A' Ghàidhlig an Canada'.

64. MacDonnell, *The Emigrant Experience*, p. 7.

65. The poem is sometimes entitled 'Am Bàrd an Canada' ('The Poet in Canada'), which is the case for Neill's translation.

66. For Gaelic poetry of the Clearances, see Maclean, 'The Poetry of the Clearances'; and Meek, *Tuath Is Tighearna*. For a discussion of examples that complicate the dominant mythology and historiography on Highland emigration that depicts the immigrant in a perpetual state of nostalgic mourning for a lost Highland homeland, see Kennedy, '"Lochaber No More"', which provides literature and correspondence of Highlanders actively looking forward to life in the colonies.

67. For the alienating and oppressive effect of the 'huge and unresponsive' Canadian landscape on the literary imagination, see Frye's 'Haunted by Lack of Ghosts'. Frye's essay makes explicit reference to the Canadian poet and critic Earle Birney, who commented in 1947 that 'it's only

by our lack of ghosts we're haunted'. Birney was referring not to the Canadian landscape but to the nation's preoccupation with its apparent 'lack' of history in comparison with the United States. For a recent discussion of aboriginal haunting as the 'neocolonial uncanny' in non-Native literature and culture, however, see Cariou, 'Haunted Prairie'.
68. As nineteenth-century Canadian culture became increasingly racialised, the history of cross-cultural relations between Highlanders and First Nations peoples were largely erased, as Highlanders became part of white settler culture, the vanguard of civilisation. This is exemplified in the accounts of Alexander Ross, a native of Nairn, who came to the Red River Settlement in the 1820s. In 1856 Ross published the first full-length historical account of the colony, *The Red River Settlement*. In it, Ross would describe Selkirk's colonising scheme as a noble attempt to establish an outpost of civilisation in the region that would bring benefit to its aboriginal people, an ambition that Ross, looking back forty years, concludes was a complete failure. Yet, as Van Kirk recounts in '"What if Mama is an Indian?"', Ross himself married the young daughter of a chief of the Okanagan people of the Upper Columbia River, and brought her and their children to Red River, where he hoped they would be able to benefit from a 'Christian education'. Ross himself would become one of the most influential members of the Red River community, but his mixed-race children would later be ostracised in the increasingly race-conscious culture of the settlement.
69. Laurence, *The Diviners*, pp. 40, 69.
70. For a critique of Laurence's treatment of Métis dispossession, see Rocard, 'The Métis in Margaret Laurence's Manawaka Works'.
71. For a fruitful re-examination of Scottish diaspora culture, as an aspect of the fragmentation and hybridity of national subjectivity in the postcolonial world, see Harper and Vance, *Myth, Migration and the Making of Memory*; and Davis '"Coming to the Past"'.
72. Morton describes the unique pattern of land use and settlement in the Red River area in the early nineteenth century, in which the framework of narrow lots running back from a river front established in the old seigneurial system of the French 'was filled with a content not French and not Canadian'. Instead, the pattern of land use, begun by Selkirk's Scottish settlers, resembled the traditional infield and outfield system of the Highlands. In short, Morton writes, 'the Red River Settlement was a Scottish valley-side spread flat on a North American plain, within the framework of a French-Canadian survey' ('Introduction', p. xxv).
73. Selkirk's treaty with the local tribal people rather than cementing relations with them instead created conflicts and ill will that would plague the region for years after. Selkirk believed the Hudson's Bay Company

charter made it unnecessary to enter into a formal treaty of land surrender with the Indians. However, after the North West Company's campaign of open warfare against the settlement, Selkirk came to accept the expediency of formalising relations with tribal bands. On 18 June 1817 Selkirk gathered a group of local Cree, Assiniboine and Salteaux Indians who had been prominent in relations with the settlement and whom he deemed tribal 'chiefs'. The treaty stipulated that Indians would relinquish lands around the settlement in exchange for an annual gift of 'one hundred pounds weight of good merchantable tobacco'. Indian understanding of what the treaty implied, however, was more in the way of a lease, signalled by an annuity, but with actual payment for the land to follow at a later time. Since no payment was ever forthcoming, Indians believed they still held title to the land. This interpretation became more insistent in later decades, when conflict erupted between Indians and settlers over hay rights in lands adjacent to the treaty area. In the early 1860s Peguis, a prominent spokesman for the Salteaux, complained that the Hudson's Bay Company had marked out and sold their lands without permission and that his people 'had never sold our lands to said Company, nor to the Earl of Selkirk'. A statement of his claim appeared in the settlement newspaper, *The Nor'-Wester* ('Native Title to Native Lands'). Debate on the issue went on throughout the 1860s and was not fully resolved even after the Red River Resistance of 1869–70 and passage of the Manitoba Act. See also McDermot, 'Peguis Refuted'; and Peers, *The Ojibwa of Western Canada*, pp. 198–9.
74. Allen, *Blood Narrative*, p. 17.
75. For the contemporary internationalisation of the concept of 'indigenous', see Merlan, 'Indigeneity: Global and Local'. Merlan divides definitional frameworks into two categories: 'criterial' and 'relational'. Criterial definitions 'propose some set of criteria, or conditions, that enable identification of the "indigenous" as a global "kind"'. Relational definitions 'emphasize grounding in relations between the "indigenous" and their "others" rather than in properties inherent only to those we call "indigenous" themselves' (305). While not wanting to enter too deeply into the waters of this debate, my own discussion on the emergence of the Highland aborigine in a Scottish post-Enlightenment discourse that served colonial and imperial interests emphasises a relational definition of the term.
76. Allen, *Blood Narrative*, p. 9.
77. For the importance of treaty language in indigenous sovereignty claims, see Allen, *Blood Narrative*; and Hoxie, 'Why Treaties?'. See Womack, *Red on Red* for a critique of anti-essentialism.

78. For the post-Clearance land reform movement, see Devine, *Clanship to Crofter's War* and Hunter, *The Making of the Crofting Community*.
79. A recent report from the Scottish Crofting Foundation argues that both Sammi and Highlanders 'found themselves inside the boundaries of newly formed, aggressive and acquisitive nation states, which soon took steps to try to wipe out their way of life' (MacKinnon, *Crofters*, p. 8). See also Miller, *Invisible Indigenes*, pp. 156–207.
80. Bryden and Geisler, 'Community-Based Land Reform', p. 2.
81. Quoted in Mackenzie, *Places of Possibility*, p. 40.
82. Allen identifies the blood/land/memory complex as a discursive trope that 'makes explicit the central role that land plays both in the specific project of defining indigenous minority personal, familial, and communal identities (blood) and in the larger project of reclaiming and reimagining indigenous minority histories (memory)' (*Blood Narrative*, p. 16).
83. Quoted in Mackenzie, *Places of Possibility*, p. 37.
84. Recent years have seen increasing examples of transatlantic cultural, historical and kinship ties and expressions of mutual affinity among indigenous peoples and Scots. Witness the recent opening ceremonies of the Abernethy Highland Games for which Cherokee Nation Principal Chief Chadwick 'Corntassel' Smith served as honorary chieftain. Smith, who led a delegation of thirty Cherokee from Oklahoma, claims his Scottish heritage as a sixth-generation grandson of Ludovic Grant, who, banished to South Carolina after the failed Jacobite revolt of 1715, later became a successful trader among the Upper Cherokee, marrying a Cherokee woman. Smith, however, also makes explicit the shared history between Cherokee and Gaels as 'repressed indigenous nations' and acknowledges 'their common challenges in regaining self-determination and preserving ancestral cultures and languages'. A David Grant from Edinburgh is quoted as saying 'All of our hearts go out to the Cherokee . . . We know what it is like to fight to keep your culture and language alive. And because of the Highland Clearances, we can relate to them' (Prins and McBride, 'Cherokee Chief Opens Highland Games in Scotland').
85. For a discussion of the varied and complex contemporary invocations of the term 'diaspora', see Clifford, 'Diasporas'. Examining the definitional borders of diaspora, Clifford argues diasporas are defined not only against the 'norms of nation-states', but also 'indigenous, and especially autochthonous, claims by "tribal" peoples' (307).

Chapter 4

Memory, Identity and the Scottish Remembrance of Slavery

Slavery and the Politics of Memory in Scotland

For too long, we are told, Scotland has forgotten its slavery past, and only now have historians and writers in Scotland begun to make amends for that collective amnesia. As part of renewed interest in the UK on the subject, commencing around the two hundredth anniversary of the abolition of the slave trade in 2007, the historical investigation into Scotland's contribution to transatlantic slavery has sought to remind the nation that slavery is not just England's shame. Though the traffic of the enslaved by ships from Scottish ports was small compared to the tremendous traffic associated with the major English ports, recent commemorative museum exhibits, historical writing and prominent feature articles in Scotland have begun to inventory the country's significant contribution to the economics of West Indian slavery, not just to the trade itself but through the establishment and maintenance of the plantation system, and of mercantile and commercial interests dependent on the trade of commodities produced by the labour of the enslaved.[1] Scotland's deep involvement is reflected in the public record and in the often strident defence of slavery and the plantocracy that appeared in the pages of the periodical reviews and partisan newspapers. In the pages of *Blackwood's* and *The Glasgow Courier*, and in the pronouncements of lobbying groups such as the West India Association, Scottish advocates for slavery lambasted the arguments and evidence of abolitionist reformers while defending the system of enslavement as, while capable of amelioration, necessary to the prosperity of Britain's Atlantic empire.

It is this aspect of slavery that Scotland has forgotten; the rare previous instances of memorialisation had been limited to commemorating Scotland's past of anti-slavery, a past of the abolition societies and their Scottish leaders, and of the outsize public commitment in Scotland to eradicating colonial enslavement.[2] The *other* slavery past – the past of Scottish-born plantation landowners and their clerks, overseers and slave drivers; the Scottish captains and ship's surgeons of the slaver ships; the merchants in Glasgow and Edinburgh who traded in tobacco, indigo, cotton and sugar; and the Scottish apologists for slavery – has been, in the words of a recent influential collection of historical writing, 'long lost to history' and is only now being recovered.[3] Carla Sassi has charted Scotland's disavowal of its slavery past, arguing that Scottish literary tradition is largely one of protracted silence on the subject, part of a larger dynamic of alternating 'willed' and 'unwilled amnesia'.[4] In a similar vein, Michael Morris has written that Scottish writing on the subject of Caribbean slavery has been largely characterised, until only recently, by its distancing strategies, through which the 'West Indies became removed from the mainstream of Scottish cultural memory'.[5] Only in recent years have Scottish writers – such as Robbie Kyd, Andrew O. Lindsay and James Robertson – sought both to commemorate the dark forgotten chapter in Scotland's past and to confront the nation's collective desire to forget. The work of these writers, Sassi writes, witnesses 'a deeply changed attitude toward Scotland's colonial past, by articulating a desire to inquire into the country's involvement in West Indian slavery and to assume historical responsibility'.[6]

Protracted silences in Scotland's historical memory of slavery is also the theme of a commemorative piece by the poet and novelist Jackie Kay that appeared in *The Guardian* in 2007 to mark the anniversary of the abolition of the slave trade. The anniversary, Kay writes, is a moment for Scots 'to try and remember what we should not have forgotten'.[7] For Kay, the anniversary of the trade's end evokes the accumulation of silences: 'from African people who do not want their children to hear about slavery, and from white people who do not want to discuss the family tree with its roots in a plantation in the Caribbean'. Commemorating the end of the slave trade is also to grant recognition to the 'missing faces' of this past: not only 'the people buried at sea, the deaths in the tobacco and sugar fields' but 'the Scottish plantation owner who was often as cruel as his English or American counterpart'. For Kay, the unseen and voiceless witnesses to slavery are part of Scotland's contemporary self-image as a 'hard-done-to wee nation', which has required a 'canny' process of selective memory – remembering one historical trauma while forgetting another. 'It's time', she concludes, 'that Scotland included the history of the plantations alongside the history of the Highland clearances. A people being cleared off their land, and taken from the Slave Coast, the Ivory Coast, the Guinea Coast to a new land. Forced to board a ship and taken on a nightmare journey from Hell.' For Kay, the ethical implications involved in acts of remembering and forgetting are clear. The price of Scotland's collective amnesia, its failure to acknowledge its own responsibility for the crimes of slavery and to memorialise its victims, is to deny a rich legacy, not only to the descendants of enslaved Africans but to all Britons. The processes of historical memory are therefore irrevocably bound up with national identity – which past we remember and which past we forget are questions ultimately of who we are and how we define ourselves.

The imagining of West Indian slavery as historical memory in contemporary writing in Britain emphasises both its catastrophic force in the lives of those who were engulfed by it and the strong traces it has left on the national consciousness, whether or not they are acknowledged openly. In these accounts, mnemonic tropes of remembrance and forgetting configure slavery as a moment of collective trauma; its 'recovery' in the historical consciousness signals a therapeutic rearticulation, the initial stage of a final 'working through' a repressed traumatic past that had continued to disturb the national psyche. As it frames an understanding of past events through a psychoanalytic model of repression, denial and recovery, the call to remember slavery also asserts an ontological certainty about the significance of those past events identified as traumatic. Trauma, it is assumed, inheres in the event itself, and the call by a later generation to remember is therefore a natural, if delayed, response to the traumatic nature of the event. Yet, as recent critics have suggested, 'cultural trauma' is itself a particular mode of thinking about the past, a 'socially mediated attribution' evoked in retrospect, often as the collective memory of a particular social group.[8] Neil J. Smelser defines cultural trauma as 'a memory accepted and publicly given credence by a relevant membership group and evoking an event or situation which is a) laden with negative affect, b) represented as indelible, and c) regarded as threatening a society's existence of violating one or more of its fundamental cultural presuppositions'.[9] Cultural trauma is a mode of historical understanding in which the past is deemed to be insufficiently known or understood ('distorted' or 'forgotten') and is only now becoming publicly recognised ('remembered'). Often both self-reflexive and part of an activist historiography, cultural trauma demands a reimagining of national or collective identity. To think of cultural trauma in this way, as a mode of historical consciousness rather than as a category of historical event, is to emphasise its imaginative and symbolic dimension, as it seizes upon the 'inchoate experience from life' and forms it 'through association, condensation, and aesthetic creation into some specific shape'.[10] Such an understanding of cultural trauma as a mode of historical representation is not to deny the reality of transatlantic chattel slavery, or of the Highland Clearances, for that matter, nor of its unspeakable brutality and dehumanisation. Rather, it is to make visible the symbolic contestations at work in trauma's affirmation (remembrance) or denial (forgetting) and how the politics of cultural memory shape collective identity in contemporary Britain and in its former colonies.[11]

The recent call in Britain for an active remembering of slavery's legacy has inspired a revisit to the historical archive in the hopes of recovering the voices of those who experienced the effects of slavery in the late eighteenth and early nineteenth centuries first-hand, and first-person eyewitness accounts, which themselves often took the form of retrospective 'memory' of past experience, fittingly have provided a critical glimpse into transatlantic slavery while also helping to shape collective identities in the present. As the debate on slavery intensified in the time period, and writing on slavery became increasingly polemic, 'eyewitness testimony' became a prominent mode of discourse on the subject, to speak the truth of slavery, granting powerful authority for a writer to lay claim to the truth of his or her assertion while casting doubt on the claims of others.[12] The prominence of testimony in the debate meant that the relative power to persuade or dissuade an audience became indexed to the past experiences of the writer and to his or her relative position and proximity to slavery. In abolitionist polemics particularly, eyewitness testimony, like many other forms of abolitionist writing, sought to forge a sympathetic connection between reader and the enslaved by drawing upon tropes of sensibility and sympathy established in large part through sentimental literature, which in turn had roots in Scottish Enlightenment discourse on feeling associated with writers such as Francis Hutcheson, David Hume and Adam Smith.[13] Testimonial accounts were called upon both to bear witness to the horrors of slavery and to provide unmediated first-hand scenes of suffering to inspire humanitarian compassion on the part of its readers for the enslaved. In the often memoirist structure of their narratives, such retrospective testimonies open a window into the day-to-day experiences of slavery while also giving voice to national and transnational subjectivities that arose from the unprecedented individual and cultural disruptions of the transatlantic slave trade. From the often fragmented, multivocal and diasporic testimony of the eyewitness to slavery, new identities emerge, and older identities are forged anew.

Scots, who took an active role in the debate on slavery, also took part in shaping transatlantic identities through retrospective eyewitness testimony. This chapter explores the contribution of Scottish writers to these testaments to slavery, which reflect the complexities of Scottish national culture in the late eighteenth and early nineteenth centuries. I highlight these complexities by examining the work of two Scottish writers associated with seminal first-hand accounts of slavery, both of which lay claim to providing an unvarnished account of the horrors of transatlantic enslavement. The first, John Gabriel Stedman's *Narrative of a Five Years Expedition against the Revolted Negroes of Surinam*, which recounts his 1773–7 stay in the Dutch plantation colony, was published in 1796, as the debate on abolishing the slave trade was intensifying.[14] The second, the slave narrative *The History of Mary Prince* – with extensive supplementary material provided by her benefactor and editor, Thomas Pringle – was published in 1831, at the height of the debate over the total abolition of slavery in the British colonies, which would be achieved less than two years later. Both accounts have received much critical attention in recent years, as they exemplify how memory-texts of slavery were crucial to the emergence of hybrid, intercultural identities in the transatlantic world. Yet the Scottish dimensions of both these contributions have been consistently overlooked or elided.

Both Stedman and Pringle were shaped by the circum-Atlantic and transperipheral conduits in which they moved, and which conditioned their perspectives on slavery and their own national allegiances and affinities. Stedman, born to a Scottish father and Dutch mother at Dendermonde, was, like his father before him, an officer in the Scottish-Dutch Scots Brigade, and he arrived in Surinam as part of an expeditionary force sent by the Dutch Republic to quell an uprising of escaped slaves. Pringle was born into a Scottish Borders family, and, after a short-lived residence in Edinburgh, where he was – among other things – the first editor of *Blackwood's*, emigrated to the Cape Colony where he helped to establish a Scottish settlement. He later was forced to return to London, where he eventually became Secretary of the Anti-Slavery Society, met the former slave Mary Prince, and made his contributions to her *History*. Though the circumstances in which both writers encountered transatlantic slavery and wrote about it were very different, their writing reflects the unique complexities of Scottish experiences in the transatlantic world. As Britain's post-Union empire provided an immense new arena for Scottish ambition and energy, it also established the conditions for an unprecedented level of migration and uprootedness, and the writings of Stedman and Pringle, both of whom self-identified as Scots throughout their lives, reflect these mutually entangled experiences of diasporic and expatriate migration and colonial occupation and settlement. Scottish writings on slavery like Stedman's and Pringle's provide an important dimension to our understanding of British discourse on slavery in the era, reminding us that this discourse was not monolithic, but was itself comprised of multiple voices, which were subject to widely varied relations of economic, cultural and social power.

I also wish to take up, in the last section of my discussion, the ways in which transatlantic slavery informed the construction of a specifically Scottish national past, as one itself born out of an experience of collective trauma. Donald Macleod's 1857 *Gloomy Memories of the Highlands of Scotland*, which would become a seminal work in an emergent historiography of Clearance in the late nineteenth century, was published as a response to Harriet Beecher Stowe's travel memoir *Sunny Memories of Foreign Lands*, in which Stowe lauded the abolitionist sympathies of her patron, the Duchess of Sutherland, while dismissing out of hand accounts like Macleod's of Sutherland cruelty and injustice during the Clearances. Though Macleod did not take a direct position on abolition, transatlantic slavery plays a prominent role in his work, as he seeks to dismantle what he saw as the hypocritical polemics of an abolitionist landowning elite, who profess sympathy with the African slave while at the same time wilfully 'forgetting' the plight of the Scottish Gael. Reader sympathy for the Gael in *Gloomy Memories*, however, comes at the expense of sympathy for the African enslaved. With the understanding that cultural trauma is itself often forged in the very call to remember historical events as 'traumatic', I argue *Gloomy Memories* is an important Scottish cultural-memory text, one that continues to shape notions of collective trauma and identity, and the ways in which slavery has been 'remembered' – or 'forgotten' – in Scotland.

This chapter examines a collection of Scottish writing that spans half a century and which recounts experiences in four different continents; however, all of the works I examine share common aspects and themes. All three works functioned as retrospective eyewitness accounts, which invited their readers to share in scenes of cruelty and suffering as they actually occurred and to sympathise with the victims. All three were written in the context of their author's own experience of displacement, migration and diaspora. Taken together, all three provide a glimpse into the significant Scottish contribution to a transatlantic discourse on slavery and to the politics of collective memory.

Memoirs of a Stranger in a Strange Land

John Gabriel Stedman offered the reading public his memories of his four-year sojourn in Surinam through what Pratt has aptly described as 'a vivid discursive compendium interweaving the whole repertoire of eighteenth-century European encodings of the imperial frontier: ethnography, natural history, military reminiscence, hunting stories, social description, survival tales, anti-slavery critique, and interracial love'.[15] Published by the prominent Radical and abolitionist publisher Joseph Johnson, Stedman's *Narrative* caused a sensation when it first appeared; his particularly lurid descriptions of the cruel treatment of slaves, his minute observations on the social and economic relations of the colony's Dutch plantocracy, and the dramatic story of his own love for, and ultimate tragic separation from, a mulatto slave woman made Stedman's a prominent abolitionist text on both sides of the Atlantic.[16] Enhanced by over eighty engraved plates – sixteen of them by William Blake – the *Narrative* remains one of the richest and most detailed accounts of slavery of the period and is the subject of numerous recent critical studies.[17] While many of these studies are careful to observe the ambiguity of Stedman's cross-cultural affiliations, few trace in any detail the particular threads of his national or ethnic background.[18]

Though he was shipped off to Scotland at an early age to complete his education, Stedman spent the majority of his early life in the Low Countries, where he enlisted in the Scots Brigade. As a young officer, he led a dissolute life of misadventure, drunkenness, and debauchery in various postings throughout the Low Countries before, hoping to pay off his debts, he volunteered for the expeditionary force to Surinam. In later life, Stedman summarised his life as one of perpetual, if not permanent, ostracisation:

> in all places I have been beloved by the inhabitants when known but at first cald mad in Scotland, mased [confused] in England, fou [crazy] by the namurois [Belgians], gek or dol [crazy or mad] by the Duch and law [Sranan for insane] by the Negroes in Surinam, owing intirely to my studying to be singular in as much as can be so.[19]

While demonstrating his linguistic ambidexterity – in Surinam, Stedman acquired Sranan, the English-based creole used by slaves, to add to his fluency in English, Dutch and French – this summary of a lifelong 'studying to be singular' exemplifies the importance Stedman placed in his autobiographical writing in representing himself as worthy of admiration and sympathy while also an iconoclast and nonconformist. Stedman in his writing often employed terms that highlighted his alienation from the societies he encountered, defining himself as a perpetual outsider, a stranger in a strange land. This self-fashioning of identity through disassociation is perhaps also expressive of the particular kind of expatriate life he chose for himself and which provided a common outlet for Scottish male ambition in the eighteenth century – the life of a professional soldier-for-hire. The Stedman family tradition of service in the Scots Brigade provided the circumstances for his Surinam sojourn and also shaped the tenor of his *Narrative*, which is heavily weighted with the particulars of military life: endless marching and bivouacking, bad food, the meting out of military discipline and punishment, disputes among officers and men, and the constant threat of death by violence or disease. Service as a Scottish mercenary, a role for which Scott would provide a celebrated gloss in the character of Dugald Dalgetty, also demanded a complex and at times seemingly contradictory interplay of loyalties and affinities.[20] On the one hand, Stedman offered his sword and, potentially, his life to the Dutch Republic while on the other swore ultimate fealty to his British king. Though membership in the Scots Brigade, which had served in the Dutch Republic since 1572, arguably encouraged or even necessitated an ambivalent or contingent national consciousness, its officers and men nevertheless maintained a distinct national identity that derived from the circumstances of their profession. Though the paymasters of the Brigade, Joachim Miggelbrink writes, were Dutch:

> the majority of the commanding officers were Scottish, and the commands were given in the soldiers' vernacular. When in battle, the soldiers played the Scots March, their uniforms were the standard red of the British army, and they wielded specific colours that were associated only with their regiments and Great Britain and had no connection with the Dutch Republic. These were the symbols they identified themselves with.[21]

For members of the Scots Brigade, national identity was expressed not so much through references to a putative Scottish homeland where they or their families might have once resided; instead, their national identity was expressed through a profession-based sign system that evoked traditions and ideals belonging to the unique expatriate life they shared in common. The lasting power of this sign system was made clear when, after the outbreak of the Fourth Anglo-Dutch War in 1780, the Dutch Republic nationalised the Scots Brigade and merged it into the Dutch national army, eliminating the Brigade's unique uniforms and symbols and requiring its officers to take an oath 'abjuring all allegiance to their native Land'.[22] Some sixty officers of the Brigade, including Stedman, refused to take this oath and returned to Britain, where they sought the king's patronage and were put eventually on the half-pay list of the British army.[23]

Throughout his life, Stedman proudly laid claim to the symbols and traditions of the Scots Brigade, from which he derived his greatest sense of familial and national identity. Stedman often expressed in his writing a sentimental Scottishness, which was invested in the signs, rituals and affinities he associated with patriotic devotion to one's country. His *Narrative* and unpublished diaries and journals, for example, reveal Stedman's rigorous devotion to celebrating St Andrew's Day, no matter what his circumstance; and while living in England in retirement, Stedman writes of paying the funeral expenses of an acquaintance who had committed suicide because of a 'duty to which ... I owed to his relations, and my country, he being from Scotland'.[24] Remarking on the united nations that was his own small family ('4 people only, yet four different nations ... who speak no less than 6 different languages'), Stedman identifies himself as the sole member who is 'Scotch' (*Stedman Archive: Journal*, p. 36).[25]

Slavery-in-Memoir

The instability and ambiguity that pervade Stedman's self-fashioning reflect not only his rebellious personality and his expatriate social background but are also a product of the textual uncertainties associated with the *Narrative*. Stedman himself was never happy with the published version of his manuscript. The final product was reworked so intensely and was so heavily bowdlerised – ironically to suit in part the pro-slavery sentiments of its Scottish-born editor – that Stedman would come to disavow the published *Narrative* as 'mard intirely' and 'good for nothing' (*Narrative*, p. l).[26] Yet the manuscript that Stedman submitted for publication was itself ostensibly based on the diaries and journals he had kept while in Surinam. These original journals and diaries provide a very different picture of Stedman's life in Surinam than even Stedman's original manuscript of the *Narrative*. Summarised by Marcus Wood, the fragmented, often terse entries of the diaries reveal a Stedman who is 'a practical, frequently brutal, occasionally kind and charming, mercenary soldier', and whose 'defining motivations . . . were the demonstration of his valor and the preservation of his honor, within the military code, and display of his sexuality, which is explored, defined, and finally asserted through his multiple relations with white and black women which he records'.[27] The most dramatic difference between the diaries and the manuscript is perhaps the recounting of the relationship between Stedman and the mulatto slave Joanna. In the *Narrative*, Joanna is the woman he loves, a figure of stoic virtue and high moral character who nurses him back to health and eventually bears him a son. Their ill-fated interracial love story, which culminates with her death by poison after Stedman is unable to emancipate her and bring her back to Europe, amounts to a retelling and revision of the immensely popular eighteenth-century tale of Inkle and Yarico, in which an English castaway falls in love with, but later abandons, a beautiful Indian maiden.[28]

The love story of Stedman and Joanna furnished one of the most compelling examples of slavery's cruelty, and their story was reproduced and adapted in Britain and the United States.[29] In his diary, however, Stedman describes his first encounters with Joanna as one of several sexual liaisons he had with enslaved women in the early months of his stay. Stedman concludes a 9 February 1773 entry describing the disembarkation of troops at the capital Paramaribo with 'Go to sleep at Lolkens who was in the country. I f – k one of his negro maids –'.[30] Soon after, he writes:

> Feb. 25 Dine at the mess-house and soop in me room with two mallatto girls, on bread, chese, and bottle of clerret
>
> March 26 Dine at Kennedys. B – e comes to stay with me and stays the whole night
>
> April 11 Dine at Demelly's. J – a, her mother, and Q – mother come to close a bargain we have, we put it off for reasons I gave them.
>
> April 12 Dine and soop Lolkens B – e and J – a both breakfast with me, I call meself Mistire
>
> April 13 was before the Fort Zealandia. B – e sleeps with me.
>
> April 23 J – a comes to stay with me. I give her presents to the value of ten pound sterling and am perfectly happy. (*Journal, diaries, and other papers: 1772–1796, 1772–1774*, 22–5)

Stedman's description of sexual encounters with several slave women, including Joanna, sometimes in the same evening, and his reference to the 'bargain' he attempts to work out with her mother, reveal the underlying reality of sexual relations in Surinam's plantocracy, which Stedman glosses over and sentimentalises in his *Narrative*. 'Stedman's marriage to Joanna,' Pratt writes,

> like many transracial love affairs in the fiction of this time, is a romantic transformation of a particular form of colonial sexual exploitation, whereby European men on assignment to the colonies brought local women from their families to serve as sexual and domestic partners for the duration of their stay.[31]

Stedman's diaries reveal he was well aware of this practice of contingent concubinage – termed 'Surinam marriage' in the colony – yet he elides the economic, and sexual, dimension of his relationship with Joanna in the *Narrative*.

Given such discrepancies it is perhaps tempting to read the diary accounts as an unmediated and authentic description of a young officer's day-to-day experiences, recorded in private and as they were happening, and the *Narrative* as a semi-fictionalised and highly wrought account, composed many years later in the service of the anti-slavery cause. Yet the passage of time bears its stamp even on some of Stedman's seemingly unmediated unpublished 'diary' material. Among his diaries is a thirty-two-sheet folded 'journal' of pages written on both sides that recount Stedman's family origins and document his life up to the time he left for Surinam. Although these pages take the form of a diary, with dated entries in chronological order, they were not written until 1785 or 1786, after Stedman had already commenced work on his *Narrative*, and they include 'comments written well after the dates under which they were entered' (*Narrative*, p. lxxxvi). Though this autobiographical sketch was never published and it is unclear what connection, if any, Stedman intended between this sketch of his life leading up to the events recounted in the *Narrative*, the former highlights the degree to which retrospection informs even his supposed 'as-it-happened' diarist accounts. With this in mind, the bare diary entries of his time in Surinam operate less as an unmediated and authentic alternative to the *Narrative* and more as a kind of aide-memoire for the fuller account of Stedman's life for which he would devote the whole of his later years. Though Stedman would enter into the abolitionist social circles of his publisher, who clearly envisioned the *Narrative* as a powerful statement against slavery, Stedman's post-Surinam journal entries suggest that he always set out to produce an engaging memoir of his life and mercenary adventures rather than a polemical testimonial. The bulk of Stedman's writing, unpublished and published, provides an overall impression of an ageing ex-soldier, now settled in the Devon countryside with a Dutch wife and children, who, rather than taking a principled stand against slavery, seeks through retrospection to give form and meaning to the questionable experiences and actions of his younger days.

Remembering Slavery and the Limits of Sympathy

Though part of a larger body of writing that recounts a 'singular' life, the *Narrative* nevertheless provides some of the most harrowing accounts of slavery ever put on paper, which would prove the basis for its influence as an anti-slavery polemic. Stedman's confrontation with slavery's dehumanising cruelty begins immediately after he disembarks in Surinam. The first image he lays eyes on, he writes, is that of:

> a most miserable Young woman in chains simply covered with a Rag round her Loins, which was like her Skin cut and carved by the lash of the Whip in a most Shocking Manner. Her Crime was in not having fulfilled her Task to which she was by appearance unable. [. . .] She was a beautiful Negroe Maid and while I was Meditating on the shocking Load of her Irons I myself nearly escaped being rivitted by Fascination – I now took a draft of the wretched Creature upon paper which I here present to the Sympathizing Reader and which inspired me with a very unfavorable Opinion of the Humanity of the Planters residing in this Colony toward theyr negro Slaves – (39)[32]

This first scene sets the tone for Stedman's descriptions of the treatment of the enslaved throughout the *Narrative*, and the juxtaposition of thinly veiled eroticism with sadistic cruelty, which is dependent on the objectification of the black female body through a masculine voyeuristic gaze, provides evidence of the pornographic quality that a number of recent critics have identified in Stedman's work.[33] Yet Stedman's *Narrative* also makes explicit a set of assumptions about the production and exchange of feeling that borrowed heavily from sentimental literature and served as the driving impetus of much Romantic-era anti-slavery writing. Without preconceptions and with no natural affinities in the strange world in which he finds himself, Stedman figures as, in Adam Smith's formulation, an 'impartial spectator', a disinterested and therefore objective eyewitness to the scenes of distress he recounts. For Smith, whose theories drew upon and reacted to those of David Hume, the production of sympathy hinges on the imaginative faculty of the mind, which speculates on the feelings of the observed, rather than receiving a direct impression of them, as Hume had envisioned.[34] Perhaps as a corrective to Hume's potentially wild and anarchic spontaneous production of powerful emotion, Smith argues that the transmission of actual states of feeling from one person to another is an impossibility: 'as we have no immediate experience of what others feel, we can form no idea of the manner in which they are affected, but only by conceiving what we ourselves feel in the like situation'.[35] Because, for Smith, one cannot actually feel what another feels, sympathy is less a process of shared feeling than an imaginary, conjectural, substitution of the observed by the observer. To drive home the limits of fellow feeling, Smith adopts a stark example of witnessing a member of one's own family as a victim of torture: 'Though our brother is upon the rack, as long as we ourselves are at our ease, our senses will never inform us of what he suffers. They never did, and never can, carry us beyond our own person, and it is by imagination only that we can form any conception of what are his sensations'.[36]

Sympathy, then, is for Smith, as Rae Greiner observes, less a feeling itself than a 'mechanism of feeling-production, an activity with the capacity to generate feelings ("moral" or otherwise)'. Because it is not a feeling in its own right, she continues, sympathy 'is incapable of certifying which feelings result' and cannot therefore ensure the creation of compassion or moral altruism.[37] Yet the social and intersubjective character of Smith's idea of sympathy, and its ability to inspire, through imaginative projection and substitution, pity for the suffering or sorrow of others who are at quite a distance from us, became key operating features of abolitionist polemics. The identificatory power of sympathy is crucial to the anti-slavery narrative as it is, Jenny Sharpe writes, the 'source of the ability to feel pity and compassion and to act benevolently', but sympathy's power to forge an identification 'with the suffering Other also distances the spectator from the one who is suffering, for the observer alone is in a position to ameliorate their condition'.[38] As he first sets foot upon Surinam's shores, Stedman casts his gaze relentlessly and unflinchingly onto scenes of cruelty and torture perpetrated against the victims of slavery, inviting his 'Sympathizing Reader' to share in his horror and his fascination, while maintaining a relatively comfortable, and superior, distance.

The most dramatic instance of Stedman's attempts to mobilise reader sympathy, however, is a scene in which Stedman is emphatically a most *interested* spectator, the moment when he discovers his beloved Joanna is to be sold off to satisfy the creditors of her master's sugar estate. Unable to purchase her for himself, Stedman becomes distraught at the thought of Joanna's fate at the hands of her new masters: 'Me thought I saw her, mangled, ravished, ridiculed and bowing under the weight of her Chains calling aloud for my assistance – I was miserable . . .' (*Narrative*, p. 176). This imagining of

Joanna's plight would have struck a chord with British and American abolitionists, Sharpe writes, as Stedman 'sees her as a forlorn and pitiable slave calling for his aid' (81). Reading this passage in the context of other descriptions in the *Narrative* and the autobiographical sketch that Stedman composed but never published, however, highlights aspects of Stedman's work that undermine its position as an anti-slavery polemic. For one, Stedman's descriptions of plantocratic cruelty are only one category of description in a work that, among other things, seeks to provide a precise account of local flora and fauna, and whose stated intent is broaden the scope of British world knowledge, to make more perfectly 'known to this Kingdom' [of Great Britain] the 'Colony of *Surinam* in Dutch Guiana' (27). The decentring of the figure of the enslaved is arguably one facet of the disinterested stance of its author, yet it also brings into focus his ultimately profoundly ambivalent outlook on plantation life, an outlook conditioned by his background as a Scottish mercenary and predicated on his overriding motive to portray himself as the hero of his own sentimental narrative – as one who is singularly sensitive to suffering. If the power of Stedman's *Narrative* to strike a chord with abolitionists lies in its ability to produce sympathy through various witnessings of scenes of cruelty, the shifting orientation of that sympathy often undermines its power. Throughout the *Narrative*, Stedman imagines himself as a superior individual with a particularly heightened sense of fellow feeling, but his sympathetic gaze seems to be directed everywhere – and to nowhere in particular.

In many scenes, Stedman is seen to feel sympathy for the suffering at the hands of despotic masters of those who are not actually enslaved. Frequent examples are the common soldiers of the colony, who suffer horribly under the callous neglect and wilful cruelty of tyrannical commanders. For example, early in the *Narrative* Stedman notes the assassination of a former governor of the colony – a man Stedman says 'had the character of a Tyrant; he was under the mask of Religion – Brutal – Despotic – hasty and Cruel'. This governor and his commandant 'were murdered by their own Soldiers' not only because they had starved the men with meager rations, but because they had also 'forc'd the Men to work like Negroes . . .' (61–2). Nevertheless, Stedman's account of the tyrannical governor is counterbalanced by moments when he orders beatings and other forms of physical punishment for his men. When discord breaks out between black soldiers and white marines under his command, for example, Stedman 'tied up the ring leaders of both parties' and ordered 'the first to be well flog'd and the latter horsewhipt for an hour' (126). Stedman's willingness to inflict physical pain on blacks and whites alike, while also condemning acts of cruelty towards the African enslaved and European soldiers, points to an alternative understanding of 'humanitarian compassion' within the context of the military culture of which Stedman was a part, a culture that above all demands the maintenance of order and discipline.[39] Summarising his duty as a soldier, Stedman writes he must always adhere to the 'Articles of War, viz., bluntly obey and ask no Questions' (128). Stedman's appreciation of the strict hierarchies of military life, and its rigid distinctions between officers and enlisted men, superiors and inferiors, carries into his general views on civil society and the relationship between the rulers and the ruled. 'A Proper subordination and discipline is certainly the foundation of all good order', Stedman writes, but in enforcing that discipline, a good ruler must achieve the proper balance between 'too much Severity or too much Lenity'. Regardless of whether the subordinate is a soldier or a slave, 'a certain Medium' must be 'kept in View which tends so much to Secure the happiness of both the Ruler and the Subject and Strengthen the Bands of Society in General' (78). It is the failure to achieve this medium, rather than the institution of slavery itself, that Stedman witnesses and condemns in Surinam, and that has made the West Indies 'dangerous, and is striking at its root points to over through [overthrow] it –' (78).

An indictment of cruelty in all its forms and perpetuated on all living beings is Stedman's greatest target in the *Narrative*, not slavery itself. That Stedman can, with near equal intensity, sympathise with the plight of tortured slaves, overworked and beaten white soldiers, and dead or dying animals ultimately diminishes the *Narrative*'s power as an anti-slavery tract.[40] In calling for an end to the slave system's abusive and degrading cruelties and for accountability for its worst perpetuators, Stedman instead adopts what would become a common position of defenders of slavery, particularly those who argued against total abolition after the banning of the slave trade in 1807. Advocating an 'ameliorist' stance, Stedman calls for a reform rather than total dismantling of the plantation system, a stance which perhaps reflects a military (albeit sensitive) mindset that privileges the maintenance of existing social hierarchies through the proper, balanced employment of disciplinary punishment.⁴¹

'Poor John Stedman!' Sympathy and Heroic Self-Fashioning

Sharpe has argued that Stedman's sympathetic description of his beloved 'wife' Joanna beaten and raped by her new enslavers is representative of the *Narrative*'s dramatic shift in the tropic force of the figure of the mixed-race woman in British writing, a shift that ultimately served the gender politics of white female anti-slavery advocates.⁴² Yet the scene also exemplifies the way in which Stedman fashions his own subjectivity through a reorientation of focus, away from the observed and back to the observer (himself). Significantly, the scene of her suffering is already a figment of Stedman's imagination: 'Me *thought* I saw her . . .' (my emphasis). As such, the scene emphasises the conjectural processes of sympathy, focusing not on the feelings or experiences of Joanna herself but the distressed state of Stedman's own mind and emotions, to which he immediately returns:

> I was miserable – Indeed I was truly wretched labouring under such Emotions as had now nearly deprived me of my faculties, til restored by the assurance of my Friend, Mr. Lolkens, who providentially was appointed to Continue Administrator of the Estate . . . [and] who brought Joana again to my presence . . . (*Narrative*, p. 176)

Here, Stedman effectively redirects the sympathetic gaze of his reader, turning it away from Joanna and back towards himself, as one who is sympathising and, therefore, himself worthy of sympathy.

Such invitations to the reader to pause and reflect on the self-description of the writer's own pitiable state are frequent throughout the *Narrative* and Stedman's other autobiographical writings. For example, after a day spent bivouacking in the bush, Stedman describes awakening in the middle of the night to find himself covered in blood, bitten by a vampire bat. His clothing already reduced to rags and his body emaciated by the hardships of military life, Stedman is a miserable figure, 'with my Face most Horrible Pale and Ghastly – My Sword and Pistol Slung Across my Meagre

Shoulders, My Whole Carcass all over Besmeared with Clotted Blood . . .' (*Narrative*, p. 428). Throughout his writing, Stedman shapes a protagonist whose trials and tribulations are meant to elicit at times shock and awe, but also sympathy and pity. This often requires the use of self-pitying interjections, to alert his readers where sympathy is indicated: 'poor John Stedman!' (or 'poor Johnny' 'poor Jack, or 'poor Stedman').[43] At the same time, the *Narrative* displays a keen awareness of the spectatorial dynamics of sympathy and of the social capital acquired through the proper display of compassion for the plight of others. Stedman, for example, reports that his own overwrought state while imagining the horrible fate awaiting his 'Dear Mullatto' is vindicated when the new plantation manager tells Stedman that he will be committed to rendering 'every service' to Stedman 'as well as the virtuous Joana, whose deserving character has attracted the attention of so many People, while your laudable Motive redounds to your lasting Honour throughout this Colony' (291). The scene of Stedman in anguish and then relieved therefore mimics similar scenes in eighteenth-century sentimental novels, which seek to instruct the reader in how to recognise and emulate a sympathising subject, largely through an identification with the feeling protagonist. For Stedman, the words of the new plantation manager represent a welcome reprieve from his misery, but an even more satisfying experience comes immediately after:

> I was surrounded by several Gentlemen and Ladies, / to whom my Friend had Communicated this very romantic adventure / Some of whom pleased to Call me *Tom Jones*, and others *Roderick Random* – They all indeed congratulated me on my Sensibility, and my having met with so valuable an Acquaintance, all seem'd to partake in the pleasure that I now felt, and the day being Spent in Mirth and Conviviality, I return'd to the Hope much better Pleased than I had left it . . . (291)

This moment of supreme self-satisfaction, as Stedman is bathed in the glow of admiration of those around him, exemplifies the picaresque mode of his memoirs, as Stedman casts himself as the hero of his own (mis)adventures. Stedman's own self-fashioning as one who sympathises and is sympathetic is reinforced in his final farewell to the Reader, for which he offers his apologies for the potentially upsetting intensity of some of his descriptions:

> And now Farewell my Patient Friends who had been pleas'd to peruse this Narrative of my Sufferings with any Degree of Sensibility, particularly those whose Simpathetick Feelings have been Rous'd by the Distressing scenes they may have met with in reading, & and whose good nature is ready to forgive inacuracies annext to the pen & pencil of a Soldier debar'd from his youth from a Classical Education – I say Farewell . . . (626)

In his final statement, Stedman reveals the underlying impetus of his *Narrative*: to create a sentimental portrait in which 'distressing scenes' are not meant to instil reader sympathy for enslaved Africans, but to represent Stedman himself as one who can sympathise and is worthy of sympathy. In this, the *Narrative* is, alongside the autobiographical sketch, part of a larger project to portray a lifelong disdain for the hypocrisy, duplicity and cruelty of polite society while contextualising the most extreme aspects of his character – the dissolute recklessness, melancholia and fiery devotion to Joanna – as the lineaments of a dissipated younger self, fondly recalled in old age.

The Stedman that offers a dramatic farewell at the end seems to epitomise the persona that Wood argues Stedman consciously creates in the *Narrative*, as 'he works around the events recorded in the earlier journal and uses them as a series of opportunities to fictionalize himself as, to use McKenzie's [sic] notorious title, a "Man of Feeling" . . . who writes for a "Feeling reader"'.[44] For Wood, this self-fictionalising gives shape to Stedman's exploitative emotionalism, in which:

> [t]he displays of extreme and perverse brutality against the black body become competitive sites for white pornographic projection. Stedman expresses his extreme revulsion at slave torture by trying to convince us that he suffers as witness more exquisitely than the slave suffers as victim. It is then our [the readers'] duty to see how fully we can appropriate his fantasy.[45]

This summary reintroduces the prevailing image of Steadman as a purveyor of the 'pornography of pain'. Yet Wood's reading of Mackenzie's *The Man of Feeling* as a precursor to the *Narrative* also allows us to reorient the critical frame to bring us back to the Scottish elements of Stedman's work, particularly in regard to his own self-fashioning.

The Anglo-Scottish Man of Feeling

The national and imperial dimensions of the eighteenth-century Scottish discourse on feeling recently have come into sharp critical focus, as a number of studies have linked philosophical and literary explorations of sympathy with cultural anxieties brought on by the post-Jacobite consolidation of the British state.[46] Luke Gibbons, for example, sees the 'abiding intellectual concerns' of Scottish and Irish philosophers 'as densely mediated responses to the acute crisis of identity precipitated in their respective cultures by the formation of modern Britain'.[47] For Adam Smith in particular, the beneficial forging of ties between nations through economic exchange finds its analogue in the workings of sympathy among individuals, as, Gibbons writes, the 'self is constituted through networks of sentiment or "fellow-feeling"'.[48] Taken in total, Smith's work, Seamus Deane writes, amounts to 'an account of the union of Scotland and England which effected a conciliation between the two on the grounds of commerce, sociality, politeness, and aesthetics'.[49]

Gibbons and Deane both emphasise what Gibbons terms the 'assimilative thrust' of Smith's theory of sympathy: in Gibbons's formulation, Scots are placed in the subordinate position of the observed, who must temper their own emotions in order to cultivate the sympathy of an imagined impartial (read English) spectator.[50] In contrast to this idea of sympathy as a process of internal colonisation, however, Gottlieb and Shields, who both trace the development and refinement of Smith's ideas on sympathy in the work of prominent Scottish writers such as Smollett and Mackenzie, argue that Scots were active agents in the formation of, in Gottlieb's term, a 'sympathetic Britishness', which did not entail the subsumption of a Scottish identity.[51] At once 'insiders and outsiders, familiar and unfamiliar, Britons and foreigners', writes Shields, Scots played the role of both 'authoritative spectators and actors hungry for approval'.[52] Smith provided the theoretical framework for this complex stance, describing sympathetic exchange as a product of both self-expression and self-control. Sympathy, the force which, for Smith, binds together the disparate interests of a civilised nation, 'requires', Shields summarises, 'both the self-control necessary to regulate or moderate emotion and sensibility necessary to imaginatively change places with others'.[53]

As do the fictions of Smollet and Mackenzie, Stedman's memoirs chart a constant tension in his deployment of sympathy as he strives to maintain a balance between the cultivation of delicate sensibility and the assertion of a rigorous self-discipline. Though Stedman was partly educated in Scotland, his writing bears no obvious traces of Adam Smith's influence. But Stedman perhaps gleaned Scottish Enlightenment theories of sympathy from the Scottish novels he not only knew well but moulded his life after. The story of Stedman's life at times seems to be playing out a version of his favourite novel, Smollet's *Roderick Random*, to which Stedman frequently alludes in his writing and whose title character, Stedman declares in his autobiographical sketch, he 'resolved to take for my models' in his youth: a Scottish military man who makes his way through the world in alternating scenes of 'victimization and vindication', as he exploits the hypocrisy of others while seeking always to degrade his enemies.[54] In the same vein, though Stedman never makes reference to *The Man of Feeling* in any of his autobiographical writings, his life often seems in the *Narrative* to parallel that of Mackenzie's protagonist, Hartley, a young man whose excess of sensibility continually overwhelms him and threatens to lead to his dissipation and death. In one of the *Narrative*'s few scenes of an actual skirmish between rebel slaves and colony troops under his command, Stedman admits to a momentary failure of nerve, when, he writes, 'my Sensibility Got so much the Better of my Duty', and, taking pity on the 'poor miserable, ill-treated' rebel slaves, he is compelled to fire his musket with his eyes shut (405). Like the 'excessive sensibility' of Mackenzie's Hartley, which, Shields writes, debilitates him as it 'jeopardizes his moral and economic autonomy', Stedman's propensity towards extreme emotion often renders him distraught, undermining his social status and career, and at times even threatening his life.[55] By the end of the *Narrative*, however, Stedman seems to have mastered the necessary self-regulation lacking in Mackenzie's Man of Feeling. Finally, under sail bound for the Dutch Republic and utterly wretched because, unable to secure Joanna's freedom, he had been forced to abandon her in Surinam with their son, Stedman begins to modify his sensibility:

> [W]hy should I torment the Reader longer with what I Could not help feeling on this Occasion both in mind & Body – Suffice it to say that in a few days Reason so far Prevail'd again as almost to make me Ashamed

of my too Great Sensibility / *not of my love* / And that I Gradually became once more a man like the Rest of my Shipmates, that is, I got the better of my *Passion*, but not of my *Affections*, which Heaven knows never more Can Forsake me while I Live – (606)

Time and distance help Stedman regain composure, and upon his re-entry into European society, he has regained what Smith might term a 'masculine firmness of character', which makes him, in Smith's formulation, a figure much more worthy of sympathy himself, as one who has converted a potentially emasculating excess of sensibility into an attractive sentimentality – expressed as a temporary reverie on what might have been.

But how does Stedman acquire this emotional self-control? The answer in part points to a particular feature of Stedman's descriptions of enslaved Africans that adds an intriguing dimension to the role that sympathetic distancing plays in the formulation of Stedman's self-image. In what amounts to a real-life example of Smith's hypothetical 'brother on the rack', Stedman recounts the horrifying torture and execution of a recalcitrant slave who had escaped but was then recaptured. After first tying him to the rack, the executioner had cut off the prisoner's left hand and then proceeded to break the bones in his body with an iron crow bar, while the victim, writes Stedman 'never Uttered a Groan or Sigh' (*Narrative*, p. 546). Instead, Stedman is astonished that the prisoner's only response is mocking disdain; he asks for a pipe of tobacco, sings songs and jokes with his torturers, declaring 'you Christians ... have mis'd your aim, and I now Care not where I to lay here Alive a month Longer' (547). For Stedman, the scene engenders an overwhelming sympathetic response, as he regards the tortured prisoner as a figure of classical nobility, a martyr to the inhumanity of slavery. The scene also seems to epitomise the desired 'flatten[ing]' of emotion on the part of the sufferer that Smith argues effects the most 'complete sympathy' between observer and observed. By 'lowering his passion to that pitch which the spectators are capable of going along with him', the stoic slave is seen to achieve a greater 'concord of the affections' between himself and the spectator.[56] We see Stedman himself wanting to emulate the example of the stoic African, but in a scene of suffering where much less is at stake. Infested with chiggers, Stedman describes how Joanna is forced to pick them out of his foot with a needle, which 'caused / as may be imagined / the most excrusiating torments but which I bore without flinching with the resolution of an affrican Negroe –' (*Narrative*, p. 284).

Stedman's admiration for the stoic resolution of the 'affrican Negroe' and his desire to emulate it seem to hold out the possibility that sympathy may establish not only bonds of common interest among individuals within a civil society but among all human beings. Yet if Stedman painstakingly and unflinchingly provides his eyewitness observations of the cruelty perpetuated on the enslaved in Surinam, he does so within the context of a retrospective account of his own life which uniformly seeks to (re)direct reader sympathy onto himself. The power of the *Narrative* to promulgate a sense of moral outrage at the plight of the enslaved is undermined by its author's constant desire to enshrine his reputation as one who is 'virtuous and humane', by means of an incessant demonstration of his 'exquisite sensibility'.[57] In one of the many descriptions of his own suffering, Stedman cannot help but admire his own clever awareness of the operations and power of sympathy:

> [I] was at this moment in a burning fever, forsaken by all my Officers and Men without a friend, or assistance of any kind, except what the poor remaining negroe Slaves could afford to give me in boyling a little Water to make some tea – One consolation I feel while I am writing this, which is that my hardships have a chance to attract some Pity, and who would not undergo a little Pain to see the Pretty Girls sigh for their Sufferings? (145)

The Stedman who asks his reader to sympathise with the enslaved and with himself is also the Stedman who can provide a winking meta-commentary for the reader, revealing perhaps his rather 'mercenary' motives – to manipulate reader sympathy so as to garner attention and selfish gain. Such a self-revelation highlights the contradictions of Stedman's self-image, of one who is at once rakish raconteur and feeling sentimentalist, apologist for the plantocracy he serves and naive but sympathetic bystander. This ambivalent insider/outside stance has led some critics to suggest that Stedman's *Narrative* offers a radical destabilisation of the British colonial discourse on slavery. Helen Thomas, for example, has identified the *Narrative* as providing a 'fitting precursor to the discussion of the "mutant" or "creolised" strategies contained within the autobiographical narratives by slaves', as the work 'explodes cultural divisions in its exposure of interracial sex relations and "miscegenations," which confuse the boundaries between coloniser and colonised, enslaved and free'.[58] For Thomas, Stedman's ultimate return to England and his subsequent marriage after abandoning Joanna amount to a 'reintegrate[ion] with his former cultural self' as they 'portray the author's ultimate loyalty to both his nation and his employers'.[59] Yet the Scottish dimensions of Stedman's cross-cultural subjectivity complicate the notion that his residence in England, a country to which he had no personal connection nor ever likely visited before, constitutes a return to a former self. More an 'ending-up' than a return, Stedman's last sojourn instead highlights the nomadic expatriate life of a late eighteenth-century Scottish soldier-for-hire, whose ultimate stance towards the transatlantic world of slavery he witnessed first-hand remains deeply ambivalent.

'Cultural Diaspora-isation' and *The History of Mary Prince*

As a first-hand account of slavery written by former slave, *The History of Mary Prince* manifests no ambiguity as to where the reader's sympathy is to be directed, even as Mary Prince's narrative shares with Stedman's the status of a retrospection shaped by the expatriate life of its author. First published in pamphlet form in 1831, Prince's *History* is the first narrative of the life of a black woman to be published in Britain and one of the last examples of British slave narratives published before abolition in 1833. The *History* provides a valuable historical record of a former slave called upon to bear irrefutable witness to the 'the horrors of slavery', to give voice to memories of the break-up of her family, endless toil, disease, physical and emotional brutality, and sexual exploitation. At the same time, as autobiographical retrospective accounts, slave narratives such as Prince's have become recognised as key contributors to the emergence of collective identities forged in the crucible of transatlantic slavery: African-American, Afro-Caribbean, Black Atlantic and Black diasporic.[60] Stuart Hall neatly summarises the transnational and cross-cultural processes at work in the formulation of these identities:

> The final point which I think is entailed in this new politics of representation has to do with an awareness of the black experience as a diaspora

experience, and the consequences which this carries for the process of unsettling, recombination, hybridization and 'cut-and-mix' – in short, the process of cultural *diaspora-ization* (to coin an ugly term), which it implies.[61]

Slave narratives reveal this process of what Hall terms 'diaspora-ization' in the fragmentation and hybridity of the black (writing) subject. Prince's *History* is not a straightforward memoir of her experiences of enslavement. Because Mary Prince is unable to authorise the story of her own experience, her *History* must rely heavily on the textual interventions of her editor, Thomas Pringle, who is called upon to represent an irreproachable authority who can verify and lend credence to her eyewitness claims, and who can himself testify to her character as an upright Christian woman. As a Christian, male, abolitionist, Pringle authorises her voice, and her body, to speak the truth of slavery.[62] As Williams L. Andrews summarises, 'Slave narratives usually required a variety of authenticating devices, such as character references and reports of investigations into the narrator's slave past (almost always written by whites), so that the slave's story might become operative as a linguistic act'.[63] Prince's *History*, writes Sara Salih, 'is not the simple narrative of a black woman's experiences'. Instead, 'it is a composite text assembled by an editor who had a clear agenda in mind', and Pringle's 'preface, supplement and appendices' are, therefore, 'an inseparable part of the text' (xiii). The mediated, dialogic quality of the *History* characterises transatlantic black women's writing in general, which Carole Boyce Davies argues 'should be read as a series of border crossings' within a framework of 'cross-cultural, transnational, translocal, diasporic perspectives'.[64]

Thomas Pringle's paratextual contributions are therefore a crucial component of Prince's creolised Caribbean subjectivity as expressed in her writing, yet few recent studies of Prince's work have paid much attention to the transnational character of Pringle's own background and writing career beyond the *History*.[65] After abandoning a failed literary career in Edinburgh, faced with the loss of his family's small tenant farm in the Scottish Borders, Pringle found himself in 1820 leading the vanguard of Scottish settlement in the newly pacified 'Neutral Territory' in the Cape Colony of South Africa, as part of a state-supported emigration-assistance scheme.[66] In Cape Town, he continued to write and founded a newspaper and literary journal, but after only six years in the colony – during which time he witnessed the brutality of slavery first-hand – Pringle returned to Britain, forced out by financial hardship and by the colonial governor, whom Pringle had offended. In London, Pringle began a new career as editor of the *Anti-Slavery Reporter* and paid secretary for the Anti-Slavery Society, one of the most prominent and powerful abolitionist organisations in the city, where his life and work intersected with Mary Prince's.[67] When his position as secretary came to an end in 1834, after abolition, he had already made plans to leave London and return, not to Scotland, but to the Cape Colony, where he hoped to live out his days. Pringle's Cape experiences and writings led later critics to claim him as 'the father of South African poetry', while others have sought to reclaim him as a Scottish writer.[68] Yet studies which place Pringle's writing within a single national literary historiography belie the ways in which his voice, like Mary Prince's, is a product of the 'process of cultural diaspora-ization'. Exile, displacement and dispossession – experiences that brought him to Mary Prince and her *History* in the first place – inform Pringle's own contribution to her slave narrative. As the product of a Scottish diaspora, Pringle's contribution manifests a partial identification with Prince's condition of exile, while providing its own powerful yet distinct expression of diaspora.

A Scottish Double Consciousness

In his preface to the *History*, Pringle lays out his editorial agenda, stating that, while he 'retain[ed] as far as was practicable, Mary's exact expressions and peculiar phraseology', so that 'no fact of importance has been omitted and not a single circumstance or sentiment has been added', he had 'pruned [her narrative] to exclude redundancies and gross grammatical errors, so as to render it clearly intelligible' (3). Pringle's rendering of Prince's oral testimony represents, for many recent critics, an act of colonial appropriation. Jessica L. Allen, for example, describes Pringle's editorial decisions, particularly his exclusion of redundancies, an instance of 'white imperialist domination', as it demonstrates his profound ignorance concerning the uses of repetition in creole patois.[69] While Pringle indeed spent no time in the Caribbean and was probably completely unfamiliar with the linguistic structures of West Indian patois, his desire to render Prince's language reflects perhaps his own linguistic anxieties, as a native Scottish speaker seeking a metropolitan audience. The impetus to linguistic compromise and collaboration that informs Pringle's editorial interventions in the *History* manifest a Scottish 'double consciousness', a conflicted, hybrid subjectivity derived from long habits of subsuming traces of 'native' vernacular while adopting the language of the British metropole in public speech. Calder argues that Pringle's Scottish university training predestined him to resist the vernacular and accept genteel (English) standards of diction in his own poetry. At the same time, Scots words and phrases in Pringle's writing often serve as linguistic markers of his national identity, and he retained the use of Scotticisms in his personal and informal writing.[70] Pringle's career as a poet, Calder writes, parallels that of the Scottish poet Pringle idolised, Thomas Campbell, who 'epitomised the tension in Scottish literary circles between the claims of native culture and the wish not to seem uncouth in Southern eyes'.[71]

While Pringle also exhibited a keen, if patronising, awareness and interest in indigenous African tongues as well as the Dutch and English creoles he encountered in the Cape Colony, aspects of which he sometimes deployed in his own writing, he also stressed the importance of using what he defined as plain style to move a reader. In a letter written to his friend John Fairbairn in 1825, Pringle defends this stylistic approach in his poem 'The Bechuana Boy', which describes the plight of one member of a group of displaced refugees who roamed near his settlement and who were often sold into slavery.[72] This poem, Pringle writes,

> is adapted to please a class of readers whom you too much neglect ['women, children, counting house clerks, country functionaries, and aides de camp'] . . . [I] have tried this *very simple* style with something of a further view – to excite some sympathy in very *common* readers, for this class of unfortunate strangers . . .[73]

The language politics of Pringle's Scottish background, coupled with his ideas on plain style's ability to move most dramatically a 'common' reader to sympathy, suggests that something more complex than colonial ignorance is at work in Pringle's later editorial interventions in the *History*. Instead, his editorial agenda suggests the anxieties of a writer who himself has felt perpetually on the outside, one who has had to constantly modulate his voice in order to speak with authority in the metropolis. As the product of a Scottish-British poet/colonial settler/abolitionist secretary, the 'white written text' of *The History of Mary Prince*, through which its subject must speak – creating the hybrid 'double-voiced' quality that been identified as the hallmark of Black diaspora literature – is itself already double-voiced.[74]

'The Stranger and the Exile Who is in Our land within Our Gates'

As a retrospective looking-back, the *History*, like many other slave narratives, plots a transformation of its author's subjectivity – from brutalised human chattel to self-autonomous writing subject, who is able to speak for those still enslaved. Yet Prince's narrative differs from many other slave narratives in expressing the precariousness not only of her past but also of her here and now. The *History* recounts how she was forced to leave behind a husband in Antigua and brought to London by her masters, the Woods, who were attending to their children's education. Prince's London visit initially represents a hopeful future, a possible cure for the rheumatism that she had acquired from lifetime of hard labour and, more crucially, an escape from thraldom, as she hears that, once in London, 'my master would free me' (31). Yet the hopefulness that London holds out is contingent in her mind on an eventual return to Antigua, where she could live out the rest of her life with her husband as a free woman. In London, however, Prince, too ill and weak from her rheumatism to accomplish the work demanded of her from her masters, is threatened with dismissal from their household. Prince describes the decisive moment when the Woods make a final ultimatum that she must accede to their demands or face eviction:

> [Mrs Wood] supposed I thought myself a free woman, but I was not: and if I did not do it directly I should be instantly turned out of doors. I stood a long time before I could answer, for I did not know well what to do. I knew that I was free in England, but I did not know where to go, or how to get my living; and therefore, I did not like to leave the house. But Mr. Wood said he would send for a constable to thrust me out; and at last I took courage and resolved that I would not be longer thus treated, but would go and trust to Providence. This was the fourth time they had threatened to turn me out, and, go where I might, I was determined now to take them at their word; though I thought it very hard, after I had

lived with them for thirteen years, and worked for them like a horse, to be driven out in this way, like a beggar. (33)

This scene represents a pivotal moment in the transition of Prince's subjectivity, the moment when she asserts her autonomy as a 'free woman' in England against the dictates of the Woods who would have her remain a slave. Yet the scene also recounts Prince's ambivalence when confronted with the sacrifice freedom requires of her, which she characterises as a casting out, to become penniless and alone. Finding temporary shelter with the Moravians, Prince eventually made her way to the offices of the Anti-Slavery Society, where she met Pringle. Pringle not only championed her cause but took her into his home. Yet she continues to characterise her life in London as one of permanent exile from home and family life she had established in Antigua. As she exclaimed to Pringle at their first meeting:

> I would rather go to my grave than go back a slave to Antigua, though I wish to go back to my husband very much – very much – very much! I am much afraid my owners would separate me from my husband, and use me very hard, or perhaps sell me for a field negro; – and slavery is too too bad. I would rather go into my grave! (39)

Unable to return 'home' to Antigua without also returning to a condition of enslavement, Prince was trapped in a legal limbo in London, 'shipwrecked', in Sandra Pouchet Paquet's words, 'by laws that made slavery illegal in England, while it was still legal in the colonies'.[75] Far from signalling the achievement of autonomous selfhood, Prince's London domicile is only the final in a series of displacements recalled in her *History*: born into slavery in Bermuda but separated from her family at the age of twelve and sold off to succession of masters, Prince was for a time on Grand Turk Island before returning to Bermuda and then moving to Antigua, before sailing to London with the Woods.

Prince's predicament, as one whose freedom is contingent upon permanent exile from her Antiguan 'homeland', represents an unresolved disjuncture in her transformation in the *History* from slave to former slave, a disjuncture that eventually forms part of its polemicist agenda. By publishing Prince's story, and by sponsoring a petition to parliament, the Anti-Slavery Society hoped not only to provide further evidence of the cruelty of slavery but to draw attention to a particular anomaly in British slavery laws, originating in the 1722 case of Grace Jones. Like Mary Prince, Grace Jones had accompanied her mistress from Antigua to England. Jones's later return to the Caribbean with her mistress was deemed a violation of her rights; her defenders argued that Jones's stay in England had made her a free British subject, but the judge in the case, Lord Stowell, had ruled that Jones was only a free woman while residing in England, and that when she returned to the West Indies she had forfeited her freedom.[76]

Pringle makes explicit reference to the Jones case at the end of his Supplement to the *History*, suggesting that the particular significance of Prince's story is its bearing upon the status of slavery in Britain itself:

> I may observe that the history of Mary Prince furnishes a corollary to Lord Stowell's decision in the case of the slave Grace, and that it is most valuable on this account. Whatever opinions may be held by some readers on the grave question of immediately abolishing Colonial Slavery, nothing assuredly can be more repugnant to the feelings of Englishmen than that the system should be permitted to extend its baneful influence to this country. Yet such is the case, when the slave landed in England still only possesses that qualified degree of freedom, that a change of domicile will determine it. Though born a British subject, and resident within the shores of England, he is cut off from his dearest natural rights by the sad alternative of regaining them at the expence of liberty, and the certainty of severe treatment. (*History*, p. 62)

Expanding on the legal questions, Pringle makes an appeal to readers' sympathy, asking them to imagine the emotional ramifications of a life of perpetual freedom-in-exile:

> It is true that [the slave] has the option of returning; but it is a cruel mockery to call it a voluntary choice, when upon his return depend his means of subsistence and his re-union with all that makes life valuable. Here he has tasted 'the sweets of freedom,' to quote the words of the unfortunate Mary Prince; but if he desires to restore himself to his family, or to escape from suffering and destitution, and the other evils of a climate uncongenial to his constitution and habits, he must abandon the enjoyment of his late-acquired liberty, and again subject himself to the arbitrary power of a vindictive master. (62)

Pringle's elaboration of vexed legal issues moves to an empathetic imagining of the anguish that Prince must suffer, as one whose freedom is contingent on permanent estrangement from home and family. References to Prince's exiled status appear frequently in Pringle's contributions to the *History*. He writes that, after waiting for nearly a year and 'seeing the poor woman's spirits sinking under the sickening influence of hope deferred' while her legal case remained unresolved, he promised to intervene on her behalf, referring to her as the 'exiled negro woman' (42). In a postscript to the second edition of the *History*, which is also quoted in the preface to the third edition, Pringle reports that Prince's legal status remains unchanged – she remains 'cruelly and hopelessly severed from her husband and her home' – but her health has deteriorated, and she has become afflicted with 'a disease in the eyes' which may lead to 'total blindness' (4). Pringle makes a final appeal, on the grounds of sympathy, to those 'friends of humanity' to promote the sale of her narrative so that she receives much needed funding. '[T]he seasonable sympathy thus manifested in her behalf', Pringle writes,

> will neither be fruitlessly expended nor unthankfully received; while in accordance with the benign Scripture mandate, it will serve to mitigate and relieve, as far as human kindness can, the afflictions of 'the stranger and the exile who is in our land within our gates'. (4–5)[77]

Perhaps a fitting summary of the overall impetus of his contributions to Prince's work, Pringle's postscript paints her as a figure worthy of great sympathy, a woman broken in body and mind after a lifetime of physical and mental cruelty. Pringle's reference to the Christian mandate to lend aid and shelter to the outcast and the homeless also places both him and Prince within a narrative of Christian charity, in which Pringle can play the role of the compassionate Christian householder, who will take the exiled Prince into his home and tutor her on the path to salvation. In casting their relationship this way, however, Pringle is also repeating a narrative similar to the one he had established in his poem 'The Bechuana Boy' and in his other South African writings. In 'The Bechuana Boy', Pringle recounts his relationship with the eponymous subject of the poem, 'a swarthy Stripling', who is an orphan and a refugee from war and slavery. As he recounts their first meeting, Pringle encounters the Bechuana Boy one day, when he comes out of the desert and suddenly appears, half-naked and forlorn, before Pringle's tent, exclaiming 'in the language of his race', 'I have no home!' (*African Poems*, p. 4). The boy then relates a story of violent dispossession and exile: the destruction of his village by mountain banditti, wandering in the wilderness before being sold into slavery by Boers, and his escape to Pringle's home where, Pringle writes, 'We took him for "our own".' Pringle eventually comes to regard the boy as his own child and sets him on the path of conversion to Christianity (7).[78]

As he had done for the real-life inspiration for 'The Bechuana Boy', Hinza Morassi, Pringle 'takes in' Mary Prince, in an act of benign paternalism that plays out the dynamics of sympathy that Sharpe describes as characteristic of British anti-slavery polemic, which, while it established a 'kinship of Europeans and Africans', places the suffering black 'other' in a position of inferiority in relation to a sympathetic white observer who alone has the power to help them.[79] Parallels in the accounts of refugee and former slave provided in 'The Bechuana Boy' and the *History* have led Matthew Shum to read the former as a 'prehistory' of the latter, in which Morassi prefigures Prince as an object of readerly sympathy.[80] But the associative quality of Pringle's recollections of his life in South Africa extends beyond parallels between Pringle's accounts of his two black protégés. Pringle's contributions to the *History* reverberate with the echo of his own memory of estrangement and multiple displacement, both from his native Scotland and from the Cape Colony where he had hoped to make a lasting home but never did.

Scottish Diaspora in South Africa

Wonder at the vast unknown, coupled with hopes for future settlement, permeates Pringle's initial impressions of South Africa. In poems he composed while living in the Cape Colony and in the *Narrative of a Residence in South Africa* he published in 1834 as part of his two-volume collection *African Sketches*, Pringle provides a retrospective account of his arrival in the colony, which encapsulates the psychology of a Scottish settler diaspora, as he describes the journey to the fertile valley in which he and the small band he lead planned to established their initial settlement. In his *Narrative*, Pringle describes the differing reactions of English and Scots upon seeing the colony for the first time from the ship:

the sublimely stern aspect of the country, so different from the rich tameness of ordinary English scenery, seemed to strike many of the Southron with a degree of awe approaching to consternation. The Scotch, on the contrary, as the stirring recollections of their native land were vividly called up by the rugged peaks and shaggy declivities of this wild coast, were strongly affected, like all true mountaineers on such occasions. Some were excited to extravagant spirits; others silently shed tears.[81]

Pringle narrates a communal diasporic consciousness, which commences the moment the new world landscape comes into view with fond remembrances of the departed homeland. The 'rugged peaks and shaggy declivities' of the South African landscape provide a comforting analogue to a native landscape left behind, while also prompting, perhaps, an equally comforting assertion of a continued Scottish identity in opposition to an English one. Nevertheless, the topography of this new world initiates a strong conflictedness on the part of Scottish emigrants, who hope for a better future but for whom memories of the homeland they have left behind appear unbidden and without warning. At a temporary sojourn on their long trek to their intended settlement, for example, Pringle describes the reaction of a long-time resident, one Mr Hart – 'a Scotch gentleman' – who, even though he has resided in the colony for more than twenty years, is overcome when he overhears a conversation of a large party of his fellow expatriates:

> A numerous party of us were assembled at tea in the officers' dining hall, when Mr. Hart joined us. The Scottish accent, seldom entirely lost even by the most polished of the middle ranks of our countrymen, was heard from every tongue; and the broad 'Doric dialect' prevailed, spoken by female voices, fresh and unsophisticated from the banks of the Teviot and the Fields Lothian. Hart, a man of iron look and rigid nerve, was taken by surprise, and deeply affected. The accents of his native tongue, uttered by the kindly voice of woman, carried him back forty years at once and irresistibly, as he afterwards owned, to the scenes of his mother's fireside; and recalled freshly before him the softened remembrances of early life – those tender and sacred remembrances which, though apparently buried beneath the cares and ambitious aims of after years, are never, in any good heart, entirely effaced. (28)

Pringle's description of the affective power of the sound of the Scottish dialect echoes early nineteenth-century theories of the 'malady of nostalgia', which gave emphasis to aural sensory impression – native songs and voices, particularly, were thought to bring memories of a former life to the forefront of the imagination.[82] Such sensory impressions can, 'at once and irresistibly', bring memories of a former life to the forefront of consciousness. An ode to the associative power and sanctity of remembrance, the passage suggests how a national consciousness can be retained and even cultivated in new surroundings. Remembrances tied to homeland and family are never 'entirely effaced', no matter how long one has been away.[83] The lingering anguish of exile, the persistent memory of a home left behind, reminds Mr Hart that he remains an alien in the colony.

Conflictedness summarises the sentiment of much of Pringle's poetry on the theme of emigration, as his tone from poem to poem swings dramatically, from morbid despondency to hopeful optimism. Pringle adopts the ballad form in 'An Emigrant's Song' (date of composition unknown but first published in 1834), in which the poet asks the 'maid of Tweed' to sail with him to 'the wilds of South-Africa, far o'er the sea', where he will build her a 'cabin beside the clear fount'. The poem concludes with the image of a future life of prosperity, free from the burden of memory: 'there, rich in the wealth which a bountiful soil / Pours forth to repay the husbandman's toil; / Content with the Present, at peace with the Past, / No cloud on the future our joys to o'ercast' (*African Poems*, p. 34). In 'The Exile's Lament', published in 1824, Pringle again adopts the ballad form, and presents us with another 'Scottish Maiden'. But the maiden of 'The Exile's Lament' is *already* in South Africa and, 'mournfully pour[ing] her melting lay / In Teviot's Border Tongue', she sings a much different song. The sunny and fertile landscape that surrounds her brings no optimism or hope: 'bright are the skies – and these valleys of bloom / May enchant the traveller's eye; / But all seems drest in death-like gloom / To the exile – who comes to die!' (44). The poem concludes with a final lament: 'Oh, light, light is poverty's lowliest state, / On Scotland's peaceful strand, / Compared with the heart-sick exile's fate, / In this wild and weary land!' (45).

In perhaps his most sustained and personal exploration of the diaspora experience in South Africa, 'The Emigrant's Cabin' (first published in 1834 but dated 'Glen-Lynden 1822'), Pringle recounts his motives for emigration. In the poem, he imagines a visit to his rustic cabin by his friend John Fairbairn, who chides him, suggesting he embraced self-exile on the Cape due to a 'disappointed pride' in the failure of his literary career back in Scotland. Pringle retorts,

'You've missed the mark, Fairbairn: my breast is clear. / Nor Wild Romance nor Pride allured me here: / Duty and Destiny with equal voice / constrained my steps: I had no other choice' (*African Poems*, p. 29). Alluding to the destitution that had threatened his family amid the harsh new economic realities of post-war rural Scotland, Pringle configures his motive to emigrate as the duty to secure financial prosperity for his immediate family and their descendants. Pringle makes this motive of familial preservation explicit at the beginning of his *Narrative*, as one of the 'two distinct objects in view' when he decided to emigrate to the Cape: 'to collect again into one social circle, and establish in rural independence, my father's family, which untoward circumstances had broken up and begun to scatter over the world' (3). As was the case for many Scottish emigrants to the British colonies, and in stark contrast to Mary Prince – for whom the price of freedom was exile and permanent estrangement from 'all that makes life valuable' – Pringle envisions his displacement as a means to secure and perpetuate past ties and affiliations, rather than as a hopeless break from them. Migration to rural Africa in 'The Emigrant's Cabin' signals a hoped-for continuation of a communal way of life, built upon ties of kinship and compatriotism, which had become untenable back 'home' in Scotland. Though Pringle's deft and knowing incorporation of indigenous and Dutch-Afrikaans terms and phrases has led the editors of his collected African poems to identify 'The Emigrant's Cabin' as one of the first depictions of 'an embryonic indigenous culture definably "South African" in character' (*African Poems*, p. 96), the poem also gives sentiment to the particular aspects of the Scottish diasporic experience of the period – the global 'scattering' of extended families and whole communities that sought to hold on to a distinctly 'Scottish' way of life.

In the autumn of 1824, however, Pringle was in poor health and hounded by the colonial governor, whom he had publicly criticised in the pages of the newspaper he had helped establish. Increasingly despondent, describing his 'prospects in the Colony' as 'entirely blasted', Pringle began to consider a return to Britain. In October, Pringle sent Fairbairn a poem entitled 'To Scotland'.[84] '[W]hen I think of all I've lost', he writes, 'In leaving thee to seek a foreign home, / I find more cause the farther I roam / To mourn the home I left the favoured Coast' (*South African Letters*, p. 132). Given Pringle's disappointed hopes for a prosperous life in South Africa, there is bitter irony in the poem's expression of loss and exile, as Pringle confronts the possibility of a double displacement – imminent dispersal from a colonial domicile that had already established the diasporic conditions of his earlier writings. This history of multiple displacement weighs heavily on Pringle's contributions to *The History of Mary Prince*. As residence in London represents for Mary Prince a kind of doubled 'exile' – from a Caribbean 'homeland', of no certain nation or territory in a transatlantic circuit that exemplified a 'diaspora-ised' Black Atlantic – so too does Pringle's stay in London represent a kind of doubled exile – from the colonial settlement on which he had staked a claim for a new life and a new beginning, as he departed his native Scotland. As Pringle perhaps drew out and amplified Prince's own lamentations of exile, his contributions to her story suggest more than white British abolitionist sympathy-at-a-distance; rather, they manifest a recognition and partial identification with a diasporic voice he found that, in some ways, corresponded with his own: the voice of a stranger in the metropolis, an outcast from a national and colonial 'home' that had ultimately proved untenable.

Scottish Imperialist Humanitarianism

To emphasise affinities and parallels in the circumstances that brought Mary Prince and Thomas Pringle together in the metropolis, and helped shape the dialogic structure of Prince's narrative, is not to suggest that those circumstances are in any way the same. Although Pringle's writing, like Prince's, reflects the conflicted wavering between a hopeful optimism and the despondency of the exile who is alienated from his or her surroundings, Pringle, of course, was always a free citizen of the British Empire, and his writings reflect the peculiar conditions of the nineteenth-century Scottish diaspora. As part of the great wave of Scottish emigration during the period, Pringle acquired a special knowledge and sympathetic insight into the local black African cultures he encountered, while also providing a consistently pointed critique of the British slave system and its denial of the basic humanity of black Africans. Nevertheless, his South African writings also rehearse familiar assumptions of Scoto-British Christian abolitionism, expressing the absolute conviction of his country's moral, intellectual and social superiority. This conviction is evident in his description of his earliest encounters with native African peoples in the *Narrative*. Setting out on horseback to survey the environs of his party's initial camp, Pringle recounts his impressions of a native village he suddenly comes upon, emphasising the stark juxtaposition of the familiar and the strange:

> The bleating of flocks returning to the fold, the lowing of the kine to meet their young, and other pleasant rural sounds, recalling to my recollection all the pastoral associations of a Scottish glen, gave a very agreeable effect to my first view of this missionary village. When I entered the place, however, all associations connected with the rural scenery of Europe were at once dispelled. The groups of woolly-haired, swarthy-complexioned natives, many of them still dressed in the old sheep-skin mantle or *caross*; the swarms of naked or half-naked children; the wigwam hovels of mud or reeds; the long-legged, large-horned cattle; the broad tailed African sheep, with hair instead of wool; the strange words of the evening salutation (*goeden avond* – 'good evening'), courteously given, as I passed, by old and young; the uncouth clucking sounds of the Hottentot language, spoken by some of them to each other; these, and a hundred other traits of wild and foreign character, made me feel that I was indeed far from the glens of Cheviot, or the pastoral groups of a Scottish hamlet – that I was at length in the Land of the Hottentot. (14)

Here again is the emigrant's search for familiar analogues of the homeland he has left to make sense of the new world in which he now resides. These, however, must yield to the disorienting unfamiliar aspects of this new world, for which no analogues can be found. However, in his lengthy description of his first encounter with the 'Land of the Hottentot', Pringle also seeks to contain the African Other through what would become a familiar colonialist alignment of race and primitiveness that reasserts a confidence in his own superiority. Relying on the universalist theories of the Scottish Science of Man that his description adumbrates, Pringle reasserts a social, cultural and epistemological authority on the natives through a careful ethnographic cataloguing of their salient characteristics. Though this passage describes his first encounter with African village life, the knowing references to African social and linguistic practice betray their later composition, after Pringle already had resided sometime in the colony and after his cultivation of knowledge of its various cultures.

All of Pringle's writing on South Africa is shot through with the sympathetic and tolerant but patronising view of black Africans that this passage displays. In his *Narrative*, 'The Bechuana Boy' and 'Song of the Bushman' – which provide a representative of what Pringle describes as an outcast wandering people, 'the South African "Children of the Mist"' (*African Poems*, p. 86) – or 'The Captive of Camalú', a poem dedicated to 'those Caffers and Gohnaquas . . . who . . . were forced to become bondmen among the boors or imprisoned in Robben Island' (105), Pringle demonstrates his sympathy not only with the plight of the enslaved, but with that of displaced indigenous peoples who are victims of the colony's long history of internecine warfare and European encroachment. His sympathy for the latter often inspires a condemnation of British colonial policy. After recounting in the *Narrative* a conspicuous act of criminal duplicity on the part of a Scottish commander overseeing the violent removal of Xhosa people from lands they occupied, during an earlier attempt at native 'pacification', Pringle sums up the general tenor of British colonial attitudes: '[I]t is a lamentable truth that in our treatment generally of savage nations, all respect for common honesty, justice, or humanity, appears to be often utterly forgotten, even by men otherwise generous, kind, and sensitively honourable' (292). Pringle's tolerance for cultural difference and his sympathy for the native victims of 'unchristian' British violence and dispossession, however, at times give way to expressions of strong hostility against resistance to the colonial social order, especially when that resistance threatens his own settlement. For example, he characterises as 'banditti' the nomadic groups of displaced peoples, runaway slaves, and what he described as mixed-race thieves and deserters from the colonial militia, who occasionally harassed Glen Lynden. In a June 1825 letter to Fairbairn, Pringle described a group of 'Bushmen' who

> continue to plague us – *ungrateful schelms*! Even after I have celebrated them in song [i.e. in 'The Bushman']. They stole all my brother's riding possessions last week and severely wounded a Bastard [mixed-race] Hottentot with poisoned arrows. So I have declared war against them and have written to the Landdrost for a commando to attack them in their rocky dens. You see we back Settlers grow all savage and bloody by coming in continual collision with savages. (*South African Letters*, p. 192)[85]

In the formal letter he sent to the to landdrost, the colonial authority in the region, Pringle tempers his rhetoric, saying 'both on the count of humanity and for the ends of justice' it would be preferable to force the capture of 'these Banditti' by surrounding and blockading them in their strongholds, rather than adopting the 'usual mode' of 'firing upon them indiscriminately'. Nevertheless, he continues:

> there cannot surely be a doubt either of the justice or necessity of extirpating (under proper guidance of course) a band of thieves and murderers from the territory ceded by the Caffers – a country in the first place, which . . . they can have no claim to occupy; and secondly . . . are composed of runaway *Schelms* from the Colony, deserters from the Cape Corps, and other criminals, whom it is otherwise expedient to put down. (*South African Letters*, p. 194)

The ambiguity and ambivalence illustrated in Pringle's alternating depictions of sympathetic outcasts and lawless wandering banditti suggest the contradictions of Pringle's own transperipheral experiences and background. Intentionally established as a kind of buffer zone between the British colony and warring Xhosa groups, the 'Ceded Territory', at the very frontier at which Pringle's settlement was situated, was frequented by the dispossessed and the displaced, including refugees from recent frontier wars and Xhosa people who had recently been pushed off their lands. In his transoceanic migration from one 'borderland' to another, Pringle is, on the one hand, particularly attuned to the complexity of cross-cultural contact and the disruptive consequences of the uncertain and constantly shifting allegiances and loyalties at work along national and imperial frontiers. He is also deeply sympathetic to the plight of what he terms 'enthralled aborigines', refugees of war who have been sold into slavery. On the other hand, as the leader of his settlement he fancies himself a 'petty "border chief," able to muster upwards of thirty armed horsemen (including our own party and the six Hottentot soldiers) at an hour's notice', to defend his small isolated community from marauding outsiders (*Narrative*, p. 114).[86] Pringle ultimately sees himself as belonging to the vanguard of Christian progress in the Cape Colony, and his South African writings display a special interest in the theory and practice of colonial settlement. His recounting of his six-year Cape residence prefigures accounts of the great Scottish imperial icon David Livingstone, whose missionary work and sympathetic concern for the welfare of the native would come to exemplify Scotland's contribution to the civilising mission in Africa, later in the century. In his concluding remarks in the *Narrative*, Pringle provides a vision of an African future in which emancipation and justice are achieved through a programme of unbridled imperial expansion:

> The Native Tribes, in short, are ready to throw themselves into our arms. Let us open our arms cordially to embrace them as MEN and as BROTHERS. Let us enter upon a new and noble career of conquest. Let us subdue savage Africa by JUSTICE, by KINDNESS, by the talisman of CHRISTIAN TRUTH. Let us *thus* go forth, in the name and under the blessing of God, gradually to extend the moral influence, and, if it be thought desirable, the territorial boundary also of our Colony, until it shall become an Empire, embracing Southern Africa from the Keisi and the Gareep to Mozambique and Cape Negro – and to which, peradventure, in after days, even the equator shall prove no ultimate limit. (342)

Pringle's narrative of material and spiritual improvement in Africa informs much of his South African writings. Traces of this narrative also surface throughout his contributions to the *History of Mary Prince*, revealing a correspondence with the diasporic conditions that shape her story. In this way, the story of the exiled but free and Christianised African Mary Prince was also, perhaps, for Pringle a particularly Scottish allegory of empire.

A Land of No Return

But what became of Mary Prince and Thomas Pringle? In London, Prince lived in Pringle's home for a time, yet her ultimate fate became entangled in the competing public narratives of her virtue. In the Christian abolitionist polemic that Pringle helped shape, Prince's story was made to conform to an 'evangelical model of womanhood' in which, Moira Ferguson writes, 'acceptance of conversion necessitates admission as well as absolution of formal sinfulness'.[87] Yet Prince was also subject to the racialised sexual stereotyping of her former owner and his sympathisers. Her most prominent critic was the Scottish-born James MacQueen, the editor of the *Glasgow Courier*, who publicly portrayed her as a licentious and deceitful woman. MacQueen was one of the most prominent pro-slavery advocates of the time, and, as a former plantation overseer in Grenada, belonged to what David Lambert identifies as 'an Atlantic system of patronage and kinship that was of profound importance in the manning and maintenance of Scottish-owned plantations across the Caribbean'.[88] MacQueen took up Prince's *History* in the pages of *Blackwood's* and other pro-slavery publications to launch a scathing attack on the truthfulness of her claims while seeking to cast doubt on her character, in part through an imputation that she had been addicted to 'immoral habits', which 'led her to commit the most disgraceful lascivious acts'.[89] Pringle, in MacQueen's account, plays the role of Prince's hypocritical dupe, one who 'sees nothing but purity in a prostitute'.[90]

MacQueen's vicious insinuations prompted Pringle to sue MacQueen's London publisher, Thomas Cadell, and Pringle himself would be sued by Prince's former master, John Wood, in early 1833; Prince's sexual past would again become the subject of public scrutiny in the context of these libel suits.[91] Also, though she remained in contact with the Pringles after publication of her *History* and attended the wedding of her transcriber, Susanna Strickland, Prince ultimately became the victim of the sexual politics of the white missionary world that had once given her sanctuary. The Moravian church gave her immediate shelter in London after she had left the Woods, and Moravian missionaries in Antigua had taught her to read. The church, however, refused her appeal for readmittance in London in 1834; 'the sexual nature of MacQueen's public character attacks on Prince and Pringle and her pecuniary situation and prospects', writes Sue Thomas, 'clearly affected their decision'.[92] Exiled once again because her sexual identity had become incompatible with a Christian antislavery idea of proper victimhood, Prince disappears from the public record, and nothing is known of her life afterwards.

As for Pringle, a self-awareness of his own unsettled predicament perhaps underlay his desire to help Prince, as London represented for both of them not a centre, but a meeting point at the crossroads of exile. Like Prince, who, as far as is known, never made the return trip 'home', to the West Indies, so did Pringle remain in London, estranged from the Cape Colony where the rest of his family had permanently settled. Alienated from his immediate surroundings and nostalgic for the African 'home' he had sought to make – in an ideal re-creation of his native Scotland – yet retaining a faith in Christian progress and the potential of native Africans to become 'civilized', Pringle began to plan for his return to South Africa. In declining health, Pringle wrote in July 1834: 'If I had now a few hundred pounds I would go out to the Caffer frontier, buy and stock a farm, and settle myself for life in the wilderness' (*South African Letters*, p. 366). Failing to obtain compensation for losses suffered at the hands of the colonial governor several years earlier, however, Pringle was unable to make a purchase of land. Still resolved 'to go to the Cape, where I have . . . relations, among whom I may either regain my health or find a not unmourned grave and leave my wife among kind friends', Pringle sold off all his furniture and household goods while making a final appeal to his Anti-Slavery Society friends, who supplied him with sufficient funds to finance the voyage (*South African Letters*, p. 369). While awaiting embarkation, however, Pringle became too ill to sail and died in London.[93] Pringle thus ended his days where his life had intersected with Mary Prince's; he, like her, remained in 'exile', unable to make the return journey 'home'.

Clearance, Slavery and Cultural Amnesia: Macleod's *Gloomy Memories*

Although the written testimony of former slaves like Mary Prince had become a prominent feature of the slavery debate on both sides of the Atlantic by the 1830s, Harriet Beecher Stowe's depictions of the degradations suffered by the enslaved in *Uncle Tom's Cabin* set off a firestorm of emotion that changed the course of the debate after its publication in 1852. With the unprecedented success of *Uncle Tom's Cabin*, Stowe demonstrated the uses of white-authored sentimental fiction, rather than eyewitness testimony, in engendering widespread sympathy in America and Britain for the plight of the enslaved. On the heels of the novel's publication, the Glasgow Ladies New Anti-Slavery Society became the first organisation to invite Stowe to Britain, and in the spring of 1853 she was feted by enthusiastic abolitionists among all ranks of British society. Stowe's visit to Great Britain revitalised the ties of an already well-established transatlantic anti-slavery network, established through correspondence and exchange.[94] Soon after her return to the United States, Stowe penned a memoir of her travels entitled *Sunny Memories of Foreign Lands*, in which she recounts her recollections 'of a most agreeable visit'; chapters on her travels in Scotland are particularly replete with enraptured first-hand remembrances of places associated with Scottish history and literature, particularly those concerning her favourite author, Walter Scott.[95]

Stowe, as recent critics have argued, had both professional and political motives for penning *Sunny Memories*, which was intended (among other things) to help heal factional schisms and national rivalries that threatened to undermine the transatlantic network *Uncle Tom's Cabin* had helped build.[96] Yet one section of *Sunny Memories*, which Stowe likely intended to highlight Anglo-American anti-slavery solidarity and cooperation, instead sparked an unanticipated controversy that only indirectly involved the slavery debate. In a chapter recounting her visit to Stafford House, the London residence of prominent anti-slavery sympathiser the Duchess of Sutherland, Stowe praised her host, who, along with the Earl of Shaftesbury, had organised an anti-slavery address signed by 577,000 British women. Presenting herself as an unbiased character witness, Stowe also defended the duchess against the 'ridiculous stories' of her detractors, the most prominent of whom was Donald Macleod, whose outraged accounts of the dispossession and displacement of Sutherland tenants in the first half of the nineteenth century had been widely circulated in Britain and North America.[97] Stowe's defence of the duchess and her easy dismissal of accounts of Sutherland cruelty in *Sunny Memories*, which Judie Newman argues were 'designed from the outset to combat Macleod', prompted him to publish his own rebuttal, in a collection he entitled *Gloomy Memories*.[98] Called upon to defend his assertions of widespread, systematic injustice on the Sutherland estate, Macleod lays claim to the truth of his own account by adopting a discursive mode familiar in the anti-slavery debate: the eyewitness testimonial, derived from his recollections of events he experienced first-hand and from other eyewitnesses who also experienced the events and could therefore corroborate his own account. Macleod's bitter condemnation of Stowe's claims, as deriving from 'one who was not there', validates and authorises his own counter-claims, deriving from one who was. Reading the interrelation between these two 'memoirs' provides insight into an important moment in Scottish national history: when memory, in the form of irrefutable eyewitness testimony of past experiences 'as they really happened' speaks truth to power, and in doing so helps shape a new understanding of the nation's past. In

Gloomy Memories, Macleod ironically adopts the testimonial mode of the slave narrative to take on the most influential abolitionist writer of his time, deploying a first-person testimonial to confront what he saw as a denial of the past and a collective will to forget. In doing so, Macleod was instrumental in forging a powerful cultural memory of what is now termed the Highland Clearances.

I Who Was Once There

By 1853, when Stowe penned *Sunny Memories*, Macleod, a mason by trade, had long since emigrated to Canada, residing in Ontario in a district largely settled by immigrants who, like himself, had been cleared from the Sutherland estate. Macleod's account of the Clearances in Sutherland, largely spanning the 1810s and 20s, was first published as a series of letters in the *Edinburgh Weekly Chronicle* in 1840 and 1841, which were then bound into a single volume entitled *History of the Destitution in Sutherlandshire*, published in 1841. The appearance of *Sunny Memories* incited Macleod to revisit his earlier written recollections of events that were themselves now nearly forty years past. In 1857 he published his original letters in Toronto, along with updated material pertaining specifically to Stowe's visit to Scotland, in a new compilation, the complete title of which was *Gloomy Memories of the Highlands of Scotland versus Mrs. Harriet Beecher Stowe's Sunny Memories in (England) a Foreign Land: or a Faithful Picture of the Extirpation of the Celtic Race from the Highlands of Scotland*. No longer a 'history' but a collection of 'memories', Macleod's revised title not only makes for a bitterly ironic retort to Stowe's work, it also signals the ways in which, for him, the terms of their contest ultimately come down to a question of the validity of their respective remembrances. Laying out his aims and methods, Macleod emphasises his impartiality and the crucial role that eyewitness testimony will play in his account:

> [I] shall produce a selection of such facts and incidents, as can be supported by sufficient testimony, to many of which I was an eyewitness, or was otherwise cognizant of them. I have been, with my family, for many years, removed, and at a distance from those scenes, and have no personal malice to gratify, my only motive being a desire to vindicate my ill-used countrymen from the aspersions cast upon them, to draw

public attention to their wrongs, and, if possible, to bring about a fair inquiry, to be conducted by disinterested gentlemen, as to the real causes of their long-protracted misery and destitution, in order, that the public sympathies may be awakened in their behalf, and something effected for their relief. With these observations I now conclude, and in my next letter I will enter upon my narration of a few of such facts as can be fully authenticated by living testimony.[99]

Declaring himself an eyewitness to many of the 'facts and incidents' which he recounts, Macleod establishes his personal bona fides to speak on his subject, as one who can himself authenticate through 'living testimony' the truth of what he describes. Though Stowe never refers specifically to Macleod, he often employs direct address when defending his version of past events and rebutting her assertions. For example, bitterly condemning Stowe's primary informant, James Loch, who was factor of the estate in 1812 and whom Macleod held responsible for the worst outrages of the clearances, he writes, 'Of those vile executors of atrocities I have been describing . . . it seems the chief were left to give you all the information you required about British slavery and oppression' (93). In response to unreliable second-hand reports such as Loch's, Macleod offers his own eyewitness recollection of actions committed under Loch's direction:

> I was at the pulling down and burning of the house of William Chisholm, I got my hands burnt taking out the poor old woman from amidst the flames of her once comfortable though humble dwelling, and a more horrifying and lamentable scene could scarcely be witnessed. I may say the skeleton of once a tall, robust, high cheek boned respectable woman, who had seen better days, who could neither hear, see, nor speak, without a tooth in her mouth, her cheek skin meeting in the centre, her eyes sunk out of sight in their sockets, her mouth wide open, her nose standing upright among smoke and flames, uttering piercing moans of distress and agony, in articulations from which could be only understood, oh, *Dhia, Dhia., tein, tein* – oh God, God, fire, fire. When she came to the pure air her bossom [*sic*] heaved to a most extraordinary degree, accompanied by a deep hollow sound from the lungs, comparable to the sound of thunder at a distance. When laid down upon the bare, soft, moss floor of the roofless shed, I will never forget the foam of perspiration which emitted and covered the pallid death looking countenance. This was a scene, Madam, worthy of an artist's pencil, and of a conspicuous place on the stages of tragedy. (93)

This description is one of many in which Macleod offers direct testimony, not only as way to counter the validity of Stowe's own 'witnesses', but to offer his readers his own authoritative testimony of the horrible suffering of Clearance victims. Deploying strategies that Stowe herself deployed in *Uncle Tom's Cabin*, Macleod seeks to bring through 'horrifying and lamentable' scenes of individual suffering, particularly of women and mothers, a powerful immediacy to the plight of the victims of Clearance and to offer a pointed response to the callous dismissal of their suffering in Stowe's own blanket generalisation of 'ridiculous stories'.

The horror of Clearance is 'brought home' to Macleod himself in his relation of the sudden eviction of his own family from their cottage, which took place while he was working several miles away. After failing to erect a temporary shelter against their former home, Macleod's wife and children are forced to spend the night exposed in a raging storm, their neighbours, Macleod writes, too fearful of reprisal to take in an evicted family:

> Death seemed to be staring them in the face, for by remaining where they were till morning, it was next to impossible even the strongest of them could survive, and to travel any distance amid the wind, rain, and darkness, in that rugged district, seemed to afford no prospect but that of death by falling over some of the cliffs or precipices with which they were surrounded, or even into the sea, as many others had done before. (*Gloomy Memories*, p. 49)

In this passage, Macleod moves from distanced eyewitness to victim of the suffering he describes, and in scene after scene of suffering and cruelty, Macleod's work adopts the common rhetoric and narrative techniques of anti-slavery accounts. Even as he exclaims 'the English language fails to supply me with words to describe' the 'painful picture[s]' of the suffering Gaels, Macleod continually places his readers in the position of spectators of that suffering so that they will sympathise and, ultimately, demand redress for the victimised (129). Yet *Gloomy Memories*, for all the striking immediacy of its eyewitness scenes, also relies heavily on other historical material that places Highland Clearance in the larger context of the after-effects of Union – the disintegration of clanship and the dramatic changes in land tenure and in the social and cultural life of rural Highlanders. Macleod's work also provides detailed statistics on, among other things, the numbers of the evicted, the extent of destitution, and the relative paucity of funds provided for relief in the Highlands; newspaper accounts of the trial of Patrick Sellar, with witness testimonies; and letters and other published eyewitness descriptions relating to events on the Sutherland estate, from both sides of the Atlantic.[100] Through the thick accumulation of paratextual material that frames his account, Macleod positions himself as not only an individual eyewitness to the trauma of the recent past in the Highlands but also the compiler of its collective memory, drawing upon a wide range of sources to draft that memory in a war against what he sees as a systematic plan of cultural genocide. Appealing to 'all Christian people', Macleod asks rhetorically:

> Are sheep walks, deer forests, hunting parks, and game preserves, so beneficial to the nation that the Highlands must be converted into a hunting desert, and the aborigines banished and murdered? I know that thousands will answer in the negative; yet they will fold their arms in criminal apathy until the extirpation and destruction of my race will be completed. Fearful is the catalogue of those who have already become the victims of the cursed clearing system in the Highlands, by famine, fire, drowning, banishment, vice, and crime. (129)

Memory is both a record of Macleod's individual suffering and a testament to the suffering of the Gaels as a people. In *Gloomy Memories*, the 'Highland Clearances' coalesce in Scottish historical consciousness *as* cultural trauma.[101]

'I am a native of Sutherlandshire, and remember . . .' (1): so Macleod commences his *Gloomy Memories*, the personal and public repository of the cultural trauma of Clearance, to be retrieved in the service of communal identity. As the living embodiment of these memories, Macleod casts himself as one keenly aware of the fragility of memory, and of his obligation to preserve the past: 'I am now an old man', he writes, 'bordering upon seventy years of age, symptoms of decay in the tabernacle convinces me that my race through time towards eternity is near at an end, when I will have to give an account for what I write and leave on record' (208). At the end of his account, Macleod presages the ultimate demise of the 'tabernacle' of his memory, which prompts a nostalgic retrospection to happier times in the Highlands long ago:

> when inhabitants of that country lived comfortably and happily, when the mansions of proprietors and the abodes of factors, magistrates, and ministers, were the seats of honor, truth, and good example – when people of

quality were indeed what they were styled, the friends and benefactors of all who lived upon their domains. (1)

Here Macleod adopts the memorialist mode of recalling the recent past in a time of unprecedented change. Like other Scottish writers who had adopted this memorialist mode, Macleod assumes the mantle of the preserver of a collective memory that is in danger of becoming lost; but, in contrast to writers like Scott, Cockburn and Chambers, Macleod offers more than a nostalgic, but ultimately inert, lament for a lost way of life that has faded through the inevitable forces of historical progress. Instead, Macleod's retrospection of a happier time serves to foreground the destitution and misery of more recent times and to lay the blame for this squarely on the 'avarice and tyranny' of the landlords and factors. For Macleod, and for the late-century advocates of Highland land reform who were influenced by his work, the memory of a lost world can *only* signify in the context of cultural trauma – in the context of an activist present that seeks recognition for a past of injustice and communal dispossession. Nostalgia in *Gloomy Memories* functions in the service of a fervent political agenda for social change that seeks both to elicit the sympathy of readers outside the Highlands and, just as importantly, to marshal the collective righteous anger of the Gaels themselves.[102] For Macleod, remembering Clearance is an act of personal and public vengeance against the oppressor:

> I am a Highlander, and must have revenge for the wrongs I have suffered. The revenge I desire is that these letters may be preserved for many a day in my native country, to keep up the remembrance of the evil that was done to many an innocent individual, and among others to Donald M'Leod. (54)

The activist impetus of Macleod's remembrances is highlighted in his claim to being both an eyewitness to a collective cultural trauma and the spokesman for the 'people', who cannot speak for themselves:

> It was thought an illiterate people, speaking a language almost unknown to the public press, could not make their wrongs be heard as they ought to be, through the length and breadth of the land. To give their wrongs a tongue – to implore inquiry by official, disinterested parties into the cause of mal-practices which have been so long going on, so as if possible to

procure some remedy in future – has been my only motive for availing myself of your kindness to throw a gleam of light on Highland misery, its causes and its consequences. (44)

Macleod takes up the 'burden of the witness', which, 'in spite of his or her alignment with other witnesses', Shoshana Felman and Dori Laub write, 'is a radically unique, noninterchangeable and solitary burden'.[103] Yet, if Macleod takes up the solitary task of witness to cultural trauma, he at the same time appoints himself transmitter of its memory. In this respect, Macleod represents what sociologist Jeffrey C. Alexander, following Max Weber, describes as a member of a 'carrier group', collective agents who initiate the process of the cultural construction of trauma by making 'a claim to some fundamental injury, an exclamation of the terrifying profanation of some sacred value, a narrative about a horribly destructive social process, and a demand for emotional, institutional, and symbolic reparation and reconstitution'.[104] Neither a personal memoir, autobiography nor straightforward historical account, *Gloomy Memories* is instead a social memory-text, which serves a cultural as well as political agenda. Memory is mobilised in the service of enunciating a collective trauma that, as a wrong perpetuated on the community as whole, also helps to consolidate a sense of shared identity. Indeed, as Smelser writes, cultural trauma and collective identity are intertwined, as 'any given trauma may be community- and identity-disrupting or community- and identity-solidifying – usually some mixture of both'.[105]

Macleod's memory of Clearance embodies, Charles W. J. Withers writes, 'a shared or collective memory held – or so Macleod argued – by all Gaels'.[106] In a rhetorical gesture deployed many times in his work, Macleod begins a rebuttal of one of Stowe's defences of the Sutherlands by reminding her that he is not alone: 'Now, Madam, I can tell you, and hundreds of my countrymen in Canada, and thousands of them at home can tell you . . .' (*Gloomy Memories*, p. 99). In enlisting the testimony of a vast community of 'my countrymen', Macleod lays claim to his work as a 'communal utterance', that, like the slave narrative, comes to stand for the collective memory of a people, a memory that Macleod emphasises now circulates throughout the transatlantic world.[107] Mustering the transnational collective memory of the Gael, Withers writes, Macleod aims 'not just to prick the British social conscience but that of the Gaelic diaspora in Canada (of whom, as a result of clearance, he was one)'.[108] In his final paragraph, Macleod reminds the Gaelic diaspora of their shared identity and summons them to act by evoking their near-sacred duty to remember:

> You have now before you the substance of my labour in behalf of my people and race for many years. Highland oppressors dealt out unsparingly to me the remuneration they thought I deserved, IN MANY A BITTER CUP. You will deal with me now as you deem proper in my advanced years; but my request is, whether this will find you among the mountains of Scotland or upon a foreign strand, *Cuinichibh air, na daon hannig roimbdh*. Remember those who were before you. (212)

Claiming to speak for the voiceless, translating their collective memory into English and into text, Macleod bestows the sacred repository of that memory as he enunciates its mnemonic ideal. 'Remember those who were before you' becomes the watchword for Macleod's activist account, demanding that the traumatic memory of the past come to the forefront of public consciousness.[109]

Gloomy Memories represents a counter-memory of cultural trauma, in response to an official memory in which the systematic dispossession of the Gael is either denied or dismissed as a scattered, localised phenomenon – in other words, 'forgotten' – in the larger narrative of national progress and prosperity. Stowe had offered a version of this official memory in *Sunny Memories*, summarising Sutherland's behaviour on the estate as 'the benevolent employment of superior wealth and power in shortening the struggles of advancing civilization, and elevating in a few years a whole community to a point of education and material prosperity, which, unassisted, they might never have obtained' (1:313). In his pointed and acrimonious rebuke to Stowe's abstracting, Macleod presents a commemorative retrospection on Clearance that could be said to inaugurate a nineteenth-century 'politics of recognition' for Gaeldom, in which 'culture, history and memory', as Laurajane Smith describes, 'become important arenas of struggle for equity'.[110] Macleod's emotional appeal to remember the victims of Clearance as a counter to an official 'misrecognition' of historical truth parallels in many respects the contemporary cultural politics of recognising the past of slavery – remembering the 'blank spots', as Smith terms it – in the collective memory so that 'a recognition or re-recognition of British identity [can be] undertaken'.[111]

The Hierarchy of Cultural Trauma: Clearance, Not Slavery

Even though, as I have argued, *Gloomy Memories* adopts the testimonial mode of the slave narrative to construct a memory of the past as cultural trauma, there are relatively few examples in Macleod's work where he directly takes up the plight of enslaved Africans, and he does so always within the context of drawing comparison between black chattel slavery and Clearance. For example, in one of his most emphatic condemnations of the former, Macleod writes, 'Slavery is damnable, and the most disgusting word in the English or any other language; and it is to be hoped that the Americans will soon discern its deformity, pollution and iniquity, and wipe away that old English polluted stain from their character' (*Gloomy Memories*, p. 76). Yet he evokes American attitudes only to serve as a contrast to the character of the 'British aristocracy', whom he believes will never willingly give up their 'system of slavery' (meaning Clearance) because it is too profitable. Macleod's more general practice is to draw parallels between the two oppressive systems to generate a sympathetic understanding of Clearance victims by pointing out commonalities between their experiences and those of the enslaved. In one example, where Macleod seeks to provide corroborating testimony to support his claims of widespread and ongoing Highland misery, he recounts an episode that took place in Barra only a year before Stowe's visit to Britain, in which evicted tenants were forced onto immigration ships:

> Were you to see the racing and chasing of policemen, constables, and ground officers, pursuing the outlawed natives you would think, only for their colour, that you had been by some miracle transported to the banks of the Gambia on the slave-coast of Africa. (139)

Macleod's point here is that Clearance is ongoing and not simply a thing of the past. In making this oblique analogy between African slaves and Highland victims of Clearance, Macleod hopes to remind his readers that, though slavery had been abolished in the colonies, the eradication of oppressive thraldom within the nation itself is unfinished business. Even so, Macleod's desire to draw slavery into his argument to generate sympathy for the plight of the Gael reveals a deep ambivalence about the ultimate condition of the African enslaved. This ambivalence becomes most pronounced in passages in the updated sections of Macleod's work, which specifically take up Stowe's claims in *Sunny Memories*. In these, Macleod's appeal for sympathy for the Gael depends on a pointed discounting of the suffering of enslaved Africans.

Implying a kind of zero-sum theory of reader sympathy, Macleod makes clear that, in the hierarchy of victimhood, the cleared Gael outpaces the enslaved African. He asks rhetorically whether the Gael, whom he characterises as a 'brave, moral, intelligent and enterprising race of people, who were born free' and who were 'robbed and deprived of all the liberties and rights they were told and taught by their fathers to be their indisputable inheritance, and enthralled to the lowest degree of degradation, submission, and poverty', should 'not much more be pitied' than the African, whom he summarises as a race 'denounced, consigned, and designated to be slaves and the servants of servants – consequently despised, left untold, untaught in the science of enterprise, progress, or civilization, and totally ignorant of the rights and privileges of human beings' (*Gloomy Memories*, p. 74). While acknowledging that '[b]oth cases are to be pitied and lamented', Macleod makes clear that Gaels are more worthy of sympathy because their suffering is of a greater degree: African slaves, unlike cleared Gaels, can never recall a happier life they once knew. Like a blind child who never knew what light was, writes Macleod, the African, so long enslaved, cannot 'lament over the loss of [light]; besides, in most cases natural instincts will, to a certain extent, make up for the deficiency'; whereas for the 'poor fellow who knew what light was', the 'loss of his sight' is the 'principle cause of his bewailing and sufferings' (75). Macleod offers a dramatic hypothetical transatlantic emigration of the enslaved in America to the Scottish Highlands to highlight how the Gaels have it much worse:

> [I]f it was possible or practicable to try the experiment, that is, to bring nineteen thousand of the American slaves to Sutherlandshire, and give them all the indulgence, all the privileges, and comforts the aborigines of that county do enjoy, I would risk all that is sacred and dear to me, that they would rend the heavens, praying to be restored to their old American slave owners, and former position. (74)

Macleod's 'experiment' is meant to highlight the unrecognised suffering of the Gael and to expose the hypocrisy of those (like Stowe) who make apologies for Highland landlords while championing the anti-slavery cause, yet the affective force of this passage comes at the expense of feeling for the enslaved, who, in Macleod's hypothetical case, need only to live the far more pitiable life of the Highlander to pray for a return to thraldom in America.[112] It is in such passages as these, expressing Macleod's resolute scorn for the hypocritical British elite, that he displays his greatest rancour at the injustice of what he sees as misdirected sympathy. Because, Macleod writes, there is 'no class under heaven' more unlikely to have any influence on 'republic Americans' than the 'English inhuman, ambitious, slave making aristocracy', he is convinced that the object of Stowe's visit to Stafford House could only have been 'English gold'. With bitter irony, however, he poses an alternative scenario that he imagines would have brought her even greater renown as a champion of the oppressed:

> [H]ad you come to Britain, and got up an Uncle Donald, Uncle Jock, and Uncle Geordy's Cabin, where you would not need *colouring*, nor steep your brains to get up sublime falsehood, and impossible achievements of runaway slaves, where the naked unvarnished truths were more than could be believed. Then to return with these British cabins to the United States you would have a good chance to reap as rich a harvest of them in the States, as you have reaped of Uncle Tom in Britain, and establish your name and memory immortal and unsullied. (*Gloomy Memories*, p. 105)

Adopting overtly racist language in this passage, Macleod assails what he sees as an unconscionable displacement of sympathy. By championing what he emphatically views as the lesser of two evils – slavery – while ignoring the atrocities of her Sutherland patrons, Stowe reveals her fundamental moral and ethical failings, which, Macleod implies, will leave a lasting stain on her reputation. Macleod's lifelong frustration and anger that his own polemics had not received the attention he felt they were due crystallise in a long passage, which amounts to a self-pitying diatribe against Stowe and the enslaved for whom she demands sympathy. Once again seizing on the idea of an alternative, Highland-inspired version of *Uncle Tom's Cabin*, and once again adopting overtly racist language, Macleod imagines a scenario in which his own eyewitness account of Clearance finally receives the recognition it deserves:

> 'Uncle Tom's Cabin' has aroused the sympathy and compassion of the Duchesses of Sutherland, Argyle, Bedford, and Ladies Blantyre

and Trevellyan, and many thousands of the women of England, over the fate of Ham's black children. But we would seriously advise the Duchess of Sutherland and her host to pause until Uncle Donald M'Leod's Cabin comes out, and until he himself comes across the Atlantic with it among the thousands of those and their offsprings [sic] who have fled from their iron sway and slavery to our shores. He, poor man, has been expostulating with you for the last twenty years against your cruel, unnatural, irrational, unchristian, and inhuman treatment of the brave, athletic, Highland *white sons of Japhet*, but no English or Scottish Duchesses and Ladies took any notice of him, nor convened a meeting to sympathise with him or to remonstrate with Highland despotic slave-making proprietors to discontinue their unrighteous depopulation of the country, and their ungodly draining away of the best blood from the nation. Hence we aver that these ladies would never convene a sympathising meeting for the benighted Africans, should their own African chiefs, kings, and queens destroy them by the thousand; but because they sell them, and we buy them and take care of them, English feminine hearts sympathise with them. This is a fine opportunity for Donald M'Leod. Let him now speak out, and make haste, and we promise him a quick and an extensive sale for his Cabin of unvarnished facts. (107)

Casting himself as a long-suffering Uncle Tom–like figure on the other side of the Atlantic, Macleod's plea for sympathy for victims of the Clearances is reduced to bitter invective directed not only to those who would not listen to him but to the victims of slavery upon whom sympathy has been unjustly bestowed.

Slavery and Clearance in Scottish Collective Memory

The analogies that Macleod draws upon in *Gloomy Memories*, comparing Highland victims of Clearance to enslaved Africans in America, echo similar analogies in reform writings of the time; these likened working-class labourers in Britain as 'white slaves', whose degradation was deemed sometimes even greater than enslaved Africans. Analogies first drawn in eighteenth-century pro-slavery polemics that asserted the good treatment of enslaved black labourers in the West Indies, relative to their white counterparts, became, Catherine Gallagher writes, 'fundamental to nineteenth-century criticism of industrial society'.[113] Though these criticisms recast the analogy to serve the cause of labour law reform, 'metaphoric likening of English workers to slaves', she writes, 'tended to retain a certain proslavery residue in both substance and tone'.[114] Indeed, when he alludes to the 'curse of Ham' shibboleth that Africans are an accursed race and therefore acclimated to degradation, when he asserts that Africans are naturally more inured to physical pain, and when he argues that their very condition as property ensures some level of concern on the part of their masters, Macleod reiterates some of the most oft-repeated racist arguments of pro-slavery advocates on both sides of the Atlantic.

Macleod died in 1860 and so did not live to see the renewed appreciation of his work he himself had envisioned amid the Stowe controversy. But as the Highland land reform movement dramatically took hold in the wake of crofter agitation in the 1880s, interest in *Gloomy Memories* saw a dramatic revival. In 1883 the prominent writer, editor and land reform advocate Alexander Mackenzie published his seminal *History of the Highland Clearances*, which relies heavily on verbatim extracts from Macleod's work. The Report of the Napier Commission, formed after the crofter agitations to enquire into conditions in the Highlands, was influenced by *Gloomy Memories* and relied heavily on the kind of eyewitness testimony that Macleod provided in his work. Some of those in the Napier report providing testimony as to the truth of landlord injustices made reference to accounts in *Gloomy Memories*, which they corroborated. Mackenzie's work would become a standard source of material for historical writing on the Highland Clearances in the twentieth century, and later accounts would come to adopt the testimonial mode and narrative style of Macleod's work. John Prebble's popular 1963 history of the Clearances, for example, relies on Macleod's material, privileging memory and testimony as well as adopting his often bitterly ironic tone.[115] By the turn of the twenty-first century Macleod's mode of retrospection had achieved the status of official memory as a part of a national heritage, furnishing *lieux de mémoire* in the Highlands. As the Highland Council in the 1990s considered a 'Gloomy Memories Trail' of Strathnaver, 'using a combination of waterproof route cards, interpretive panels at the sites and "in car" tape cassettes, "providing an audio guide" to the strath', 'memory' has become the primary mode of comprehending Scotland's Clearance past.[116]

Tracing *Gloomy Memories'* journey from counter-memory to official memory along a transatlantic axis highlights the complexity of collective memory as it is tied to cultural and political debates that recall the past in order to make change in the present. Macleod's frequent dismissal of slavery and the suffering of the enslaved may not constitute, in the contemporary parlance of historical memory, an 'active forgetting', but it does represent a powerful elision. *Gloomy Memories* evokes the memory of black chattel slavery only to dismiss it as unequal to the memory of the suffering of the Gaels: if the work gives shape to a Scottish memory of Clearance as cultural trauma, it also carries with it a troubling residue of racist apology for enslavement. For Macleod, to remember slavery is somehow to play into the hands of a British landowning elite, and their apologists – like Stowe – who sought to misdirect sympathy away from the victims of their own brutality. In this way, Macleod's counter-memory of Clearance forestalls a memory of transatlantic slavery, through processes of substitution and displacement.[117] The logics of equivalence and misdirected sympathy that figure in *Gloomy Memories* continue to do their work – in contemporary accounts of historical 'white slavery' that seek to neutralise or redirect demands for recognition of racial injustice or for compensation.[118] Perhaps we must return to Jackie Kay's call for an 'alongside-ness', rather than a hierarchy, in contemporary Scotland's memory-as-cultural trauma. If Donald Macleod's gloomy 'memory' of Clearance has firmly established itself within Scottish historical consciousness, then it is perhaps time to assert a 'memory' of slavery that exists alongside rather than in place of it. This memory is of a much different experience, but, like the memory of Clearance, it reminds us how Scotland's present and, most likely, its future is indebted to an understanding of its transatlantic past.

Notes

1. For recent historical accounts, see Devine, *Recovering Scotland's Slavery Past*; and Hamilton, *The Caribbean and the Atlantic World*.
2. For example, the 1 June 1883 edition of the *Glasgow Herald* commemorated the fiftieth anniversary of abolition with the statement: 'It is to Glasgow's lasting honour that while Bristol and Liverpool were up to their elbows in the slave trade, Glasgow kept out of it. The reproach

can never be levelled at our city, as it was at Liverpool that there was not a stone in her streets that was not cemented with the blood of a slave' (quoted in Devine, 'Lost to History', p. 21).
3. Devine, 'Recovering', p. 2. For recent studies on Scottish abolitionism, see Rice, *The Scots Abolitionists*; Whyte, *Scotland and the Abolition of Black Slavery*; and Shyllon, *James Ramsay*. For studies on Scottish apologists for slavery, see Hall, '"The Most Unbending Conservative in Britain"'; and Lambert, 'The "Glasgow King of Billingsgate"'.
4. Sassi, 'Acts of (Un)willed Amnesia', p. 142. Recent critical studies on slavery in Scottish literature have tended to focus on poetry and, particularly, the work of Robert Burns. Burns, who often evoked the theme of slavery in his poetry, infamously considered immigrating to Jamaica in 1786 to take a position as plantation bookkeeper. See Nigel Leask, 'Burns and the Poetics of Abolition'. See also Rieley, '"Wha sae base as be a slave?"'; and Andrews, '"Ev'ry Heart can Feel"'. For an analysis of the use of the term 'slavery' in Scottish literature and culture of the Romantic era, see Pittock, 'Slavery as a Political Metaphor in Scotland and Ireland in the Age of Burns'.
5. Morris, 'Yonder Awa', p. 44. See also Morris, *Scotland and the Caribbean*.
6. Sassi, 'Acts of (Un)willed Amnesia', p. 187.
7. Kay, 'Missing Faces'.
8. Alexander, 'Toward a Theory of Cultural Trauma', p. 7.
9. Smelser, 'Psychological Trauma and Cultural Trauma', p. 44.
10. Alexander, 'Toward a Theory of Cultural Trauma', p. 9.
11. For studies of historical memory and commemorations in the UK upon the two hundredth anniversary of ending the slave trade, see Wallace, *The British Slave Trade and Public Memory*; and Smith, '"Man's Inhumanity to Man"'.
12. See Foster, *Witnessing Slavery*.
13. For discussion of Scottish Enlightenment contributions to this discourse, see Dwyer, *The Age of the Passions*, and *Virtuous Discourse*; Pinch, *Strange Fits of Passion*; and Mullan, *Sentiment and Sociability*. For a discussion of the cult of sensibility, sentimentalism and slavery, see Barker-Benfield, *The Culture of Sensibility*; Langford, *A Polite and Commercial People*, pp. 516–18; and Jordan, *White Over Black*.
14. Though the title of Stedman's *Narrative* makes a claim for a five-year stay, he was in the colony for just over four years.
15. Pratt, *Imperial Eyes*, p. 91.
16. By 1840 Stedman's work had been translated into six languages and had gone through several editions in Britain, the United States, and throughout Europe.

17. See, for example, Gikandi, *Slavery and the Culture of Taste*, pp. 183–7; Sharpe, *Ghosts of Slavery*, pp. 44–86; Sollers, *Neither Black Nor White Yet Both*, pp. 189–219; Thomas, *Romanticism and Slave Narratives*, pp. 125–53; Gwilliam, '"Scenes of Horror", Scenes of Sensibility'; Klarer, 'Humanitarian Pornography'; Pratt, *Imperial Eyes*, pp. 86–102; Price, *Masks of Difference*, pp. 86–107; Wood, *Slavery, Empathy, and Pornography*, pp. 87–140, and *Blind Memory*, pp. 230–9.
18. Depending on the critical frame of reference, 'John Gabriel Stedman' has represented a wide array of author-subject positions in recent studies, but Wood's influential study of Stedman's *Narrative* in *Slavery, Empathy, and Pornography* is typical in making no reference to Stedman's Scottish background. On the other hand, Klarer introduces Stedman 'as an English officer in Surinam in the 1770s' ('Humanitarian Pornography', p. 559).
19. Diary entry of 29 November 1785, quoted, with gloss, in Price and Price's 'Introduction' to the *Narrative* (p. xx). All subsequent references to Stedman's *Narrative* are given in abbreviated form in the body of the text, or by page number alone where unambiguous.
20. Dalgetty appears in *A Legend of the Wars of Montrose*. Though the setting of Scott's novel is seventeenth-century Scotland and Dalgetty serves a Swedish nation, not a Dutch one, the novel explores the vexed position of the Scottish mercenary. Though the royalist Earl of Mentieth accepts Dalgetty's services, he is sharply critical of the mercenary profession. Scott also briefly alludes to the Scots Brigade in *The Heart of Midlothian*: the ill-fated John Porteous had in his youth served in the 'corps long maintained in the service of the States of Holland, and called the "Scotch-Dutch"' (26).
21. Miggelbrink, 'The End of the Scots-Dutch Brigade', p. 85.
22. Ibid. p. 89.
23. Stedman, *Journal of John Gabriel Stedman*, p. viii. All subsequent references to the *Journal* are given in abbreviated form in the body of the text, or by page number alone where unambiguous.
24. Stedman, *Stedman Archive: Journal*, p. 46. All subsequent references to this source are given in abbreviated form in the body of the text, or by page number alone where unambiguous.
25. Stedman reports that his own father displayed 'such partiality' for 'the English nation' that he kept carefully in his possession a jaw-bone he found on the battlefield of Fontenoy, which he presumed to belong to an Englishman. Though he settled in Devon with a Dutch wife who bore him several children, Stedman always seemed to regard England as foreign soil. In a diary entry dated 20 February 1787, he reports that on 'Shrove Tuesday – everybody eats pancakes in England, – and so do

we notwithstanding we 4 are from 4 different nations . . .' (*Stedman Archive: Journal*, p. 52).
26. Johnson engaged William Thomson to edit Stedman's transcript. Thomson ended up rewriting the manuscript sentence by sentence, making it 'less radical (and more pro-slavery)' (*Narrative*, p. lxiv). For the most detailed comparison of Stedman's original manuscript and the printed version, see *Narrative*, pp. xlvii–lxvi.
27. Wood, *Slavery, Empathy, and Pornography*, p. 138.
28. Stedman alludes to the story several times in the *Narrative*. The version he knew first appeared in *The Spectator* in March 1711 and went on to inspire forty-five different versions in the eighteenth century, in English, German and French. For a discussion of the Inkle and Yarico story in the *Narrative*, see Sollors, *Neither Black Nor White Yet Both*, pp. 193–219; Hulme, *Colonial Encounters*; and Ferguson, *Subject to Others*, pp. 76–90.
29. Lydia Maria Child adapted Stedman's love story in her abolitionist piece *Joanna*, published in Boston in 1834. The work sparked an outpouring of interracial romance writing in the United States. See Sollors, *Neither Black Nor White Yet Both*, pp. 189–219; and Sharpe, *Ghosts of Slavery*, pp. 81–6. For a contemporary version of the story, see Gilroy, *Stedman and Joanna – A Love in Bondage*.
30. Stedman, *Journal, diaries, and other papers: 1772–1796*, 1772–1774, p. 20. Stedman's original diaries and manuscript are housed in the James Ford Bell Library at the University of Minnesota and have been recently digitised. All subsequent references to this source are given in abbreviated form in the body of the text, or by page number alone where unambiguous.
31. Pratt, *Imperial Eyes*, p. 91.
32. The Price and Price 1988 critical edition, based on Stedman's personal manuscript copy of the *Narrative*, retains most of Stedman's sometimes idiosyncratic orthography.
33. Wood in *Slavery, Empathy, and Pornography*, for example, sees Stedman's *Narrative* as a very early example of 'plantation pornography'. See also Klarer, 'Humanitarian Pornography'; and Halttunen, 'Humanitarianism and the Pornography of Pain in Anglo-American Culture'.
34. In *A Treatise of Human Nature*, Hume defines sympathy as the spontaneous exchange of feeling, in which the general emotional state of another is first 'known only by its effects and by those external signs in the countenance and conversation, which convey an idea of it' to the observer. Presently converted into 'an impression', this idea ultimately 'acquires such a degree of force and vivacity, as to become the very passion itself, and produce an equal emotion, as any original affection' (206).

35. Smith, *Theory of Moral Sentiments*, p. 9.
36. Ibid.
37. Greiner, 'Sympathy Time', p. 293.
38. Sharpe, *Ghosts of Slavery*, p. 79.
39. Immediately afterwards, however, Stedman writes, he 'pardoned them all without one Lash – this had equally the effect of the Punishment, and Peace was perfectly established . . .' (127).
40. Stedman often sympathises with the suffering of animals. Horrified, for example, when he fails to kill a monkey even after first shooting it out of a tree and knocking its brains out against the side of his canoe, Stedman is forced to drown it: 'while my heart felt Sick on his account . . . never Poor Devil felt more than I on this occasion'. So overwhelmed by the experience, he writes, he is even unable to eat the animal, which, he says, 'afforded to some others a delicious repast . . .' (*Narrative*, p. 141). The death of the monkey prompts a long discursion into the natural history of humankind, in which Stedman rehearses common eighteenth-century assumptions on the Great Chain of Being, the 'wonderful chain of Gradation', he writes, 'from Man to the most diminutive of the above Species [monkey]' in which the 'african Negroe' is placed somewhere in between: 'does not the Face, Shape, and Manner of the african Negroe / whom in every respect I look on as my brother / I say does this not often put us in Mind of the Wild Man of the Woods or *Orangoutang*? While on the other hand what is *this* still'd more than a large Monkey?' (144).
41. Thus, though Stedman declares that he read Thomas Clarkson's anti-slavery essays 'with pleasure', and that 'African Negroes . . . Are made of no Inferior Clay but in every one Particular are our Equals' (*Narrative*, p. 514), Stedman's summary of the slave system he encountered in Surinam rehearses familiar arguments of slavery apologists: that enslavement is part of a long-standing tradition of warfare, and that the lives of Africans enslaved in the Caribbean are no worse than those living under cruel regimes back home – and are certainly better than the lives of many Europeans. Stedman rejects immediate emancipation outright and suggests an evolutionary or 'ameliorist' approach, in which only measures to abolish slavery's wonton cruelty, torture and disenfranchisement need be immediately effected. For discussion on the increasing consensus in the 1790s on amelioration, rather than outright abolishment, of slavery, see Boulukos, *The Grateful Slave*, pp. 201–32.
42. See Sharpe, *Ghosts of Slavery*, pp. 81–6. See also Sollors, *Neither Black Nor White Yet Both*, pp. 221–45.
43. Typical is an entry in his autobiographical sketch describing a pitiable moment early in his military career while stationed in the Netherlands: 'Poor Jack Stedman without a friend in the world to assist him, and in

an employment howsoever honorable he detested on account of scantiness of income, little more than a d-mned 20 pence a day' (*Journal, diaries, and other papers: 1772–1796*, 1772, p. 70).
44. Wood, *Slavery, Empathy, and Pornography*, p. 138.
45. Ibid. pp. 138–9.
46. See Shields, *Sentimental Literature and Anglo-Scottish Identity*; Gottlieb, *Feeling British*; Gibbons, *Edmund Burke and Ireland*, pp. 83–120; and Deane, *Strange Country*.
47. Gibbons, *Edmund Burke and Ireland*, p. 86.
48. Ibid.
49. Deane, *Strange Country*, p. 37.
50. Gibbons, *Edmund Burke and Ireland*, pp. 94–5.
51. Gottlieb, *Feeling British*; and Shields, *Sentimental Literature and Anglo-Scottish Identity*.
52. Shields, *Sentimental Literature and Anglo-Scottish Identity*, p. 86.
53. Ibid. p. 11.
54. Stedman writes of 'throwing aside Plutarch's Lives, Flavius Josephus, Spectator, &c.' and reading 'romance, Setting out with Joseph Andrews, tom Jones, and Roderick Random', of which *Roderick Random*, Stedman writes 'I liked best . . .' Stedman duly introduces Diana Bennet, with whom he fell in love in his younger days, as '*Narcissa*', the love interest in *Roderick Random* (*Journal, diaries, and other papers: 1772–1796*, 1772, p. 36). The phrase 'victimization and vindication' is Bjornson's term in his study of Smollett's novel, to summarise the pattern of Random's life ('Victimization and Vindication in Smollett's *Roderick Random*', pp. 196–210).
55. Shields, *Sentimental Literature and Anglo-Scottish Identity*, p. 72.
56. Smith, *Theory of Moral Sentiments*, p. 22.
57. Ibid. p. 10. The relative impotence of sympathy, or sensibility, to effect social change was a theme taken up by many of Stedman's contemporaries. For example, see Coleridge, 'On the Slave Trade' (p. 139), published in the same year as the *Narrative*.
58. Thomas, *Romanticism and Slave Narratives*, p. 9.
59. Ibid. p. 132.
60. For recent studies on slave narratives as the earliest examples of Afro-Caribbean autobiography, see Paquet, *Caribbean Autobiography*; Thomas, *Telling West Indian Lives*; Sharpe, *Ghosts of Slavery*; and Ferguson, *Subject to Others*.
61. Hall, 'New Ethnicities', p. 448.
62. The Birmingham Ladies' Society for Relief of Negro Slaves was hesitant to provide relief funds for Prince until they received corroboration from credible sources that she indeed bore the marks of repeated

beatings that she claimed in the *History*. In response, Pringle's wife, Martha, provided her and three other women's first-hand examination of Prince in a letter to the society, confirming 'that the whole of the back part of her body is distinctly scarred, and, as it were, *chequered* with the many vestiges of severe floggings' (Prince, *History*, p. 64). See also Baumgartner, 'The Body as Evidence'. All subsequent references to Sara Salih's edition of Mary Prince's *History* are given in abbreviated form in the body of the text, or by page number alone where unambiguous.

63. Andrews, '"Ev'ry Heart can Feel"', p. 23. Robert Wedderburn's slave narrative, *The Horrors of Slavery*, published in London in 1824, is unusual in that it does not rely on a white editor to bolster its credibility. Wedderburn's account, however, runs to only a few pages, and provides only a brief sketch of his birth and early life in Jamaica. Instead, accusations and counter-accusations as to Wedderburn's true paternity occupy much of *The Horrors of Slavery*, which amounts to a scathing critique of his Scottish planter father, who abused and raped his enslaved mother.

64. Boyce Davies, *Black Women, Writing and Identity*, p. 4.

65. See Glissant's seminal account of creolisation in *Caribbean Discourse*. Morris notes that Prince's work might be considered more broadly within the framework of a Scoto-British transnational network in the Caribbean, which includes not only Pringle but also his Scottish-born pro-slavery nemesis in the libel cases that followed publication of the *History*, James MacQueen (*Scotland and the Caribbean*).

66. Even though Pringle, along with James Cleghorn, was fired from his job as co-editor of *Blackwood's* after only six issues, Pringle continued to be the target of ridicule among John Wilson and John Gibson Lockhart, two of the magazine's most influential contributors. Wilson and Lockhart made mocking reference to the disability which forced Pringle to walk on crutches his whole life. In the satirical 'Translation from an Ancient Chaldee Manuscript', Pringle takes up the fight against 'the man whose name is ebony [William Blackwood]' in the service of 'the man who is crafty [rival publisher Archibald Constable]'. The latter exclaims, 'Unprofitable generation! ye have given unto me . . . a horse which hath no feet' (93).

67. Pringle wrote an account of slavery on the Cape of Good Hope just before setting sail for Britain in January 1826. Pringle alludes to this account in his Supplement to the *History*, writing he could state 'many cases which fell under my own personal observation, or became known to me through authentic sources, at the Cape of Good Hope' (*History*, p. 60). Pringle thus plays not only the role of corroborating witness in

the *History* but provides his own first-hand eyewitness observances to supplement Prince's own.
68. The first edition of the *Companion to South African English Literature* in 1986 echoes the claim of Wahl, who, in the 'Introduction' to his 1970 edition of Pringle's *Poems Illustrative of South Africa*, writes 'For well over a century Thomas Pringle has been regarded as the "father" of South African poetry' (xi). Low, writing in the midst of the Second Boer War, some sixty years earlier, states emphatically '[t]he poet of South Africa is Thomas Pringle' ('The Poet of South Africa', p. 208). Thompson, writing in 1868, just thirty-four years after Pringle's death, declares 'Pringle is more to us than simply one of the minor poets of Great Britain. He was *the* South African poet, colonist, and philanthropist' (*Poems, Essays, and Sketches*, p. 136). The editors of the most recent collection of Pringle's poetry ask rhetorically, 'Can we still – after Mtshali, Serote, Sepamla, after *The New Classic, Staffrider*, and the performance poetry of Qabula and Mzwakhe – continue to describe Pringle as the "father of South Africa poetry"?' (Pringle, *African Poems*, p. xi). See, however, Calder's insistence that we see Pringle as 'a poet typifying a Scottish school which flourished in his lifetime' ('Thomas Pringle [1789–1834]', p. 1). Calder points out that Pringle spent only six of his forty-six years in South Africa. For recent reassessments of Pringle as neither a South African nor a Scottish but a 'British' colonial writer, see Klopper, 'Politics of the Pastoral'; and Voss, 'The Personalities of Thomas Pringle'. See also Coetzee, *White Writing*; and Bunn, '"Our Wattled Cot"'.
69. Allen, 'Pringle's Pruning of Prince', p. 511.
70. For example, in a letter to his friend and fellow Scottish emigrant John Fairbairn, Pringle refers to the Cape colonial governor who eventually ruined him as 'the muckle sumph' (grand idiot) (Pringle, *South African Letters*, p. 231). In his *Narrative of a Residence in South Africa* (p. 26), Pringle describes the laughter of the native Africans in his camp as 'wild and *eldritch*', the latter a word appearing frequently in Scottish literature from the Middle Ages onwards, that connotes 'weird, ghostly, uncanny, unearthly, hideous, esp. of sound' (Maggie Scott, 'Scots Word of the Season: *Eldritch*').
71. Calder, 'Thomas Pringle [1789–1834]', p. 7.
72. Pringle first refers to 'The Bechuana Boy' in a letter to John Fairbairn dated 12 October 1825, but the poem did not appear in print until 1830, when it was published in *Friendships' Offering*. Pringle refers to the poem again in 1829, and it appears that this poem is a completely rewritten version of the earlier poem (*African Poems*, p. 77). All subsequent references to *African Poems* are given in the body of the text, or by page number alone where unambiguous.

73. Pringle, *South African Letters*, p. 260. All subsequent references to the *Letters* are given in the body of the text, or by page number alone where unambiguous.
74. For a discussion of double-voiced discourse in black literature, see Gates, *The Signifying Monkey*. See also Baker, *Modernism and the Harlem Renaissance*; and Gilroy, *The Black Atlantic*.
75. Paquet, *Caribbean Autobiography*, p. 31.
76. For a discussion of the case, see Fryer, *Staying Power*, pp. 130–2; and Prince, *History*, pp. xix–xx.
77. See, for example, Deuteronomy 14:21, 5:14; and Exodus 20:10.
78. Pringle provided a brief account of the real-life particulars of the circumstances recounted in 'The Bechuana Boy' in his notes to the poem. Marossi was 'apparently nine or ten years of age', when he had been 'carried off from his native country by the Bergenaars . . . and sold to a boor (for an old jacket!) . . .' Pringle adopted him in September 1825, and Morassi accompanied the Pringles to England where in 1827, Pringle writes, he 'took on himself . . . his baptismal vows, in the most devout and sensible manner. Shortly afterwards, Pringle reports, 'he died of a pulmonary complaint under which he had for many months suffered with exemplary meekness' (*African Poems*, p. 78).
79. Sharpe, *Ghosts of Slavery*, p. 79. Indeed, Voss labels 'The Bechuana Boy' 'a slave narrative' ('The Personalities of Thomas Pringle', p. 94).
80. Shum reveals discrepancies between Pringle's published accounts of his relationship with Marossi and other sources. For example, though Pringle described their meeting as accidental in his notes to the poem and in his *Narrative*, Pringle's correspondence reveals that he was aware that the colonial government was 'distributing stranded refugees', and that he had requested '"a few of them" for the Scottish party and "a single young man or boy of 14 years of age" for himself'. See Shum, 'The Prehistory of *The History of Mary Prince*', p. 296.
81. Pringle, *Narrative of a Residence in South Africa*, p. 7. Subsequent references to Pringle's *Narrative* are given in the body of the text, or by page number alone where unambiguous.
82. For a discussion of the 'acoustical theory of nostalgia', see Starobinski, 'The Idea of Nostalgia'; and Illbrick, *Nostalgia*. Roth quotes from a French medical dissertation of 1830, which lists some of the 'occasional causes' of nostalgia: 'a love letter, a picture, a conversation, a song', or 'hearing the accent of one's native country' ('Returning to Nostalgia', p. 30).

83. Even Pringle's name for their new settlement, 'Glen Lynden', was meant to remind them of their Scottish origins, even though it had no correspondence to an actual location in Scotland (Vigne, *Thomas Pringle*, p. 79).
84. The poem was first published in *Ephemerides* in 1828, reprinted in the anti-slavery journal *The Tourist* in 1832 as 'Colonial Exile', and, with some revision, in *African Sketches* (1834); and as 'My Country' in the posthumous *Poetical Works of Thomas Pringle* (1838). See Pringle, *South African Letters*, p. 132.
85. *Schelms* is a derogatory Dutch term, akin to English 'rogues' or 'rascals'. 'Commando' describes the vigilante border patrols, historically organised by local (Boer) farmers in the Cape Colony.
86. Pringle wrote a poem on the Ceded Territory, 'The Forester of the Neutral Ground', which he subtitled 'A South-African Border Ballad'. In it, he adopts the Scottish ballad form to dramatise the ambiguities of social and cultural exchanges that characterise borderlands. The poem recounts the tale of a Dutch provincial functionary's son, who falls in love with the family's house slave. Outraged, his father sells 'Brown Dinah', who is borne away to 'far Bovenland', but the son finds her, and together they escape to live as outcasts in the wilderness, where they raise a family. Pringle's modern-day editors describe 'the Forester of the Neutral Ground' as the first South African poem to treat the theme of miscegenation (Pringle, *African Poems*, p. xxiii). In other writing, Pringle makes more explicit the benefits of marriages between free whites and enslaved blacks, which he sees as way of bringing Christianity and civilistion to indigenous Africans. See, for example, his notes to lines 215–16 of 'The Emigrant's Cabin' in *African Poems*, p. 98.
87. Ferguson, *Subject to Others*, p. 377, n. 31.
88. Lambert, 'The "Glasgow King of Billingsgate"', p. 392.
89. MacQueen, 'The Anti-Slavery Society and the West-India Colonists', p. 1.
90. Ibid. As for Pringle's own view of black female sexuality in the context of slavery, he condemned the Cape Colony practice of the 'rearing and educating of handsome female slaves, as objects of licentious traffic with the European, and especially with the rich Indian residents' in his article on 'Slavery at the Cape of Good Hope' (295). He also in the *Narrative* lamented the 'evil example' of 'habitual concubinage' commonly practised among landowners near his settlement (115).
91. For a detailed account of the libel trials, see Thomas, 'Pringle v. Cadell and Wood v. Pringle'.
92. Thomas, 'New Information', p. 85.

93. Vigne, *Thomas Pringle*, pp. 245–7.
94. For an overview of Stowe's visit and its significance in renewing and extending links between abolitionist organisations, see Kohn, Meer and Todd, *Transatlantic Stowe*; Bolt, *The Anti-Slavery Movement and Reconstruction*; and Fladeland, *Men and Brothers*. For the internationalisation of the abolitionist movement, see Rice, *The Scots Abolitionists*. For a study of women abolitionists in Britain, see Midgley, *Women against Slavery*.
95. Stowe, *Sunny Memories of Foreign Lands*, p. iii. (Subsequent references to this work are given in the body of the text, or by volume and page number alone where unambiguous.) Kohn, Meer and Todd in *Transatlantic Stowe* note that Scott's novels were the first ones to be welcomed into Stowe's childhood home, and that she read them hungrily. Stowe later returned to the Waverley Novels and read them in chronological order as she composed *Uncle Tom's Cabin* (p. xv).
96. See Foster, 'The Construction of Self in *Sunny Memories*'; and Ross, '*Sunny Memories* and Serious Proposals'. For an account of the schisms within British and American anti-slavery societies, see Rice, *The Scots Abolitionists*.
97. Among Sutherland's other critics was the Irish writer Thomas Mulock, who visited the estate in October 1849 and who wrote a series of letters published in the *Inverness Advertiser* recounting the extirpation of local tenants and their current state of destitution. Mulock relied heavily on Macleod's work in his own accounts. After Mulock recanted and apologised publicly to the Duke of Sutherland, Macleod disavowed him in *Gloomy Memories*, accusing him of selling out. (See Prebble, *The Highland Clearances*, pp. 239–48.) Karl Marx also published an indictment against the Duchess of Sutherland, whom he termed 'a female Mehemet Ali' in the *New York Daily Tribune* in February 1853, the year before *Sunny Memories* appeared (quoted in Shepperson, 'Harriet Beecher Stowe and Scotland', p. 41). Though she references stories of the duchess that had appeared in the United States, Stowe clearly had in mind Macleod's writings, which had achieved widespread circulation in Britain and from which she quotes in *Sunny Memories*.
98. Newman, 'Stowe's Sunny Memories of Highland Slavery', p. 31.
99. Macleod, *Gloomy Memories*, p. 4. Subsequent references to this work are given in the body of the text, or by page number alone where unambiguous.
100. For example, a letter to the editor written by 'Late Emigrants of Sutherland', which appeared in the *Pictou Observer* in 1832, recounts the recent history of evictions, burnings, destitution and famine on

the Sutherland estate and ends with '[L]et us hear no more of munificence or magnanimity, or princely domains ruled by such hands of iron as the petty tyrants of Sutherland.'
101. For a nuanced study of how Macleod's work shaped a cultural memory of the Highland landscape, see Withers, 'Landscape, Memory, History'.
102. For examples of this activist nostalgia in the Gaelic tradition, see Màiri Nic a' Phearsain, *Soraidh leis an Nollaig ùir* / 'Farewell to the New Christmas' and *Nuair bha mi òg* / 'When I was Young'.
103. Felman and Laub, *Testimony*, p. 3.
104. Alexander, 'Toward a Theory of Cultural Trauma', p. 11.
105. Smelser, 'Psychological Trauma and Cultural Trauma', p. 44.
106. Withers, 'Landscape, Memory, History', p. 35.
107. For the slave narrative as a 'collective tale' of an entire community, see Gates, *The Classic Slave Narratives*, p. x. For a study of the changing and polyvalent structure of social 'memory' among the Highland diaspora in Canada, see Bitterman, 'On Remembering and Forgetting'.
108. Withers, 'Landscape, Memory, History', p. 35.
109. For discussion of a 'diasporic discourse' largely derived from textual accounts – such as published histories, websites and other forms of media – and contemporary 'folk memory' of the Highland diaspora, see Basu, *Highland Homecomings*, pp. 187–98.
110. Smith, '"Man's Inhumanity to Man"', p. 194.
111. Ibid. For the politics of recognition, see Fraser, 'Social Justice in the Age of Identity Politics'.
112. For an earlier example of this line of argument against misplaced sympathy, see Stewart, *Sketches of the Character, Manners, and Present State of the Highlanders*. Stewart remarks on the public outcry concerning the enslaved of the West Indies – who, Stewart argues, have no local attachments – when they are removed from their estate to one only a few miles distant. He compares this outcry to the general apathy concerning dispossessed Highlanders – who have the strongest of attachments (1:150).
113. Gallagher, *The Industrial Reformation of English Fiction*, p. 6.
114. Ibid.
115. See Prebble, *The Highland Clearances*. Prebble also borrows Macleod's strategy of attacking the credibility of Stowe, 'a woman', Prebble writes, 'whose personal knowledge of [slavery] had been gathered during a weekend in Kentucky' (*Highland Clearances*, p. 286). For a discussion of the 'Prebble-isation' of the Clearances as amounting to an usurpation of 'genuine' memory of the Clearances, see Basu, 'Narratives in a Landscape', and *Highland Homecomings*.
116. Basu, 'Narratives in a Landscape', p. 35.

117. For a general discussion of Scottish displacement of the memory of its slavery past, see Morris, 'Yonder Awa'.
118. For the Irish 'white slave' myth and related memes, see, for example, Hogan, 'Debunking the Imagery of the "Irish Slaves" Meme", in which a 'forgotten' history of Irish bondage is employed to advance a historical equivalence between white and black oppression. For a study of the distancing strategies at work in reaction to contemporary exhibitions marking the 1807 bicentenary, see Smith, '"Man's Inhumanity to Man"'.

Chapter 5

John Galt and Circum-Atlantic Memory

Who (and Where) is John Galt?

The first part of the question, for *our* John Galt, the Romantic-era writer – not Ayn Rand's fictional character and philosopher-hero of the US libertarian right – is met now with fewer shrugged shoulders than in decades past. But the question of '*Where* is John Galt?' or more precisely 'On which side of the Atlantic should we situate John Galt?' remains a vexed one. After his death in 1839, Galt's reputation largely went underground; not until the latter half of the last century was there a much needed reappreciation and reappraisal of Galt's significance. This renewed interest in Galt, however, took two parallel but largely distinct tracks. The 1979 collection of essays that marked the centenary of Galt's birth announced a revival of interest in Galt and his achievement within the context of a much-needed cultural self-reassessment in Scotland. The cultural nationalist impetus behind this reappraisal is made clear in the editor's claim that Galt's reputation had gone into decline because of his use of Scots vernacular. Those readers in past decades, 'especially north of the border', Christopher Whatley writes, whose linguistic indoctrination perhaps began with 'a taste of MacIvor's *First Aid in English*', moving to 'large helpings of Shakespeare, Dickens and Charles Lamb', and finally 'topped up with tawse enforced strictures about the merits of speaking "correctly"' would find Galt's work 'well-nigh incomprehensible'.[1] 'Fortunately, the modern Scot', he writes,

> is in some areas being allowed to consider the study of his own linguistic history on a par with that of medieval English, and that, allied to the general awareness that there is a Scottish cultural past (and present), is

helping to bring the work of John Galt very much to the forefront of Scottish literary studies.²

The collection itself, which tends to restrict its scope to Galt's fiction with Scottish settings, seeks to advance this renewed awareness of a Scottish cultural past and present by placing 'the name of John Galt even more firmly amongst the ranks of Scotland's literary successes', and to 'convince the public, teachers, students and academics that Galt's writings are both a unique and inseparable part of the Scots literary tradition'.³ This line of critical reappreciation that situates Galt within a Scottish national literary tradition has continued with Duncan's account, which establishes Galt as a key contributor to a literary field of post-Enlightenment Scottish Romanticism.⁴ Galt, in Duncan's account, alongside James Hogg, struggled to define his own rival brand of fiction-making within the Scott-dominated world of literary Edinburgh. In the novels he wrote in the early 1820s – *Annals of the Parish*, *The Entail* and *The Provost* – Galt works out a mode of historical fiction that, though it is indebted to the unprecedented demand for 'Scotch Novels' that *Waverley* and its successors inspired, nevertheless represents a crucial alternative to Scott's brand of historical fiction.

The critical reassessment of Galt's work that arose from Scottish academic circles in the late 1970s, however, was matched, and perhaps exceeded, by a body of work emanating from Canada that made claims for Galt's significance also in the context of a national recovery project. Largely in reaction to the increasing cultural domination of its own neighbour to the south, critics in Canada sought afresh the antecedents in Canada's own literary historiography. In 1977 McClelland & Stewart published, as part of its New Canadian Library series, a new mass paperback edition of Galt's transatlantic emigrant's tale *Bogle Corbet*, first published in three volumes in London in 1831. This reissue, edited by Elizabeth Waterston, recounts the journey and early travails of its title character, as he attempts to establish a settlement in Upper Canada, in latter-day eastern Ontario. The front cover blurb establishes the work's Canadian literary bona fides, describing the title character as 'the first and still typical Canadian anti-hero in a long tradition of anti-heroes'. As if to remove any possible ambiguity as to the work's intrinsic Canadianness, Waterston chose to omit more than half of the original novel, beginning the story at the moment Corbet decides to emigrate, which does not take place in the original until four chapters from the end of the second volume. The Waterson edition leaves out a wide and varied collection of experiences, as the novel's eponymous character charts his life history across several sites in the British Atlantic world.[5] In this, the publishers and editor of the reissue laid claim to *Bogle Corbet* as a key, if distorted, example in the opening chapters of Canada's national literary history. Galt's national significance in Canada was further emphasised by a collection of critical essays published in 1985 by the University of Guelph and edited by Waterston that also called for a reappraisal of Galt.[6] By this time, Galt was already an established figure in Canada's colonial historiography, noted more for his direct role in its early settlement than for his literary output, and even much of the 1985 essay collection is devoted to Galt's thinking on economics and economic development, particularly in the colonies.

The two-pronged trajectory of recent critical treatment of Galt is perhaps echoed and encouraged by the trajectory of Galt's own professional life, which itself followed two distinct tracks. Galt's writing career began when his family moved to Greenock and he began to contribute, when he was in his early twenties, small pieces to the *Greenock Advertiser* and Constable's *Scots Magazine*. Relative success would take root after Galt's move to London at age twenty-five, and he would afterwards produce a large volume of work in a wide range of genres, including verse drama, historical biography, travel narrative and essays on political economy. Galt's steady output would culminate in the contributions he made to *Blackwood's Magazine* in the 1820s, where some of his most famous and best-received works were first serialised. At the same time, throughout his life Galt embarked on a variety of entrepreneurial and business ventures, many of which came to little or failed entirely. An early partnership established in his first year in London went bankrupt and a later import venture, which would have placed Galt in Gibraltar, to get around the French trade embargo, became moot after Wellington's victory over Napoleon's forces in Spain. A stint as a lobbyist for loyalists seeking compensation for lands lost due to the American invasion of Upper Canada during the War of 1812 led to Galt's greatest business success. Though his attempts to secure compensation ultimately were not successful, the work prompted him to come up with a scheme designed to encourage settlement through the purchase and distribution of government lands in Canada. This led to the creation in 1826 of the London-based joint-stock Canada Company, which, with a share capital of a million pounds and control of close to 2.5 million acres (over 1 million hectares) of land, proved to be one of the largest land development corporations in Canada's history.[7] A key player in the company's inception, Galt was given authority to oversee in Canada the sale of company lands and to direct 'public works and improvements'. As superintendent of the Canada Company, Galt was instrumental in opening for settlement a vast tract of land in southern Ontario, part of a larger parcel that only very recently had been surrendered by Anishinaabe peoples.[8] In the role on which his contribution to Canada's early settler history would be staked, Galt founded the town of Guelph in 1827 – in 2006 the town renamed its August civic holiday 'John Galt Day' in his honour.[9] Galt was in Canada for a little more than two years directing the Canada Company, but after he ran afoul of the colonial administration and had trouble balancing the books, the company's board of directors summarily recalled him to London, where he was promptly placed in prison for debt, and where he began his most significant fiction on colonial subjects – the emigrant novels *Lawrie Todd* and *Bogle Corbet*.

The varied professional experiences, movements and writerly interests of John Galt make him perhaps uniquely positioned, even among highly mobile Scots of the time, to survey the complexity of the Atlantic world, and to chart its troubled history, and recent critics – looking at both his fiction dealing with West Country provincial life and his emigrant novels – have adopted this frame of reference, positioning Galt not as simply a Canadian or Scottish writer but an Atlantic one. Most prominently, studies by Trumpener and Shields, and two recent essay collections devoted to Galt, have begun to scrutinise more deeply Galt's cross-Atlantic connections.[10] Shields describes Galt's emigrant novels as exemplary of the 'migrant fictions' that are the subject of her study, as his Canadian novels are particularly revealing of the intersections and divergences of what she sees as two bodies of literature circulating in the British Atlantic – what she defines as the archipelagic Atlantic – English, Welsh, Scottish and Irish literatures and the literature of the early America Republic – and British colonial literatures. Trumpener's work represents a pioneering identification of the transatlantic dynamic of Galt's writing. His novels, she writes, form not only 'a panoramic historical survey of modern Scotland worthy of Balzac or Zola', but 'also suggest the influence of the British imperial economy on Scotland'.[11]

The picture that emerges from this recent critical examination is that of a writer who is unmatched in capturing the culture of modernity in the Atlantic world. In his writing, Galt takes on the themes that occupy the present study – revolution, war and political upheaval; the slave trade and the West Indies; Highland dispossession, clearance and emigration; indigenous peoples and their land claims; and colonial emigration and settlement. Galt took up these themes from a wide variety of perspectives, in a wide variety of writing modes: the three-volume novel, short tale or sketch, joint-stock prospectus, economic travelogue, fictional annals or memoir, and statistical account. In all these, Galt brought the unique understanding of his Scottish education and training. Steeped in ideas on political economy and natural history, which had shaped a distinctly Scottish Romantic literary tradition, Galt also brings to his work the unique inflections of his West Country and Glaswegian upbringing and experiences. Able to delineate in minute detail the peculiarities that mark provincial life but always from the perspective of the world traveller, political economist and colonial policymaker, Galt sees at once the social and economic interconnections between Britain's core, its colonies and its peripheries, as they are writ large on an increasingly globalised scale. In Galt's work, we see how events on the eastern seaboard of North America, the Blue Mountains in Jamaica, or the Isthmus of Panama can reverberate on the other side of the Atlantic, having profound social or economic effects in rural Scotland. At the same time, Galt's writing, and career, is full of 'comings and goings', as he traces the migrations of peoples within and across the regional and national boundaries, emphasizing the cultural or economic interconnections that connect together discrete national or regional entities in the Atlantic. In this, Galt's writing charts what could be termed a 'circum-Atlantic' cartography that imagines the Atlantic world, in David Armitage's words, 'as a particular zone of exchange and interchange, circulation, and transmission' that is 'distinct from any of the particular, narrower, oceanic zones that comprise it'.[12]

Trumpener's study situates Galt firmly in this world of exchange and interchange, circulation and transmission, while also emphasising the unique example of his historical fiction. She situates Galt's three best-known works – *Annals of the Parish*, *The Provost* and *The Entail* – within the context of emergent Romantic-era Anglo-Celtic fiction genres that follow the national tale and that represent an alternative to Scott's historical novels, presenting a different attitude towards historical change. While both Galt's 'annalistic fictions' and Scott's historical novels describe the destructive effects of historical change on organic national communities, she writes, the latter insists that such upheaval shapes a new national community in place of the old. Annalistic fictions, on the other hand, 'refuse this happy ending to stress instead the traumatic consequences of historical transformations and the long-term uneven development, even schizophrenia, it creates in "national characters"'.[13] I want to take up Trumpener's suggestive reading of Galt's work, but look more closely at the mode in which he took up the circum-Atlantic world. I hope to show how Galt's annalistic mode of fiction, and, adding into the equation, a 'statistical' mode of fiction – what he labelled 'theoretical history' or 'theoretical biography' – provided not just a *history* of this world, but, more precisely, a cultural memory of it. I examine not only his two late-career emigrant novels, *Lawrie Todd* and *Bogle Corbet*, but also his earlier writing set in Scotland – particularly the work which established his reputation as a fiction writer and which proved his greatest success, *Annals of the Parish* – to examine ways in which Galt, even early in his career, began to erect a circum-Atlantic past, a past which can be measured in the lifespan of a generation or two and is transmitted in the form of a (fictive) retrospection. The cultural memory of this world is one of fractures and upheavals, revolutions, violence, dislocations and migrations, affecting all those who inhabit the circum-Atlantic. Having spent much of his adult life navigating the spaces of this world, Galt was uniquely positioned among Scottish fiction writers to chart the complexity of its proximate past, as he brought the full range of his thinking – historical, literary and political-economic – to his subject. Like Scott, Galt evokes an individual remembrance that is called upon to bear witness for the collective in an epoch of modernity, in which unprecedented and accelerated historical change has split the present from the past. Galt, however, radically expands the spatial range of *Waverley*'s 'aftermath' temporality to encompass the whole of the Atlantic world, and, by extension, the globe. At the same time, however, there is no single historical crux upon which to anchor this collective remembrance, no Atlantic 'Forty-Five', which can be recalled and reiterated. Without a historical centre or fixed point of reference, Galt's collective memory of the circum-Atlantic provides no identificatory power. The circum-Atlantic remains a world to which nobody belongs. Instead, in Galt's account, circum-Atlantic memory turns out to be a series of traumatic disruptions which, in their sheer accumulation, begin to bear oppressively on the individual psyche and which ultimately call into question not only the past but the future as well. Galt, perhaps better than any other writer of his time, brings into view a circum-Atlantic world of which no one is a 'native', yet which nevertheless stamps its own distinct features, its own distinct collective past, on those who traverse its contours.

Theoretical History/Cultural Memory: *Annals of the Parish*

In the work that established his reputation, *Annals of the Parish*, Galt set out to provide his own brand of historical fiction. If, as Duncan argues, Scott worked out a phenomenally successful fusion of romance and history, setting the (improbable) plots of individual characters against a broad historical backdrop of the clash of cultures and the unfolding of historical progress, Galt would eschew the categories of 'novels or romances' altogether, which he felt were too devoted to the contrivances and artifices of plot.[14] Galt would later recount his motives for writing *Annals of the Parish*, and, in doing so, stake a claim for offering an alternative mode of historical fiction he labelled 'theoretical history', in which historical 'truth' is grounded in the logic of probability and exemplarity.[15] Galt derives his theoretical history from the conjectural historiography of Scottish Enlightenment writers such as Lord Kames, Adam Ferguson, John Millar and Dugald Stewart, who sought to deduce probable motives behind historical events by extrapolating universal stages of development from the knowledge of universal principles.

Galt applied the scientific method of the theoretical historian to his narratives of Scottish society, extrapolating the actions and psychology of individual characters from a broad understanding of the economic forces that shape a society over time. De-emphasising a unified or coherent plot, Galt's 'theoretical history', writes Duncan, 'is a register of hypothetical instances unfolding general laws'.[16] In doing so, Galt 'works out a new modern rhetoric of typology, what might be called empirical or statistical typology, in relation to an older allegorical mode'. As Galt 'dismantles "fable" for a series of interwoven anecdotes, episodes and micronarratives, which carry an exemplary force . . . [t]he narrative is given unity by the scheme of autobiography, the narrative of a singular subjectivity occupying a definite space and time'.[17] The plotlessness of *Annals of the Parish*, links it, in Trumpener's mind, to the anterior mode of historical narrative named in its title: the medieval annal 'with its apparently naïve listing of narrated events in an order dictated only by chronology'.[18] Galt himself, however, did not originally label the work an annal. A previous manuscript, presented to Constable in 1813 but rejected, was entitled 'The Pastor of the Parish'; Galt would have to wait several more years to see the work in print, after the success of *Waverley* created a whole new market for Scotch novels. In 1821 William Blackwood agreed to publish the manuscript, but only after suggested revision, including a new title, to which Galt agreed.[19] Galt himself referred to the work as a 'chronicle', and it is this label that most precisely describes the historical mode that Galt was imitating. In Hayden White's account, although the medieval chronicle, like the annals that preceded it, employs 'chronology as an organizing principle' and 'lacks closure', the chronicle can be distinguished from the annal by its 'greater comprehensiveness, its organization of materials "by topics and reigns," and its greater narrative coherency'. Also, unlike the annal, the chronicle 'has a central subject – the life of an individual, town or region; some great undertaking . . . or some institution'.[20] For White, what particularly distinguishes the narrative structure of a chronicle like Richerus of Rheims' *History of France* (c. 998) – a work that, like the annal, does not conclude 'but simply terminates' – is the presence of a single 'self-conscious' narrator, one who states his desire to preserve in writing the past events of a particular society of which he is a member, and who positions himself as uniquely qualified to narrate these events, 'as his own personal observations gave him insight into facts that no one else could claim'.[21] It is the relative self-consciousness of the narrator that also furnishes Galt's *Annals of the Parish* with its narrative coherence. As Galt himself summarised:

there is nothing that properly deserves to be regarded as a story; for the only link of cohesion, which joins the incidents together, is the mere remembrance of the supposed author, and nothing makes the work complete within itself, but the biographical recurrence upon the scene, of the same individuals.[22]

Narrative unity in Galt's fictive 'annal' is provided by the 'singular subjectivity' of its self-conscious chronicler – Micah Balwhidder, the parish minister of Dalmailing – who, 'occupying a definite space and time', intervenes throughout his narrative, infusing his recounting of past events with the moral judgements, preoccupations and perspectives of his own class and professional position.

Generations Past

Annals of the Parish's status as a fictive chronicle, with its mix of 'objective' chronology and highly personalised autobiography, highlights the complex interplay of competing modes of narrative at work that is contained within its pages. This interplay tends to complicate the claims Galt made for his work as a theoretical or conjectural history, for as Balwhidder lays claim to preserving the proximate past of his own local community, his historical narrative adopts the preoccupations, tropes and forms that are associated with collective or cultural memory. Announcing his own narrative situation in the present day, as one looking back from a position of retirement in old age, Balwhidder begins his history by recalling two disparate past experiences at once – the occasion of his very last sermon, on the last sabbath of the year 1810, and the circumstances which brought him to the parish in the first place, fifty years before that date:

> In the same year, and on the same day of the same month, that his Sacred Majesty King George, the third of the name, came to his crown and kingdom, I was placed and settled as the minister of Dalmailing. When about a week thereafter this was known in the parish, it was thought a wonderful thing, and every body spoke of me and the new king as united in our trusts and temporalities, marvelling how the same should come to pass, and thinking the hand of Providence was in it, and that surely we were pre-ordained to fade and flourish in fellowship together; which has really been the case, for in the same season that his Most Excellent

Majesty, as he was very properly styled in the proclamations for the general fasts and thanksgivings, was set by as a precious vessel which had received a crack or a flaw, and could only be serviceable in the way of an ornament, I was obliged, by reason of age and the growing infirmities of my recollection, to consent to the earnest entreaties of the Session, and to accept of Mr. Amos to be my helper. (*Annals*, p. 1)

In its precise fixing of its narrative to specific years – each successive chapter commences a new year – *Annals of the Parish* could be said to reinforce a the 'homogenous empty time', fixed by clock and calendar, which, in Anderson's influential account, is the ascendant temporality that underlies the growth of modern national consciousness.[23] Yet the paralleling of the trajectory of Balwhidder's career as parish minister with that of George III's reign suggests that an alternative measure of time is at work, oriented through the lifespans of individual human beings. The organising principle of Balwhidder's account may be chronological, the simple passing of each successive year, but the account is also keyed to the range of collective memory. As Balwhidder and his generational counterpart George III are 'united in their trusts and temporalities', the historical narrative of their respective communities is indexed to the passing of their respective years, as they both 'fade and flourish in fellowship together'. In the same year that George III was stripped of his royal prerogatives due to increasing infirmities and mental illness in old age – what Balwhidder euphemistically describes as being 'set by as a precious vessel which had received a crack or a flaw' – so does Balwhidder consent to step down from his pulpit, 'by reason of age and the growing infirmities of my recollection'.

As he aligns his own 'reign' as parish minister with that of his sovereign, Balwhidder authorises himself to speak, not only for his village but for his generation. Bidding his community farewell in his last sermon, and, boasting there was not a 'dry eye in the kirk', Balwhidder imagines himself as an idol taken away from the heathens, for, he writes, 'I had been with the aged from the beginning – the young considered me as their natural pastor' (1). In the sermon that marks his own retreat from public life, and which commences his historical narrative, Balwhidder sees his community in generational terms, dividing his flock into two groups, the aged, of which he himself is a member, and the young who will soon succeed them. Turning to members of his own generation, he offers them his final words, and in doing so summarises the attributes they share in common and which distinguish them from the young:

> As for you, my old companions, many changes have we seen in our day, but the change that we ourselves are soon to undergo will be the greatest of all. We have seen our bairns grow to manhood – we have seen the beauty of youth pass away – we have felt our backs become unable for the burthen, and our right hand forget its cunning – Our eyes have become dim, and our heads grey – we are now tottering with short and feckless steps towards the grave; and some, that should have been here this day, are bed-rid, lying, as it were, at the gates of death, like Lazarus at the threshold of the rich man's door, full of ails and sores, and having no enjoyment but in the hope that is in hereafter. What can I say to you but farewell! Our work is done – we are weary and worn out, and in need of rest – may the rest of the blessed be our portion! – and, in the sleep that all must sleep, beneath the cold blanket of the kirk-yard grass, and on that clay pillow where we must shortly lay our heads, may we have pleasant dreams, till we are awakened to partake of the everlasting banquet of the saints in glory. (3–4)

In stark awareness that the increasing frailties of the body and mind are only a harbinger of the inevitable oblivion of the grave, Balwhidder reminds his generation that they, and he, will soon be passing from the scene. *Annals of the Parish*, like *Waverley*, gives shape to a memorialist temporality of 'generationality', as its narrator reminds his reader that his understanding of the past is one shared by those of a similar age.[24]

As part of an elder generation, Balwhidder also grants himself privileged authority to provide advice for the younger generation among his flock. 'To my young friends,' Balwhidder begins his parting words, 'look to the lives and conversation of your parents – they were plain, honest, and devout Christians, fearing God and honouring the King' (2–3). Balwhidder here strikes a seemingly conservative note, advising the rising generation to hew to the political and social status quo. Yet after evoking the wisdom of the generation that immediately preceded that of his audience, Balwhidder's advice takes a sudden swerve into the more radical beliefs of the generations that had come even before. Look to your parents, he tells them, for: '[t]hey bore in mind the tribulation and persecution of their forefathers for righteousness-sake, and were thankful for the quiet and protection of the government in their day and generation' (3). The dark days of Covenanter persecution are gone, but their memory remains, passed down to succeeding generations, and though they live in a time of prosperity and a just government, Balwhidder reminds the young, the memory of their righteous forebears will guard them from complacency:

> [B]elieve that the laws of the land are administered with a good intent, till in your own homes and dwellings ye feel the presence of the oppressor – then, and not till then, are ye free to gird your loins for battle – and woe to him, and woe to the land where that is come to, if the sword be sheathed till the wrong be redressed. (3)

Though Balwhidder's narrative displays in most respects a 'theoretical' understanding of history as a linear unfolding of social progress – aligned with Providence – he nevertheless here offers an alternative understanding of the past grounded in a collective memory that is passed down among a community of Presbyterian Scots from generation to generation and that warns of the possibility of historical recurrence and repetition; it therefore grants to the community a transhistorical 'divine right of resistance'.[25] Occupying a narrative situation that resembles that of Scott's narrator in *Waverley*, the sentimental but sincere parish chronicler of *Annals of the Parish* offers Galt's own particular brand of historical fiction as memory-text. Balwhidder takes on a solemn duty to act as intermediary, to set down in writing the memory of his own generation and those of generations past, and to pass down this memory to newer generations, as part of their communal inheritance.

Memory and the capacity for remembrance set the boundaries for the past that Balwhidder seeks to record. Galt's annalist is no antiquarian. With no recourse to archival material, diary or journal, or any written documents – save for the epitaph he himself wrote for the grave of his first wife, in a deeply personal act of memorialisation – Balwhidder's history is tied to the limits of his powers of recollection. Galt's fictive recounting does not extend beyond the horizon of his narrator's individual experience, or observation. Balwhidder restricts his narrative to what he has experienced, observed or heard from firsthand testimony; and, most importantly, to what he can 'remember' or 'recall' from the vantage point of old age. Balwhidder assumes the role of village historian, but his total reliance on memory tends to offset the narrative's strict chronological structure. Though Balwhidder is careful to fill in every chapter, every successive year, with detail, the extent of this detail is not much determined by chronology – each year as a separate vessel of time with its own internal coherence shaped by clock and calendar – but by the contingencies and priorities of his own memory, as he recounts each passing year, in his words, 'to the best of my recollection' from a single narrative vantage point (152). Beginning the fourth chapter, and fourth year, of his annals, for example, Balwhidder writes 'The An. Dom. 1763, was, in many a respect, a memorable year, both in private and public', adding later that 'the most memorable thing that befell among my people this year, was the burning of the lint-mill on the Lugton Water . . .' (21, 23). In a similar passage, he wraps up his account of the year 1761 with 'I do not recollect any other remarkable thing that happened in this year' (15). Relying completely on his memory of events, Balwhidder will record only what is memorable in the first place, and the circularity of his reasoning is suggested in the passage that begins the year 1762: 'The third year of my ministry was long held in remembrance for several very memorable things' (16). Memory, more than chronology, sets the terms by which Balwhidder will record the past, as memory determines what is worthy of record in the first place. But this mode of historical narrative always carries with it the implication that there are occurrences that lie beyond its recounting – 'things' unremarkable and therefore not memorable, events which may have happened in the past but which are now forgotten and therefore cannot be retrieved or recorded. To remember is always also to forget, and there are places in Balwhidder's narrative where the traces of this forgetting are made visible. For example, describing a troop of 'wild Irish' who, in the year 1766, suddenly appeared in the village but were forced off after killing one of his own prized sows, Balwhidder rebukes his mnemonic skills, as he is unable to recall with accuracy events he now deems significant. The troop ended up in Glasgow, he recounts, 'where one of them was afterwards hanged for a fact, but the truth concerning how he did it, I either never heard, or it passed from my mind, like many other things I should have carefully treasured' (40). Galt's portrayal here of what constitutes 'treasured' knowledge for Balwhidder is perhaps a bit of burlesque, but it also reminds us that Balwhidder is remembering, rather than strictly chronicling, from a vantage point of many years later, and the historical record he provides is wholly contingent upon his, often inconsistent, memory.

The contingencies of a past transcribed through remembrance are also brought to the forefront in moments when Balwhidder struggles to maintain his chronicle framework by not revealing the outcome of events before the chapter/year in which they actually occur. When he recounts the death and burial of his first wife, for example, he begins to make reference to his second wife (whom he will eventually bury alongside the first, thirty-three years later), but then checks himself: 'But I must not enter here on anticipation.' The impulse to narrate events of the future year – events that have already taken place long ago, in relation to the 'present' of Balwhidder's narrative situation – is again connected to remembrances of those intimately connected to him. Prefacing his recording of the events of the year 1768, Balwhidder remarks on the 'surprising' pace of time's progression:

> Gilbert, my son, that is now a corpulent man, and a Glasgow merchant, when I take up the pen to record the memorables of this An. Dom., seems to me yet but a suckling in swaddling clothes, mewing and peevish in the arms of his mother, that has been long laid in the cold kirk-yard, beside her predecessor, in Abraham's bosom. (46)

The largely associative operations of Balwhidder's memory can compress time so that two moments separated by twenty years seem to overlap and occupy nearly the same point in time. At the same time, compression reminds Balwhidder of the speed in which time can take its toll on the body. 'It's a surprising thing', he writes, 'how time flieth away, carrying off our youth and strength, and leaving us nothing but wrinkles and the ails of old age' (46). Moreover, with each successive chapter, each successive year, Balwhidder's narrative reveals the changes in his memory as he ages, and his account is increasingly interrupted by the acknowledgement of the frailties and inconsistencies of his own failing memory. Commencing the year 1809, the penultimate chapter of his history, Balwhidder makes note of the surprising shifts in his memory: 'As I come towards the events of these latter days, I am surprised to find myself not at all so distinct in my recollection of them, as in those of the first of my ministry; being apt to confound the things of one occasion with those of another . . .' (201). In what strikes Balwhidder as a peculiar state of affairs, he finds himself able to remember events of longer ago with better acuity than events that occurred only recently, and as much as it is a memoir of past experiences and observations, *Annals of the Parish* is an exploration of the operations of human memory. With no outside documentary evidence, no material artefact to corroborate the accuracy of anything that he recounts, we are left with a look-back at the recent past of the village of Dalmailing that, like the memory of its parish minister, is both rich and varied yet ultimately indeterminate, a quality that led many of its initial readers to assume it was an actual autobiography.[26] Like the fictive retrospective of John Neal's aged Revolutionary War veteran or Anne Grant's memoirs of her youth, the memoir of Galt's aged parish minister evokes the very limited range of collective memory, its fragility and ephemerality – as it is embodied in a member of an ageing generation.

But what, in the shifting contingencies of his own memory, constitutes for Micah Balwhidder a 'remarkable' event, an event worth 'remembering'? The answer seems to be a hodge-podge of occurrences that reflect both on the contingencies of Balwhidder's own life and on his idiosyncratic understanding of what constitutes village life. A Presbyterian parish minister who is also a devoted reader of the *Scots Magazine* miscellany, Balwhidder recounts the great and cataclysmic events of his time – revolutions in America and France, religious dissent and schism, the Napoleonic wars, the rise of industrialism, and Radical politics; yet he also remarks on particular moments that weighed heavily on his own intimate circle (the death of his first wife), in addition to occurrences of natural oddity ('a cow that calved two calves in one calving') or of the locally unprecedented (Charlie Malcolm being the 'first that ever went from our parish, in the memory of man, to be a sailor'). What breathes particular life into Balwhidder's count, however, and what made *Annals of the Parish* long valued as an actual social history, is its careful tracking of the changes in 'customs and manners', the almost imperceptible shifts in the repetitive mundane commonplaces of everyday village life.[27] At times, these shifts in everyday life come into sharp focus. Balwhidder remembers well, for example, that the drinking of tea was little known in the village until the year 1761, when it became 'rife' (12). In other times, Balwhidder locates the shifting pattern of community life in the changes of its urban spaces. He recounts the fate of the spacious residence in the middle of the village, which, after the death of its widowed occupant, fell into disrepair and for a time 'began to wear the look of a waste place'. The village change-house proprietor then 'took "the Place," as it was called, and had a fine sign, THE

CROSS KEYS, painted and put up in golden characters, by which it became one of the most noted inns any where to be seen . . .' (123). This 'vast amendment' to the village, however, brought little corresponding 'amendment of manners', Balwhidder laments, 'for the farmer lads began to hold dancings, and other riotous proceedings there, and to bring, as it were, the evil practices of towns into the heart of the country' (124). In its description of the 'transmutation' of 'the Place', Balwhidder's narrative echoes the particular memorialist accounts of Robert Chambers or Henry Cockburn, providing a kind of local archaeology that charts the changes of everyday life in the community through a description of the material changes to its urban landscape.

As much as Balwhidder, in the precise chronology he establishes, would like to fix changes in village to precise years in which they occurred, the nature of 'custom' poses a special challenge to this effort. Dating the increase of 'worldly prosperity' in the village to 1788, when local farmers began to do a brisk business in an open market in the village itself instead of having to travel to neighbouring towns, Balwhidder admits that he 'cannot say whether this can be said to have well begun in the present Ann. Dom, although I know that in the summer of the ensuing year it was grown into settled custom', when the plenitude of the burgeoning local market inspired a memorable meal at the home of one of his parishioners: she 'bought in the market for dinner that day, both mutton and fowls, such as twenty years before could not have been gotten for love or money on such a pinch' (129). The indeterminism of Balwhidder's tracing of changes in 'settled custom' – the routine practices upon which collective memory is constituted, suggests there can be no annalist tracing of the changes in custom and manners. Their very repetitiveness makes it impossible to identify the exact year of changes to them, since these changes only come into focus long after they have occurred.

Progress and the Road of Time

As a self-proclaimed member of an elder, and elderly, generation, Balwhidder acknowledges he is often out of step with the contemporary times, and that both his body and his mind are becoming increasingly frail; yet he also insists that advanced age grants to him and by extension, other members of his generation, a privileged understanding of the present times, and of the mechanisms of historical change that shaped them, mechanisms that are all but invisible to the younger generation. A long lifetime's worth of experience and observation, for example, allows him to testify to the acumen of his second wife's father, Mr Kibbock, a man 'beyond the common', a 'far forcasting man'. With an insight that enabled him 'to draw profit and advantage where others could only see risk and detriment', Kibbock

> planted mounts of fir-trees on the bleak and barren tops of the hills of his farm, the which every body, and I among the rest, considered as a thrashing of the water, and raising of bells. But as his tack ran his trees grew, and the plantations supplied him with stabs to make stake and rice between his fields, which soon gave them a trig and orderly appearance, such as had never before been seen in the west country; and his example has, in this matter, been so followed, that I have heard travellers say, who have been in foreign countries, that the shire of Ayr, for its bonny round green plantings on the tops of the hills, is above comparison either with Italy or Switzerland, where the hills are, as it were, in a state of nature. (34)

Kibbock's example of acute commercial foresight, to which Balwhidder, in retrospect, can bear witness, is echoed in his description of Mr Coulter, who receives a small tack from the parish landowner and who, after removing all 'unprofitable plants' on his land 'turned all to production, and it was wonderful what an increase he made the land bring forth. . . . Truly, when I look back to the example he set, and when I think on the method and dexterity of his management, I must say, that his coming to the parish was a great God's-send . . .' (37).

The fulsome praise that Galt places in the mouth of his parish minister is significant, as Kibbock and Coulter represent a relatively early appearance in Galt's fiction of a figure that would come to exemplify a kind of a beau idéal for him: the careful but speculative entrepreneur whose scientific-based expertise gives him special foreknowledge that enriches both his pocketbook and his good reputation, as a contributor to the overall prosperity of his community. This figure will feature prominently in many of Galt's works, particularly in the emigrant novels that are the topic of the discussion below, and it perhaps represents the standard that Galt set for himself in his commercial life. Kibbock and Coulter represent individual agents of history, bringing small but cumulative changes to village life. The insight and careful planning of right-minded individuals, keyed ultimately to the dictates of the market-place, are the active agents of historical progress in Balwhidder's account, yet if such moments of material improvement are the markers in Balwhidder's narrative that make such progress visible, at least to his well-trained eye, there are also examples where improvement seems to be instigated by happenstance or by accident rather than careful human planning. These examples are often ironic or comical, most notably in Balwhidder's recounting of the building of the new 'trust-road' in the village, which came about through the goading of the enraged local landowner, who, after he was thrown from his carriage while riding from London on the old narrow and decrepit king's road, had landed in a manure pile. The outcome of a remarkable chain of coincidences, the new road is to Balwhidder 'clear proof how improvements came about, as it were, by the immediate instigation of Providence' (43).

Though improver-hero figures like Kibbock and Coulter represent instances of the importance of human agency in effecting material improvement, Balwhidder's alignment of improvement with Providence suggests that it lies beyond the realm of human intervention, and that its workings are often inscrutable to the mass of human kind. This is especially the case in places when Balwhidder recounts the destruction and unrest that improvement often brings to his community. The establishment of a cotton mill in the year 1788, for example, on the one hand meets with Balwhidder's excited approval. He describes the year of its construction, as one 'of great activity', in which 'the minds of men were excited to new enterprizes; a new genius, as it were, had descended upon the earth, and there was an erect and out-looking spirit abroad that was not to be satisfied with the taciturn regularity of ancient affairs' (128). On the other hand, the coming of the cotton mill brings an influx of skilled labourers into the village, and with them new social relations and unrest, as 'the ancient families' of the village resented the infusion of new capital and new wealth, which 'sank their pride into insignificance' (128). Even more insidiously, 'in the midst of all this commercing and manufacturing', Balwhidder detects more pernicious threats to the 'wonted simplicity of our country ways'. 'Among the cotton-spinners and muslin weavers', he writes,

> were several unsatisfied and ambitious spirits, who clubbed together, and got a London newspaper to the Cross Keys, where they were nightly in the habit of meeting and debating about the affairs of the French, which were then gathering towards a head. They were represented to me as lads by common in capacity, but with unsettled notions of religion. (128)

The emergence of Dalmailing's own home-grown branch of the Radical Corresponding Society signals the first of a host of challenges that progress brings to the village, and which threaten Balwhidder's ministry. The most insistent of these is the growth, concomitant with increasing prosperity, of 'the evil and vanity of riches': 'for in that same spirit of improvement, which was so busy every where, I could discern something like a shadow, that shewed it was not altogether of that pure advantage, which avarice led all so eagerly to believe' (137). At the same time, Balwhidder questions whether the prosperity that improvement brings is spread equitably among the villagers. 'For with wealth come wants', he writes, concluding his record for the year 1768, 'like a troop of clamorous beggars at the heels of a generous man, and it's hard to tell wherein the benefit of improvement in a country parish consists, especially to those who live by the sweat of their brow' (50). Though he fails to delve more deeply in the implications of his observations on the unevenness of economic development, ending the chapter instead with a disavowal – '[b]ut it is not for me to make reflections' – Balwhidder, at least for a moment, casts a critical eye on the effects of improvement. Yet this moment of scepticism is balanced by his more general pronouncements on social progress. In his last chapter, for example, Balwhidder acknowledges the fluctuations and eddies in the flow of time, yet suggests that ultimately time's river runs ever forward and for the better: 'I have lived longer than the common lot of man, and seen many mutations and turnings', yet these are 'notwithstanding the great spread that has been our national prosperity' (203). Soon after his last sermon, Balwhidder reports, even those who had broken with his ministry to form their own church presented him with a silver server with a 'well-penned inscription, written by a weaver lad' (204). 'Such a thing', he writes, 'would have been a prodigy at the beginning of my ministry, but the progress of book learning and education have been wonderful since, and with it has come a greater spirit of liberality than the world knew before' (204). Balwhidder's complex, often conflicted, ideas on improvement, as he notes both its destructive and productive aspects, are part of what many critics have suggested is a larger exploration in Galt's novels about the nature of historical progress and its effects on human societies.[28] 'Swaying between an investment in the value of Scottish cultural forms and a confidence in modernization', Gerard Lee McKeever writes, 'Galt's Scottish novels dovetail and exemplify the conflicting pressures which improvement brings to bear' (71). Though at times ambivalent about the material and spiritual effects of progress on his parishioners, Balwhidder's ultimate faith in its benefits is manifested, as befits the general outlook of his whole retrospective, not in grand pronouncements of prosperity on a nationwide scale, but in the smallest of customary gestures, made by a local lad in a small rural community.

Annals of the Parish displays a conjectural historical methodology through its general alignment between historical progress and economic and social improvement, as these unfold – in the narrative's careful recounting – with each passing year. It is this alignment which provides the 'theoretical' for Galt, in his 'theoretical history'; it allows Balwhidder to move deductively, for example, from observations on changes in fashion in the village to a general conclusion that the benefits of improvement are not uniform: 'with wealth come wants'. This bit of scepticism on Balwhidder's part, however, is prefaced with a telling description of the vantage point that allows him to deduce this: '[a]t the time, these alterations and revolutions in the parish were thought a great advantage; but now when I look back upon them, as a traveller on the hill over the road he has passed, I have my doubts' (50). Only because he has already journeyed quite a way down the road of time is Balwhidder, looking back, able to see its overall direction and its differing contours. Like Scott's figurative time-travellers in *Waverley*'s Postscript, 'who drift down the stream of a deep smooth river . . .' and who 'are not even aware of the progress we have made until we fix our eye on the now-distant point from which we set out', Balwhidder can see the changes wrought in his own small society by turning to look backwards from whence he came, fixing his eye on a distant point. Progress, for both Galt and Scott, is a fundamental mechanism of historical change, but it is also often imperceptible from day to day. What grants to Scott's narrator the ability to detect the powerful effects of progress in his own society is the accelerated temporality of modernity, anchored, as I have argued, by a fateful turning point in the proximate past. The culmination of the Forty-Five marked the starting point of the speeding up of Scottish history, bringing an unprecedented rate of change; so much so that the nation's heritage, embodied in its store of collective remembrances, was in danger of becoming lost. Balwhidder, though he identifies no specific turning point in the past, nevertheless describes his own 'aftermath' moment, in which the unprecedented pace of change has bestowed upon his own historical account perhaps some extra merit. 'Writing for a vain world', he writes, was never his aim, 'but only to testify to posterity anent the great changes that have happened in my day and generation – a period which all the best informed writers say, has not had its match in the history of the world, since the beginning of time' (201). Balwhidder's sense of his own unique periodicity – which distinguishes his own time from all previous historical periods and which allows him to recall a past profoundly different than the present, within the space of a lifetime – gives expression to the particular temporality of modernity that is echoed in other works by Galt and that was the insistent preoccupation of Scottish writers of the time.[29] Only in the accelerated pace of change that marks his 'day and generation' is Balwhidder, with his reader, able to see the social and economic changes wrought by improvement, and the ways in which it can radically split the past from the present, over the relative short span of the life of a parish minister.

Balwhidder divides the fifty-year-span of his ministry into three distinct (sub)'epochs', each with its own relative tempo of significant events, indexed to the relative increase in the size of the village. Beginning the chapter that describes the first year of the new century, he writes:

> It is often to me very curious food for meditation, that as the parish increased in population, there should have been less cause for matter to record. Things that in former days would have occasioned great discourse and cogitation, are forgotten, with the day in which they happen; and there is no longer that searching into personalities which was so much in vogue during the first epoch of my ministry, which I reckon the period before the American war; nor has there been any such germinal changes among us, as these which took place in the second epoch, counting backward from the building of the cotton-mill [in 1788] that gave rise to the town of Cayenneville. (172)

Yet, though he can subdivide his history into even smaller segments of time, the overall measure of Balwhidder's 'epochs', and the frame which contains his overall retrospective, remains generational, as each new 'day and generation' potentially brings its own shifts in custom and habit, its own tempo of change. As a testament to this 'generational' marking of social change, Balwhidder sees a growing ideological clash in the village, in the wake of the French Revolution, as a problem of a growing generation gap. Dividing them into two opposing camps – 'Jacobin' supporters of the Revolution and conservative 'government-men' – Balwhidder devises a plan to neutralise the former, whose members he describes as 'the rising generation', who 'were taught to jibe at [the Christian religion's] holiest ordinances'. Perceiving his sermon would have no effect on the Jacobin (men) themselves, Balwhidder devised a stratagem to couch his arguments 'in a familiar household manner' instead, which successfully 'took the fancies of the young women',

> which was to me an assurance that the seed I had planted would in time shoot forth; for I reasoned with myself, that if the gudemen of the immediate generation should continue free-thinkers, their wives will take care that those of the next shall not lack that spunk [spirit] of grace . . . I saw, as it were, the children unborn, walking in the bright green, and in the unclouded splendour of the faith. (148)

Though changing times and upheavals from the outside world may bring changes to manners and attitudes that threaten to divide his community, Balwhidder finds salvation in a vision of generational transformation, if not in his own lifetime, then in the next one.

Local/Atlantic

Because Balwhidder is not assisted by documentary source material, his historical account is profoundly limited in both its range and scope. *Annals of the Parish*, unlike *Waverley*, provides no mediating English narrator through which a reader can comprehend the novel's scenes and actions. We see only what is recounted in the West Country–inflected Scottish vernacular of its character-chronicler. In Galt's self-avowed anti-romance non-novel, which de-emphasises both plot and the actions of an individual protagonist, Balwhidder is both a central figure and near non-presence. Originating outside the parish and remaining somewhat isolated from it, by virtue of his education and profession, Balwhidder positions himself as a kind of 'auto-ethnographer' of his community; both insider and outsider, he is able to transcribe local custom and manners of the parish for his readers. As such, *Annals of the Parish*'s restrictive chronicle of a relatively short fifty-year span adheres, like Scottish memorialist writing, to the restrictive contours of its locality. The much smaller setting of Galt's fiction, however, also makes it one of the most prominent examples of 'tales of locale', which, in Martha Bohrer's account, rose to prominence in the Romantic period. With their own unique narrative strategies, and in their 'focus on the social life and environment of a small community', Bohrer writes, the 'particular fictional power of tales' can be differentiated from, and exist in tension with, 'more sweeping, privileged, and canonical, and nationalistic genres'.[30] A focus on a small community is highlighted by the mnemonic mode of Balwhidder's historical narrative, which emphasises both the peculiarities of custom and manner that are unique to the parish, as well as the narrow confines that delimit it. Yet the narrative's focus on historical change provides a view to the outside world, as Dalmailing proves, not immune to disruptive forces that emanate from far away. At the start of what proves to be the momentous year of 1776, Balwhidder reminds his readers that 'it belongs to the chroniclers of the realm, to describe the damage and detriment which fell on the power and prosperity of the kingdom' by reason of the rebellion in the American colonies. His only 'task is to describe what happened within the narrow bound' of his own ministry (*Annals*, p. 80). Yet the American Revolution proves to have a dramatic and immediate effect on the parish community, for in February of that year Balwhidder writes:

> a recruiting party came to our neighbour town of Irville, to beat up for men to be soldiers against the rebels; and thus the battle was brought, as it were, to our gates, for the very first man that took on with them was one Thomas Wilson, a cotter in our clachan, who, up to that time, had been a decent and creditable character. (80)

Throughout Balwhidder's chronicle, Atlantic revolution – in America, Ireland and France – intrudes into village life, shaping the lives of its inhabitants as 'the battle is brought to its gates'. As knowledge of great upheavals of the time taking place elsewhere is made known through the effect they have on everyday life in the community, Balwhidder's history of Dalmailing becomes a narrow portal through which to glimpse the history of the British Atlantic, a world, Balwhidder's account always reminds us, of which his own small village is a part. Thus, a description in the category of 'natural oddity' becomes noteworthy as it takes on an exemplary force, showing the processes of socioeconomic integration that tie Dalmailing to the rest of this world:

> I have now to note a curious thing, not on account of its importance, but to shew to what lengths a correspondence had been opened in the parish with the farthest parts of the earth. Mr. Cayenne got a turtle-fish sent to him from a Glasgow merchant, and it was living when it came to Wheatrig-house, and was one of the most remarkable beasts that had ever been seen in our country side. It weighed as much as a well-fed calf, and had three kinds of meat in its body, fish, flesh, and fowl, and it had four water-wings, for they could not be properly be called fins; but what was little short of a miracle about the creature, happened after the head was cutted off, when, if a finger was offered to it, it would open it mouth and snap at it, and all this after the carcase was divided for dressing. (184)

Afterwards, at a feast to mark the occasion, Balwhidder reports, 'we drank lime-punch as we ate the turtle, which I understand, is the fashion in practice among the Glasgow West Indy merchants, who are famed as great hands with turtles and lime-punch' (184). Through the small detail of eating turtle and drinking lime-punch, Balwhidder imagines the imperial network that connects village and plantations of the British Caribbean as a set of 'correspondences', brought about by the circulation of people and commodities in the Atlantic world. The changes to the economic and social fabric of the village that these correspondences engender exemplify the ways in which, as Bohrer writes, *Annals of the Parish* 'stretched the parochial boundaries' of the 'tales of the locale' genre,

> representing a porous community open to the flow of goods and people between village, nation, and empire with engaging analysis of the social friction, changing power dynamics and shifting ideologies that accompanied fifty years of major socioeconomic and political change.[31]

In its acute observation of larger historical dynamics at work on the village in *Annals of the Parish*, Bohrer's summary echoes the sentiments of Galt's own narrator, who himself identifies the fifty-year span of his recounting as one of unprecedented historical change. The great national and transregional conflicts of the time leave their mark, yet it is trade and commerce that Balwhidder identifies as the true driver of change in the village. This is made clear in his 1808 account of the failure of the cotton mill, which overnight threw a large contingent of the village out of work: '[O]n the Monday, when the spinners went to the mill, they were told that the company had stopped payment. Never did a thunderclap daunt the heart like this news, for the bread in a moment was snatched from more than a thousand mouths' (*Annals*, p. 198). The failure of the mill represents an unprecedented calamity in the village, its disruptiveness perhaps symbolised by the self-inflicted deaths of the ruined English mill director and his wife, the bodies of whom Balwhidder discovers in their bedroom, as their young children play outside. Though the wars that Balwhidder had seen as parish minister have left their trace in the village, even in the last, American, war 'those that suffered were only a few individuals, and the evil was done at a distance, and reached us not until the worst of its effects were spent' (197). 'By the building of the cotton-mill', however, he writes, 'and the rising up of the new town of Cayenneville, we had intromitted so much with concerns of trade, that we were become part of great web of commercial reciprocities, and felt in our corner and extremity, every touch or stir that was made on any part of the texture' (197). The failure of the mill testifies to the immediate and direct effects of economic integration, effects which are of a different order than effects felt from all the previous Atlantic conflicts of his tenure. Balwhidder's metaphor of a 'great web of commercial reciprocities' imagines, or attempts to imagine, a single economic entity, linked through interconnected strands that tie together its discrete spaces, so that its 'every corner and extremity' suffers 'every touch or stir' that is made upon it.[32] As Balwhidder's chronicle reaches the present day of its narrative situation, the Atlantic world has not so much come to Dalmailing as Dalmailing has come to it, through the intensifying integration of national and imperial economies. This picture of small locale as a single corner of a larger economic zone of commerce is perhaps testament also to the preoccupations and energies of Galt's own professional life in the 1820s, as he struggled to make a name for himself, in both commercial and colonial policy arenas, in the circum-Atlantic world.

Past and Future: Conjectural History and the Statistical Account

The 'new, modern rhetoric of typology, what might be called an empirical or statistical typology', that Galt, Duncan argues, works out in *Annals* 'imitates the genre of the parish register or chronicle', which was 'given canonical form in the *Statistical Account of Scotland*', Sir John Sinclair's multivolume eight-year-long effort to provide a complete account of the state of the nation through a massive accumulation of critical data.[33] Initial readers of Galt's work themselves picked up on parallels between the statistical account and Balwhidder's chronicle, which for many gave *Annals* its quality of verisimilitude and for which it was chiefly prized, even long afterwards.[34] In her review of the novel in the *Inverness Courier*, for example, Christian Isobel Johnstone wrote approvingly that 'Micah Balwhidder is among our modern historians what Wilkie is among the Scottish painters; and we think that the Statistical Account of Scotland will never be complete, till the faithful annals of this homely and veracious Chronicler are added to the appendix'.[35] In a later entry in his history, the chapter that begins the year 1800, Balwhidder telescopes some ways into the future, to give his reaction to being credited by the village with the gift of prophecy after the 1802 Peace of Amiens, having preached on the subject beforehand:

> I got great credit for my foresight, but there was no merit in't. I had only lived longer than most around me, and had been all my days a close observer of the signs of the times; so that what was lightly called prophecy and prediction were but a probability that experience had taught me to discern. (*Annals*, p. 170)

Experience and long life have given Balwhidder the power to discern the universal mechanisms that govern historical change, which, for the trained observer, are apparent at any point in time. While this passage demonstrates salient features of conjectural history, as Balwhidder anticipates the ending to a historical narrative that has not yet quite concluded, it also demonstrates a key distinction, in both the method and ultimate application, between the conjectural method that supplies the 'theoretic' in Galt's 'theoretical history' and the statistical account that it imitates. The same universalised set of assumptions that allows the historian to *conjecture* about the past, to fill in the gaps in the historical record, also allows the political economist to *speculate* about the future.[36]

The links between conjectural history and the statistical methodology of political economy, with its increasing valuation of numerical data, have been traced by Mary Poovey, who locates the intellectual roots of political economy in the mid- and late eighteenth century, when Scottish philosophical historians 'began to convert the universalized assumption embraced by the experimental moralists (that human nature is everywhere the same) into another kind of theoretical entity – a form of abstraction that seemed capable of acting in the world'.[37] Because it was grounded in a belief in providential design, she writes:

> [t]his new kind of abstraction – William Robertson's figure of 'the human mind,' for example – was conceptualized as the agent of history; as a historical agent, 'the human mind' could be inferred from its effects, many (though not all) of which had been documented by eyewitnesses who recorded particulars whose larger significance they did not understand.[38]

It thus became the task of the 'philosophical historians to know what no one could actually see: the invisible (but consistent) agent whose agenda was realized in phenomena both observed and yet to be seen'.[39] Adam Smith, in Poovey's account, like his philosophical historian predecessors, was always interested in identifying larger systems fomented through abstraction – for example 'the division of labour'; but whereas philosophical historians had been willing to 'conjecture' on a past they could not document, 'content to construct theories from a combination of abstractions, introspection, and experience', Smith, whose work was explicitly oriented in the here and now, was more interested in the material effects that theoretical systems had on society, effects which he presumed could be measured or quantified.[40] As Smith brought a new, scientific empiricism to the study of economics, in which observable facts proved the basis for understanding human economic and social activity, he also brought a predilection for numerical representation. For Smith, 'political economic knowledge' would be based on numbers, and, as his extensive use of them in the tables he produced for *The Wealth of Nations* show, he would 'confer on them connotations of impartiality, transparency, and methodological rigor', while also helping 'to neutralize the old connotations (of necromancy and sorcery) that had once made numerical representation suspect'.[41]

Though *The Wealth of Nations* signalled the ascendancy of political economy, and with it the primacy of empirically based numerical quantification of human social and economic activity, Smith was sceptical of the numerical data available to him in 1776 when he wrote his work. Describing much of the numerical record as inaccurate or inadequate, Smith longed for what Poovey summarises as a 'new kind of numerical information, informed by theory at every level' that could provide both information about an abstraction that could not be seen (the market system) and proof that such a system was subject to a governing set of laws.[42] It would be up to Scottish MP and landowner Sir John Sinclair to answer the call for a new kind of numerical information, and he published in 1791 the first volume of his great brainchild and professional preoccupation, *The Statistical Account of Scotland*. A parish-by-parish compilation of statistical information, *The Statistical Account* would eventually run to twenty-one volumes, the last of which was published in 1799, and include reports from all 938 parishes of Scotland that existed at the time. Perhaps ironically, Sinclair quotes Dugald Stewart in asserting that general principles can only be derived by a prior study of particulars. 'The foundation of all human knowledge', Sinclair writes, 'therefore, must be laid in the examination *of particular facts* and it is only so far as general principles are resolvable into these primary elements, that they possess either truth or utility'.[43] Only through a relentless grounding in the empirical can the principles of the political economist have any purchase on the truth. In what amounts to a mass accumulation of information and reportage gathered over a lengthy span of time, *The Statistical Account* seeks no less than

> to prove the advantages of statistical inquiries, and the practicability of ascertaining the real political state of a country, by inquiries into its minute details. The justness of this great maxim would thence be evident, 'That the science of statistics is, in politics, what anatomy is in medicine, the only sure foundation of happiness and of useful improvement.'[44]

In his likening of the relation between the science of statistics with the science of anatomy, Sinclair suggests the social body is analogous to the human body, while also perhaps acknowledging the mind-numbing monotony of the *Statistical Account*'s seemingly endless parade of numbers on population, wool production, kelp harvests, ship tonnages, cotton manufactures and the like. Nevertheless, in the same way that a thorough understanding of anatomy is the foundation of the study of medicine, so do statistics provide the basis for more imaginative and useful political economic exploration. For all of Sinclair's tireless enthusiasm for collecting empirical data, he is always ultimately interested in abstract systems and principles, and he would follow up his monumental *Statistical Account* with a work he considered to be a more significant contribution to the science of political economy, the *Analysis of the Statistical Account of Scotland*. Envisioned by Sinclair years before, as a 'Code of Political Economy' – a kind of systematic approach to a system – the *Analysis* was fundamentally a work of the imagination, in which Sinclair would demonstrate the necessary relation between numerical information – statistics – and the abstract systems of the political economist. Together, the *Statistical Account* and its *Analysis* would affirm the primacy of numbers as the basis for fomenting abstract systems of political economy, thus inoculating the field against the spectre of (mere) conjecture.

While providing what its author felt was the ultimate in statistical compilation, the *Statistical Account* also marks a shift in late eighteenth-century political economic discourse. Where writers in the earlier part of the century had concerned themselves largely with investigating economic agents and activities limited to those which had an effect on matters of state finances, particularly on matters involving state revenues, Sinclair's new science of statistics was aimed at estimating the general state of the nation, in his words, 'for the *purpose of ascertaining the* quantum *of happiness enjoyed by its inhabitants and the means of its future improvements*'.[45] In this Sinclair saw himself not only as a scientist but as a patriot, for, he writes,

> the facts which [*The Statistical Account*] will bring forward, and the discussions which it will contain, will elucidate many of the most important questions of political economy. In this enlightened age, also, real statesmen, whether in the cabinet, or on the throne, seem

truly anxious to promote the welfare of those they govern. They feel, that the possession of power, the distribution of patronage, or the emoluments of office, produce pleasures which are only fleeting and transitory; whereas, the reflexion of having contributed, – 'To the improvement and prosperity of their country, and the comfort and happiness of its inhabitants,' – furnishes enjoyment of a permanent nature, which they can recollect with exultation and pride, to the latest period of their existence, and which will endear their memories to the latest posterity.[46]

The Statistical Account presented a powerful reordering of national categories, indexed to the state of national health – manufactures, agriculture, transportation, population – all of which could be measured, quantified and, in theory, adjusted. As Withers argues, statistical analysis like Sinclair's reimagined Scotland's national geography: 'Scotland as a national space was, in some respects, only understood at all in consequence of the inductive integration of local knowledge to form a picture of the nation' ('How Scotland Came to Know Itself' 373). The nation's present was comprehended not in isolated actions of an elite few or the metonymic actions of exemplary individuals but in the sheer accumulation of empirical observation of every nook and cranny in the national space. Underlying all of Sinclair's mass of numerical data was a fundamental assumption of, and faith in, historical progress. Improvement, for Sinclair, was the touchstone of national 'prosperity' and individual 'comfort and happiness', and he finds its benefits working everywhere in the 'impartial' numbers of his multi-volume compilation.[47] The inheritor of Scottish Enlightenment ideas and preoccupations, Sinclair's *Statistical Account* embraced the local in all its vivid peculiarity and distinctiveness while also subjecting it to a universalised set of assumptions that could be replicated anywhere on the globe.

Sinclair's aim in providing accurate and useful data for the 'real statesman' concerned about the welfare of his country is also keenly focused on the here and now of his present day, and though they are rooted, as Poovey demonstrates, in the discourse of Scottish conjectural history, statistical accounts like Sinclair's had moved a long way from the historical focus of their predecessors. Yet even in his attempt to provide, despite the eight-year gap between publication of its first and last volumes, the most up-to-date information, Sinclair acknowledges that an understanding of the historical changes leading to the 'present state' of the nation can be invaluable. 'A knowledge of local facts', Sinclair writes,

> and comparisons of the ancient and modern state of the same districts, are also of importance, for enabling us, to make a proper estimate of the advantages peculiar to our own times; and though farther improvements ought not to be lost sight of, yet it is certainly safer, and more candid, to compare our political condition, with that of our fathers, rather than with refined and visionary theories of perfection, which perhaps never were, nor will be attained in any age or country.[48]

A knowledge of the past is therefore subordinated to the regime of speculation, as it provides a basis of comparison to effect 'farther improvements' in the future. When Galt's parish minister describes his own powers of prediction, as 'but probability that experience had taught me to discern', he shifts slightly the temporal orientation of his account, and begins to resemble less the conjectural historian, or even the local informant of the *Statistical Account* that Johnstone had claimed for him, and more Sinclair's ideal political economist (*Annals*, p. 170). Balwhidder grounds his own ability to foresee the future not on any special insight into Providence, but on his knowledge of the protocols of probability, derived from a lifetime of close observation. His ability to observe the minutiae of everyday life and from these deduce larger historical trends – in other words to make visible what is invisible – allows him to affirm the 'theoretic' principles of Galt's history as they are manifest in the proximate history of his small parish. Also, because Balwhidder's predictions for the future have already come about, he can testify to how experience allows the trained observer to speculate, with some accuracy, on the future. As a parish minister and local annalist, however, Balwhidder is not in the business of prognostication. His narrative for the most part unfolds the parish's proximate past only in the service of taking stock of its present day. In later works, however, Galt would deploy statistical typology in a pointedly 'speculative' mode, to make authoritative pronouncements on the future.

Theoretic Biographies of Emigration

Galt's own keen interest in political economy and the statistical account is evident throughout his writing and activities. One of Galt's earliest publications was 'A Statistical Account of Upper Canada', which was based on information he obtained from his ship's-captain cousin, William Gilkison, who had recently returned from Canada. In it, Galt aimed to offer 'an arranged view of a few statistical recollections'.[49] Much of Galt's rather extensive travels in adult life were devoted to the accumulation of 'useful', in a Sinclarian sense, observation – travelling for information', as Galt would term it in *Bogle Corbet*, not mere sightseeing.[50] A trip to Sicily in his early thirties, for example, was meant to furnish material for a statistical account of the island, and Galt would provide his own, updated statistical account of Upper Canada in 1832, based on his own experiences in the colony.[51] These statistical accounts display an ambition to which Galt would devote much of his writing – fiction and non-fiction alike: bringing a collection of observations and facts together under 'correct theoretical purposes' in order to make them useful for economic and social improvers. In this, Galt followed Sinclair, who wrote that '[p]olitical knowledge . . . cannot be intuitively attained. It is the result of information and experience; and what is experience, but a record of facts?'.[52] The two-part fictional exploration of the emigrant experience that Galt began with *Lawrie Todd* in 1830 and then followed with *Bogle Corbet* in 1831 represents perhaps his most powerful working-out of the relation between statistical methodology and the attainment of correct 'political knowledge' in order to ensure an economically prosperous future. In keeping with his earlier 'theoretical histories', *Lawrie Todd* and *Bogle Corbet*, which Galt labelled 'theoretic biographies', offer a mode of historical realism in which claims to truthfulness are located in the domain of the probable and the empirical. Their narratives unfold a fictionalised accumulation of knowledge that demonstrates the abstract principles the narrative seeks to make visible. As Galt describes his method in the preface to *Lawrie Todd*, 'the narrative embraces the substance of [the author's] knowledge, whether obtained by inquiry, observation, or experience'.[53] In the second of his emigrant series, the statistical typology is not only rhetorical. Galt appended to *Bogle Corbet* a formal 'statistical account of Upper Canada', divided into eight sections, each one representing a district of the region and describing the most pertinent information on the situation of townships, condition of the soil, access to water, and relative condition of settlement roads and waterways. For readers of the present day, perhaps, Galt's statistical appendix sits like a lead weight at the end of the story proper (although Waterston chose to include it in her otherwise expurgated edition). For Galt's intended readers, however, neither the empirical data of the Appendix nor the narrative that comes before is meant to supersede the other. Instead, both parts of the work are interdependent, as the 'theoretic biography' provides a 'case history', embodied in his life experiences and observances, of Corbet's particular emigrant type, which the numbers at the end of the work are meant to illuminate and serve. *Bogle Corbet* represents perhaps the crowning achievement of Galt's innovative brand of 'theoretical' fiction as a 'vehicle for instruction or philosophy teaching, by example'. In *Bogle Corbet*, felicity of characterisation is subordinated, Galt writes, to 'an attempt to embody facts and observations, collected and made on actual occurrences ... restraining the scope of invention entirely to probabilities' (*Autobiography*, vol. 2, pp. 209–10). Galt's theoretic biographies provide a bridge between the conjectural, retrospective mode of his earlier West Country fiction and the speculative, future-oriented political economy of his colonial writings.[54] Intended more as a political economic 'wealth of colonies' than a historical 'annals of Canada', each novel employs the mode that Galt developed from his previous writing to provide useful knowledge for a colonial setting that was, for its intended audience, terra incognita, in which an accurate understanding of the state of the country could mean the difference between prosperity or ruin, and even life or death.

Galt's case histories represent his foray into a genre that rose in prominence in the late 1820s and early 1830s, 'the emigrant novel', the general aim of which was to provide essential advice and guidance for its intended reader, the would-be emigrant to the British colonies. Galt's work shares similarities with other such guidebooks that circulated throughout the British Empire, and their increasing popularity reflected a larger shift in public attitude towards emigration and colonial settlement, in which the Earl of Selkirk's writings and settlement schemes played an important part.[55] In a political environment in which emigration was not simply tolerated but actively encouraged, writers with colonial experience and backgrounds competed to promote their own indispensable expertise on how to succeed in the colonies. For example, William 'Tiger' Dunlop, who was Galt's principal surveyor when they both worked for the Canada Company, published the *Statistical Sketches of Upper Canada for the Use of Emigrants written by a Backwoodsman* the year following publication of *Bogle Corbet*. Like Galt, Dunlop would lay claim to be an authority on emigration based on his career in Canada. Like *Bogle Corbet*, Dunlop's work includes statistical information: dividing the region into smaller districts based on their soil types, Dunlop provides up-to-date information on the state of agriculture and manufactures; wages and the cost of labour, land, and essential commodities; and ease of transportation. Basing his authority on the exemplarity of his own true-life experiences as a bona fide Canadian 'backwoodsman' Dunlop sought to position himself as one who could

> give such information to emigrants . . . that they may know how to proceed and where to go, and not as too often happens, waste their time and their money in the great towns, making fruitless inquiries of people just as ignorant of the nature and capabilities of the country as themselves . . .[56]

Dunlop, like Galt, became a frequent contributor on colonial subjects to *Blackwood's* in the late 1820s and early 1830s.[57] Dunlop's experiences in Canada – also paralleling Galt's – earned him the sobriquet 'Blackwoodian Backwoodsman', a label that could also be readily applied to Galt, as both he and Dunlop were members of a coterie of circum-Atlantic writers, all of whom had devoted much of their professional lives to opening up British North American colonies to settlement.[58] The Canada Company itself disseminated a variety of material in the 1830s – in the form of posters, handbills and newspaper advertisements – in an effort to attract more emigrants seeking land to the area controlled by the company. These gave 'practical advice' on 'settling wild lands', providing detailed testimonies of now prospering emigrants, who recounted their experiences settling on lands recently purchased from the company.[59] Much of this material was distributed widely in the United States, the British Isles and continental Europe, where it was printed in several languages.[60] The company even hired its own promoter, William Cattermole, who in 1832 embarked on a sixteen-month speaking tour in England, touting the advantages of emigrating to company lands. Cattermole, who claimed to have influenced the emigration decisions of 6,000 people, published his own guidebook, which amounted to a slick brochure for the Canada Company.[61]

Galt's own contributions to the emigrant-novel genre represent a major salvo in his campaign in the early 1830s to publicly promulgate and defend his owns views on emigration, both in terms of the views of his competitors and in direct response to company board members who had summarily dismissed him a few years before.[62] Though Galt's contributions to the genre differed from Dunlop's in the latter's claim to a truthfulness unmediated by fiction, Galt nevertheless makes the case for the authenticity and utility of his fictional approach. Because his description is based on his own knowledge and experiences in North America, as he writes in the preface to *Lawrie Todd*, it 'may be considered authentic', and such a description 'of the rise and progress of a successful American settlement, cannot but be useful to the emigrant who is driven to seek a home in the unknown wilderness of the woods' (iv–v). Meant to be taken in tandem, Galt's emigrant novels share similarities. Both are first-person narratives framed as a retrospective, fictive memoirs that recount the experiences of their respective male protagonists, both Scottish-born and both compelled by social and economic circumstances to emigrate to North America. As he did in his earlier works set wholly in Scotland, Galt sets the adventures of his two emigrant protagonists against a broad backdrop of social and economic change, much of which overlaps with his Scotland-set fiction. Both *Bogle Corbet* and *Lawrie Todd* display a digressiveness that is perhaps symptomatic of an author whose publisher demanded three volumes worth of material for each, even though Galt himself preferred a much shorter format.[63] In keeping with Galt's 'case history' approach, *Bogle Corbet* and *Lawrie Todd* represent complementary depictions of emigrant life, cast as the experiences of two distinctive emigrant types. Lawrie Todd is 'a humbly-educated Scotchman, who arrives in America with little more than the clothes on his back' (*Lawrie Todd*, vol. 1, p. iii); whereas in *Bogle Corbet*, Galt wanted to 'give expression to probable feelings of a character upon whom the commercial circumstances of the age have had their natural effect, and to show what a person of ordinarily genteel habits has really to expect in emigrating to Canada' (*Bogle Corbet*, vol. 1, p. iii). Galt therefore sought to communicate his principles on correct settlement practices and emigrant wealth accumulation through two parallel tracks determined by a relative access to capital, as each of his protagonists suffers trials and tribulations but largely overcomes them, achieving eventual success in the New World. Yet as was the case in *Annals of the Parish*, abstract principles in Galt's theoretic biographies are often subservient to the dictates of memory, as each of his emigrant protagonists becomes 'unsettled' by his remembrances of elsewhere. Differences in each character's social background yield significant differences in their individual outlook, disposition and decision-making. Beyond differences of class and education, however, generational difference – with the operations of memory that are shaped by this difference – also plays a defining role in Galt's emigrant stories. Lawrie Todd's life as an emigrant commences at age twenty, when he sets sail for America, and, increasingly disturbed by the memory of his native Scotland while adrift in a country with no collective memory of its own, he ultimately abandons emigrant life. Bogle Corbet, on the other hand, is well into middle age when he sets out for Canada, having already spent most of his life struggling to overcome a continuous series of personal and business disappointments. Though Bogle Corbet remains in Canada, his own emigrant story comes to represent a middle-generational cultural memory-text of the entire circum-Atlantic world, as it bears the cumulative effects of the region's violent recent past.

Lawrie Todd and the Romance of Speculation

The first of Galt's emigrant novels was also by far the most successful. The first, three-volume, edition of *Lawrie Todd* sold well and was quickly followed by a cheaper, one-volume edition with illustrations, which was popular throughout the nineteenth century, particularly in the United States.[64] Based on the manuscript memoir of real-life Scottish emigrant Grant Thorburn, *Lawrie Todd* recounts the adventures of its protagonist, born in the village of Bonnytown on the River Esk and brought up in the trade of his father, a nailer.[65] Todd gets involved with the Radical politics of the Corresponding Societies and finds himself on trial for high treason. He is acquitted, but his father decides to put him and his brother on a ship bound for New York City. Arriving with only three shillings and sixpence between them, Todd sets out to make his fortune in America. He builds his own nail-making shop in the city, only to have it fail as industrialisation makes his skills obsolete. A stint at selling mercantile goods then leads him to the seed-selling business, which prompts an interest in buying land to produce his own seeds. All of his endeavours, however, bear little fruit until a chance encounter sets him on a journey upstate, where he successfully establishes himself as both a settler and land speculator.

In his introduction to the second edition, Galt described in greater detail how he made use of Thorburn's original material: only the first two parts, in a novel Galt divides into nine parts, derive from the manuscript material. Beginning with part three, Galt writes, 'the narrative might claim the epithet of invention, were it not more strictly described as a compilation; it contains stories that I have heard, and incidents that have befallen actual settlers' (*Lawrie Todd*, 1832, p. 450). In reworking Thorburn's original, Galt also refashions its overall theme. Thorburn's intent is made clear in the subtitle he gave his narrative when it was published in 1834 (with an introduction by Galt): *The Doctrine of a Particular Providence Exemplified in the Life of Grant Thorburn (The Original Lawrie Todd)*. Though Galt faithfully replicates Thorburn's frequent references to Providence in his own fictional account, he also devoted an entire chapter of his *Literary Life* to disavowing Thorburn's notion of 'particular providence' – his belief that God directly intervened in the trajectory of his life. Galt dismissively describes the doctrine as one that 'implies a temporary meddling and uncertainty in the Universe' (1:286).[66] In his own work, Galt identifies an alternative principle of causality in Todd's life story, one that is in keeping with *Annals of the Parish*'s alignment of Providence and historical progress. The transformation of Todd's fortunes comes at a critical nadir in his life: with all his early mercantile and trading endeavours coming to a fruitless end, Todd finds himself debt-free but as penniless as the day he first landed in America. After the sudden death of his daughter provokes a deep despondency and near-fatal fever, Todd journeys upstate, in search of better health. While on his travels, he meets with a fellow Scottish settler, Mrs Micklethrift, who provides him with some unlooked-for insight, thoroughly grounded in the material, rather than spiritual, realm. Todd sees his own misfortune as part of a general decline in trade that he foresees will 'bring both the old and new world almost to an end', but his interlocutor offers an alternative understanding:

> Trade's just like the farming, sometimes a good and sometimes a bad harvest; and so it will to the conclusion. There's no steadiness in trade more than in the seasons. It was this persuasion that made my son loup off the treadles and go into the woods, where, if he now and then meet with a bad crop, he's still as certain of making a living; and as men

increase and multiply, the value of his land will rise in the natural way, and without the artifice of speculation. (1:168)

Micklethrift's distinction between the instability of wealth derived from the speculative world of trade and manufacturing and the 'naturally' upward-trending stability of wealth derived from the improvement of wildlands inspires an immediate turnaround in Todd's fortunes, as he realises the wisdom of her words. 'Trade, in the generality, will always be fluctuating,' he states, 'whereas, the settler in the woods, when he has cleared enough to maintain his family, and does not let his wants outgrow his means, rises, of necessity, with the progress of the community, in comparative safety and steadiness' (1:169). After this encounter, Todd decides to make a go of it in the local area, where he eventually establishes a homestead and begins to venture, with ever-increasing success, in the business of buying and developing land. In the process, Todd meets up with variety of characters who exemplify both good and bad land speculation practices on the frontier. Mr Hoskins, who typifies the 'Yankee' entrepreneur that Galt would later lampoon in other writing, is not without his faults; nevertheless, in his shrewd ability to spot a good investment – a good 'spec', as he terms it – and to negotiate the best possible terms in his transaction, Hoskins represents an admirable figure for emulation. When Todd himself manages to arrange for the purchase of 20,000 acres of land from an Albany land agent at a price much lower than the land proves to be worth, Hoskins compliments him on his acumen. 'Had the old man himself made all the amount or the value in profit hard in hand,' Todd reports, 'he could not have been more pleased, so well did he think of the bargain, and of "the handsome ability," as he called it, which I had shown in the business' (2:39). Galt's description of the immense windfall that the pious Todd derives from his less-than-forthright negotiations with the land agent suggests the critique of the corrupting effects of speculative behaviour that Angela Esterhammer has traced in Galt's writing, and that Galt characterised as 'irresponsible and manipulative' in affairs both public and private.[67] A later passage, however, seems to foreclose this reading of Todd's dealings:

> I agree with the generality of the public in thinking the Agent was, maybe, rather quick in acceding to my proposal. But then this should

be said for him, he had been several years in the management, during which his business had moved very heavily, and experience did not warrant him to expect the sudden tide of immigration which came flowing upon the country after the war. In fact, it is to Mr Hoskins' sagacious discernment of what was coming to pass, that I am indebted, under a higher power, for all the benefits derived from the speculation. He foresaw where the people were coming from by whom the western territory was to be inhabited, and he it was that pointed out to me the advantage of acquiring as much land as possible in the earliest stage of the settlement . . . [T]he chief merit of it, as a stroke of business, consisted, as far as I was concerned, in there being no risk . . . (2:101–2)

Todd assigns no moral opprobrium to himself or to others in his dealings with the land agent. Instead, he reorients the question to one of relative foresightedness. The 'good' speculator is one who maximises potential profitability through acute powers of observation informed by a shrewd understanding of human economic activity, which at the same time eliminates as much as possible the contingencies that constitute 'risk'.

Todd's story charts an increasing speculative savvy, which is linked to the advancement of the colonial prosperity through public works and urban development. When Todd proposes that he and Hoskins share the costs of a building a road that would run through both their land parcels, potentially increasing their value, Hoskins is initially wary, fearing Todd may be seeking to profit at Hoskins's expense. But he eventually sees the potential in Todd's scheme and agrees. 'Thus it came to pass, that in the course of three months', Todd writes,

> two spacious and capital roads were cut through the heart of my speculation, by which the value of the land was at once doubled, so that, although I had realized nothing, I was made at once a man of good property. There is indeed no way of raising the value of wild land, but by making it accessible. The forest is a raw material, and it must be manufactured for the market before you can hope to make profit. (2:52–3)

Through his ultimate success as a land developer, imagined as adding value to raw material by 'manufacturing it' – opening it to future settlement as opposed to farming it himself – Todd becomes the embodiment of Galt's own vision of colonial expansion and settlement effected through the unfettered workings of a market economy, a vision he worked out in much of his non-fictional writing of the mid-1820s and early 1830s. In several essays on the subject of emigration he wrote under the pseudonym 'Bandana' that appeared in *Blackwood's* in 1824 and 1826, Galt offered a careful reworking of the prevailing Malthusian assumptions of advocates of government-assisted emigration. These had argued that Britain's 'excess population', particularly in Ireland and Scotland, could be transplanted to the colonies, thereby alleviating the problem of unemployment, pauperisation and the social unrest which followed. As a social 'safety valve' to reduce pressures brought on by industrialisation, writes Galt, quoting from a speech made by a chief proponent of assisted emigration, Robert Wilmot-Horton, 'the inconvenient excess of population could always be carried off imperceptibly'. At the same time, Wilmot-Horton had declared, 'the pauper, for whose labour no remuneration can be afforded at home, will be transmuted by this process into an independent proprietor, and at no distant period will become a consumer of the manufactured articles of his native country'.[68] For Galt, however, the problem of emigration was not one of surplus population in the British peripheries but undercapitalisation in the colonies. Without an adequate circulation of capital, any plan to send the destitute to the colonies would result in even greater destitution. Instead, Galt envisioned a system that encouraged an influx of capital so that the colonies could support the large-scale development activity for which emigrant labour would be needed.

Galt's writing on the colonies represents a sophisticated and ambitious foray into early nineteenth-century political economy, and, unlike many proponents of assisted emigration, who saw it primarily as a means to alleviate problems at home, Galt links the continued prosperity of one region of the British Atlantic with the future prosperity of another. Galt would make admiring reference to the Earl of Selkirk's Highland settlement schemes, but in offering a vision of a circum-Atlantic world in which the interdependence of markets and spaces and the fluctuating demand for labour necessitate a trans-oceanic circulation of not just people but capital, Galt himself laid out a much grander plan for colonial development, one that would be dependent not on government approval or funding but on the activities of individual entrepreneurs acting, like Lawrie Todd, on economic self-interest. Colonial settlement, Galt argued, 'can never be a legitimate application of the powers and means of Government'.

Instead, the 'future business', he argued, 'of removing the redundant population, should be left to the enterprise of private or of associated speculators'.[69] For Galt, the ideal instrument for effecting such enterprise was a commercial entity that could purchase undeveloped land in the colonies; make it accessible by building roads, bridges and canals; and then sell parcels at a profit to would-be settlers, who would 'manufacture' it. Galt saw an opportunity to bring about his vision of colonial settlement, by opening up the vast acreages of 'Reserve' lands in the newly surveyed townships of Canada:

> Both in Upper and Lower Canada, but especially in the former, there are certain portions of land reserved in all the settled parts of the provinces, at the disposal of the crown. These RESERVES have become a dead weight on the improvement of the country ... As it never could have been intended that these reserved lands should be held in perpetuity by the crown ... I would ask, why it is that they are suffered to remain as so many obstacles to the improvement of the country? Or rather, why is it that they are not brought to sale, and a fund created out of the proceeds, to assist in the business of emigration? – not directly, but by making such facilities of intercourse in the country as would induce private adventurers to embark their capital in clearing and settling these lands. (439)[70]

In all his political economic writing on British colonial policy, Galt positions himself as one who only lacks the authority and power to unleash the forces of market capitalism in the colonies. In 1826 Galt believed he had been granted just that authority and power, when he was given control of the day-to-day operations of the Canada Company, with its Galt-inspired charter to purchase and develop Reserve lands in Upper Canada.[71] Galt's work for the company presented a chance to implement his vision of privately financed settlement he had described in his essays on emigration, summarised in the reassurances he gives to hypothetical 'capitalists' perhaps sceptical about investing: 'You are not to count on great immediate profits to be obtained from the produce of the soil, but on the improved value which the land will derive from the capital expended in clearing and bringing it to cultivation.' With patience, profits will come, derived not from the production of the land itself, but 'in the difference between the value of the land, in a state of nature, and in a state rendered habitable and arable, with a constant flow of emigrants from Europe, becoming purchasers of lots, or tenants at great rents'.[72] Through the creation of the Canada Company, Galt believed improvement of public infrastructure in Upper Canada would proceed apace, alongside the improvement of privately held lands. As the company's Superintendent, Galt set about to do the work of capital improvement – road and canal building and town planning – that he considered fundamental to the creation of prosperity and wealth, and that he dramatised in his emigrant 'theoretic biographies'. After several years of judicious speculation by himself, Hoskins and others, Lawrie Todd observes its improving effects on his own settlement, Judiville, which Galt modelled after Rochester, New York:

> The progress of the town has been very wonderful. In less than five years from the date of 'The festivaul,' it contained upwards of two thousand seven hundred inhabitants, and at this present writing, the population exceeds ten thousand souls. Mr. Hoskins is one of the richest men in many counties; and when the instalments are paid up on my twenty thousand acres, which were all settled for in the five years, I shall have no cause to grumble at the reward vouchsafed for my courage in that speculation. But let me not brag. (2:246)

Emigration and the Persistence of Memory

Lawrie Todd, Galt's first emigrant novel, brought to the forefront his ideas on colonial settlement, as he established a kind of entrepreneurial exemplar through which he set out to demonstrate his theories of social and economic progress in a colonial context. Galt's own emigrant experiences, however, ended in failure, when the London-based Court of Directors of the Canada Company became unhappy with their superintendent. Not satisfied with the rate of return on shareholder investments, or with Galt's irregular bookkeeping and inability to make nice with the prevailing factions of government in both Canada and London, the Court of Directors recalled him. In London, suddenly jobless and with debtors' prison staring him in the face, Galt became a victim of the speculative world in which he sought to manoeuvre.[73] In contrast, the trajectory of his fictional emigrant's life in America seems ever upward. His Radical associations and sympathies having made life in Scotland untenable for him, Todd is initially unfazed by his forced departure and seems to thrive in the democratic culture of his new homeland. Todd displays a fierce egalitarian streak when he admonishes an Englishman of a genteel family background, newly arrived at the settlement, who deems the local schoolmaster an unsuitable suitor to his widowed mother:

> Mr. Bradshaw, you will neither find comfort nor increase here, unless you conform, not only to the customs of those among whom your lot has been cast, but to their opinions and ways of thinking. The people on this side of the Atlantic have no ancestors; it is not more than two hundred years, since the Adam and Eve of this world were formed out of the waters of the sea in the hollow of a ship. (2:238)

In his insistence on conforming to the 'opinions and ways' of the New World, Todd's attitude is in keeping with the sentiments of many emigrant guidebooks. Wholly oriented on the future world that awaits, guidebooks such as Dunlop's or Cattermole's express no regard for what the emigrant must leave behind in order to secure the promise of a better life in the colonies.[74] For the sake of their future 'comfort and increase', emigrants must be prepared to cast off their former pretensions and customs and embrace the 'opinions and ways of thinking' of the New World. Todd also configures this rejection of the past in generational terms – with no ancestors to pass down old ways, Americans are free to craft their own. As his life story progresses, however, the New World's notable absence of ancestral memory begins to weigh heavily on Todd's state of mind, as he begins to see his own life less as a linear unfolding of ever-increasing prosperity and more a part of a larger cyclical story of generations who had come before and who will come after. When Todd's own son Robin is forced to flee to England, accused of murder after shooting a man in a duel, Todd thinks of his own father in Scotland, whom Todd, 'intoxicated with the democratic vapours of the French Revolution', had left all those years ago:

> I discerned then the truth . . . on the difference of feeling, between the regard which the young entertain for their seniors, and the tender affection of the old for those whom they have seen growing up from merry schoolboys into sober-visaged men; and the thought of my own recklessness made me suffer the heart-burn of remorse. Strange! that I should have lived, insensible to the grief I had inflicted on my father, until the errors of my own son made me to feel the sting. (2:215)

Todd's renewed sense of familial attachment corresponds increasingly to renewed feelings of attachment to his native land, and he begins to feel its insistent pull upon him. When Todd's father requests to see his son one last time before he dies, Todd, in the final volume of the novel, makes the return journey to Scotland after an absence of twenty years, which also allows him to undertake a simultaneously synchronic and diachronic comparative study of progress. Taking note of the relatively puny steamboat that is to take him from Greenock to Glasgow, Todd begins to think 'for the first time, like the Yankees, that surely, indeed, Europe was far behind America in improvements' (3:7). At the same time, Todd is acutely aware of changes made to a once familiar landscape in the space of twenty years. The village landmarks of his childhood have fallen into some disrepair, but, he notes:

> [i]f the hand of time was seen working detriment on the town, it had been far otherwise exercised in the country. The hills that I had left broomy and pastoral were ploughed to the top, and many of them bonneted with fir-trees, and belted with plantings. It was impossible to view the improvements without satisfaction; but I wondered where the schoolboys would find nests, and allowed myself to fancy that for lack of the brave sports of their fathers, the next generation would, may be, show themselves, in the dangers of other wars, a less venturesome race. (3:20)

With an improver's eye, Todd scans the countryside of his youth and is heartened by the changes while at the same time suggesting a growing nostalgia for the simpler world now lost to progress. The jocular descriptions of Todd's travelogue, which replicate Galt's own statistical style of 'travelling for information', eventually cease altogether, however, and his narrative becomes increasingly sentimental as he anticipates his return to America. While preparing to depart, Todd becomes engaged for a final time – matching Balwhidder's three marriages – but on the eve of his impending nuptials, he writes:

> although I had before me a fair and rational prospect of conjugal comfort, I yet was sensible to a chilliness creeping, like an icy incrustation, on my spirit. I was again about to bid my native land adieu – perhaps for ever – and why? because it seemed to offer me no resting-place. My early friends were all dead and gone; I had acquired notions and ways,

both of thinking and or acting, not in harmony with those of the new generation, with whom, had I remained, I should have been obliged to associate. Of all the passages of my life, this visit to Scotland was the most unsatisfactory, notwithstanding I wooed and won an excellent wife in it . . . (3:117)

Though the exile of his own son and the death of his father have made him acutely aware of his own generational position, Todd, like Rip Van Winkle, suffers a twenty-year gap in memory that has severed him from the community of his birth. Without this memory to sustain him, Todd instead is left to brood at sites that recall him to his early life. As he makes one last visit to his village birthplace, he is overcome by a nostalgic melancholia:

> I spent the afternoon in revisiting every well known object, and the few sad living relics of the olden time, who, though they were never my companions, were yet mixed up with recollections of those that were, and of harmless adventures, which it was a mournful happiness to remember. (3:119)

'Mournful happiness', an apt characterisation of Romantic-period nostalgia, overtakes Todd.[75] Standing before his father's grave, Todd feels only deep remorse for the misery he had caused him:

> [A]ll the sluices of affection were then opened in my bosom, and every tender feeling was overflowing. Endearing Memory brought also her earliest tablets, and read me many a long-forgotten tale of the sufferings which my father had endured, and the tears he had wept, as he thought unseen, when his means failed, and his hands knew not where to find the wherewithal to support me, for whom he implored Heaven to pity as his helpless one. (3:120)

The 'enduring memory' of familial attachments will neither sustain Todd in his settlement in America nor in the Bonnytown of his birth. Instead, the very persistence of memory serves as a constant reminder that Todd is a stranger in his circum-Atlantic world, wherever he chooses to abide: Todd knows he cannot go home again, but neither is he ever completely settled in the New World. Back in Judiville, Todd, by now a prominent figure in the community, is put up for election to the state legislature. Standing before the townspeople at a clamorous public meeting, Todd declines the nomination. Sidestepping the issue of his political allegiances, he instead bases his decision on filial duty to his country – to Scotland, not America:

> 'It may seem to some of you that the land which contains a man's business, property, and family, is his country – and I know that this is a sentiment encouraged here – but I have been educated in other opinions, and where the love of country is blended with the love of parent – a love which hath no relation to condition, but is absolute and immutable – poor or rich, the parent can neither be more nor less to the child than always his parent, – and I feel myself bound to my native land by recollections grown into feelings of the same kind as those remembrances of parental love which constitute the indissoluble cement of filial attachment.' (3:210)

For Todd, national allegiance derives from the experiences of the past, no matter what his present circumstances. Echoing Anne Grant's sentiments on patriotic feeling, Todd's love of country is akin to love of one's progenitors, as fond recollections of native land are blended in his mind with the fond remembrances of parental love: 'Nature makes up the obligation of our attachment to [our country], from the reminiscences of our enjoyments there, just as she forms our filial affection from the remembrance of the caresses of our parents' (3:211). The moment of Todd's nomination ought to signal the culmination of Todd's emigrant story – as he goes from pennilessness outcast to successful and respected member of a thriving and prosperous settler community, a figure fully integrated into the national polity of his adopted land. Instead, Todd's nomination represents the culmination of his struggle with his conflicted national loyalties: divided between those based on filial devotion and childhood memory and those based on the circumstances of the emigrant's here and now. As he lays claim at the end of the novel to an immutable attachment to the country of his birth and childhood, Todd enacts a figurative return to origins that is at odds with the narrative arc that had preceded it. The future for Lawrie Todd turns out not to lie in the New World, but elsewhere, in the old. Hounded by a deranged former minister of the settlement and secure in the knowledge that, as his wife tells him, 'Your family are now settled, . . . and their happiness and prosperity are in their own and the Lord's hands; for their worldly circumstances you can have no anxiety', Todd abandons Judiville and makes his way back to Britain (3:256).

Galt's ending represents a dramatic departure from his source material: in Thorburn's own published memoir, he remains in New

York and becomes a successful seed merchant.[76] Modern-day readers might wonder what would-be emigrant readers would have made of Galt's ending. Despite the novel's role in establishing a pattern for emigrant stories that followed it, Lawrie Todd is ultimately a failure as a colonist, as the 'obligations' of his attachment to his native country, analogous to intergenerational bonds among family, take precedence. *Lawrie Todd* turns out to be not a story of settlement, of the emigrant successfully putting down roots in the New World. Instead, it becomes a migrant story of restless movement and the struggle to reconcile the competing obligations of 'home' and 'away'. As Todd takes his final leave of America, Galt's novel swerves away from the exemplary case study he claimed it to be and becomes something else: a sentimental exploration of a prolonged and ultimately unresolved 'unsettling' nostalgia that haunts the migrant subject and that only deepens, as the years pass by.

Bogle Corbet and Circum-Atlantic Memory

As a man of 'ordinarily genteel habits', with long experience in the circum-Atlantic world of trade through which he has already acquired some wealth, Bogle Corbet seems ideally suited to exemplify the kind of middle-class emigrant who could bring about the vison Galt had laid out in his colonial writing policy and that he had sought to put into practice through the Canada Company: the importation of surplus capital and commercial know-how from the mother country to the colonies, in the figure of the emigrant-speculator-investor who would seek profit 'in the difference between the value of the land, in a state of nature, and in a state rendered habitable and arable'. In shaping a 'theoretic biography' of both a middle-aged and middle-class emigrant, one who, Galt wrote to a friend, is meant to represent 'no bad specimen' of 'the manufacturers of the first crop – that is, those who began their career about 1792', Galt creates a character whose general outlook on life is more in line with Micah Balwhidder's than Lawrie Todd's.[77] Corbet's retrospection casts much further into the past than does Todd's, and the vagaries of memory that strike at the ageing minister of Dalmailing also assail Bogle Corbet. He, for example, admits to 'imperfect recollections of his sailing to Canada' (1:275) and defends his use of direct quotation for a conversation that took place quite some time in the past, when he was a young man:

> The courteous reader cannot expect, after the lapse of so many years, that I should be able to recollect exactly the conversation which took place between my curators on the ever-memorable Monday. The substance, however, can never fade from my mind; it was prospective to an event that was to bias and colour all my future life, and it made an indelible impression. (1:25)

Already in the 'October of [his] days', Bogle Corbet, we find out, has seen and done much in life, and, at the vantage point from which he recounts his experiences, he is already much further down the road, to use Balwhidder's metaphor of the passage of time, than is Lawrie Todd. But Corbet seems less enlightened by his lifetime's accumulation of experiences than he is more worn out by them, as he has found himself frequently entangled in 'the commercial circumstances of the age', which he has witnessed first-hand and which he seeks to narrate. *Bogle Corbet* represents Galt's greatest fictional rendition of the 'great web of commercial reciprocities' that comprises the circum-Atlantic world; and though Galt's avowed aim for the work was to provide practical advice on what the genteel emigrant 'has really to expect' in the colonies, the speculative, statistical impetus of Galt's second emigrant case history, like his first, is largely overshadowed by a troubling and debilitating persistence of memory, as its protagonist recalls his first-hand experiences of the debasing horrors of transatlantic slavery, of economic collapse and financial ruin brought on by war and revolution, and of constant dislocation and uprootedness.

Bogle Corbet's emigrant journey commences after the slow but relentless downturn is his business dealings, attended by a precipitous decline in his standard of living, induces him to leave. As he stands on the deck of the ship that is to take him and his family to Canada and sees the lights of the English coast for the last time, he is overcome with a sudden melancholy – 'farewell my native land! England, good night – alas!' (2:250). This leave-taking scene, a recurring trope of the emigrant stories then and now, is located in the opening chapters of the expurgated 1977 Waterston edition of the novel, which is in keeping with the editor's argument that *Bogle Corbet* is significant because it inaugurates a new national tradition, the inception of which, from her own historical vantage point, is manifest. Bogle Corbet's story becomes 'Canadian' for Waterston at this moment of looking back, which commences the rupture – demarcated by the vast (largely unnarrated) blankness of the Atlantic crossing – between the past and future. Waterston's assumption that this future is Canada is of course the impetus behind her own critical project, which makes *Bogle Corbet* useful to her in ways that *Lawrie Todd* is not. But Bogle Corbet's sentimental farewell moment, with its melancholic recollection of a time and place never to be reclaimed, is replicated in several instances in the novel and in multiple sites of the Atlantic world it narrates. In the opening chapter of the first, 1831 edition, it is not the English coastline of Corbet's 'native land' that he is fondly recalling but Jamaica, his actual birthplace. And it is not the remembrance of his family that the memory of Jamaica brings to mind, but his black nurse, Baba, who accompanied him on his journey back to Scotland as a child. Though it has been more than fifty years since the 'ever-caressing' Baba departed from Corbet (and he can still count back to the exact day that she left him), the 'the wound of our parting', he writes, 'is still fresh and painful' (1:4). This leave-taking is echoed when Corbet makes an adult journey to Jamaica, after an initial sojourn that had taken him from Scotland to London. He refers to the voyage to Jamaica as a return home to his native land, but the island also represents renewed hope for the future, as it provides a possible escape from his troubled finances. Later in the novel, after having lived in London for a time, and just before departing for Canada, Corbet makes a return journey to the Scottish village where he grew up and the home of his ailing childhood guardian. But this journey to Scotland represents no more a return to origins, on the eve of his permanent exile, than does his journey to Jamaica or to Canada for that matter – his 'long home', as his wife describes it. Instead, Corbet's nostalgia for a lost 'homeland' is replicated and doubled with each migration, each departure and return. *Bogle Corbet*'s 'migrant narrative', to use Shields's suggestive phrase, recounts a long chain of substitutions and displacements, of multiple leave-takings in an Atlantic world marked by impermanency and the constant circulation of goods and people. In the context of this larger mapping of circum-Atlantic movement, which the expurgated edition obscures, Corbet's migration to Canada is merely one destination in a personal history of many destinations and journeys, back and forth along the routes and conduits that connect the varying locales within the Atlantic world and which necessitate a continuous accumulation of farewells.

The troubled experiences of each sojourn in Corbet's Atlantic experience leaves its trace, its sediment, which accumulates through multiple reiterations and repetitions. This accumulation poses an alternate trajectory to the narrative of Corbet's eventual prosperity in the New World. Instead, in his middle-age retrospective, we see that each moment of departure and return is accompanied by the reappearance of a peculiar melancholy, a sense of unease and disorientation, that is compounded as he traces and then retraces the routes of his circum-Atlantic world. Bogle Corbet – Galt's embodiment of New World 'facts and observations, collected and made on actual occurrences' – turns out to be weighed down by the accumulated past of traumatic experiences that have happened elsewhere. By the time of his actual arrival in Canada, Corbet, in Trumpener's words, is 'a figure haunted by a suppressed past . . . depressed by the cumulative weight of British history'.[78] The weight of this history manifests itself not only in apprehension of the immediate present, but the future as well, supplanting the abstracted, statistical vision that the novel as a whole is supposed to serve. Corbet's dis-ease is not Lawrie Todd's nostalgic loss upon leaving his homeland, but an ever-increasing anxiety brought on by the accumulating weight of the proximate past of the British Atlantic, a past that is largely configured as traumatic.

The perpetual feeling of displacement is echoed in the sentiments of characters that Corbet meets throughout his life and travels. Early experiences in the Glasgow cotton mills, where he witnesses the same rise of Jacobinism that had forced Lawrie Todd into American exile, lead to mercantile ventures which, given the conduits of Glasgow's circum-Atlantic trade, almost inevitably take him to the West Indies. After his merchant business fails, Corbet is forced by his creditors to take charge of assets held by his company in Jamaica. In his return journey to the island of his birth, Corbet recounts his encounter with an old woman on the voyage, who, long settled in Kingston, was returning from England where she had gone to see friends: 'perhaps with the intention of spending the remainder of her days there, but few she found alive, and every thing so changed' that England 'was no longer her native land – Jamaica was more homely' (1:277). For

Corbet himself, the 'return' visit he makes to the island as a younger man does not replicate the childhood memory of comfort and security he would recall in later years. Instead, Jamaica turns out to be the space of unsettled historical memory itself. During Corbet's visit, curiosity prompts him to seek a community of maroons, fugitive slaves who had fled their white masters and now eke out subsistence lives in the interior mountains of the island. It is there he meets with an old woman who recounts a horrifying past. Some sixty years before, she had helped her lover to kill his master, burning the master's house down in the process. What is more, Corbet discovers, to his 'inexpressible amusement', that she speaks a Scots-inflected patois – 'Negro Scotch', he terms it – that she had learned from her lover's Scottish master (1:299).

The encounter with the old maroon woman provides a telling glimpse into Galt's own complex attitude to the Atlantic slave trade and to the abolition debate, which was coming to a head while he was writing his emigrant novels. On the one hand, the scene suggests an acute awareness of the insistent legacy of Britain's, and particularly Scotland's, slavery past, while also rehearsing common tropes of abolitionist slave narratives: the righteous resistance of the enslaved and the intimacy between enslaved women and their masters that exposed the moral depravity and hypocrisy of slavers. The past of slavery, sixty years since, is recalled to the present, when Corbet visits the estate of an English planter who recently had married a Quadroon woman after the death of his English first wife. This marriage had so disturbed the man's young daughter that she shoots herself after an argument with the new wife during a fancy-dress ball at their home (2:15). The awful scene of discovering her body is, declares Corbet, too horrible for him to record. Though it cannot be recounted, the traumatic memory of Jamaican maroonage has lived on, deep within its mountains, while it also reverberates beyond them, replicating its tragic effects and creating a residual unease in succeeding generations long after. A constant feeling of impermanence pervades the plantation world, Corbet observes, and an 'apprehension of possession', had prompted a haste in all activities, 'as if everything were prepared for a sudden abandonment' (1:305).

On the other hand, the 'self-emancipated' maroon woman that Corbet encounters in Jamaica also adumbrates a key aspect of Galt's theoretical ideas on the future of the Atlantic slave trade, which he articulated in a series of essays that appeared in the late 1820s and early 1830s on what he termed 'the West Indian question'. These essays had placed Galt conspicuously on one side of the slavery debate in Scotland, much of which was playing out in the Edinburgh periodical reviews and in Glasgow newspapers.[79] While accepting 'that slavery is contrary to rights of man and privileges of all who live under British law', Galt nevertheless argues that the slave 'should still remain bound to do a certain labour for his owner, and bound to remain on his estate till he received his owner's assent to quit it'.[80] Galt holds up for ridicule abolitionist arguments based on experiential testimony that operated on the precepts of sentiment and sympathy. In a rather vehement rebuttal to what he termed the 'fanatics for emancipation', who adopt 'tricks, stratagems, and frauds' in their 'mealy-mouth[ed]' disregard for proper 'philosophy', Galt insists that a proper understanding of the future of slavery must be grounded in principles of probability and political economy. In typical fashion, Galt offered several alternatives to immediate emancipation, which he argues are more in line with correct economic principles.[81] The essays Galt wrote on West Indian slavery established him as a forceful and ardent champion of planter interest, and he adopted common lines of argument in anti-abolitionist writing that, Iain Whyte summarises, 'sought to postpone abolition indefinitely and to eke out the life of slavery'.[82] Galt joined a cadre of Scottish writers sympathetic to planter interest – such as Archibald Alison, James MacQueen, Alexander Barclay, Michael Scott and John Gibson Lockhart – many of whom had ties to the Glasgow-based planter community.[83] In the lead-up to eventual emancipation in 1833, Galt, like many of these apologists for slavery, while not defending it as an institution, called for gradual emancipation and compensation for planters.

As for Bogle Corbet himself, Galt's anti-hero is ultimately ambivalent on the matter, having 'never been able to form a decided opinion; for although, abstractedly, all philanthropists are agreed as to the political rights which ought to belong to the negroes', the relative conditions of West Indian slaves when compared to the conditions of common labourers elsewhere 'must ever give us pause' (2:31). Yet the story of the old maroon woman, a kind of case history of the enslaved within Galt's emigrant case history, functions as an important exemplar of Galt's apprehensions concerning the West Indian question, as it stood in 1831. The maroon's memories of slave uprisings of the not-too-distant past are perhaps meant to register as a portent of the monstrous violence and destruction that Galt felt would erupt if immediate and total emancipation were granted.[84] Perhaps in ways Galt did not intend, his description of the woman as a 'hideous Sycorax', with a visage that 'was something horrible, between a toad's and a baboon's' and 'odiously protruded' lips that 'revealed a ghastly grin of four or five long unequal yellow teeth', reveals deep-seated anxieties about a West Indian world dominated by free Blacks (1:299). Yet the traumatic memory of the violence of slavery, the past that refuses to stay in the past, in *Bogle Corbet* is at odds with the theoretical realism that Galt insists on in his non-fiction writings on the West Indies. Corbet's experiences in the haunted landscape of his birthplace offer no reassurance, no exemplary case by which the would-be emigrant, or colonial policy-maker, can gauge the future. All that these experiences can offer is an explanation for Corbet's increasing melancholia, which takes the form of a dread anxiety for an unsettled future that seems to lurk always just beyond the horizon.

Corbet's disturbing encounters with the past during his adult return to Jamaica, which also marks a key moment in his gradual economic decline – the failing of his West Indies trading partnership – are repeated in other contexts, other places, and serve as an index for the novel's apprehension of the past and its accumulative effects on those living in the present. The process begins early on in Corbet's life: after an early foray into cotton manufacturing, his first attempt at establishing a business fails after a ship carrying money intended for the firm is seized and Corbet and his partners are unable to meet the payment demands of their creditors. Public knowledge of their troubles instantly undermines confidence in the partnership, and it is ruined, an experience that parallels Galt's own entrance into the world of business.[85]

As such experiences begin to accumulate, they begin to weigh on Corbet's psyche, producing an array of symptoms – 'hypochonderics' or 'alloverishness', as Corbet calls it – sleeplessness, chronic depression, weariness, and bouts of aimless melancholic reminiscing. On one occasion, the ghost of Corbet's past reveals itself in a startling waking nightmare, prompted by the letter Corbet receives from his childhood guardian, describing her declining health. In what he describes as a state of perfect consciousness, he beholds the vision of an open coffin with a body in it, in 'the final aged helplessness of life' and dressed as one in a 'sick chamber' (2:185). This spectral vision fills Corbet with a dread anxiety of the death it presages. Like the Jamaican Sycorax, the spectre in the coffin embodies calamities past but also prefigures calamities yet to come. Corbet's impending emigration and the illness of his guardian prompts him to return to the village of his youth, where familiar objects and sights recall him to his past. When his guardian dies shortly after his arrival, Corbet's spectral vision is realised: the past finds its fulfilment in what had yet to happen.

The feeling of the past in the future and the future in the past is repeated when Corbet travels to the Scottish Highlands, to meet with a landowner arranging for the emigration of some of his tenants. Corbet views this unfamiliar world with an improver's eye, remarking favourably that the introduction of the steamboat has converted 'what would have been formerly an undertaking of hardship and hazard, into a jaunt of pleasure, salutary to invalids' (2:202), his utterances also reflecting Galt's characteristic dismissiveness towards the language and culture of the Gael.[86] Yet in Corbet's sojourn with the old Highland landowner, who himself plans to emigrate with his tenants, the novel offers a surprising swerve away from the rhetoric of improvement that had saturated much Galt's writing – including *Annals of the Parish* – and that was busily being used to transform the Highlands. Describing a world upended by the post-war collapse of temporarily inflated grain and cattle prices, the old Highlander observes to Corbet:

> The Highlands have seen their best days: the chieftains are gone, and the glory of the claymore is departed for ever . . . [T]he olden time has long been dead, its spirit walks the mountains, and scowls upon me when I dare to repine . . . This country is now but for sheep – Men have no business here . . .' (2:219–20)

The old man's lament reveals Galt's own acute understanding of how the integration of Highland agricultural markets in British imperial economy, and the accelerated restructuring of land use on the part of Highland landowners, had led to widespread displacement in the region. Bound for Canada himself, Galt's old Highlander echoes the sentiments of writers of the Highland Diaspora such as Donald Macleod and John MacLean, whose recounting of Highland dispossession and displacement became an integral feature of a collective memory of Clearance that circulated throughout the Atlantic world.

In the Highlands, nothing remains the same for Galt's old Highlander: 'After an absence of many years, I came back to this old spot, which often was remembered in distant scenes as the pleasantest the earth could contain; but on my return all that had endeared it in recollection existed no more' (2:220). The old man, however, refuses to sentimentalise the bleak picture of exile. Instead, he is resigned to the transience of time and place. Alone in the Highlands, all previous attachments having gone save his old housekeeper, he can only conclude: 'it is only by missing early friends that we discover how little aspect of our native land contributes to the sentiment with which it is pictured on the memory. In truth, I am weary of this empty place, and although past the season of adventure, I have resolved to seek another scene' (2:220). As a lifelong soldier, he is indifferent to all local attachments:

> all countries are alike to me . . . Before my return, every place had something about it inferior to my home, but the delusion is gone. I think, however, that Canada will probably have my bones; for several officers whom I knew in the army, have settled with their families there. I have no comrades left and it sweetens death to fall among companions. (2:221)

Conditioned by a nomadic existence required by a lifetime's service in the British military, the old Highlander embodies a particular conduit of migration throughout the circum-Atlantic world that foments, as we saw in the real-life memoirs of the Scottish soldier-of-fortune John Gabriel Stedman, a general rootlessness. What is left is not so much a feeling of hope for the future, for the promise of a new life and new attachments, nor a diasporic sense that a vital and identity-sustaining link to a Highland homeland has been cruelly broken. Instead, we are left with the feeling that the Highlander, like Bogle Corbet himself, has simply endured.

While in the Highlands, in a scene that echoes his previous Jamaican confrontation with the premonitional world of futures past, Corbet encounters another unworldly woman in the mountains. While on a leisurely walk with his host, Corbet is accosted by an old woman, leaning heavily upon her staff. Known to the old Highlander as one with the power of 'second sight', she recounts a mysterious vision of death: of the local churchyard and Corbet acting as pallbearer, carrying a coffin. The old woman's vision unnerves both Corbet and his host, and they hasten back to the inn where they had left their ailing travelling companion, arriving just in time for the man to fall dead in Corbet's arms. By the latter half the novel, the eve of Corbet's emigration, the presage of death brought on by the cumulative memory of Corbet's circum-Atlantic experiences weigh heavily against the predictive confidence Galt's novel is intended to provide. Dread anxiety, not sunny optimism, accompanies Corbet to Canada, as he is wearied by the realisation that the past is his future, and that his future is already past. Even the change of water colour, as Corbet's vessel enters the Gulf of St Lawrence, prompts an unexpected sense of dread, as it, in his words, seems to arise from some, 'portentous extraordinary event that had either taken place or was about to come to pass' (2:258).

(Scottish) Memories of the Circum-Atlantic

Galt set out to write his *Autobiography* a few years after his dismissal as superintendent of the Canada Company, and much of the work is related to his own circum-Atlantic experiences. As such, the *Autobiography*, and its follow-up, *Literary Life and Miscellanies*, could be said to provide their own (non-fictional) 'case history' of one middle-class emigrant's transatlantic experience, to go alongside *Bogle Corbet*.[87] Though it is perhaps a mistake to read Galt's telling of his life story as the 'auto' variation of a theoretic biography, it is not unreasonable to suggest that Galt's circum-Atlantic experiences, which informed much of his writing in later years, informed the narrative of the exemplary emigrant whose background and fortunes so closely paralleled his own. Galt wrote in his *Literary Life*, published five years before his death, that the months after the publication of *Bogle Corbet* were, save for his youthful residence in London when he went bankrupt, 'the most uncomfortable of my whole life'. Expressing an awareness of 'having attained the climacterical period of life', Galt had decided to ease up on his literary work and devote more time to leisure pursuits, but the ensuing idleness provoked in him a deep and lasting moroseness that he associated with old age:

> [A]s a man advances in years, his mind invariably becomes more acrid. The world no longer appears the same; many things which in the coming seemed gay and desirable have passed by, and when he looks on their backs, they appear scarcely worth half the thought which they had once

excited; mean, too, and slovenly, altogether undeserving of that attention which so short-lived a being as man bestows upon the hopes that cajole him onward unto age and ailing. Another unpleasant result of this kind of indescribable 'all-overishness' of the mind ... You discern that the rising generation begins to affect you in a manner not before imagined; wholly engrossed with your seniors, you had previously regarded those around you, and particularly your juniors, as objects of no care. But when you see the old making their exit, and the young coming upon the scene, and who push you from your stool – the tables are turned indeed. (*Literary Life*, vol. 1, pp. 314–15)

'All-overishness', the term that Galt puts in the mouth of the middle-aged Bogle Corbet to describe his psychological malaise, is the term that Galt uses to describe his own condition at fifty-two, already aware that he is nearing the final in the cycles of his life.[88] At the end of his narrative, even though Corbet, like Galt, was instrumental in founding a town and helping to expand settlements in Lower Canada, he can only lament that he has 'been too late'; as one who emigrated above the age of fifty, 'the habits and notions of the old country are too riveted upon him' and so he should not have expected 'aught much better than discomfort' in the New World (3:302). But at the end of *Bogle Corbet*, the question remains, which 'old country'? Is it the Scotland where Corbet was raised and educated, or the Jamaica of his birth? Or is it London, where he went to seek his fortune? It is not the habits or notions of any of Corbet's sojourns in the circum-Atlantic world that have worn away his optimism for the future. Rather it is the memory of that region's troubled past that permanently discomforts him – the past that haunts his present, a memory of death and of failure that only seems to replicate itself in each new scene, each new situation.

In this way, *Bogle Corbet*, which Trumpener labelled 'Galt's most explicit, sustained mediation on the British imperial project', encapsulates within a single work two distinct strands, two discursive modes, that Galt took from Scottish literary, historical and economic writing.[89] The speculative, conjectural register of *Bogle Corbet*'s political economy is set against the melancholic tenor of the circum-Atlantic history it recounts. The latter does not supplant the speculative hopeful sense of future which the narrative is supposed to serve, but instead unsettles it, infusing the future with the dread anxiety of the past. Galt brings both modes to bear in his emigrant novels. As they engage with, and ultimately exceed, the topologies and temporalities of the emigrant novel, the early Canadian national tale, the Scottish historical romance, or the statistical account, both *Bogle Corbet* and *Lawrie Todd* bring into high relief the unique social history of the Atlantic world, and its critical relation to the culture of modernity. Galt's emigrant novels therefore stand as the capstone to Atlantic memorialist writing by Scots in the Romantic era, as they assume the mantle of cultural memory. 'Preserved' in the retrospective fictions of *Lawrie Todd* and *Bogle Corbet*, the legacy of the Atlantic world lives on, but there will be no one community that can lay claim to its inheritance.

Notes

1. Whatley, 'Introduction', p. 15.
2. Ibid.
3. Ibid. p. 9.
4. See Duncan, *Scott's Shadow*.
5. To be precise, Waterston's edition begins on the fourth paragraph of Chapter 30 of Volume Two of the original (229).
6. Waterston, *John Galt*. In her own study of Canadian literature, Waterston saw Galt's work, particularly *Bogle Corbet*, as a prominent thread in the Scottish plaid that had been woven into the fabric of Canada's literary tradition. See *Rapt in Plaid*, pp. 102–19.
7. See Lee, *The Canada Company and the Huron Tract*, pp. 173–83.
8. This was the nearly three-million-acre 'Huron Tract', a large part of which the Chippewas of Chenail Ecarté, St Clair and Aux Sauble had surrendered in April 1825, for a perpetual annuity of £1,100 to be divided equally among the 440 tribal people thought to inhabit the area at the time. The annuity would decrease if the population declined, which was the presumption (see Surtees, *Indian Land Surrenders*, pp. 79–85). An area of land, Walpole Island, at the outlet of the St Clair River into Lake St Clair, was not included in any land cessions and remains unceded land of the Bkejwanong First Nation ('Chief & Council').
9. For an account of Galt's Canadian urban development projects and ideas, see Waterston, 'John Galt, the Founder of Guelph'; and Stelter, 'John Galt: The Writer as Town Booster and Builder'. Urban historian and Guelph resident Stelter led the movement to name the holiday in Galt's honour and to erect a statue of Galt in 1979 in front of the Guelph City Hall (see 'Why Do We Celebrate John Galt Day?'). In

2008 the online *Guelph Mercury* reported that the statue was mysteriously defaced with red paint sometime during the night of the second annual Galt Day ('Guelph's John Galt Statue Defaced with Red Paint over Long Weekend'). A blogger on Infoshop.Com, an 'anarchist news blog', claimed the statue was defaced to protest Galt's role in the colonisation and genocide of indigenous peoples in Canada ('Guelph, Ontario: Anarchists Paint Bomb Statue of John Galt'). For Galt's experiences in Canada, see Lee, *The Canada Company and the Huron Tract*; and Timothy, *The Galts*.
10. See Trumpener, *Bardic Nationalism*; Shields, *Nation and Migration*; Hewitt, *John Galt: Observations and Conjectures*; and Carruthers and Kidd, *International Companion to John Galt*.
11. Trumpener, *Bardic Nationalism*, p. 277.
12. Armitage, 'Three Concepts of Atlantic History', p. 18. Armitage distinguishes between 'circum-Atlantic', 'trans-Atlantic' and 'cis-Atlantic' historiographies ('Three Concepts of Atlantic History'). For recent studies that adopt a circum-Atlantic framework, see Baucom, *Specters of the Atlantic*; Bailyn, *Strangers within the Realm*; Gilroy, *The Black Atlantic*; and Roach, *Cities of the Dead*.
13. Trumpener, *Bardic Nationalism*, p. xiii.
14. Duncan, *Scott's Shadow*, pp. 215–23.
15. For a discussion of Galt's use of the term, see Costain, 'Theoretical History and the Novel'. Costain argues that *Annals of the Parish* is, strictly speaking, the only theoretical history Galt wrote.
16. Duncan, *Scott's Shadow*, p. 221. Summarising the reputation of his two most successful fictional works in his *Literary Life*, Galt seems to accede to popular opinion while suggesting his intent continued to be misunderstood: 'The Annals of the Parish and the Provost have been generally received as novels, and I think, in consequence, they have both suffered, for neither of them have, unquestionably, a plot. But as novels they are regarded, and I must myself as such now consider them; but still something is due to the author's intention, for ... notwithstanding the alleged liveliness of some of the sketches, as stories they are greatly deficient' (1:226).
17. Duncan, *Scott's Shadow*, p. 224.
18. Trumpener, *Bardic Nationalism*, p. 152.
19. Galt's letter to Blackwood of 27 February 1821 appears in the Appendix of Kinsley's edition of the novel: Galt, *Annals*, p. 206. All subsequent references to *Annals of the Parish* are given in abbreviated form in the body of the text, or as a page number alone where unambiguous.
20. White, *The Content of the Form*, p. 16.
21. Ibid. p. 20.

22. Galt, *Autobiography*, vol. 2, p. 219. All subsequent references to the *Autobiography* are given in the body of the text, or as a volume and page number alone where unambiguous.
23. See Anderson, *Imagined Communities*, especially pp. 22–36.
24. For 'generationality', see Erll, 'Generation in Literary History'.
25. Galt would explore this theme in detail in his 1823 multigenerational saga, *Ringan Gilhaize*.
26. Blackwood wrote that his own 'worthy old Mother' had thought '"Micah an honest and upright minister of the gospel" but being told by one of her grandchildren that the book was a *novel*, was very angry at having been deceived' (Gordon, *John Galt*, p. 38).
27. For example, so much did the Whig historian G. M. Trevelyan find the work 'the most intimate and human picture of Scotland during . . . the reign of George III' that he used the novel as source material for his *English Social History* (quoted in Whatley, 'Annals of the Parish and History', p. 51). Whatley, in the same essay, offers a careful critique of the validity of Galt's fictional retrospect as historical documentation.
28. See McKeever, '"With Wealth Come Wants"'; and Costain, 'The Spirit of the Age and the Scottish Fiction of John Galt'.
29. Galt in *The Bachelor's Wife* provides further commentary on his own historical 'cycle' in a conversation between Benedict and his sage counsellor wife, Egeria, who observes: 'We are now, I think, evidently entered into a new cycle. All the past has become, in some degree, obsolete, or is only drawn on to furnish illustrations to characters, possessing something in common with that high state of excitement into which we have ourselves been raised by the vast and wonderful events of the age' (351).
30. Bohrer, 'John Galt's *Annals of the Parish*', p. 96.
31. Ibid.
32. For a nuanced discussion of the representational logics, and limits, of Balwhidder's 'web' metaphor, see Wickman, 'John Galt's Logics of Worlds'.
33. Duncan, *Scott's Shadow*, pp. 223–4.
34. Dickinson, for example, wrote in 1954 that 'Galt's Provost Pawkie and the Rev. Micah Balwhidder have placed on record a contribution to the social history of Scotland which takes its place beside the massive volumes of the old *Statistical Account*' ('John Galt: "The Provost" and the Burgh', p. 4).
35. Quoted in Moir, 'Memoir of Galt', pp. 309–10.
36. For an examination of Galt's work in the context of the speculative and imaginative aspects of Scottish conjectural history, see Hewitt, 'Introduction', especially pp. 3–12.

37. Poovey, *A History of the Modern Fact*, p. 215. See also Bender, 'Enlightenment Fiction and the Scientific Hypothesis'; Davis, *Factual Fictions*; Packham, 'Feigning Fictions'.
38. Poovey, *A History of the Modern Fact*, p. 215.
39. Ibid. p. 216.
40. Ibid. p. 239.
41. Ibid.
42. Ibid. p. 243.
43. Sinclair, *Analysis of the Statistical Account*, p. 59; italics in original.
44. Ibid. 'Preface', p. 6.
45. Sinclair, *Statistical Account*, vol. 1, p. 26; italics in original.
46. Sinclair, *Analysis of the Statistical Account*, p. 6; italics in original.
47. Though Sinclair's informants were meant to provide the raw data to ascertain theoretic principles, the reports of many betray their own theoretical and ideological orientation. Anticipating perhaps Sinclair's own perspective, many of these accounts remark approvingly on large-scale changes put into effect in the name of improvement. On the other hand, some, particularly among those who served parishes in the Gàidhealtachd and who were often themselves Gaelic-speakers, used the occasion of providing statistical information to provide a scathing indictment of improving landowners who had violated their solemn obligations as putative guardians of their people. Intended as the ultimate affirmation of the principles of improvement, Sinclair's *Statistical Account* instead reveals deep-seeded ideological and cultural resistance to the disruption of traditional farming practices in Scotland.
48. Sinclair, *Analysis of the Statistical Account*, p. 63.
49. Galt, 'A Statistical Account of Upper Canada', p. 3.
50. Galt, *Bogle Corbet*, vol. 1, p. 62. All subsequent references to *Bogle Cobet* are given in abbreviated form in the body of the text, or as a volume and page number alone where unambiguous.
51. This appears as an appendix to the first edition of *Bogle Corbet*. For an account of Galt's trip to Sicily and the Mediterranean, see his *Autobiography* (vol. 1, pp. 117–226).
52. Sinclair, *Analysis of the Statistical Account*, p. 56.
53. Galt, *Lawrie Todd*, p. iv. All subsequent references to *Lawrie Todd* are given in abbreviated form in the body of the text, or as a page number alone where unambiguous.
54. For an analysis of the interrelationship between Galt's two emigrant tales, his own political economic writings, and writing on emigrant subjects by others, see Halliwell, 'John Galt and the Paratext'.
55. For an analysis of this shift and Galt's role in it, see Irvine, 'Canada, Class, and Colonization in John Galt's *Bogle Corbet*'.

56. Dunlop, *Statistical Sketches*, p. 4.
57. Though *Blackwood's* would publish much of Galt's non-fictional writing on the colonies, it rejected both *Lawrie Todd* and *Bogle Corbet*.
58. This coterie also included Andrew Picken. For discussion of the professional and intellectual reciprocity between Galt, Dunlop and Picken, see Jennifer Scott, 'Reciprocal Investments'.
59. Quoted in Coleman, *The Canada Company*, p. 98.
60. Coleman, *The Canada Company*, p. 98.
61. See Cameron and Maude, *Assisting Emigration to Upper Canada*, pp. 46 and 306 n. 18.
62. Galt's *Autobiography*, published two years after *Bogle Corbet*, continues the work of self-justification, as more than half of the two-volume work is devoted to his role in the Canada Company. Galt's literary endeavours receive only scant attention. Those wanting an account of his literary career would have to wait a year later, for the publication of his *Literary Life and Miscellanies*.
63. *Bogle Corbet*, Galt writes in his *Literary Life*, 'is another proof, if one were wanting, that booksellers step from their line when they give orders, like to an upholsterer for a piece of furniture. Short and simple tales, any person may suggest, but to write three volumes at the request of another, in a satisfactory manner, and without an occasional sense of drudgery, is beyond my power' (1:311–12). Subsequent references to Galt's *Literary Life* are given in abbreviated form in the body of the text, or as a volume and page number alone where unambiguous.
64. Jennifer Scott reports that *Lawrie Todd* 'ended up being Galt's most popular novel, undergoing multiple American editions, eight British ones, a German translation, and was one of the most popular books sold in America in 1830' ('The Invisible Hand of the Literary Market', p. 54).
65. For a discussion of the cross-influences between Galt and Thorburn, see Jennifer Scott, 'The Invisible Hand of the Literary Market'.
66. In place of Thorburn's 'particular Providence', Galt substituted his own belief in 'predestinarianism', which places emphasis on the general principles of motion in God's creation. Predestination, for Galt, is 'a foreknowledge of whatsoever is to come to pass' operating at the level of systems not individuals (*Literary Life*, vol. 1, p. 286). See Jennifer Scott, 'The Invisible Hand of the Literary Market'; Carruthers, 'Remembering Galt'; and John MacQueen '*Ringan Gilhaize* and Particular Providence'.
67. Esterhammer, 'Galt the Speculator', p. 45.
68. Galt, 'Bandana on Emigration, Letter First', p. 438.
69. Galt, 'Bandana on Emigration', p. 474.

70. Galt, 'Bandana on Emigration, Letter First'.
71. Galt originated the idea of developing Reserve lands during his stint as parliamentary lobbyist for the Loyalists who sought compensation for lands lost during the War of 1812. Galt dates the inception of the Canada Company to a conversation he had in London with Scottish-born Bishop Alexander MacDonnell of Upper Canada, who had encouraged and aided Scottish emigrants, particularly those from his family's Glengarry estates in the Highlands (*Autobiography*, vol. 1, p. 294). For Galt, the chartered protection of a joint-stock company represented the perfect instrument to achieve the public good of bringing much needed capital to the colonies. This was in contrast to 'mining adventures, and all speculations, the success of which depends on chance', which, Galt wrote, seemed 'of the nature of gambling associations, and were not fit objects of chartered protection (*Autobiography*, vol. 2, p. 246).
72. Galt, 'Bandana on Emigration, Letter First', p. 439.
73. As a joint-stock company, the Canada Company was comprised of shareholders whose return on investment took the form of the rising value of their stock. When stock value did not rise as expected, investors began to lose confidence in the company. To preclude panic-selling, the court of directors informed Galt that his position as superintendent had been abolished and that two commissioners would succeed him. Galt would later express his frustration and disappointment concerning his dismissal. As the enterprise originally had been, he writes in his *Autobiography*, 'fraught with benevolence, calculated to assuage distress in the mother country, and to improve the condition of victims which that pressure forced to emigrate, I repine to see it sunk in a mere land-jobbing huxtry, and abortive in all the promises, but the payment, by which the government was induced to part with the lands' (2:158).
74. These are uniformly dismissive of the emerging public debate on the plight of dispossessed emigrants. Cattermole, for instance, rejects as absurd: 'the [so-called philanthropists] talk of expatriation, banishment, the severing of ties, and other sentimental phrases. Surely this is either very childish, or something worse. It is enough to say in reply, that the emigration is voluntary on the part of the pauper; that it is for his vast and permanent benefit; that, if he has a family, he will take it with him; and that his separation from his native home and country, is only what thousands of professional persons in the higher class of life are constantly undergoing for the same all-sufficient reason; namely to better their fortunes' (*Emigration*, p. 121).
75. For a discussion of Romantic ideas on nostalgia and melancholy, see Austin, *Nostalgia in Transition*; Boym, *The Future of Nostalgia*; and Turner, 'A Note on Nostalgia'.

76. Thorburn's seed catalogue, which allowed him to expand his sales dramatically, was the first of its kind in America. In seeking to advance his own literary aspirations, Thorburn, who subtitled his own published memoir *The Original Lawrie Todd*, explicitly traded on the fame that Galt's novel had brought to him. See Jennifer Scott, 'The Invisible Hand of the Literary Market'.
77. Quoted in Moir, 'Memoir of Galt', pp. lxxxix–xc.
78. Trumpener, *Bardic Nationalism*, pp. 88, 87.
79. Galt wrote three letters 'on West Indian Slavery', which appeared in *Fraser's* between November 1830 and January 1831. Other essays on West Indian Slavery are 'Means of Lessening West Indian Stress' and 'The Whole West Indian Question'.
80. Galt, 'Letters on West Indian Slavery, Letter 1', pp. 448, 447.
81. One of Galt's solutions was to divide freed-slave labour into two types: agricultural and manufacturing ('field negros and boiling-house negros'). The former would lease land from their former masters on which to produce crops, thereby providing revenue compensation for the loss of (slave) property. The latter would allow for the expansion of sugar production thereby providing for general improvement of the West Indian economy, which otherwise would decline due to global competition with regard to their chief commodity, sugar cane (see 'The Whole West Indian Question').
82. Whyte, *Scotland and the Abolition of Black Slavery*, p. 163. Much of Galt's pro-slavery work appeared in the imitative offshoot of *Blackwood's*, the London-based *Fraser's*, which, like its more prominent rival, provided a forum in the late 1820s for anti-abolition arguments made largely on political economy grounds – on the deleterious effects that immediate abolition would have on trade and on the health of empire. The co-founder and editor of *Fraser's* was William Maginn, who had been a major contributor for *Blackwood's* (see Brake, 'Maga, the Shilling Monthlies, and the New Journalism').
83. For an analysis of Galt's writing in the context of pro-slavery political economic theory, see Taylor, 'Conservative Political Economy and the Problem of Colonial Slavery'. Lamont identifies a 'Glaswegian inflection' in *Bogle Corbet*, particularly in its treatment of slavery (see 'Finding Galt in Glasgow').
84. Galt described *Bogle Corbet*'s Jamaican scenes as largely fictitious but, referring to what he characterises as the two opposed views on the state of West Indian society, writes 'what I consider as the true state is described in the work'. Alluding perhaps to his informal network of Glasgow friends and colleagues involved in the West Indian trade, Galt writes 'I felt it to be a kind of duty, to old associations, to point out the

evils that might arise, in my opinion, from giving liberty to the slaves, without due checks and restraints' (*Autobiography*, vol. 2, p. 210).

85. Galt relates in his *Autobiography* how his first partnership with a certain McLachlan went under when they were unable to pay their creditors after one of their clients was forced to stop payment. The credit crunch was exacerbated by the British blockade of the Danish West Indies, and Galt's firm went bankrupt (1:99–111).

86. When first encountering the Highland landowner, Corbet is struck by 'the politeness of his English', expecting to hear only 'the dislocated Celtic gibberish in use among the lower classes who frequent the Lowlands' (2:213).

87. In letter to his friend David Moir, Galt wrote of *Bogle Corbet*: 'It is an autobiography in the better sphere of life, and I have endeavoured to throw into the story every incident calculated to illustrate both the sept it belongs to, and his own individual portraiture, which I have hitherto succeeded in representing as no bad specimen of that mingled professional and philosophical character, which may sometimes be met with among the of the manufacturers of the first crop – that is, those who began their career about 1792' ('Memoir of Galt', p. lxxxix). Galt commenced his own professional life in 1795, as a clerk in the Greenock customs house, when he was sixteen.

88. The *OED* defines 'climacterial' as 'any of certain supposedly critical years of human life, when a person was considered to be particularly liable to change in health or fortune. Aulus Gellius identified every seventh year as climacteric, with the sixty-third being the most critical' ('climacterial, adj. and n.'). As it happened, Galt died seven years after the publication of his *Literary Life*, aged fifty-nine.

89. Trumpener, 'Annals of Ice', p. 45.

References

'aborigine, n. and adj.', *OED Online*, Oxford University Press, June 2019, www.oed.com/view/Entry/243055.

Adam, R. J., *Papers on Sutherland Estate Management, 1802–1816* (Edinburgh: Constable, 1972).

Adey, David, Ridley Beeton, Michael Chapman and Ernest Pereira (eds), *Companion to South African English Literature* (Johannesburg: Ad. Donker, 1986).

Alexander, Jeffrey C., 'Toward a Theory of Cultural Trauma', in Jeffrey C Alexander, Ron Eyerman, Bernhard Giesen, Neil J. Smelser and Piotr Sztompka, *Cultural Trauma and Collective Identity* (Berkeley: University of California Press, 2004).

Allen, Chadwick, *Blood Narrative: Indigenous Identity in American and Maori Literary and Activist Texts* (Durham, NC: Duke University Press, 2002).

Allen, Jessica L., 'Pringle's Pruning of Prince: *The History of Mary Prince* and the Question of Repetition', *Callaloo*, 35(2), Spring 2012, pp. 509–19.

Almeida, Joselyn, *Reimagining the Transatlantic, 1780–1890* (Burlington, VT: Ashgate, 2011).

Anderson, Benedict, *Imagined Communities* (London: Verso, 1991).

Andrews, Corey E., '"Ev'ry Heart can Feel": Scottish Poetic Responses to Slavery in the West Indies, from Blair to Burns', *International Journal of Scottish Literature*, 4, Spring/Summer 2008, pp. 1–22.

Andrews, William L., *To Tell a Free Story: The First Century of Afro-American Autobiography, 1760–1865* (Chicago: University of Illinois Press, 1988).

Anderson, Fred, *The Crucible of War: The Seven Years' War and the Fate of Empire in British North America, 1754–1766* (New York: Knopf, 2000).

Archer, Martin, *The Hudson's Bay Company's Land Tenures and the Occupation of Assiniboia by Lord Selkirk's Settlers* (London: William Clowes and Sons, 1898).

Armitage, David, 'Three Concepts of Atlantic History', in David Armitage and Michael J. Braddick (eds), *The British Atlantic World, 1500–1800*, 2nd edn (London: Palgrave Macmillan, 2009), pp. 13–29.

Armitage, David, and Michael J. Braddick (eds), *The British Atlantic World, 1500–1800*, 2nd edn (London: Palgrave Macmillan, 2009).

Ash, Marinell, *The Strange Death of Scottish History* (Edinburgh: Ramsay Head Press, 1980).
Ashcroft, Bill, Gareth Griffiths and Helen Tiffin, *The Empire Writes Back: Theory and Practice in Post-Colonial Literatures* (London: Routledge, 2010).
Assmann, Jan, 'Collective Memory and Cultural Identity', trans. John Czaplicka, *New German Critique*, 65, Cultural History/Cultural Studies, Spring–Summer, 1995, pp. 125–33.
Aubert de Gaspé, Phillipe-Joseph, *Les Anciens Canadiens* (Montreal: Fides, 1994).
Aubert de Gaspé, Phillipe-Joseph, *Cameron of Lochiel*, trans. Charles G. D. Roberts (Boston: L.C. Page, 1905).
Aubert de Gaspé, Phillipe-Joseph, *The Canadians of Old*, trans. Georgiana M. Pennée (Quebec: G & G. Desbarats, 1864).
Aubert de Gaspé, Phillipe-Joseph, *The Canadians of Old*, trans. Charles G. D. Roberts (New York: D. Appleton, 1890).
Aubert de Gaspé, Phillipe-Joseph, *Canadians of Old*, trans. Charles G. D. Roberts (Toronto: McClelland and Stewart, 1974).
Aubert de Gaspé, Phillipe-Joseph, *Canadians of Old*, trans. Jane Bierly (Montreal: Véhicule Press, 1996).
Austin, Linda M., *Nostalgia in Transition, 1780–1917* (Charlottesville: University of Virginia Press, 2007).
Axtell, James, *The Invasion Within: The Contest of Cultures in Colonial North America* (Oxford: Oxford University Press, 1985).
Bailyn, Bernard, *Atlantic History: Concept and Contours* (Cambridge, MA: Harvard University Press, 2005).
Bailyn, Bernard (ed.), *Strangers within the Realm: Cultural Margins of the First British Empire* (Chapel Hill: University of North Carolina Press, 1991).
Bailyn, Bernard, and Patricia L. Denault (eds), *Soundings in Atlantic History: Latent Structures and Intellectual Currents, 1500–1830* (Cambridge, MA: Harvard University Press 2011).
Bain, Robert C., 'Introduction', in John Neal, *Seventy-Six, 1823* (Bainbridge, NY: York Mail-Print, 1971).
Baker, Jr., Houston A., *Modernism and the Harlem Renaissance* (Chicago: University of Chicago Press, 2013).
Barash, Jeffrey Andrew, *Collective Memory and the Historical Past* (Chicago: University of Chicago Press, 2016).
Barker-Benfield, G. J., *The Culture of Sensibility* (Chicago: University of Chicago Press, 1992).
Barkwell, Lawrence, Leah M. Dorion and Audreen Hourie (eds), *Metis Legacy II: Michif Culture, Heritage, and Folkways* (Saskatoon: Gabriel Dumont Institute/Pemmican Publications, 2006).
Basu, Paul, *Highland Homecomings: Genealogy and Heritage Tourism in the Scottish Diaspora* (London: Routledge, 2007).

Basu, Paul, 'Narratives in a Landscape: Monuments and Memories of the Sutherland Clearances', Unpublished MSc thesis, University College London, 1996.
Baucom, Ian, 'Introduction', *The South Atlantic Quarterly*, 100(1), Winter 2001, pp. 1–13.
Baucom, Ian, *Specters of the Atlantic: Finance Capital, Slavery, and the Philosophy of History* (Durham, NC: Duke University Press, 2005).
Baumgartner, Barbara, 'The Body as Evidence: Resistance, Collaboration, and Appropriation in "The History of Mary Prince"', *Callaloo*, 24(1), Winter 2001, pp. 253–75.
Becker, John P., *The Story of Old Saratoga and History of Schuylerville* (Albany: Fort Orange Press, 1900).
Belich, James, *Replenishing the Earth: The Settler Revolution and the Rise of the Angloworld, 1783–1939* (Oxford: Oxford University Press, 2011).
Bender, John, 'Enlightenment Fiction and the Scientific Hypothesis', *Representations*, 61, Winter 1998, pp. 6–28.
Bergland, Renée L., *The National Uncanny: Indian Ghosts and American Subjects* (Hanover: University Press of New England, 2000).
Berkhofer, Robert F., *The White Man's Indian: The History of an Idea from Columbus to the Present* (New York: Knopf, 1978).
Beveridge, Craig, and Ronald Turnbull, *The Eclipse of Scottish Culture* (Edinburgh: Polygon, 1989).
Bierly, Jane, 'Introduction', Phillipe-Joseph Aubert de Gaspé, *Canadians of Old*, trans. Jane Bierly (Montreal: Véhicule Press, 1996).
Binnema, Theodore, Gerhard J. Ens and Rod Macleod (eds), *From Rupert's Land to Canada* (Edmonton: University of Alberta Press, 2001).
Bitterman, Rusty, 'On Remembering and Forgetting: Highland Memories within the Maritime Diaspora', in Marjory Harper and Michael Vance (eds), *Myth, Migration and the Making of Memory* (Halifax: Fernwood Press, 1999), pp. 253–66.
Bjornson, Richard, 'Victimization and Vindication in Smollett's *Roderick Random*', *Studies in Scottish Literature*, 13, 1978, pp. 196–210.
Black, Fiona A., 'Bookseller to the World: North America', in Bill Bell (ed.), *The Edinburgh History of the Book in Scotland: Vol. 3 Ambition and Industry* (Edinburgh: Edinburgh University Press, 2007).
Black, Ronald I., 'The Gaelic Academy: The Cultural Commitment of the Highland Society of Scotland', *Scottish Gaelic Studies*, 14(2), 1986, pp. 1–38.
Blakemore, Steven, 'Family Resemblances: The Texts and Contexts of "Rip Van Winkle"', *Early American Literature*, 35(2), 2000, pp. 187–212.
Bloodgood, S. Dewitt, *The Sexagenary: or, Reminiscences of the American Revolution* (Albany: W. C. Little and O. Steele, 1833).
Bobbé, Dorothie, *The New World Journey of Anne MacVicar* (New York: G. P. Putnam's Sons, 1971).
Bohrer, Martha, 'John Galt's *Annals of the Parish* and the Narrative Strategies of Tales of Locale', in Regina Hewitt (ed.), *John Galt: Observations*

and Conjectures on Literature, History, and Society (Lewisburg: Bucknell University Press, 2012), pp. 95–118.
Bolt, Christine, *The Anti-Slavery Movement and Reconstruction: A Study of Anglo-American Co-Operation, 1833–1877* (Oxford: Oxford University Press, 1969).
Boulukos, George, *The Grateful Slave* (Cambridge: Cambridge University Press, 2008).
Boyce Davies, Carole, *Black Women, Writing and Identity: Migrations of the Subject* (London: Routledge, 1994).
Boym, Svetlana, *The Future of Nostalgia* (New York: Basic Books, 2001).
Brake, Laurel, 'Maga, the Shilling Monthlies, and the New Journalism', in David Finkelstein (ed.), *Print Culture and the Blackwood Tradition, 1805–1930* (Toronto: University of Toronto Press, 2006).
Brantlinger, Patrick, *Dark Vanishings: Discourse on the Extinction of Primitive Races, 1800–1930* (Ithaca: Cornell University Press, 2003).
Bryden, John A., and Charles Geisler, 'Community-Based Land Reform: Lessons from Scotland', *Land Use Policy*, 24, 2007, pp. 24–34.
Buell, Lawrence, 'American Literary Emergence as a Postcolonial Phenomenon', *American Literary History*, 4(3), Autumn 1992, pp. 411–42.
Bumsted, J. M., 'Introduction', in Thomas Douglas Selkirk, *The Collected Writings of Lord Selkirk*, ed. J. M. Bumsted (Winnipeg: Manitoba Records Society, 1984).
Bumsted, J. M., *Lord Selkirk: A Life* (Winnipeg: University of Manitoba Press, 2008).
Bumsted, J. M., *The People's Clearance: Highland Emigration to British North America, 1770–1815* (Edinburgh: Edinburgh University Press, 1982).
Bunn, David, '"Our Wattled Cot" Mercantile and Domestic Space in Thomas Pringle's African Landscapes', in W. J. T. Mitchell (ed.), *Landscape and Power* (Chicago: University of Chicago Press, 1994), pp. 127–73.
Burke, Peter, 'History as Social Memory', in Thomas Butler (ed.), *Memory: History, Culture and the Mind* (London: Basil Blackwell, 1989), pp. 97–113.
Burnham, Michelle, *Captivity and Sentiment* (Hanover: University Press of New England, 1997).
Burnham, Michelle, 'The Journey Between: Liminality and Dialogism in Mary White Rowlandson's Captivity Narrative', *Early American Literature* 28, 1993, pp. 6–75.
Cabajsky, Andrea, 'The National Tale from Ireland to French Canada: Putting Generic Incentive into a New Perspective', *The Canadian Journal of Irish Studies*, 31(1), Spring 2005, pp. 29–37.
Calder, Angus, 'Thomas Pringle [1789–1834]: A Scottish Poet in South Africa', *English in Africa*, 9(1), May 1982, pp. 1–13.
Calloway, Colin G., *White People, Indians, and Highlanders* (Oxford: Oxford University Press, 2008).

Cameron, Wendy, and Mary McDougall Maude, *Assisting Emigration to Upper Canada: The Petworth Project, 1832–1837* (Montreal: McGill-Queen's University Press, 2000).
Campbell, Alexander, *The Grampians Desolate* (Edinburgh: John Moir, 1804).
Campbell, Matthew, Jacqueline M. Labbe and Sally Shuttleworth (eds), *Memory and Memorials, 1789–1914: Literary and Cultural Perspectives* (London: Routledge, 2000).
Canny, Nicholas P., 'Atlantic History: What and Why?' *European Review*, 9, 2001, pp. 399–41.
Canny, Nicholas P., 'Writing Atlantic History; or, Reconfiguring the History of Colonial British America', *Journal of American History*, 86, 1999, pp. 1093–114.
Cariou, Warren, 'Haunted Prairie: Aboriginal "Ghosts" and the Spectres of Settlement', *University of Toronto Quarterly*, 75, 2006, pp. 727–34.
Carruthers, Gerald, 'Remembering John Galt', in Regina Hewitt (ed.), *John Galt: Observations and Conjectures on Literature, History, and Society* (Lewisburg: Bucknell University Press, 2012), pp. 33–51.
Carruthers, Gerald, and Colin Kidd (eds), *International Companion to John Galt* (Glasgow: Scottish Literature International, 2017).
Carter, Jennifer, and Joan H. Pittock (eds), *Aberdeen and the Enlightenment* (Aberdeen: Aberdeen University Press, 1987).
Caruth, Cathy, *Unclaimed Experience: Trauma, Narrative, and History* (Baltimore: Johns Hopkins University Press, 1996).
Casgrain, Henri-Raymond, *Philippe Aubert De Gaspé* (Quebec: Legér Brousseau, 1871).
Castiglia, Christopher, *Bound and Determined* (Chicago: University of Chicago Press, 1996).
Cattermole, William, *Emigration: The Advantages of Emigration to Canada Being the Substance of Two Lectures Delivered at the Town-Hall, Colchester, and the Mechanics Institution, Ipswich* (London: Simpkin & Marshall, 1831).
Chalmers, George, Letter to Anne Grant, 21 May 1808, University of Edinburgh Library La.II.357, ff. 141–3.
Chambers, Robert, *Minor Antiquities of Edinburgh, or 'Reekiana'* (Edinburgh: W. & R. Chambers, 1833).
Chambers, Robert, *Traditions of Edinburgh* (Edinburgh: W. & C. Tait, 1825).
Chambers, Robert, *Traditions of Edinburgh*, New Edition (Edinburgh: W. & R. Chambers, 1868).
Chandler, James, *England in 1819: The Politics of Literary Culture and the Case of Romantic Historicism* (Champaign: University of Chicago Press, 1998).
'Chief & Council', Bkejwanong Walpole Island First Nation, https://walpoleislandfirstnation.ca/chief-council.

Choate, Rufus, *Addresses and Orations of Rufus Choate* (Boston: Little, Brown, 1891).
Clifford, James, 'Diasporas', *Cultural Anthropology*, 9(3), August 1994, pp. 302–38.
'climacterial, adj. and n.', *OED Online*, Oxford University Press, June 2019, www.oed.com/view/Entry/34308.
Clyde, Robert, *From Rebel to Hero: The Image of the Highlander, 1745–1830* (East Linton: Tuckwell, 1998).
Cockburn, Henry, *Journal of Henry Cockburn: Being a Continuation of the Memorials of His Time, 1831–1854* (Edinburgh: Edmonston & Douglas, 1874).
Cockburn, Henry, *Memorials of His Time* (Edinburgh: Adam and Charles Black, 1856).
Cockburn, Henry, *Some Letters of Lord Cockburn: With Pages Omitted from the Memorials of His Time*, ed. Harry A. Cockburn (Edinburgh: Grant & Murray, 1932).
Coclanis, Peter A. 'Drang nach Osten: Bernard Bailyn, the World-Island, and the Idea of Atlantic History', *Journal of World History*, 13(1), 2002, pp. 169–82.
Coetzee, J. M., *White Writing: On the Culture of Letters in South Africa* (New Haven: Yale University Press, 1988).
Cohen, Margaret, 'Traveling Genres', *New Literary History*, 34(3), 2003, pp. 481–96.
Colden, Cadwallader, *History of the Five Indian Nations of Canada* (London: T. Osborne, 1747).
Coleman, Thelma, *The Canada Company* (Stratford, ON: Cummings, 1978).
Coleridge, Samuel Taylor, 'On the Slave Trade', in ed. Lewis Patton, *The Collected Works of Samuel Taylor Coleridge, Vol 2, The Watchman* (Princeton: Princeton University Press, 1970).
Colley, Ann C., *Nostalgia and Recollection in Victorian Culture* (Macmillan: St. Martin's, 1998).
Colley, Linda, *Britons: Forging the Nation, 1707–1837* (New Haven: Yale University Press, 1992).
Corbett, Mary, *Allegories of Union in Irish and English Writing, 1790–1870* (Cambridge: Cambridge University Press, 2000).
Costain, Keith M., 'The Spirit of the Age and the Scottish Fiction of John Galt', *The Wordsworth Circle*, 11(2), 1980, pp. 98–106.
Costain, Keith M., 'Theoretical History and the Novel: The Scottish Fiction of John Galt', *ELH*, 43(3), Autumn 1976, pp. 342–65.
Craig, Cairns, *Associationism and the Literary Imagination* (Edinburgh: Edinburgh University Press, 2007).
Craig, Cairns, *Out of History: Narrative Paradigms in Scottish and British Culture* (Edinburgh: Polygon, 1996).
Crawford, Robert, *Devolving English Literature* (Oxford: Clarendon Press, 1992).

Creighton, Helen, and Calum MacLeod, *Gaelic Songs in Nova Scotia* (Ottawa: National Museums of Canada, 1964).

Cyclopedia of American Literature, Vol 1, ed, Evert A. Duyckinck (Philadelphia: W. Rutter, 1875).

Daly, Kirsten, '"Return No More!": Highland Emigration and Romantic Nostalgia', *Literature and History*, 9(1), April 2000, pp. 24–42.

Dames, Nicholas, *Amnesiac Selves: Nostalgia, Forgetting, and British Fiction, 1810–1870* (Oxford: Oxford University Press, 2001).

Davis, Leith, '"Coming to the Past": Alastair MacLeod's *No Great Mischief* and Post-Devolution Scottish Emigrant Identity', in Caroline McCracken-Flesher (ed.), *Culture, Nation, and the New Scottish Parliament* (Lewisburg: Bucknell University Press, 2007).

Davis, Leith, *Acts of Union: Scotland and the Literary Negotiation of the British Nation, 1707–1830* (Stanford: Stanford University Press, 1998).

Davis, Leith, Ian Duncan and Janet Sorensen (eds), *Scotland and the Borders of Romanticism* (Cambridge: Cambridge University Press, 2004).

Davis, Lennard J., *Factual Fictions: The Origins of the English Novel* (Philadelphia: University of Pennsylvania Press, 1996).

Deane, Seamus, *Strange Country: Modernity and Nationhood in Irish Writing since 1790* (Oxford: Oxford University Press, 1997).

Dekker, George, *The American Historical Romance* (Cambridge: Cambridge University Press, 1987).

DeLucia, JoEllen, *A Feminine Enlightenment: British Women Writers and the Philosophy of Progress, 1759–1820* (Edinburgh: Edinburgh University Press, 2015).

Deschamps, Nicole, 'Les "anciens Canadiens" de 1860: une société de seigneurs et de va-nu-pieds', *Études françaises*, 1(3), 1965, pp. 3–15.

Devine, T. M., *Clanship to Crofter's War* (Manchester: Manchester University Press, 1994).

Devine, T. M., 'Lost to History', in T. M. Devine (ed.), *Recovering Scotland's Slavery Past: The Caribbean Connection* (Edinburgh: Edinburgh University Press, 2015).

Devine, T. M. (ed.), *Recovering Scotland's Slavery Past: The Caribbean Connection* (Edinburgh: Edinburgh University Press, 2015).

Devine, T. M., *Scotland's Empire & the Shaping of the Americas, 1600–1815* (Washington, DC: Smithsonian Books, 2003).

Devine, T. M., *The Scottish Nation* (London: Penguin Books, 1999).

Dickinson, W. Croft, 'John Galt: "The Provost" and the Burgh, Being the John Galt Lecture for 1954' (Greenock: Telegraph, 1954).

Dippie, Brian W., *The Vanishing American: White Attitudes and U.S. Indian Policy* (Lawrence: University Press of Kansas, 1982).

Dodgshon, R. A., *From Chiefs to Landlords* (Edinburgh: Edinburgh University Press, 1998).

Dondore, Dorothy, 'The Debt of Two Dyed-in-the-Wool Americans to Mrs. Grant's *Memoirs*: Cooper's *Satanstoe* and Paulding's *The Dutchman's Fireside*', *American Literature*, 12(1), March 1940, pp. 52–8.

Ducharme, Michel, 'Interpreting the Past, Shaping the Present, and Envisioning the Future: Remembering the Conquest in Nineteenth-Century Quebec', in Phillip Buckner and John G. Reid (eds), *Remembering 1759: The Conquest of Canada in Historical Memory* (University of Toronto Press, 2012), pp. 136–60.

Dunbar, Rob, 'The Poetry of the Emigrant Generation', *Transactions of the Gaelic Society of Inverness*, 64, 2008, pp. 22–125.

Duncan, Ian, *Scott's Shadow: The Novel in Romantic Edinburgh* (Princeton: Princeton University Press, 2007).

Duncan, Ian, with Leith Davis and Janet Sorensen, 'Introduction', in Leith Davis, Ian Duncan and Janet Sorensen (eds), *Scotland and the Borders of Romanticism* (Cambridge: Cambridge University Press, 2004), pp. 1–19.

Dunlop, William 'Tiger', *Statistical Sketches of Upper Canada for the Use of Emigrants written by a Backwoodsman* (London: John Murray, 1832).

Dwyer, John, *The Age of the Passions: An Interpretation of Adam Smith and the Scottish Enlightenment* (East Linton: Tuckwell Press, 1998).

Dwyer, John, *Virtuous Discourse: Sensibility and Community in Late Eighteenth-Century Scotland* (Edinburgh: John Donald, 1987).

Ebersole, Gary L., *Captured by Texts: Puritan to Postmodern Images of Indian Captivity* (Charlottesville: University of Virginia Press, 1995).

Elliott, J. H., 'Atlantic History: A Circumnavigation', in David Armitage and Michael J. Braddick (eds), *The British Atlantic World, 1500–1800*, 2nd edn (London: Palgrave Macmillan, 2009), pp. 253–70.

Ellis, David M., 'Yankee-Dutch Confrontation in the Albany Area', *The New England Quarterly*, 45(2), June 1972, pp. 262–70.

Ellison, Julie, *Cato's Tears and the Making of Anglo-American Emotion* (Chicago: University of Chicago Press, 1999).

Ens, Gerhard J., *Homeland to Hinterland: The Changing Worlds of the Red River Metis in the Nineteenth Century* (Toronto: University of Toronto Press, 1996).

Erll, Astrid, 'Generation in Literary History: Three Constellations of Generationality, Genealogy, and Memory', *New Literary History*, 45(3), Summer 2014, pp. 385–409.

Esterhammer, Angela, 'Galt the Speculator: Sir Andrew Wylie, the Entail, and Lawrie Todd', in Gerald Carruthers and Colin Kidd (eds), *International Companion to John Galt* (Glasgow: Scottish Literature International, 2017), pp. 44–56.

Fairhurst, Horace, 'The Surveys for the Sutherland Clearances, 1813–1820', *Scottish Studies*, 8, 1964, pp. 1–18.

Felman, Shoshana, and Dori Laub, *Testimony: Crises of Witnessing in Literature, Psychoanalysis, and History* (London: Routledge, 1992).

Fentress, James, and Chris Wickham, *Social Memory* (Oxford: Blackwell, 1992).

Ferguson, Frances, 'Romantic Memory', *Studies in Romanticism*, 35(4), 1996, pp. 509–33.

Ferguson, Moira, *Subject to Others: British Women Writers and Colonial Slavery, 1670–1834* (London: Routledge, 1992).

Ferland, Catherine, and Dave Corriveau, *La Corriveau: de l'histoire à la legend* (Quebec City: Septentrion, 2014).

Ferris, Ina, *The Achievement of Literary Authority* (Ithaca: Cornell University Press, 1991).

Ferris, Ina, 'Melancholy, Memory, and the "Narrative Situation" of History in Post-Enlightenment Scotland', in Leith Davis, Ian Duncan and Janet Sorensen (eds), *Scotland and the Borders of Romanticism* (Cambridge: Cambridge University Press, 2004), pp. 77–93.

Ferris, Ina, 'Translation from the Borders: Encounter and Recalcitrance in *Waverley* and *Clan-Albin*', *Eighteenth-Century Fiction*, 9(2), January 1997, pp. 203–22.

Fielding, Penny, *Writing and Orality* (Oxford: Oxford University Press, 1996).

Fladeland, Betty, *Men and Brothers: Anglo-American Antislavery Cooperation* (Champaign: University of Illinois Press, 1972).

Flanagan, Thomas, *Metis Lands in Manitoba* (Calgary: University of Calgary Press, 1991).

Fliegelman, Jay, *Prodigals and Pilgrims: The American Revolution against Patriarchal Authority, 1750–1800* (Cambridge: Cambridge University Press, 1982).

Foster, Frances Smith, *Witnessing Slavery* (Madison: University of Wisconsin Press, 1994).

Foster, Shirley, 'The Construction of Self in *Sunny Memories*', in Denise Kohn, Sarah Meer and Emily B. Todd (eds), *Transatlantic Stowe: Harriet Beecher Stowe and European Culture* (Iowa City: University of Iowa Press, 2006), pp. 149–66.

Fraser, Nancy, 'Social Justice in the Age of Identity Politics: Redistribution, Recognition, and Participation', in Nancy Fraser and Axel Honneth, *Redistribution or Recognition? A Political-Philosophical Exchange* (London: Verso, 2003), pp. 7–109.

Fry, Michael, *The Scottish Empire* (Edinburgh: Birlinn, 2001).

Frye, Northrup, 'Haunted by Lack of Ghosts', in David Staines (ed.), *The Canadian Imagination* (Cambridge, MA: Harvard University Press, 1977).

Fryer, Peter, *Staying Power: The History of Black People in Britain* (Edmonton: University of Alberta, 1984)

Gallagher, Catherine, *The Industrial Reformation of English Fiction, 1832–1867* (Chicago: University of Chicago Press, 1985).

Galt, John, *Annals of the Parish*, ed. James Kinsley (Oxford: Oxford University Press, 1986).

Galt, John, *The Autobiography of John Galt* (London: Cochrane and M'Crone, 1833).

Galt, John, *The Bachelor's Wife* (Edinburgh: Oliver and Boyd, 1824).
Galt, John, 'Bandana on Emigration', *Blackwood's Edinburgh Magazine*, 20, July–December 1826, pp. 470–8.
Galt, John, 'Bandana on Emigration, Letter First', *Blackwood's Edinburgh Magazine* 15, January–June 1824, pp. 433–40.
Galt, John, *Bogle Corbet; or, the Emigrants* (London: Henry Colburn and Richard Bentley, 1831).
Galt, John, *Bogle Corbet*, ed. Elizabeth Waterston (Toronto: McClelland & Stewart, 1977).
Galt, John, *Lawrie Todd: or the Settlers in the Woods* (London: Henry Colburn and Richard Bentley, 1830).
Galt, John, *Lawrie Todd: or the Settlers in the Woods. Revised, Corrected, and Illustrated with a New Introduction, Notes, etc. by the Author* (London: Richard Bentley, New Burlington Street, [Late Colburn And Bentley]: Bell and Bradfute, Edinburgh; Cumming, Dublin; And Galignani, Paris, 1832).
Galt, John, 'Letters on West Indian Slavery, Letter 1', *Fraser's Magazine for Town and Country*, 2, November 1830, pp. 440–9.
Galt, John, *The Literary Life and Miscellanies of John Galt* (Edinburgh: William Blackwood, 1834).
Galt, John, 'Means of Lessening West Indian Stress', *Fraser's Magazine for Town and Country*, 3, April 1831, pp. 356–350.
Galt, John, 'A Statistical Account of Upper Canada', *The Philosophical Magazine*, 29(113), October 1807, pp. 3–10.
Galt, John, 'The Whole West Indian Question', *Fraser's Magazine for Town and Country*, 8, July 1833, pp. 81–90.
Games, Alison, 'Atlantic History: Definitions, Challenges, and Opportunities', *The American Historical Review*, 111(3), 2006, pp. 741–57.
Gardiner, Michael, 'Introduction', in Michael Gardiner, Graeme McDonald and Niall O'Gallagher (eds), *Scottish Literature and Postcolonial Literature: Comparative Texts and Critical Perspectives* (Edinburgh: Edinburgh University Press, 2011).
Gardiner, Michael, Graeme McDonald and Niall O'Gallagher (eds), *Scottish Literature and Postcolonial Literature: Comparative Texts and Critical Perspectives* (Edinburgh: Edinburgh University Press, 2011).
Garneau, F. X., *Histoire du Canada depuis sa découverte jusqu'à nos jours* (Quebec City: N. Aubin, 1845).
Garneau, F. X., *History of Canada from the Time of Its Discovery till the Union Year of 1840–41*, trans. Andrew Bell (Montreal: John Lovell, 1862).
Garside, Peter, 'The English Novel in the Romantic Era', in Peter Garside and Rainer Schöwerling, *The English Novel, 1770–1829: 2* (Oxford: Oxford University Press, 2000).
Garside, Peter, 'Popular Fiction and National Tale: Hidden Origins of Scott's *Waverley*', *Nineteenth-Century Literature*, 46(1), June 1991, pp. 30–53.
Gates, Jr., Henry Louis, *The Signifying Monkey: A Theory of African American Literary Criticism* (Oxford: Oxford University Press, 1988).

Gates, Jr., Henry Louis (ed.), *The Classic Slave Narratives* (Harmondsworth: Penguin, 1987).

Gibb, Andrew Dewar, *The Scottish Empire* (A. MacLehose & Co., 1937).

Gibbons, Luke, *Edmund Burke and Ireland* (Cambridge: Cambridge University Press, 2003).

Gikandi, Simon, *Slavery and the Culture of Taste* (Princeton: Princeton University Press, 2011).

Giles, Paul, *Transatlantic Insurrections: British Culture and the Formation of American Literature, 1730–1860* (Philadelphia: University of Pennsylvania Press, 2001).

Gilroy, Beryl, *Stedman and Joanna – A Love in Bondage* (New York: Vantage, 1991).

Gilroy, Paul, *The Black Atlantic* (Cambridge, MA: Harvard University Press, 1993).

Glissant, Eduoard, *Caribbean Discourse*, trans. J. Michael Dash (Charlottesville: University Press of Virginia, 1989).

Göbel, Walter, 'Washington Irving's "Rip Van Winkle," a Postcolonial Reading, or In Search of a Usable Past', *Semiotic Encounters*, 26, 2009, pp. 103–18.

Goodman, Kevis, 'Romantic Poetry and the Science of Nostalgia', in James Chandler and Maureen N. McLane (eds), *The Cambridge Companion to British Romantic Poetry* (Cambridge: Cambridge University Press, 2008), pp. 195–216.

Gordon, Ian A., *John Galt: the Life of a Writer* (Toronto: University of Toronto Press, 1972).

Gottlieb, Evan, *Feeling British: Sympathy and National Identity in Scottish and English Writing, 1707–1832* (Lewisburg: Bucknell University Press, 2007).

[Grant, Anne], *Essays on the Superstitions of the Highlanders of Scotland* (London: Longman, Hurst, Rees, Orme, and Brown, 1811).

Grant, Anne, 'Letters Concerning Highland Affairs in the 18th Century', ed. J. R. N. Macphail, in *Diary of Sir Archibald Johnston, Lord Wariston, 1639: The Preservation of the Honours of Scotland, 1651–52: Lord Mar's Legacies, 1722–1727: Letters Concerning Highland Affairs in the 18th Century, by Mrs. Grant of Laggan* (Edinburgh: T. and A. Constable, 1896).

Grant, Anne, *Letters from the Mountains*, ed. Kirsteen McCue and Pam Perkins, *Women's Travel Writings in Scotland*, Vols 1–3 (London: Routledge, 2017).

Grant, Anne, *Memoir and Correspondence of Mrs. Anne Grant of Laggan*, ed. J. P. Grant (London: Longman, Brown, Green, and Longmans, 1845).

Grant, Anne, *Memoirs of an American Lady: with Sketches of Manners and Scenery in America, as They Existed Previous to the Revolution* (London: Longman, Hurst, Rees, and Orme, 1808).

Grant, Anne, *Memoirs of an American Lady: with Sketches of Manners and Scenery in America, As They Existed Previous to The Revolution* (Albany: Joel Munsell, 1876).
Grant, Anne, *Memoirs of an American Lady: with Sketches of Manners and Scenery in America, As They Existed Previous to The Revolution* (New York: Dodd, Mead, 1901).
Grant, Anne, *Poems on Various Subjects* (London: Longman and Rees, 1803).
Gray, Malcolm, *The Highland Economy 1750–1850* (Edinburgh: Oliver and Boyd, 1957).
Greiner, Rae, 'Sympathy Time: Adam Smith, George Eliot, and the Realist Novel', *Narrative* 17(3), October 2009, pp. 291–311.
'Guelph, Ontario: Anarchists Paint Bomb Statue of John Galt', Infoshop News, 5 August 2008, http://news.infoshop.org/article.php?story=20080805143218265.
'Guelph's John Galt Statue Defaced with Red Paint over Long Weekend', *Guelph Mercury Tribune*, 7 August 2008, http://news.guelphmercury.com/News/article/364438.
Gwilliam, Tassie, '"Scenes of Horror": Scenes of Sensibility: Sentimentality and Slavery in John Gabriel Stedman's *Narrative of a Five Years Expedition against the Revolted Negroes of Surinam*', *ELH*, 65(3), Fall 1998, pp. 653–73.
Halbwachs, Maurice, *Les Cadres sociaux de la memoire* (Paris: F. Alcan, 1925).
Halbwachs, Maurice, *The Collective Memory*, trans. J. Ditter, Jr and Vida Yazdi Ditter (New York: Harper & Row, 1980).
Halbwachs, Maurice, *On Collective Memory*, ed. and trans. Lewis A. Coser (Chicago: University of Chicago Press, 1992).
Halbwachs, Maurice, *The Psychology of Social Class*, trans. Claire Delavenay (Glencoe: The Free Press, 1958).
Hall, Catherine, '"The Most Unbending Conservative in Britain": Archibald Alison and Pro-Slavery Discourse', in T. M. Devine (ed.), *Recovering Scotland's Slavery Past: The Caribbean Connection* (Edinburgh: Edinburgh University Press, 2015).
Hall, Stuart, 'New Ethnicities', in David Morley and Kuan-Hsing Chen Stuart (eds), *Stuart Hall: Critical Dialogues in Cultural Studies* (London: Routledge, 1996), pp. 442–51.
Halliwell, Kevin, 'John Galt and the Paratext: The Discourse of Authentication in North American Emigration Literature', STAR Project Website, http:// www.star.ac.uk/star-publications/e-texts.aspx.
Halttunen, Karen, 'Humanitarianism and the Pornography of Pain in Anglo-American Culture', *The American Historical Review*, 100(2), April 1995, pp. 303–34.
Hamilton, Douglas, *Scotland, The Caribbean and the Atlantic World, 1750–1820* (Manchester: Manchester University Press, 2005).

Hammerschmidt, Sören, 'Social Authorship and the Mediation of Memory in Anne Grant's Poetry', *European Romantic Review*, 30(2), DOI: 10.1080/10509585.2019.1582417, pp. 199–220.

Harper, Marjory, and Michael E. Vance (eds), *Myth, Migration, and the Making of Memory: Scotia and Nova Scotia, c.1700–1990* (Halifax: Fernwood Press, 1999).

Hay, Robert P., 'The American Revolution Twice Recalled: Lafayette's Visit and the Election of 1824', *Indiana Magazine of History*, 69(1), pp. 43–62.

Hayne, David M., 'The Historical Novel and French Canada', Unpublished PhD diss., University of Ottawa, 1945.

Hechter, Michael, *Internal Colonialism: The Celtic Fringe in British National Development, 1536–1966* (Berkeley: Berkeley University Press, 1975).

Hewitt, Regina, 'Introduction', in Regina Hewitt (ed.), *John Galt: Observations and Conjectures on Literature, History, and Society* (Lewisburg: Bucknell University Press, 2012).

Hewitt, Regina (ed.), *John Galt: Observations and Conjectures on Literature, History, and Society* (Lewisburg: Bucknell University Press, 2012).

Hinderaker, Eric, *The Two Hendricks: Unraveling a Mohawk Mystery* (Cambridge, MA: Harvard University Press, 2010).

Hobsbawm, Eric, *The Age of Revolution: Europe 1789–1848* (New York: Praeger Publishers, 1969).

Hogan, Liam, 'Debunking the Imagery of the "Irish Slaves" Meme', Medium.com., https://medium.com/@Limerick1914/the-imagery-of-the-irish-slaves-myth-dissected-143e70aa6e74.

Hook, Andrew, *From Goosecreek to Gandercleugh: Studies in Scottish-American Literary and Cultural History* (Edinburgh: Tuckwell, 1999).

Hook, Andrew, 'Scotland, the USA, and National Literatures in the Nineteenth Century', in Gerard Carruthers, David Goldie and Alastair Renfrew (eds), *Scotland and the 19th-Century World* (Leiden: Rodopi, 2012).

Hook, Andrew, *Scotland and America: A Study of Cultural Relations, 1750–1835* (Glasgow: Blackie, 1975).

Hook, Andrew, and Richard B. Sher (eds), *The Glasgow Enlightenment* (East Linton: Tuckwell Press, 1997).

Hope, Ascott R., 'A Scotch Lassie in America', *Young Days of Authors* (London: John Hogg, n.d.), pp. 243–98.

Hopfl, H. M., 'From Savage to Scotsman: Conjectural History in the Scottish Enlightenment', *Journal of British Studies*, 17(2), Spring 1978, pp. 19–40.

Horwitz, Howard, '"Rip Van Winkle" and Legendary National Memory', *Western Humanities Review*, 58, 2004, pp. 34–47.

Hoxie, Frederick E., 'Why Treaties?', in Mark A. Lindquist and Martin Zanger (eds), *Buried Roots and Indestructible Seeds: The Survival of American Indian Life in Story, History, and Spirit* (Madison: University of Wisconsin Press, 1994), pp. 85–105.

Hulme, Peter, *Colonial Encounters: Europe and the Native Caribbean, 1492–1797* (London: Routledge, 1992).
Hume, David, *A Treatise of Human Nature*, ed. David Fate Norton and Mary J. Norton (Oxford: Oxford University Press, 2000).
Hunter, James, *A Dance Called America* (Edinburgh: Mainstream, 1994).
Hunter, James, *The Making of the Crofting Community* (Edinburgh: John Donald, 1976).
Hunter, James, *Set Adrift upon the World: The Sutherland Clearances* (Edinburgh: Birlinn, 2015).
Hutton, Patrick H., *History as an Art of Memory* (Hanover: University Press of New England, 1993).
Huyssen, Andreas, *Present Pasts: Urban Palimpsests and the Politics of Memory* (Stanford: Stanford University Press, 2003).
Illbrick, Helmut, *Nostalgia: Origins and Ends of an Unenlightened Disease* (Chicago: Northwestern University Press, 2012).
Insko, Jeffrey, 'Eyewitness to History: the Antinarrative Aesthetic of Neal's *Seventy-Six*', in Edward Watts and David J. Carlson (eds), *John Neal and Nineteenth-Century American Literature and Culture* (Lewisburg: Bucknell University Press, 2012), pp. 57–74.
Irvine, Alexander, *An Inquiry into the Causes and Effects of Emigration from the Highlands and Western Islands of Scotland* (Edinburgh: Peter Hill, 1802).
Irvine, Robert P., 'Canada, Class, and Colonization in John Galt's *Bogle Corbet*', in Robert Lawson-Peebles and Kristin A. Cook (eds), *Writing the Americas, 1480–1826*, issue of *The Yearbook of English Studies*, 46, 2016, pp. 259–76.
Irving, Washington, *Diedrich Knickerbocker's A History of New York*, ed. Stanley Williams and Tremaine McDowell (New York: Harcourt, Brace, 1927).
Irving, Washington, *The Sketch-Book of Geoffrey Crayon, Gent.*, ed. Haskell S. Springer, *The Complete Works of Washington Irving* (Boston, MA: Twayne, 1978).
Irving, Washington, *The Sketch-Book of Geoffrey Crayon, Gent.*, ed. Susan Manning (Oxford: Oxford University Press, 1996).
Jarrells, Anthony, 'Short Fictional Forms and the Rise of the Tale', in Peter Garside and Karen O'Brien (eds), *The Oxford History of the Novel in English, Vol. 2. English and British Fiction, 1720–1820* (Oxford: Oxford University Press, 2015), pp. 478–94.
[Jeffrey, Francis], 'Review of *Essays on the Superstitions of the Highlanders of Scotland*', *Edinburgh Review*, 18(36), August 1811, pp. 480–510.
Johnson, Samuel, *A Journey to the Western Islands of Scotland*, ed. Peter Levi (Harmondsworth: Penguin, 1984).
Jones, Catherine, *Literary Memory: Scott's Waverley Novels and the Psychology of Narrative* (Lewisburg: Bucknell University Press, 2003).

Jones, Catherine, 'Scott's *The Heart of Midlothian* and the Disordered Memory', in Matthew Campbell, Jacqueline M. Labbe and Sally Shuttleworth (eds), *Memory and Memorials, 1789–1914: Literary and Cultural Perspectives* (London: Routledge, 2000).

Jordan, Winthrop, *White over Black: American Attitudes toward the Negro, 1550–1812* (Durham, NC: University of North Carolina Press, 1968).

Kammen, Michael, *The Mystic Chords of Memory: The Transformation of Tradition in American Culture* (New York: Alfred A. Knopf, 1991).

Kammen, Michael, *A Season of Youth: The American Revolution and the Historical Imagination* (Ithaca: Cornell University Press, 1978).

Kay, Jackie, 'Missing Faces', *The Guardian*, 23 March 2007, https://www.theguardian.com/books/2007/mar/24/featuresreviews.guardianreview25.

Kennedy, Michael, '"Lochaber No More": A Critical Examination of Highland Emigration Mythology', in Marjory Harper and Michael E. Vance (eds), *Myth, Migration, and the Making of Memory: Scotia and Nova Scotia, c.1700–1990* (Halifax: Fernwood Press 1999), pp. 267–97.

Kidd, Colin, *Subverting Scotland's Past: Scottish Whig Historians and the Creation of an Anglo-British Identity 1689–1830* (Cambridge: Cambridge University Press, 1993).

Kidd, Sheila M., 'Caraid nan Gaidheal and "Friend of Emigration": Gaelic Emigration Literature of the 1840s', *The Scottish Historical Review*, 81(1), 21 April 2002, pp. 52–6.

Killick, Tim, *British Short Fiction in the Early Nineteenth Century: The Rise of the Tale* (London: Routledge, 2008).

Klarer, Mario, 'Humanitarian Pornography: John Gabriel Stedman's *Narrative of a Five Years Expedition Against the Revolted Negroes of Surinam* (1796)', *New Literary History*, 36, 2005, pp. 559–87.

Klein, Kerwin Lee, 'On the Emergence of Memory in Historical Discourse', *Representations*, 69, Special Issue: *Grounds for Remembering*, Winter 2000, pp. 127–50.

Klooster, Wim, *Revolutions in the Atlantic World: A Comparative History* (New York: New York University Press, 2009).

Klopper, Dirk, 'Politics of the Pastoral: The Poetry of Thomas Pringle', *English in Africa*, 17(1), May 1990, pp. 21–59.

Knapp, Steven, 'Collective Memory and the Actual Past', *Representations*, 26, Special Issue: *Memory and Counter-Memory*, Spring 1989, pp. 123–49.

Kohn, Denise, Sarah Meer and Emily B. Todd (eds), *Transatlantic Stowe: Harriet Beecher Stowe and European Culture* (Iowa City: University of Iowa Press, 2006).

Konkle, Maureen, *Writing Indian Nations: Native Intellectuals and the Politics of Historiography, 1827–1863* (Chapel Hill: University of North Carolina Press, 2004).

Koselleck, Reinhart, *Futures Past: On the Semantics of Historical Time* (New York: Columbia University Press, 1985).

Kröller, Eva-Marie, 'Walter Scott in America, English Canada, and Quebec: A Comparison', *Canadian Review of Comparative Literature/Revue candienne de littérature comparée*, 7(1), Winter/Hiver 1980, pp. 32–46.

Kuczynski, Peter, 'Intertextuality in Rip Van Winkle: Irving's Use of Büsching's Folk Tale Peter Klaus in an Age of Transition', in Michael Gassenmeier, Petre Bridzun, Jens Martin Gurr and Frank Eric Pointner (eds), *British Romantics as Readers: Intertextualities, Maps of Misreading, Reinterpretations: Festschrift für Horst Meller* (Heidelberg: Universitätsverlag C. Winter, 1998), pp. 295–318.

LaCapra, Dominick, *Writing History, Writing Trauma* (Baltimore: Johns Hopkins University Press, 2001).

La Corne, Saint-Luc de, *Journal du voyage de M. Saint-Luc de La Corne, écuyer, dans le navire l'Auguste, en l'an 1761* (Montreal: Fleury Mesplet, 1778).

Lambert, David, 'The "Glasgow King of Billingsgate": James MacQueen and an Atlantic Proslavery Network', *Slavery and Abolition*, 29(3), September 2008, pp. 389–413.

Lamonde, Yvan, *The Social History of Ideas in Quebec, 1760–1896*, trans. Phyllis Aronoff and Howard Scott (Montreal: McGill-Queen's University Press, 2013).

Lamont, Craig, 'Finding Galt in Glasgow', in Gerald Carruthers and Colin Kidd (eds), *International Companion to John Galt* (Glasgow: Scottish Literature International, 2017), pp. 34–43.

Langford, Paul, *A Polite and Commercial People: England, 1727–1783* (Oxford: Clarendon Press, 1989).

La Rochefoucault-Liancourt, François-Alexandre-Frédéric, *Travels through the United States of North America, the Country of the Iroquois, and Upper Canada, in the Years 1795, 1796, and 1797* (London: R. Phillips, 1800).

'Late Emigrants of Sutherland', *The Pictou Observer*, 21 November 1832.

Laurence, Margaret, *The Diviners* (Chicago: University of Chicago Press, 1993).

Le Goff, Jacques, *History and Memory*, trans. Steven Randall and Elizabeth Claman (New York: Columbia University Press, 1992).

Leask, Nigel, 'Burns and the Poetics of Abolition', in Gerard Carruthers (ed.), *The Edinburgh Companion to Robert Burns* (Edinburgh: Edinburgh University Press, 2009).

Lee, Robert C., *The Canada Company and the Huron Tract, 1826–1853: Personalities, Profits and Politics* (Toronto: Natural Heritage Books, 2004).

Lee, Yoon Sun, *Nationalism and Irony: Burke, Scott, and Carlyle* (Oxford: Oxford University Press, 2004).

Lemire, Maurice, 'Introduction', Phillipe-Joseph Aubert de Gaspé, *Les Anciens Canadiens* (Montreal: Fides, 1994).

Lemire, Maurice, 'James Huston', *Dictionary of Canadian Biography* http://www.biographi.ca/en/bio/huston_james_8E.html.

Lemire, Maurice, '*Les Anciens Canadiens*', in Maurice Lemire (ed), *Dictionnaire des œuvres littéraires du Québec*, Vol. I: *Des origines à 1900* (Montreal: Fides, 1978), pp. 16–24.

Lemire, Maurice, *Les Grands Thèmes nationalistes du roman historique canadien-français* (Quebec City: Les Presses de l'Université Laval, 1970).

LeMoine, J. M, *Maple Leaves: A Budget of Legendary, Historical, Critical and Sporting Intelligence* (Quebec City: Hunter, Rose & Co, 1863).

Lenman, Bruce P., '"From Savage to Scot" via the French and the Spaniards: Principal Robertson's Spanish Sources', in Stewart J. Brown (ed.), *William Robertson and the Expansion of Empire* (Cambridge: Cambridge University Press, 1997).

Leys, Ruth, *Trauma: A Genealogy* (Chicago: University of Chicago Press, 2010).

Lincoln, Andrew, *Walter Scott and Modernity* (Edinburgh: Edinburgh University Press, 2007).

Linebaugh, Peter, and Marcus Rediker, *The Many-Headed Hydra: Sailors, Slaves, Commoners, and the Hidden History of the Revolutionary Atlantic* (Boston, MA: Beacon Press, 2000).

Loch, James, *An Account of the Improvements on the Estates of the Marquess of Stafford* (London: Hurst, Rees, Orme, and Brown, 1820).

[Lockhart, John Gibson], *Peter's Letters to His Kinsfolk* (Edinburgh: William Blackwood, 1819).

Looser, Devoney, *British Women Writers and the Writing of History, 1670–1820* (Baltimore: Johns Hopkins University Press, 2000).

Lord Durham's Report on the Affairs of British North America, ed. L. C. Prestwood (Oxford: Clarendon Press, 1912).

Low, Sidney, 'The Poet of South Africa', *The Anglo-Saxon Review*, 9, June 1901, pp. 207–21.

Löwy, Michael, and Robert Sayre, *Romanticism against the Tide of Modernity*, trans. Catherine Porter (Durham, NC: Duke University Press, 2001).

Lukács, Georg, *The Historical Novel*, trans. Hannah and Stanley Mitchell (London: Merlin Press, 1962).

McCracken-Flesher, Caroline, *Possible Scotlands: Walter Scott and the Story of Tomorrow* (Oxford: Oxford University Press, 2007).

McCrone, David, 'Representing Scotland: Culture and Nationalism', in David McCrone, Pat Straw and Stephen Kendrick (eds), *The Making of Scotland: Nation, Culture & Social Change* (Edinburgh: Edinburgh University Press, 1989), pp. 161–74.

McDermot, Andrew, 'Peguis Refuted', *The Nor'-Wester*, 28 February 1860.

Macdonald, Alexander, 'Alex. Macdonald to Selkirk, March 26, 1819', pp. 18:6009-10, MG19-E1, 18, Microfilm reel C-6, Library and Archives Canada.

MacDonell, Margaret, *The Emigrant Experience: Songs of Highland Emigrants in North America* (Toronto: University of Toronto Press, 1982).
MacGhillEathain, Iain/MacLean, John, 'A' Choille Ghruamaich' ('The Gloomy Forest'), trans. William Neill, in Roderick Watson (ed.), *The Poetry of Scotland* (Edinburgh: Edinburgh University Press, 1995).
MacInnes, John, 'The Panegyric Code in Gaelic Poetry and Its Historical Background', in Michael Newton (ed.), *Dùthchas Nan Gàidheal: Selected Essays of John MacInnes* (Edinburgh: Birlinn, 2006), pp. 265–319.
McKeever, Gerard Lee, '"With Wealth Come Wants": Scottish Romanticism as Improvement in the Fiction of John Galt', *Studies in Romanticism*, 55(1), Spring 2016, pp. 69–93.
Mackenzie, A. Fiona D., *Places of Possibility: Property, Nature and Community Land Ownership* (Chichester: Wiley-Blackwell, 2013).
McKillop, Alan D., 'Local Attachment and Cosmopolitanism – the Eighteenth-Century Pattern', in Frederick W. Hilles and Harold Bloom (eds), *From Sensibility to Romanticism* (Oxford: Oxford University Press, 1965), pp. 191–218.
MacKinnon, Iain, *Crofters: Indigenous People of the Highlands and Islands* (Scottish Crofting Foundation, 2008).
McLean, Marianne, *The People of Glengarry: Highlanders in Transition, 1745–1820* (Montreal: McGill-Queen's University Press, 1991).
Maclean, Sorley, 'The Poetry of the Clearances', *Transactions of the Gaelic Society of Inverness*, 38, 1939, pp. 293–324.
Mackenthun, Gesa, 'America's Troubled Postcoloniality: Some Reflections from Abroad', *Discourse*, 22(3), Fall 2000, pp. 34–45.
MacLennan, Hugh, *Scotchman's Return, and Other Essays* (Toronto: Macmillan, 1964).
Macleod, Donald, *Gloomy Memories of the Highlands of Scotland versus Mrs. Harriet Beecher Stowe's Sunny Memories in (England) a Foreign Land; or, a Faithful Picture of the Extirpation of the Celtic Race from the Highlands of Scotland* (Toronto: Thompson, 1857).
MacLeod, Margaret (ed.), *Songs of Old Manitoba* (Toronto: Ryerson, 1959).
MacLeod, Margaret, and W. L. Morton, *Warden of the Plains of Red River* (Toronto: McClelland & Stewart, 1963).
McManus, Edgar J., *A History of Negro Slavery in New York* (Syracuse University Press, 1966).
McNamara, Josephte Isabel, 'Fact or Fiction: *L'Histoire du Canada* and Its Influence on French Canadian Novels', Unpublished MA thesis, University of Concordia, 1998.
McNeil, Kenneth, *Scotland, Britain, Empire: Writing the Highlands, 1760–1860* (Columbus: The Ohio State University Press, 2007).
MacQueen, James, 'The Anti-Slavery Society and the West-India Colonists', *Glasgow Courier*, 26 July 1831, p. 1.

MacQueen, John, 'Ringan Gilhaize and Particular Providence', in Christopher Whatley (ed.), John Galt, 1779–1979 (Edinburgh: Ramsay Head Press, 1979), pp. 107–19.

Maier, Charles S., 'A Surfeit of Memory? Reflections on History, Melancholy and Denial', History and Memory, 5(2), Fall–Winter 1993, pp. 136–52.

Makdisi, Saree, Romantic Imperialism: Universal Empire and the Culture of Modernity (Cambridge: Cambridge University Press, 2003).

Manning, Susan, 'Did Mark Twain Bring Down the Temple on Scott's Shoulders?', in Janet Beer and Bridget Bennett (eds), Special Relationships: Anglo-American Affinities and Antagonisms, 1854–1936 (Manchester: Manchester University Press, 2002), pp. 8–27.

Manning, Susan, Fragments of Union: Making Connections in Scottish and American Writing (London: Palgrave, 2002).

Manning, Susan, 'Post-Union Scotland and Britishness', in Susan Manning, Ian Brown, Thomas Owen Clancy and Murray Pittock (eds), The Edinburgh History of Scottish Literature, Vol. 2 (Edinburgh: Edinburgh University Press, 2007).

Manning, Susan, 'Note on the Text', in Washington Irving, The Sketch-Book of Geoffrey Crayon, Gent., ed. Susan Manning (Oxford: Oxford University Press, 1996).

Manning, Susan, 'Ossian, Scott, and Nineteenth-Century Scottish Literary Nationalism', Studies in Scottish Literature, 1(17), 1982, pp. 39–54.

Manning, Susan, The Puritan-Provincial Vision: Scottish and American Literature in the Nineteenth Century (Cambridge: Cambridge University Press, 1990).

Manning, Susan and Francis Cogliano (eds), The Atlantic Enlightenment (Burlington, VT: Ashgate, 2008).

Marienstras, Elise, 'White Children in Captivity Narratives', American Studies International, 40(3), 2002, pp. 33–45.

Matus, Jill L., Shock, Memory and the Unconscious in Victorian Fiction (Cambridge: Cambridge University Press, 2009).

Maxwell, Richard, The Historical Novel in Europe, 1650–1950 (Cambridge: Cambridge University Press, 2009).

Meek, Donald E. (ed.), Tuath Is Tighearna, Tenants and Landlords (Edinburgh: Scottish Academic Press, 1995).

Megill, Allan, Historical Knowledge, Historical Error (Chicago: University of Chicago Press, 2007).

Merlan, Francesca, 'Indigeneity: Global and Local', Current Anthropology, 50(3), 2009, pp. 303–33.

Michaels, Walter Benn, '"You Who Never Was There": Slavery and the New Historicism, Deconstruction and the Holocaust', Narrative, 4(1), January 1996, pp. 1–16.

Midgley, Clare, Women against Slavery: The British Campaigns, 1780–1870 (London: Routledge, 1992).

Miggelbrink, Joachim, 'The End of the Scots-Dutch Brigade', in Steve Murdoch and A. Mackillop (eds), *Fighting for Identity: Scottish Military Experience, c. 1550–1900* (Leiden: Brill, 2002), pp. 83–103.

Millar, John, *Observations Concerning the Distinction of Ranks in Society* (London: John Murray, 1771).

Miller, Ashley, '"Striking Passages": Memory and the Romantic Imprint', *Studies in Romanticism*, 50(1), 2011, pp. 29–53.

Miller, Bruce Granville, *Invisible Indigenes: the Politics of Nonrecognition* (Lincoln: University of Nebraska Press, 2003).

[Moir, David], 'Memoir of Galt', in John Galt, *Annals of the Parish and the Ayrshire Legatees* (Edinburgh: William Blackwood, 1841).

Morris, Michael, *Scotland and the Caribbean, c.1740–1833: Atlantic Archipelagos* (London: Routledge, 2015).

Morris, Michael, 'Yonder Awa: Slavery and Distancing Strategies in Scottish Literature', in T. M. Devine (ed.), *Recovering Scotland's Slavery Past: The Caribbean Connection* (Edinburgh: Edinburgh University Press, 2015), pp. 41–61.

Morton, W. L., 'Introduction', in Eden Colville, *London Correspondence Inward from Eden Colville, 1849–1852*, ed. E. E. Rich (London: Hudson's Bay Record Society, 1956).

Mullan, John, *Sentiment and Sociability: The Language of Feeling in the Eighteenth Century* (Oxford: Clarendon Press, 1988).

Munsell, Joel, *Annals of Albany* (Albany: 1850–9).

Murray, Laura J., 'Aesthetic Dispossession: Washington Irving and Ideologies of (De)Colonization in the Early Republic', *American Literary History*, 8(2), July 1996, pp. 205–31.

Nairn, Tom, *The Break-Up of Britain: Crisis and Neo-Nationalism* (London: NLB, 1977).

'The Napier Commission, Vol 5', University of the Highlands and Islands, Centre for History, https://www.uhi.ac.uk/en/t4-media/one-web/university/research/centre-for-history/napier/napier-commission-vol-5.pdf.

Neal, John, *Seventy-Six, 1823* (Bainbridge, NY: York Mail-Print, 1971).

Neal, John, *Wandering Recollections of a Somewhat Busy Life; an Autobiography* (Boston, MA: Roberts Bros, 1869).

Newman, Judie, 'Stowe's Sunny Memories of Highland Slavery', in Janet Beer and Bridget Bennett (eds), *Special Relationships: Anglo-American Affinities and Antagonisms, 1854–1936* (Manchester: Manchester University Press, 2002), pp. 28–41.

Newton, Michael, *A Handbook of the Scottish Gaelic World* (Dublin: Four Courts Press, 2000).

Newton, Michael, *We're Indians Sure Enough: The Legacy of the Scottish Highlanders in the United States* (Saorsa Media, 2001).

Newton, Michael S. (ed.), *Seanchaidh Na Coille: The Memory-Keeper of the Forest, Anthology of the Scottish-Gaelic Literature of Canada* (Sydney, Nova Scotia: Cape Breton University Press, 2015).

Nic a' Phearsain, Màiri / Macpherson, Mary, 'Soraidh leis an Nollaig ùir' ('Farewell to the New Christmas'), trans. William Neill, in Roderick Watson (ed.), *The Poetry of Scotland* (Edinburgh: Edinburgh University Press, 1995).

Nic a' Phearsain, Màiri / Macpherson, Mary, 'Nuair bha mi òg' ('When I was Young'), trans. William Neill, in Roderick Watson (ed.), *The Poetry of Scotland* (Edinburgh: Edinburgh University Press, 1995).

Nilsen, Kenneth E., 'A' Ghàidhlig an Canada: Scottish Gaelic in Canada', in Moray Watson and Michelle Macleod (eds), *The Edinburgh Companion to the Gaelic Language* (Edinburgh: Edinburgh University Press, 2010), pp. 90–107.

Nora, Pierre, 'Between Memory and History: Les Lieux de Memoire', trans. Marc Roudebush, *Representations*, 26, Spring, 1989, pp. 7–24.

Nora, Pierre, *Realms of Memory*, ed. Lawrence D. Kritzman, trans. Arthur Goldhammer (New York: Columbia University Press, 1996).

[Norton, Andrews], 'Review *of Memoir and Correspondence of Mrs. Grant of Laggan*', *The North American Review*, 60(126), January 1845, pp. 126–56.

'Obituary – Mrs. Grant, of Laggan', *Gentlemen's Magazine*, 11 January 1839, pp. 97–100.

O'Donnell, Thomas F., 'Introduction', James Kirke Paulding, *The Dutchman's Fireside*, ed. Thomas F. O'Donnell (New Haven, CT: College & University Press, 1966).

Olick, Jeffrey K., and Joyce Robbins, 'Social Memory Studies: From "Collective Memory" to the Historical Sociology of Mnemonic Practices', *Annual Review of Sociology*, 24(1), 1998, pp. 105–40.

Olick, Jeffrey K., Vered Vinitzky-Seroussi and David Levy, 'Introduction', in Jeffrey K Olick, Vered Vinitzky-Seroussi and David Levy (eds), *The Collective Memory Reader* (Oxford: Oxford University Press, 2011).

Orians, G. Harrison, 'The Romance Ferment after *Waverley*', *American Literature*, 3(4), January 1932, pp. 408–31.

Packham, Catherine, 'Feigning Fictions: Imagination, Hypothesis, and Philosophical Writing in the Scottish Enlightenment', *The Eighteenth Century*, 48(2), Summer 2007, pp. 149–71.

Paquet, Sandra Pouchet, *Caribbean Autobiography: Cultural Identity and Self-Representation* (Madison: University of Wisconsin Press, 2002).

Paterson, Janet M., 'Archibald ou Arché? L'alterité dans "Les Anciens Canadiens"', in Yvan Lepage and Robert Major (eds), *Croire à l'écriture: Études de littérature québécoise en hommage à Jean-Louis Major* (Orléans: Les Éditions David, 2000), pp. 301–11.

Paulding, James Kirke, *The Dutchman's Fireside* (New York: J. and J. Harper, 1831).

Pearce, Roy Harvey, *Savagism and Civilization: A Study of the Indian and the American Mind* (Berkeley: University of California Press, 1953).

Peers, Laura, *The Ojibwa of Western Canada, 1780–1870* (Winnipeg: University of Manitoba Press, 1994).
Peers, Laura L. (ed.), *Gathering Places: Aboriginal and Fur Trade Histories* (Vancouver: University of British Columbia Press, 2010).
Peguis, 'Native Title to Native Lands', *The Nor'-Wester*, 14 February 1860.
'The People of Colonial Albany', New York State Museum, http://exhibitions.nysm.nysed.gov/albany/welcome.html.
Perkins, Pam, 'Anne Grant and the Professionalization of Privacy', in E. J. Clery, Caroline Franklin and Peter Garside (eds), *Authorship, Commerce, and the Public: Scenes of Writing, 1750–1850* (London: Palgrave, 2002).
Perkins, Pam, 'Grant: Gender, Genre, and Cultural Analysis', in Judy A. Hayden (ed.), *The New Science and Women's Discourse: Prefiguring Frankenstein* (London: Palgrave Macmillan, 2011), pp. 219–34.
Perkins, Pam, *Women Writers and the Edinburgh Enlightenment* (Amsterdam: Rodopi, 2010).
Perkins, Pamela Ann, '"Paradises Lost": Anne Grant and Late Eighteenth-Century Idealizations of America', *Early American Literature*, 40(2), 2005, pp. 315–40.
Peterson, Jacqueline, 'Many Roads to Red River', in Jacqueline Peterson and Jennifer S. H. Brown (eds), *The New Peoples: Being and Becoming Métis in North America* (Lincoln: University of Nebraska Press, 1985).
Phillips, Mark Salber, *Society and Sentiment: Genres of Historical Writing in Britain, 1740–1820* (Princeton: Princeton University Press, 2000).
Pinch, Adela, *Strange Fits of Passion: Epistemologies of Emotion, Hume to Austen* (Palo Alto: Stanford University Press, 1996).
Pittock, Murray, *Culloden (Cùil Lodair)* (Oxford: Oxford University Press, 2016).
Pittock, Murray, 'Slavery as a Political Metaphor in Scotland and Ireland in the Age of Burns', in Sharon Alker, Leith Davis and Holly F. Nelson (eds), *Robert Burns and Transatlantic Culture* (Burlington, VT: Ashgate, 2012).
Pittock, Murray G. H., *Inventing and Resisting Britain: Cultural Identities in Britain and Ireland, 1685–1789* (New York: St. Martin's Press, 1997).
Pittock, Murray G. H., *The Invention of Scotland* (London: Routledge, 1991).
Pittock, Murray (ed.), *The Reception of Sir Walter Scott in Europe* (London: Continuum, 2004).
Pochmann, Henry A., 'Irving's German Sources in *The Sketch Book*', *Studies in Philology*, 27(3), July 1930, pp. 477–507.
Poovey, Mary, *A History of the Modern Fact: Problems of Knowledge in the Sciences of Wealth and Society* (Chicago: University of Chicago Press, 1998).
Pratt, Mary Louise, *Imperial Eyes: Travel Writing and Transculturation* (London: Routledge, 1992).

Prebble, John, *The Highland Clearances* (London: Secker & Warburg, 1963).
The Present Conduct of the Chieftains and Proprietors of Lands in the Highlands of Scotland, by a Highlander (n.p., 1773).
Price, David, *Masks of Difference* (Cambridge: Cambridge University Press, 1994).
Prince, Mary, *The History of Mary Prince, a West Indian Slave, Related by Herself*, ed. Sara Salih (London: Penguin Books, 2004).
Pringle, Thomas, *African Poems of Thomas Pringle*, ed. Ernest Pereira and Michael Chapman (Pietermaritzburg: University of Natal Press, 1989).
Pringle, Thomas, *African Sketches* (London: Edward Moxon, 1834).
Pringle, Thomas, *Narrative of a Residence in South Africa* (London: Edward Moxon, 1834).
Pringle, Thomas, 'Slavery at the Cape of Good Hope', *Anti-Slavery Monthly Reporter*, 20, January 1827, pp. 289–96.
Pringle, Thomas, *The South African Letters of Thomas Pringle*, ed. Randolph Vigne (Cape Town: Van Riebeeck Society, 2011).
Prins, Harald E. L., and Bunny McBride, 'Cherokee Chief Opens Highland Games in Scotland', *Indian Country Today*, 6 October 2010, https://indiancountrymedianetwork.com/news/cherokee-chief-opens-highland-games-in-scotland.
Prucha, Francis Paul, *American Indian Policy in the Formative Years* (Cambridge, MA: Harvard University Press, 1962).
Purcell, Sarah J., *Sealed with Blood: War, Sacrifice, and Memory in Revolutionary America* (Philadelphia: University of Pennsylvania Press, 2002).
Ramsay, John, *Scotland and Scotsmen in the Eighteenth Century*, ed. Alexander Allardyce (Edinburgh and London: W. Blackwood and Sons, 1888).
Randall, Marilyn, 'Resistance, Submission and Oppostionality: National Identity in French Canada', in Charles Forsdick and David Murphy (eds), *Francophone Postcolonial Studies A Critical Introduction* (London: Arnold, 2003).
Reichart, Walter A., 'Concerning the Source of Irving's "Rip Van Winkle"', *Monatshefte*, 48(2), 1956, pp. 94–5.
Rendall, Jane, 'Bluestockings and Reviewers: Gender, Power, and Culture in Britain, c. 1800–1830', *Nineteenth-Century Contexts*, 26(4), 2004, pp. 355–74.
'Review of *Memoirs of an American Lady*', *The Southern Literary Messenger*, 2(8), July 1836, pp. 12–16.
Rezek, Joseph, *London and the Making of Provincial Literature: Aesthetics and the Transatlantic Book Trade, 1800–1850* (Philadelphia: University of Pennsylvania Press, 2015).
Rice, C. Duncan, *The Scots Abolitionists, 1833–1861* (Baton Rouge: Louisiana State University Press, 1981).
Richards, Eric, *The Highland Clearances* (Edinburgh: Birlinn, 2000).
Richards, Eric, *A History of the Highland Clearances: Agrarian Transformation and the Evictions, 1746–1886* (London: Croom Helm, 1982).

Richards, Eric, 'Scotland and the Uses of the Atlantic Empire', in Bernard Bailyn and Philip D. Morgan (eds), *Strangers within the Realm: Cultural Margins of the First British Empire* (Chapel Hill: University of North Carolina Press, 1991).

Ricœur, Paul, 'Memory–Forgetting–History', in Jörn Rüsen (ed.), *Meaning and Representation in History* (New York: Berghahn Books, 2006), pp. 9–19.

Rieley, Honor, '"Wha sae base as be a slave?": Linguistic Spaces in Scottish Historical Fiction, and Where Slavery Doesn't Fit', MA thesis, McGill University, 2011.

Rigney, Ann, *The Afterlives of Walter Scott* (Oxford: Oxford University Press, 2012).

Rigney, Ann, *Imperfect Histories: The Elusive Past and the Legacy of Romantic Historicism* (Ithaca: Cornell University Press, 2001).

Roach, Joseph R., *Cities of the Dead: Circum-Atlantic Performance* (New York: Columbia University Press, 1996).

Robertson, Fiona (ed.), *The Edinburgh Companion to Sir Walter Scott* (Edinburgh: Edinburgh University Press, 2012).

Robertson, Fiona, 'Historical Fiction and The Fractured Atlantic', in Porscha Fermanis and John Regan (eds), *Rethinking British Romantic History, 1770–1845* (Oxford: Oxford University Press, 2014).

Robertson, Fiona, *Legitimate Histories* (Oxford: Oxford University Press, 1994).

Robertson, Fiona, 'Walter Scott and the American Historical Novel', in Gerald Kennedy and Leland Person (eds), *The Oxford History of the Novel in English*, Vol. 5, *American Novels to 1870* (Oxford: Oxford University Press, 2014).

Rocard, Marcienne, 'The Métis in Margaret Laurence's Manawaka Works', *Études canadiennes*, 5, 1978, pp. 113–17.

Roeber, A. G., '"The Origin of Whatever is Not English among Us": The Dutch-Speaking and the German-Speaking Peoples of Colonial British America', in Bernard Bailyn and Philip D. Morgan (eds), *Strangers within the Realm: Cultural Margins of the First British Empire* (Chapel Hill: University of North Carolina Press, 1991), pp. 220–83.

'Romancing Scotland', Special Issue, *Modern Language Quarterly*, 70:4, December 2009.

Rosen, George, 'Nostalgia: A "Forgotten" Psychological Disorder', *Clio medica*, 10, 1975, pp. 28–51.

Ross, Alexander, *The Red River Settlement: Its Rise, Progress and Present State; with Some Account of The Native Races and Its General History, to the Present Day* (London: Smith Elder, 1856).

Ross, Donald, '*Sunny Memories* and Serious Proposals', in Denise Kohn, Sarah Meer and Emily B. Todd (eds), *Transatlantic Stowe: Harriet Beecher Stowe and European Culture* (Iowa City: University of Iowa Press, 2006), pp. 131–46.

Roth, Michael S., 'Returning to Nostalgia', in Suzanne Nash (ed.), *Home and Its Dislocations in Nineteenth-Century France* (Albany: SUNY Press, 1993), pp. 25–44.

Rubin-Dorsky, Jeffrey, *Adrift in the Old World: The Psychological Pilgrimage of Washington Irving* (Chicago: University of Chicago Press, 1988).

Russell, William, *New-York Class-Book: Comprising Outlines of The Geography and History Of New York . . . Arranged as a Reading Book for Schools* (New York: Harper & Brothers, 1847).

Sassi, Carla, 'Acts of (Un)willed Amnesia: Dis/appearing Figurations of the Caribbean in Post-union Scottish Literature', in Giovanna Covi, Joan Anim-Addo, Velma Ollard and Carla Sassi (eds), *Caribbean-Scottish Relations* (London: Mango, 2007), pp. 131–98.

Sayre, Gordon M., *Les Sauvages Américains: Representations of Native Americans in French and English Colonial Literature* (Chapel Hill: University of North Carolina Press, 1997).

'Schuyler Flatts', Friends of Albany History, https://friendsofalbanyhistory.wordpress.com/tag/schuyler-flatts/.

Scott, Jennifer, 'The Invisible Hand of the Literary Market: Authorial Self-Fashioning in Grant Thorburn and John Galt', *Nineteenth-Century Contexts*, 40(1), 2018, pp. 1–19.

Scott, Jennifer, 'Reciprocal Investments: John Galt, the Periodical Press, and the Business of North American Emigration', *Victorian Periodicals Review*, 46(3), Fall 2013, pp. 368–82.

Scott, Maggie, 'Scots Word of the Season: *Eldritch*', *The Bottle Imp*, 6, http://www.arts.gla.ac.uk/ScotLit/ASLS/SWE/TBI/TBIIssue6/Eldritch.html.

Scott, Walter, *The Antiquary*, ed. David Hewitt (Edinburgh: Edinburgh University Press, 1995).

Scott, Walter, *The Black Dwarf*, ed. P. D. Garside (Edinburgh: Edinburgh University Press, 1993).

Scott, Walter, *Journal of Walter Scott*, ed. W. E. K. Anderson (Oxford: Clarendon Press, 1972).

Scott, Walter, *The Heart of Midlothian*, ed. David Hewitt and Alison Lumsden (Edinburgh: Edinburgh University Press, 2004).

Scott, Walter, *Ivanhoe*, ed. Graham Tulloch (Edinburgh: Edinburgh University Press, 1997).

Scott, Walter, *A Legend of the Wars of Montrose*, ed. J. H. Alexander (Edinburgh: Edinburgh University Press, 1995).

Scott, Walter, *The Letters of Sir Walter Scott*, ed. H. J. C. Grierson (London: Constable, 1932).

Scott, Walter, *Waverley*, ed. P. D. Garside (Edinburgh: Edinburgh University Press, 1995).

Seawall, Samuel, *The Letter-Book of Samuel Sewall* (Boston, MA: The Massachusetts Historical Society, 1888).

Sedgwick, Catharine Maria, *The Linwoods: or, 'Sixty Years Since' in America*, ed. Maria Karafilis (Hanover: University Press of New England, 2002).
Selkirk, Thomas Douglas, *The Collected Writings of Lord Selkirk*, ed. J. M. Bumsted (Winnipeg: Manitoba Records Society, 1984).
Selkirk, Thomas Douglas, 'Communications with Government 1805-6-7 Relative to America General and Outlines of a Plan for the Settlement and Security of Canada, July 29 1805', pp. 52:13919–13926, MG19-E1, 52, Microfilm reel C-13, Library and Archives Canada.
[Selkirk, Thomas Douglas], *Observations on a Proposal for Forming a Society for Promoting the Civilization and Improvement of the North-American Indians within the British Boundary* (London: Taylor, 1807).
Selkirk, Thomas Douglas, *Observations on the Present State of the Highlands of Scotland with a View of the Causes and Probable Consequences of Emigration* [London: Longman, Hurst, Rees, Orme, 1805] (New York: Johnson Reprint Corporation, 1969).
Selkirk, Thomas Douglas, 'Plan of Settlement of Baldoon', pp. 55:14627–14652, MG19-E1, 55, Microfilm reel C-14, Library and Archives Canada.
Selkirk, Thomas Douglas, 'Suggestions Respecting Upper Canada, Delivered to Windham per Sir George Shee, March 27 1806', pp. 52:13927–13949, MG19-E1, 52, Microfilm reel C-13, Library and Archives Canada.
Sharpe, Jenny, *Ghosts of Slavery: A Literary Archeology of Black Women's Lives* (Minneapolis: University of Minnesota Press, 2003).
Shepperson, George, 'Harriet Beecher Stowe and Scotland, 1852–3', *The Scottish Historical Review*, 32(113)(1), April 1953, pp. 40–6.
Sher, Richard B., and Jeffrey R. Smitten (eds), *Scotland and America in the Age of the Enlightenment* (Princeton: Princeton University Press, 1990).
Shields, Juliet, 'Highland Emigration and the Transformation of Nostalgia in Romantic Poetry', *European Romantic Review*, 23(6), December 2012, pp. 765–84.
Shields, Juliet, *Nation and Migration: The Making of British Atlantic Literature, 1765–1835* (Oxford: Oxford University Press, 2016).
Shields, Juliet, *Sentimental Literature and Anglo-Scottish Identity, 1745–1820* (Cambridge: Cambridge University Press, 2010).
Shum, Matthew, 'The Prehistory of *The History of Mary Prince*: Thomas Pringle's "The Bechuana Boy"', *Nineteenth-Century Literature*, 64(3), December 2009, pp. 292–322.
Shyllon, F. O., *James Ramsay: The Unknown Abolitionist* (Edinburgh: Canongate, 1977).
Simpson, Kenneth, *The Protean Scot: The Crisis of Identity in Eighteenth-Century Scottish Literature* (Aberdeen: Aberdeen University Press, 1988).
Sinclair, John, *Analysis of the Statistical Account of Scotland* (Edinburgh: William Tait, 1831).
Sinclair, John, *The Statistical Account of Scotland*, ed. Donald J. Withrington and Ian R. Grant (East Ardsley: E. P. Publishing, 1983).

Sivertsen, Barbara J., *Turtles, Wolves, and Bears: A Mohawk Family History* (Bowie, MD: Heritage Books, 1996).

Sizemore, Michelle R., '"Changing by Enchantment": Temporal Convergence, Early National Comparisons, and Washington Irving's *Sketchbook*', *Studies in American Fiction*, 40(2), Fall 2013, pp. 157–83.

Smailes, Helen, *Scottish Empire: Scots in Pursuit of Hope and Glory* (Edinburgh: Scottish National Portrait Gallery, 1981).

Smelser, Neil J., 'Psychological Trauma and Cultural Trauma', in Jeffrey C Alexander, Ron Eyerman, Bernhard Giesen, Neil J. Smelser and Piotr Sztompka, *Cultural Trauma and Collective Identity* (Berkeley: University of California Press, 2004).

Smith, Adam, *Lectures on Jurisprudence*, ed. R. L. Meek, D. D. Raphael and P. G. Stein (Oxford: Clarendon Press, 1978).

Smith, Adam, *The Theory of Moral Sentiments*, ed. R. L. Meek and A. L. Macfie (Oxford: Clarendon Press, 1976).

Smith, Laurajane, '"Man's Inhumanity to Man" and Other Platitudes of Avoidance and Misrecognition: An Analysis of Visitor Responses to Exhibitions Marking the 1807 Bicentenary', *Museum and Society*, 8(3), November 2010, pp. 193–214.

Snow, Dean R., 'Searching for Hendrick: Correction of a Historic Conflation', *New York History* 88(3), Summer 2007, pp. 229–53.

Les Soirées canadiennes: Recueil de littérature Nationale (Quebec City: Brousseau et Frères, 1861).

Sollers, Werner, *Neither Black Nor White Yet Both* (Oxford: Oxford University Press, 1997).

Sorensen, Janet, 'Internal Colonialism and the British Novel', *Eighteenth-Century Fiction*, 15(1), October 2002, pp. 51–8.

Stafford, Fiona J., *The Sublime Savage: A Study of James Macpherson and the Poems of Ossian* (Edinburgh: Edinburgh University Press, 1988).

Starobinski, Jean, 'The Idea of Nostalgia', *Diogenes*, 54, 1966, pp. 81–103.

Stedman, John Gabriel, *Journal of John Gabriel Stedman*, ed. Stanbury Thompson (London: Mitre Press, 1962).

Stedman, John Gabriel, *Stedman Archive: Journal*, 1775–1796, University of Minnesota Libraries, James Ford Bell Library, umedia.lib.umn.edu/item/p16022coll187:73.

Stedman, John Gabriel, *Journal, diaries, and other papers: 1772–1796*, 1772, University of Minnesota Libraries, James Ford Bell Library, umedia.lib.umn.edu/item/p16022coll187:73.

Stedman, John Gabriel, *Journal, Diaries, and other papers: 1772–1796*, 1772–1774, University of Minnesota Libraries, James Ford Bell Library, umedia.lib.umn.edu/item/p16022coll187:73.

Stedman, John Gabriel, *Narrative of a Five Year's Expedition against the Revolted Negroes of Surinam*, ed. Richard Price and Sally Price (Baltimore: Johns Hopkins University Press, 1988).

Steele, Ian K., *Setting All the Captives Free: Capture, Adjustment, Recollection in Allegheny Country* (Montreal: McGill-Queen's University Press, 2013).
Stelter, Gilbert A., 'John Galt: The Writer as Town Booster and Builder', in Elizabeth Waterston (ed.), *John Galt: Reappraisals* (Guelph: University of Guelph, 1985), pp. 17–43.
Stewart, David, *Sketches of the Character, Manners, and Present State of the Highlanders of Scotland* (Edinburgh: A. Constable, 1822)
Stewart, Dugald, *Biographical Memoirs of Adam Smith, William Robertson, and Thomas Reid*, William Hamilton (ed.), *Collected Works of Dugald Stewart, Vol. 10* (Edinburgh: Thomas Constable, 1858).
Stowe, Harriet Beecher, *Sunny Memories of Foreign Lands* (Boston, MA: Phillips, Sampson, 1854).
Stroh, Silke, *Gaelic Scotland in the Colonial Imagination: Anglophone Writing from 1600 to 1900* (Evanston: Northwestern University Press, 2017).
Surtees, Robert J., *Indian Land Surrenders in Ontario, 1763–1867* (Ottawa: Research Branch, Corporate Policy, Indian and Northern Affairs Canada, 1984).
Sutherland, Kathryn, 'Walter Scott and Washington Irving: "Editors of the land of Utopia"', *Journal of American Studies*, 10(1), April 1976, pp. 85–90.
Szasz, Ferenc Morton, *Scots in the North American West, 1790–1917* (Norman: University of Oklahoma Press, 2000).
Szasz, Margaret Connell, *Scottish Highlanders and Native Americans: Indigenous Education in the Eighteenth-Century Atlantic World* (Norman: University of Oklahoma Press, 2007).
Taylor, Michael, 'Conservative Political Economy and the Problem of Colonial Slavery, 1823–1833', *The Historical Journal*, 57(4), 2014, pp. 973–95.
Terdiman, Richard, *Present Past: Modernity and the Memory Crisis* (Ithaca: Cornell University Press, 1993).
Thomas, Helen, *Romanticism and Slave Narratives: Transatlantic Testimonies* (Cambridge: Cambridge University Press, 2000).
Thomas, Sue, 'New Information on Mary Prince in London', *Notes and Queries*, 58(1), 2011, pp. 82–5.
Thomas, Sue, 'Pringle v. Cadell and Wood v. Pringle: The Libel Cases over *The History of Mary Prince*', *The Journal of Commonwealth Literature*, 40(1), March 2005, pp. 113–35.
Thomas, Sue, *Telling West Indian Lives: Life Narrative and the Reform of Plantation Slavery Cultures, 1804–1834* (London: Palgrave Macmillan, 2014).
Thompson, William Rodger, *Poems, Essays, and Sketches: with a Memoir*, ed. John Noble (Cape Town: J. C. Juta, 1868).

Thomson, George, Letter to Anne Grant, August 1811, University of Edinburgh Library La.II.357, ff. 201–4.

Thorburn, Grant, *Forty Years' Residence in America or the Doctrine of a Particular Providence Exemplified in the Life of Grant Thorburn (The Original Lawrie Todd)* (London: James Fraser, 1834).

Thornton, John K., *Africa and Africans in the Making of the Atlantic World, 1400–1800*, 2nd edn (Cambridge: Cambridge University Press, 1998).

Timothy, H. B., *The Galts: A Canadian Odyssey* (Toronto: McClelland & Stewart, 1977).

Todd, Emily B., 'Establishing Routes for Fiction in the United States: Walter Scott's Novels and the Early Nineteenth-Century American Publishing Industry', *Book History*, 12, 2009, pp. 100–28.

'Translation from an Ancient Chaldee Manuscript', *Blackwood's Edinburgh Magazine*, 2, October 1817, pp. 89–96.

Trumpener, Katie, 'Annals of Ice: Formations of Empire, Place, and History in John Galt and Alice Munro', in Michael Gardiner, Graeme McDonald and Niall O'Gallagher (eds), *Scottish Literature and Postcolonial Literature: Comparative Texts and Critical Perspectives* (Edinburgh: Edinburgh University Press, 2011).

Trumpener, Katie, *Bardic Nationalism* (Princeton: Princeton University Press, 1997).

[Tudor, William], 'Letters from Edinburgh', *North-American Review and Miscellaneous Journal*, 1(2), July 1815, pp. 183–95.

Turner, Bryan S., 'A Note on Nostalgia', *Theory, Culture & Society*, 4(1), February 1987, pp. 147–56.

Turner-Strong, Pauline, *Captive Selves, Captivating Others* (Boulder: Westview Press, 1999).

Van Kirk, Sylvia, ' What if Mama is an Indian?": Cultural Ambivalence of the Alexander Ross Family', in Jacqueline Peterson and Jennifer S. H. Brown (eds), *The New Peoples: Being and Becoming Métis in North America* (Lincoln: University of Nebraska Press, 1985).

Vigne, Randolph, *Thomas Pringle: South African Pioneer, Poet, and Abolitionist* (Woodbridge: James Currey, 2012).

Voss, A. E., 'The Personalities of Thomas Pringle', *English in Africa*, 18(1), May 1991, pp. 81–96.

Wahl, John Robert, 'Introduction', in Thomas Pringle, *Poems Illustrative of South Africa*, ed. John Robert Wahl (Cape Town: C. Struik, 1970).

Wallace, Elizabeth Kowaleski, *The British Slave Trade and Public Memory* (New York: Columbia University Press, 2006).

Wallerstein, Immanuel, *The Modern World-system III: The Second Era of Great Expansion of the Capitalist World Economy, 1730s–1840s* (New York: Academic Press, 1989).

Waterston, Elizabeth, 'John Galt, the Founder of Guelph', *Historic Guelph*, 17, 1978, pp. 4–15.

Waterston, Elizabeth (ed.), *John Galt: Reappraisals* (Guelph: University of Guelph, 1985).

Waterston, Elizabeth, *Rapt in Plaid: Canadian Literature and Scottish Tradition* (Toronto: University of Toronto Press, 2001).

Watts, Edward, 'Settler Postcolonialism as a Reading Strategy', *American Literary History*, 22(2), 2010, pp. 459–70.

Watts, Edward, and David J. Carlson (eds), *John Neal and Nineteenth-Century American Literature and Culture* (Lewisburg: Bucknell University Press, 2012).

Weaver, John C., *The Great Land Rush and the Making of the Modern World, 1650–1900* (Montreal: McGill-Queen's University Press, 2003).

Wedderburn, Robert, *The Horrors of Slavery and Other Writings by Robert Wedderburn*, ed. Iain McCalman (Princeton: Markus Weiner, 1991).

Whatley, Christopher, '*Annals of the Parish* and History', in Christopher Whatley (ed.), *John Galt, 1779–1979* (Edinburgh: Ramsay Head Press, 1979), pp. 51–63.

Whatley, Christopher, 'Introduction', in Christopher Whatley (ed.), *John Galt, 1779–1979* (Edinburgh: Ramsay Head Press, 1979), pp. 9–18.

White, Hayden, *The Content of the Form: Narrative Discourse and Historical Representation* (Baltimore: The Johns Hopkins University Press, 2006).

White, Richard, *The Middle Ground: Indians, Empires, and Republics in the Great Lakes Region, 1650–1815* (Cambridge: Cambridge University Press, 1991).

'Why Do We Celebrate John Galt Day?', Ward Five Guelph, 4 August 2009, http://ward5.wordpress.com/2009/08/04/why-do-we-celebrate-john-galt-day

Whyte, Iain, *Scotland and the Abolition of Black Slavery, 1756–1838* (Edinburgh: Edinburgh University Press, 2006).

Wickman, Matthew, 'John Galt's Logics of Worlds', in Evan Gottlieb (ed.), *Global Romanticism* (Lewisburg: Bucknell University Press, 2015).

Wilkinson, Charles F., *American Indians, Time, and the Law: Native Societies in a Modern Constitutional Democracy* (New Haven: Yale University Press, 1987).

Withers, Charles, 'The Historical Creation of the Scottish Highlands', in Ian Donnachie and Christopher Whatley (eds), *The Manufacture of Scottish History* (Edinburgh: Polygon, 1992), pp. 143–56.

Withers, Charles W. J., *Gaelic Scotland: The Transformation of a Culture Region* (London: Routledge, 1988).

Withers, Charles W. J., 'How Scotland Came to Know Itself: Geography, National Identity and the Making of a Nation, 1680–1790', *Journal of Historical Geography*, 21(4), 1995, pp. 371–97.

Withers, Charles W. J., 'Landscape, Memory, History: Gloomy Memories and the 19th Century Scottish Highlands', *Scottish Geographical Journal*, 121(1), 2005, pp. 29–44.

Womack, Craig S., *Red on Red: Native American Literary Separatism* (Minneapolis: University of Minnesota Press, 1999).

Womack, Peter, *Improvement and Romance: Constructing the Myth of the Highlands* (London: Macmillan, 1989).

Wood, Marcus, *Blind Memory: Visual Representations of Slavery in England and America, 1780–1865* (London: Routledge, 2000).

Wood, Marcus, *Slavery, Empathy, and Pornography* (Oxford: Oxford University Press, 2002).

Wyman, Sarah, 'Washington Irving's *Rip Van Winkle*: A Dangerous Critique of a New Nation', *ANQ: A Quarterly Journal of Short Articles, Notes, and Reviews*, 23(4), 2010, pp. 216–22.

Yokata, Kariann Akemi, *Unbecoming British: How Revolutionary America Became a Postcolonial Nation* (Oxford: Oxford University Press, 2011).

Index

abolitionism, 17, 23, 27, 141n, 201–2, 204–5, 206–7, 212, 214, 215, 216, 224–6, 228, 236, 240, 242, 244, 256n, 259n, 319–20, 332n
aborigine, 26–7, 145, 146, 148–9, 154–5, 157–8, 166, 170, 180–1, 184–5, 187, 189n, 196n, 198n, 199n, 239, 247, 252
Acts of Union
　Canada, 72
　Scotland, 5, 19, 246
Albany, 98, 107, 109, 119, 122–3, 126–7, 140n, 306
　Dutch Colony of, 97, 106, 114–16, 118–19, 125–7, 129, 131, 139n
　slavery in, 124–6, 141n
　see also Middle Ground
Algonquians, 114, 119, 138n
Allen, Chadwick, 185, 187, 200n
Allen, Jessica L., 226
Alexander, Jeffrey C., 249
American Revolution, 17, 18, 26, 36, 53, 55, 56, 58, 61–6, 68–70, 84, 128, 238, 289, 291, 293

amnesia, 56, 60, 61, 75
　collective, 154, 201–3, 244
Anderson, Benedict, 7
Andrews, William L., 225
Armitage, David, 273
Assiniboines, 176, 199
Assmann, Jan, 10, 29n, 42–4
Aubert de Gaspé, Philippe-Joseph, 71, 80–1
　Les Anciens Canadiens, 26, 37, 70–2, 75–84, 92–3n

Barash, Jeffrey, 2, 9–10
Blackwood, William, 262n, 276, 328n
Blackwood's Magazine, 7, 28, 54, 62, 201, 206, 241, 262n, 271, 302, 308, 327n, 330n, 332n
Blair, Hugh, *Critical Dissertations on the Poems of Ossian*, 138n
Blake, William, 207
Blakemore, Stephen, 60
Bohrer, Martha, 291, 292–3
Boswell, James, 13, 193n
Boym, Svetlana, 71–2
British Empire, 16, 118, 130–1, 164–6, 193n, 201, 236, 238, 273, 301, 308

British Empire (*cont.*)
  and Canada, 17, 36, 37, 72–3, 76, 81, 99, 167, 172–3, 176, 178, 179, 184, 309
  and Scotland, 3–8, 16, 18–24, 32, 76, 79, 81, 99, 130, 133–4, 134n, 145, 169, 171, 206, 209, 220, 227, 236, 251, 256, 273, 278, 291, 322
  and United States, 3, 17, 19, 36, 54, 58, 60, 109, 115, 117, 129, 195–6n
  see also modernity; nationalism; slavery; transatlanticism
Bryden, John A., 186
Bumsted, J. M., 191n
Burke, Peter, 12
Burns, Robert, 257n

Cadell, Thomas, 241
Calder, Angus, 227, 263n
Campbell, Alexander, 160, 161, 162
  Albyn's Anthology, 160
  The Grampians Desolate, 7, 157–9, 160, 165
Campbell, Thomas, 227
Canada, 77, 81, 143, 198n, 310
  and emigration, 116–17, 169, 183–4, 191, 244, 249–50, 302–4, 315, 316–18, 322–3, 324, 325
  land reform in, 145, 177–81, 183, 184–5, 196n, 200n
  see also British Empire: and Canada; Galt, John: Canada Company; nationalism; Selkirk, Thomas Douglas: National Settlements

Cape Colony, 23, 206, 225–6, 227, 232, 239, 241, 265n
Cass, Lewis, 181, 196n
Cattermole, William, 302, 311, 331n
Chambers, Robert, 25, 51, 95, 99, 111, 248, 284
  Minor Antiquities of Edinburgh, 87n
  Traditions of Edinburgh, 45, 47–51
Chandler, James, 7–8
Charles Edward Stuart (Prince), 4, 40, 49, 75
Cherokee, 18, 181, 196n, 200n
Child, Lydia Maria, *Joanna*, 259n
Choate, Rufus, 84
Clarkson, Thomas, 260n
Cockburn, Henry, 14, 25, 51–2, 95, 99, 111, 149, 248, 284
  Journal, 45
  Memorials of his Time, 45–8, 51, 135n
Colden, Cadwallader, 120
  History of the Five Nations, 138n
collective memory, 1–4, 9–10, 12, 13, 15, 25, 27, 28, 29n, 34–8, 42–3, 45, 46, 52, 55–6, 60–1, 70, 80, 154, 164, 177, 182, 184, 186–7, 197n, 203, 207, 247–50, 256, 274–5, 278, 280, 283–4, 304, 322
Colley, Linda, 8
communicative memory, 10, 29n, 42–4, 50, 72
Conquest of New France, 70–3, 75–83, 92n, 173, 179

Constable, Archibald, 54, 262n, 271, 276
Cooper, James Fenimore, 61, 62
  Satanstoe, 116, 139n
  The Spy, 53, 61, 63, 88n
Corresponding Society, 287, 304
Corriveau, Marie-Josepht, 79–80
Coureur des Bois, 74–6
Crawford, Robert, 5
Cree, 172, 176, 199n
cultural memory, 4, 10, 16, 28, 29n, 37, 43–5, 49, 52, 53, 55–6, 59–61, 64, 66–7, 70–2, 74, 77–9, 83, 95, 99, 107, 126, 134, 202, 204, 244, 249, 275–6, 294, 304, 327n
cultural trauma, 203–4, 206–7, 247–51, 256, 321

Dames, Nicholas, 31n
Daniel, Ute, 41
Davies, Carole Boyce, 225
Davis, Leith, 25
Deane, Seamus, 220
Dekker, George, 53
Devine, T. M., 5, 19–20, 134n
Dodgshon, R. A., 151
Ducharme, Michel, 92n
Duncan, Ian, 6, 16, 19, 25, 29n, 44, 45, 270, 275–6, 294, 327n
Dunlop, William, 301–3, 312
  Statistical Sketches of Upper Canada, 301–2
dùthchas, 151, 186–7

Edinburgh, 3, 6, 7, 19, 23, 40, 45–7, 83, 89n, 97, 100, 105, 110, 135n, 145, 149, 160, 202, 206, 225, 270, 320

Edinburgh Review, 62, 136n, 189n
Elliot, J. H., 18
Esterhammer, Angela, 306
ethnography, 22, 101, 104, 109, 207, 237, 291

Fabian, Johannes, 154
Felman, Shoshana, 249
Fentress, James, 14
Ferguson, Adam, 101, 102, 138n, 148, 275
Ferguson, Moira, 240
Ferris, Ina, 42, 51–2, 101
Fidler, Peter, 190n
Fielding, Penny, 14
Fraser, Malcolm, 92n
Fraser's Magazine, 332n
French Revolution, 16, 76–7, 81, 189n, 283, 290, 311

Gaelic language, 21, 104, 112, 149, 151, 168–9, 172, 173, 182–3, 186, 328n
Gallagher, Catherine, 254–5
Galt, John, 7, 28, 269–76, 288–9, 293–4, 300–3, 307–8, 310, 315, 321, 324–5, 326–7n, 331n, 333n
  Annals of the Parish, 28, 270, 274, 275–95, 299, 303, 305, 315, 316, 322, 327n, 328n
  Autobiography, 324, 330n, 331n, 333n
  The Bachelor's Wife, 328n
  Bogle Corbet, 28, 270–1, 272, 274, 300–2, 303–4, 315–26, 326n, 330n, 332n, 333n

Galt, John (*cont.*)
  Canada Company, 272, 301–2, 309–10, 315, 324, 330n, 331n
  The Entail, 270, 274
  Lawrie Todd, 28, 272, 274, 300, 303–7, 308, 310–15, 316, 317, 318, 326, 330n, 332n
  Literary Life and Miscellanies, 305, 324, 327n, 330n, 333n
  The Provost, 270, 327n
  on slavery, 319–21, 332–3n
  'A Statistical Account of Upper Canada', 300
Gardiner, Michael, 20
Garneau, François-Xavier, *Histoire du Canada*, 72–3, 92n
Garside, Peter, 29n, 40, 51, 86n
Geisler, Charles, 186
George III, 57–8, 278, 328
Gibbons, Luke, 220
Gilkison, William, 300
Gilroy, Paul, 24–5
Glasgow Courier, 201, 240
Glasgow Ladies New Anti-Slavery Society, 141n, 242
Gottlieb, Evan, 131, 220
Grant, Anne, 7, 26, 42, 97–8, 100, 103, 110, 129–31, 135–6n, 137n, 138n, 139n, 140n, 142n, 150–1, 283, 314
  Essays on the Superstitions of the Highlands, 94, 100–1, 102, 111, 113, 117
  'The Highlanders', 94, 97
  'Letters Concerning Highland Affairs', 94–6

Letters From the Mountains, 94–6, 103–5, 112
Memoirs of an American Lady, 26, 96–7, 98–9, 101, 102, 105–34, 136–7n, 138n, 139n, 170
Poems on Various Subjects, 97, 107, 112, 134n
Grant, Cuthbert, 176–7, 184
Grant, Ludovic, 200n
Great Britain *see* British Empire; transatlanticism
Greenock Advertiser, 271

Haitian Revolution, 17
Halbwachs, Maurice, 1–3, 10, 12, 28n, 42–3, 44, 46
Hall, Stuart, 224–5
Hamilton, Elizabeth, 42, 135n
Highlands, 7, 13, 21, 33, 42, 49–50, 75, 82, 94, 97, 98, 99, 100, 103–5, 112, 113–14, 131, 133, 134n, 135n, 143–4, 149, 154, 159–60, 163, 173, 175, 187, 189n, 191n, 251, 273, 322, 323, 333n
  Clearances, 3, 21, 27, 28, 117–18, 144, 147, 150–1, 152, 154, 155, 157, 162–4, 166, 178, 182–4, 186, 187, 190n, 191n
  cultural preservation of, 27, 117, 138n, 146, 148, 157–60, 164–9, 168–70, 184, 200n
  and emigration, 27, 117, 143–7, 149, 155, 157–62, 168–70, 171, 173, 182–4, 187, 191n, 193n, 235, 273, 331n

land reform, 27, 147, 150, 153, 154, 158, 163–4, 177, 184, 186–7, 193n, 197n, 200n, 203, 204, 206–7, 244–56, 273, 322–3
  see also Canada: and emigration; improvement; Kildonan; Selkirk, Thomas Douglas: National Settlements: Sutherland estate
Hinderaker, Eric, 106–7
Hofer, Johannes, 192n
Hogg, James, 270
Hook, Andrew, 18
Hudson's Bay Company, 171, 172, 173, 178, 180, 190n, 194n, 195n, 198–9n
Hume, David, 205, 213
  A Treatise of Human Nature, 259n
Huron Tract, 326n
Huston, James
  Le Répertoire national, 73, 91n, 92n
  Les Soirées canadiennes, 73, 74, 92n
Hutton, Patrick H., 12, 39
Huyssen, Andreas, 10–11, 30n

improvement, 22, 57, 144–7, 151–5, 157–62, 164–6, 168, 175, 178–82, 189n, 196n, 272, 286–9, 293–300, 306–10, 312, 329n
Indian Removal Act, 181, 196n
Insko, Jeffrey, 65–6
Intercourse Act (1796), 196n
Inverness Courier, 294
Ireland, 19, 20, 308
Iroquois, 115, 119, 120, 140n

Irvine, Alexander, 193n
Irving, Washington, 62, 139n
  History of New York, 53–5, 116
  'The Legend of Sleepy Hollow', 53, 54
  Relationship with Scott, 54–5, 89n
  'Rip Van Winkle', 26, 36, 53, 54, 55–61, 64
  Sketchbook of Geoffrey Crayon, 36, 53–4, 89n

Jackson, Andrew, 181, 196n
Jacobinism, 290, 318
Jacobite Uprising ('Forty-Five'), 2, 4–5, 8, 16, 25, 33–4, 37, 40–1, 44, 49–51, 75, 78, 82, 83, 94–6, 134n, 200n, 220, 275, 289
  Battle of Culloden, 71, 75–9, 95
Jamaica, 18, 257n, 262n, 273, 317, 319, 321, 322, 323, 325, 332n
Jeffrey, Francis, 111, 149
Johnson, Joseph, 207, 259n
Johnson, Samuel, 192n
Johnson, William, 116, 120–1, 140n
Johnstone, Christian Isobel, 134n, 294, 299
  Clan-Albin, 137n
Jones, Catherine, 16, 41–2, 60
Jones, Grace, 230

Kames, Henry Home, 101, 102, 148, 275
Kay, Jackie, 202–3, 256

Kildonan, 147, 154–5, 163, 171–2, 176–7, 183–4, 187, 190n, 194n
King Hendrick, 106–7, 137n
Klooster, Wim, 17–18
Koselleck, Reinhart, 4, 8, 154

Lambert, David, 241
Lamonde, Yvan, 91n
Laub, Dori, 249
Laurence, Margaret, *The Diviners*, 183–4
Le Goff, Jacques, 11
Le Moine, James Macpherson, *Maple Leaves*, 73–4
lieux de mémoire, 12, 45, 64, 127, 255
Livingstone, David, 239
Loch, James, 31n, 147, 149, 152–4, 157, 163, 190n, 245
  Account of the Improvements, 155, 168
Lockhart, John Gibson, 54, 262n, 320
  Peter's Letters to His Kinsfolk, 135n
London Anti-Slavery Society, 27, 206, 226, 229–30, 242
Lord Durham's Report, 72

MacDonnell, Alexander, 331n
MacDonnell, Margaret, 182
MacInnes, John, 151
McKeever, Gerald Lee, 288
McKenney, Thomas, 181, 196n
Mackenzie, A. Fiona D., 186
Mackenzie, Alexander, 173
  History of the Highland Clearances, 225
Mackenzie, Henry, 6, 160, 220
  The Man of Feeling, 219, 221

MacLean, John, 183, 322
MacLennan, Hugh, 143–4, 182, 183
Macleod, Donald, 243–4, 249, 251, 255, 322
  Gloomy Memories, 27, 206–7, 243–56, 266n
MacMillan, Calum, 187
Macphail, J. R. N., 96
Macpherson, James, 6, 104, 112, 138n; *see also* Ossian
MacQueen, James, 240–1, 262n, 320
Maginn, William, 332n
Maier, Charles S., 11
Manning, Susan, 5–6, 18
Marx, Karl, 266n
Megill, Alan, 12, 83
melancholy, 11, 28, 42, 47, 51, 64, 68, 71, 133, 156, 157–8, 159, 219, 313, 316–17, 318, 321, 325
memory
  crisis of, 8–9, 14, 34–5, 44, 56, 63
  generational, 3, 4, 9, 10, 13–14, 34–7, 38–43, 44, 46–9, 52, 56–7, 59–61, 63–6, 69–70, 71, 77, 80–2, 94–6, 111, 126–7, 146, 150, 164, 167, 184, 203, 278–80, 283–5, 289–90, 304, 311, 313, 315, 319, 325
  and history, 9–10, 11–13, 15–16, 34, 39, 41, 45, 48–9, 55, 66–7, 78, 96–7, 106–7, 110–11, 187, 202–4, 207, 243, 247, 250, 256, 281–2, 318–19
  individual, 11, 35, 45–6, 50, 66–9, 96, 105, 109, 133, 204–5, 228, 247, 274, 280

and landscape, 47–8, 55–8, 127, 130, 143–5, 151, 154, 157, 170, 183, 185–7, 233, 237, 283–4, 312, 319, 321, 323
limitations of, 11, 51, 54, 56, 64, 65–9, 96, 99, 106–8, 109–11, 127, 132–3, 281–3, 315–16
and national identity, 26, 36–7, 44, 56, 59, 61, 63–9, 72, 74, 79, 80–1, 83–4, 96, 130, 184, 203–5, 206–7, 233–4, 243, 314, 319
preservation of, 3, 13–14, 26, 27, 34–7, 39–48, 53, 55, 60–1, 63–4, 67, 70–2, 74, 78, 95–6, 110, 182, 247–8, 276–7, 280–1, 326
surrogation of, 37, 60–1, 78, 80–1, 112, 130, 132, 170, 233, 237, 256
transatlantic, 28, 98–9, 126, 133, 249–50, 182, 256, 277, 303–4, 313, 317–18, 322, 324, 325
see also amnesia; collective memory; communicative memory; cultural memory; *lieux de mémoire*; *milieux de mémoire*
Métis, 172, 176–7, 183–4, 191n, 195n
Middle Ground, 119–22, 129, 135n, 140n, 195n
Miggelbrink, Joachim, 209
milieux de mémoire, 12, 45, 87n
Millar, John, 101, 275
  The Origin of the Distinctions of Rank, 103

modernity, 1–4, 6, 7–9, 12, 15, 16–17, 25, 28, 34, 38, 39, 44–5, 47, 61, 98–9, 109–10, 113–14, 274, 276, 288–9, 294, 299, 326
and empire, 20, 115–18, 144–6, 148–9, 150, 154, 157–60, 161–5, 166, 169, 174–5, 181–2, 185, 220, 273
see also memory: crisis of; transatlanticism

Napoleonic Wars, 8, 16, 17, 271, 283
nationalism
  American, 35, 54, 59, 85n, 105, 127–8
  British, 5–6, 130–1, 134n, 135n
  Canadian, 170, 270–1, 317
  and emigration, 24, 28, 146, 159, 165, 167–8, 170, 183, 187, 207, 233–6, 272, 314, 317–19
  and empire, 36, 41, 61, 73, 97, 99, 115–16, 146, 238, 293
  Francophone Canadian, 36–7, 70, 72–5, 79–81, 83–4, 91n, 92n
  Scottish, 4–7, 24, 35, 74, 81, 105, 130–1, 153, 159–60, 161–2, 170, 205, 209–10, 220, 227, 233, 243, 269–70, 288, 298, 325
  see also British Empire; memory: and national identity; transatlanticism
Neal, John, 35, 63
  Logan, 62
  Seventy-Six, 26, 36, 62–70, 72, 283

Newman, Judie, 243
Newton, Michael, 151
Nietzsche, Friedrich, 30n
Nora, Pierre, 11–12, 45, 87n
North West Company, 172–3, 176–7, 178, 190n, 195n, 199n
Norton, Andrews, 110
nostalgia, 72, 114, 116, 157, 192n, 233–4, 241, 247–8, 312–13, 315, 317–18

Ossian, 6, 104, 112, 138n

Paquet, Sandra Pouchet, 22
Passenger Vessels Act (1803), 160, 170
Paulding, James Kirke, 139n
 The Dutchman's Fireside, 116, 139n
Peguis, 172, 199n
Penn, William, Quaker Colony, 115
Perkins, Pam, 97, 134n
Phillips, Mark Salber, 2, 13, 14, 48, 101, 102, 104–5
Pitt, William, 167
Pontiac's Rebellion, 122, 140n
Poovey, Mary, 295, 296, 298
post-colonialism, 20–1, 185–6
Pratt, Mary Louise, 119
Prebble, John, 255, 267n
primitivism, 8, 39, 98, 99, 102, 104, 112, 113, 114, 115, 116, 118, 121, 237
Prince, Mary, 206, 226, 228, 236, 240–1, 242, 262n
 The History of Mary Prince, 205, 206, 224–32, 233, 236, 238, 241, 262n, 265n
Pringle, Thomas, 7, 23, 27, 205–6, 225–7, 232, 235–6, 240–1, 262n, 265n
 African Sketches, 232
 'The Bechuana Boy', 227, 231–2, 238, 263n, 264n
 'The Emigrant's Cabin', 234
 'An Emigrant's Song', 234
 'The Exile's Lament', 234
 Narrative of a Residence in South Africa, 232–4, 237–40
 South African Letters, 235–6, 238, 242, 263n

Ramsay, John, 13–14, 31n
Randall, Marilyn, 74
Red River Colony, 146, 147, 171–3, 176–8, 184–5, 190n, 194n, 198n
Report of the Napier Commission, 255
Richerus of Rheims, *History of France*, 276
Ricoeur, Paul, 11
Riel, Louis, 184, 191n
Rigney, Ann, 16, 38
Robertson, William, 181, 296
 History of America, 181
Romanticism, 11, 34, 37, 98, 113, 134n, 157, 213, 274, 291, 313
 British, 7, 18, 31n, 88n
 Scottish, 2, 3, 4, 6, 8–9, 13–17, 19, 21, 25, 26, 28, 97, 101, 133, 171, 269–70, 273, 326
Ross, Alexander, 198n
Royal Proclamation (1763), 195–6n

Salih, Sara, 225
Salteaux, 172, 199n
Sammi, 186, 200n
Sassi, Carla, 202, 257n
Schuyler, Philip, 106, 110, 140
Scotland *see* British Empire: and Scotland; Edinburgh; Highlands; nationalism: Scottish; Romanticism: Scottish
Scots Brigade, 208–9, 258n
Scots Magazine, 271, 283
Scott, Jennifer, 330n
Scott, Walter, 2, 3, 14, 25, 33–5, 37, 42, 62, 86n, 88n, 97, 111, 149, 189n, 243, 248, 258n, 270, 274–5
  The Antiquary, 31n, 38, 52, 79
  The Betrothed, 88n
  The Black Dwarf, 52
  Guy Mannering, 38, 52
  influence of, 16, 24, 33, 35–8, 45, 53, 54, 61, 70–1, 84, 87n
  Ivanhoe, 38–9, 41
  Journal, 135n
  The Monastery, 86n
  relationship with Irving, 54–5, 89n
  The Tale of Old Mortality, 52
  The Talisman, 88n
  Waverley, 2, 3, 7, 14, 16, 25–6, 33–5, 36, 37, 38, 39–42, 43–5, 46, 47, 48, 49, 50, 51, 52–3, 54, 55, 58, 61, 64, 66, 70, 71, 75, 76, 81, 82–3, 84, 95, 266n, 270, 274, 276, 279, 280, 288, 290
Scottish History Society, 94
Sedgwick, Catharine Maria, *The Linwoods*, 61, 63

Selkirk, Thomas Douglas, 7, 26, 27, 42, 86n–7n, 156, 157, 164–7, 171–7, 178–80, 184, 186, 189n, 190n, 195n, 196n, 301, 308
  National Settlements, 117, 167–8, 170–3, 176–7, 179, 191, 194n, 290
  Observations on the Present State of the Highlands, 86–7n, 157, 160–3, 165, 167, 168, 173
  Observations on a Proposal, 179
  Sketch of the Fur Trade, 173–5, 178
  see also Red River Colony
Sellar, Patrick, 147–8, 149, 154, 163, 189n, 247
sentimentalism, 11, 42, 50, 55, 62, 78, 99, 156, 205, 209, 211, 213, 215, 218–19, 222–3, 242, 280, 312, 315, 317, 323, 331n
Seven Years War, 98, 120, 140n, 195n
Sewall, Samuel, 196n
Sharpe, Jenny, 214–15, 217, 232
Shields, Juliet, 131, 157, 220, 221, 272, 317
Shum, Matthew, 232
Sinclair, John, 300
  Analysis of the Statistical Account of Scotland, 297
  Statistical Account of Scotland, 189n, 294, 296–9, 328n
slavery, 3, 17, 22, 23, 25, 35, 124–6, 129, 160, 175, 201–4, 207, 210, 216, 225, 229–31, 251–6, 273, 316, 319–21, 332–3n

slavery (cont.)
  eyewitness accounts of, 23, 27, 204–7, 213, 223, 224, 242, 243
  see also Macleod, Donald: Gloomy Memories; Prince, Mary: History of Mary Prince; Stedman, John Gabriel, Narrative of a Five Year's Expedition
Smelser, Neil J., 203–4, 249
Smith, Adam, 174, 205, 213–14, 220, 221, 222, 296
  Wealth of Nations, 147–8, 150, 153, 161, 296
Smith, Laurajane, 250
Smith, William, Historical Account of Bouquet's Expedition, 140n
Smollett, Tobias, 220
  Roderick Ransom, 218, 221, 261n
Sorensen, Janet, 25
Speculative Society, 6, 149, 189n
Stedman, John Gabriel, 27, 205–9, 210, 212, 216, 221, 224, 257n, 258–9n, 260n, 323
  Narrative of a Five Year's Expedition, 27, 205, 207–8, 209, 210–19, 223, 224, 260n
Stowe, Harriet Beecher, 242–3
  Sunny Memories, 27, 206, 242–4, 245, 246, 249, 250, 251, 252–3, 256, 266n
  Uncle Tom's Cabin, 242, 243, 246, 253
Steaurt, Henry, 94, 96
Stewart, David, 158, 163

Sketches of the Character, Manners, and Present State of the Highlanders, 156, 267n
Stewart, Dugald, 101, 102, 103, 148, 149, 275, 296
Strickland, Susanna, 241
Sutherland Estate, 28, 147, 148, 149, 152–4, 161, 168, 171, 176–7, 184, 197n, 206, 243–4, 247, 249, 250, 252, 253, 266n
sympathy, 22, 27, 73, 98, 113, 123–4, 131, 149, 150, 155, 157, 163, 164, 181, 189n, 205, 206–7, 208, 213–14, 215, 216, 217–24, 227, 230–2, 236, 238–9, 242, 245, 248, 252–4, 256, 259n, 260n, 320

Tacksmen (Fir-tasca), 162, 193n
Terdiman, Richard, 8–9, 14–15, 44
Thomson, George, 100–1, 109, 134n
Thomas, Helen, 223–4
Thorburn, Grant, 304–5, 314–15, 332n
  Forty Years' Residence in America, 332n
transatlanticism, 17, 21, 23, 25, 35, 37, 54, 60, 62, 84, 107, 112, 114, 133, 145, 164, 174, 181, 242–3, 273–4, 291–2, 308, 316–18, 326
  and displacement, 21, 24, 26–7, 82, 144–7, 160, 164, 166, 170–1, 182–4, 187, 207, 226, 229–36, 243, 252, 317–18, 324

and historiography, 3–4, 7, 16,
18–19, 22, 23–6, 28, 98–9,
126, 133–4, 143–4, 147,
225, 272, 292, 293, 302, 325
and identity, 27, 84, 109–10,
131, 134–5, 173, 182–3, 187,
205–6, 208–10, 223–30, 232,
236, 272, 317, 319, 325
see also British Empire;
memory: transatlantic;
modernity; nationalism: and
emigration; slavery
trauma, 27–8, 40, 68, 69, 70,
77, 78, 80–2, 118, 122, 183,
275, 318; *see also* cultural
trauma
Treaty of Amiens, 294
Trevelyan, G. M., *English Social
History*, 328n
Trumpener, Katie, 18–19, 36, 37,
272–4, 276, 318, 325
Tudor, William, 135n

United States *see* Albany; British
Empire: and United States;
nationalism: American

Wales, 19, 20
War of 1812, 17, 36, 54, 271,
331n
Washington, George, 57–8,
197n
Waterston, Elizabeth,
270–1, 300, 316–17,
326n
Weaver, John C., 144
Weber, Max, 249
Wedderburn, Robert, *The
Horrors of Slavery*, 262n
Whatley, Christopher, 269,
328n
White, Hayden, 276
Whyte, Iain, 320, 332n
White, Richard, 119
Wickman, Matthew, 14
Wilkinson, Charles F., 181,
197n
Wilmot-Horton, Robert, 308
Wilson, James Grant, 110–11
Withers, Charles W. J., 249–50,
298
Wood, John, 241
Wood, Marcus, 210, 219

EU representative:
Easy Access System Europe
Mustamäe tee 50, 10621 Tallinn, Estonia
Gpsr.requests@easproject.com

www.ingramcontent.com/pod-product-compliance
Lightning Source LLC
Chambersburg PA
CBHW071826230426
43672CB00013B/2767